CRYSTAL HEALING
(5 Books In 1)

Expand Mind Power, Enhance Psychic Awareness, Achieve Higher Consciousness, Increase Spiritual Energy, Gain Enlightenment and Intuition with the Power of Crystals and Healing Stones

Crystal Lee

© Copyright 2019 by Crystal Lee - All rights reserved.

The following eBook is reproduced below with the goal of providing information that is as accurate and reliable as possible. Regardless, purchasing this eBook can be seen as consent to the fact that both the publisher and the author of this book are in no way experts on the topics discussed within and that any recommendations or suggestions that are made herein are for entertainment purposes only. Professionals should be consulted as needed prior to undertaking any of the action endorsed herein.

This declaration is deemed fair and valid by both the American Bar Association and the Committee of Publishers Association and is legally binding throughout the United States.

Furthermore, the transmission, duplication or reproduction of any of the following work including specific information will be considered an illegal act irrespective of if it is done electronically or in print. This extends to creating a secondary or tertiary copy of the work or a recorded copy and is only allowed with an expressed written consent from the Publisher. All additional right reserved.

The information in the following pages is broadly considered to be a truthful and accurate account of facts, and as such any inattention, use or misuse of the information in question by the reader will render any resulting actions solely under their purview. There are no scenarios in which the publisher or the original author of this work can be in any fashion deemed liable for any hardship or damages that may befall them after undertaking information described herein.

Additionally, the information in the following pages is intended only for informational purposes and should thus be thought of as universal. As befitting its nature, it is presented without assurance regarding its prolonged validity or interim quality. Trademarks that are mentioned are done without written consent and can in no way be considered an endorsement from the trademark holder.

TABLE OF CONTENTS

HEALING CRYSTALS
Beginner's Guide to Understanding the Healing Power of Crystals and Healing Stones

Introduction 4

Chapter 1 *Properties And Powers Of Crystals* 5

Chapter 2 *Crystals And Healing* 32

Chapter 3 *Creating Crystal Grids* 44

Chapter 4 *Crystals And Chakras* 50

Chapter 5 *Crystals In Reiki* 56

Chapter 6 *Clearing And Protection With Crystals* 58

Chapter 7 *Using Crystals For Holistic Living* 63

Chapter 8 *Crystals For Disorders, Specific Ailments, And Systems* 85

Conclusion 92

Description 93

CRYSTALS BEGINNER'S GUIDE TO CRYSTAL HEALING
How to Heal the Human Energy Field Through the Power of Crystals and Healing Stones

Introduction 97

Chapter 1 *What Are Crystals?* 99

Chapter 2 *Crystal Energy – Where Does It Come From?* 107

Chapter 3 *Benefits Of Healing With Crystals* 113

Chapter 4 *Crystals And Chakras* 122

Chapter 5 *Crystal Grids* 129

Chapter 6 *Why You Should Learn/Practice Crystal Healing* 141

Chapter 7 *Healing Fundamentals* 147

Chapter 8 *How To Choose The Right Crystals* 158

Chapter 9 *Crystals And What Ails You* 166

Chapter 10 *What Crystal For What?* 186

Conclusion 200

Description 201

CRYSTALS FOR BEGINNERS
Discover the Healing Powers of Crystals and Healing Stones

Introduction 204

Chapter 1 *The History Of Healing Stones* 205

Chapter 2 *Chakras* 220

Chapter 3 *Negative Energy Cleansing* 228

Chapter 4 *Incorporating Crystals And Their Knowledge Into Your Daily Life* 236

Chapter 5 *Starting A Crystal Collection* 251

Chapter 6 *Different Types Of Energy Healing* 258

Chapter 7 *Types Of Healing Crystals* 262

Chapter 8 *Crystal Mining And Collecting For Yourself* 327

Chapter 9 *Benefits Of Crystal And Energy Healing* 330

Conclusion 334

Description 335

CRYSTAL HEALING BIBLE
The Ultimate Guide to Gain Enlightenment and Awaken Your Energetic Potential with the Healing Powers of Crystals

Introduction 338

Chapter One *What Is Crystal Healing?* 340

Chapter Two *Health Benefits Of Crystal Healing* 358

Chapter Three *Chakra Connections And Crystals* 384

Chapter Four *Crystals To Know* 399

Chapter Five *Other Uses For Crystals* 442

Chapter Six *How To Care For Crystals* 447

Conclusion 451

Description 452

CRYSTAL HEALING FOR BEGINNERS
Introduction to Crystal Healing: Learn How to Achieve Higher Consciousness and Enhance Your Spiritual Balance with the Power of Crystals and Healing Stones

Introduction 455

Chapter 1 *Explaining Crystal Healing* 457

Chapter 2 *Guidelines For Engaging In Crystal Healing* 464

Chapter 3 *Crystal Index* 472

Chapter 4 *Explaining Chakra Healing* 507

Chapter 5 *Other Methods Of Crystal Healing* 513

Chapter 6 *Advanced Crystal Healing And Details Of The Craft* 531

Conclusion 549

Description 550

HEALING CRYSTALS
Beginner's Guide to Understanding the Healing Power of Crystals and Healing Stones

Crystal Lee

© Copyright 2018 by Crystal Lee – All rights reserved.

No part of this book may be reproduced or transmitted in any form or by any means, electronic or mechanical, including photocopying, recording or by any information storage and retrieval system without written permission of the publisher, except for the inclusion of brief quotations in a review.

The following eBook is reproduced below with the goal of providing information that is as accurate and reliable as possible. Regardless, purchasing this eBook can be seen as consent to the fact that both the publisher and the author of this book is in no way experts on the topics discussed within and that any recommendations or suggestions that are made herein are for entertainment purposes only. Professionals should be consulted as needed prior to undertaking any of the actions endorsed herein.

This declaration is deemed fair and valid by both the American Bar Association and the Committee of Publishers Association and is legally binding throughout the United States.

Furthermore, the transmission, duplication or reproduction of any of the following work including specific information will be considered an illegal act irrespective of whether it is done electronically or in print. This extends to creating a secondary or tertiary copy of the work or a recorded copy and is only allowed with express written consent from the Publisher. All additional rights reserved.

The information in the following pages is broadly considered to be a truthful and accurate account of facts and as such any inattention, use or misuse of the information in question by the reader will render any resulting actions solely under their purview. There are no scenarios in which the publisher or the original author of this work can be in any fashion deemed liable for any hardship or damages that may befall them after undertaking information described herein.

Additionally, the information in the following pages is intended only for informational purposes and should thus be thought of as universal. As befitting its nature, it is presented without assurance regarding its prolonged validity or interim quality. Trademarks that are mentioned are done without written consent and can in no way be considered an endorsement from the trademark holder.

INTRODUCTION

Congratulations on downloading your copy of *Healing Crystals: The Beginner's Guide to Understanding the Healing Power of Crystals and Healing Stones*. I am so glad you have decided to explore the healing power of crystals to help create positive changes in your life. You will soon discover the properties and healing powers of many crystals, how to use specific crystals to heal the body, mind, and spirit and how to create crystal grids. The following chapters will also discuss chakra balancing using crystals, crystals in Reiki sessions, utilizing crystals to clear negativity while attracting unconditional love, practicing crystal healing in all aspects of your life including relaxation, centering, meditation, and daily positive affirmations. Finally, crystals for specific ailments, disorders, disease, and crystal prescriptions will be explained in detail.

We have all experienced stress in a multitude of ways and on different levels including the physical, mental, and emotional. Learning the benefits of crystal healing can help balance our lives in order to feel less stressed and more energized. Some of the information in this book will allow you to open your mind, body, and spirit to the healing properties of crystals to help alleviate common stressors you may be experiencing. You will also realize how crystals initiate the power to self-heal.

This book is intended to provide you with basic information in order to utilize the functional relevance of powerful earth element crystals in your daily life. You may begin to notice small shifts at first. As you become more familiar with the practical applications of crystal use, you may experience significant changes for the better.

There are plenty of books about crystals and their healing powers on the market. Thank you so much for choosing this one! Every effort was made to ensure it is full of as much useful information as possible.

CHAPTER 1
Properties And Powers Of Crystals

What Are Crystals, Gems, Minerals, and Rocks?

Crystals are natural elements that come from the Earth. A true crystal has an organized grouping of unit cells that form a unique lattice pattern called a crystal system. There are six lattice patterns that appear within healing crystals. There is also a category of stones known as amorphous crystals, even though they are not truly crystals as they do not have an interior crystalline structure. Some of these include amber, obsidian, and opal. They each have their own unique properties.

Some use the words crystal, gem, mineral, and rock interchangeably, especially in the metaphysical aspect pertaining to crystals. Some materials that are not crystals such as amber, which is petrified tree sap, are also referred to as crystals or stones. There are technical differences among each of these. Crystals are made of minerals that are made of elements. Crystals are sometimes called gems. Crystals can be found in rocks.

Element
The chemical components of the earth are considered elements. Silver, gold, and iron are examples of elements that on their own make up crystals.

Crystal
A crystal is a mineral that has a crystalline interior structure. Agate, which is a hexagonal crystal, is also a mineral and a rock.

Gem
A gem is a cut and polished crystal, mineral, or rock. A cut diamond, which is a mineral, a crystal, and a rock, is also a gem or gemstone. Amber and pearls are organic substances that are considered gemstones but are not crystals, minerals, or rocks. Some gems come from organic matter rather than minerals. Pearls, amber, and coral are in this category. Even though they are not technically crystals, they are still used in crystal healing.

Mineral

A substance that occurs naturally with a highly ordered structure that may or may not be crystalline and with a specific chemical composition. Opal is a mineral that does not have a crystalline structure. It is a gemstone and a rock but not a true crystal.

Rock

A rock is a combination of minerals. Marble, which is made up of multiple minerals, is a metamorphic rock. It is a rock that has been subjected to heat and pressure over time.

Patterns of Crystals

Crystals are made up of three-dimensional patterns consisting of atoms, ions, or molecules.

The six crystal lattice patterns include the following:

Hexagonal - Hexagonal crystals have an interior structure that resembles a 3-D hexagon. Hexagonal crystals help with manifestation.

Isometric - Isometric crystals have an interior cubic structure. These crystals can amplify energies and improve situations.

Monoclinic - Monoclinic crystals have a 3-D parallelogram structure. They are protective crystals.

Orthorhombic - Orthorhombic crystals have a diamond-shaped crystalline pattern. They remove blockages, cleanse, and clear.

Tetragonal - Tetragonal crystals have a rectangular interior structure. These crystals are attractors. They make things more attractive and they help you attract things to you.

Triclinic - Triclinic crystals have an interior structure with three inclined axes. These crystals ward off unwanted energies or help retain energies you would like to keep.

Choosing Your Crystals

Crystals are readily available at metaphysical type stores or online. There are also many crystals, minerals, and gem shows that travel all over. It may cost to get into the show, but most vendors there are very knowledgeable. Crystals are fairly inexpensive, so stocking up on the main healing ones as well as extras you may be drawn to are pretty attainable. Be sure to store any you purchase in a soft cloth bag and if keeping all together, include clear quartz to keep them clear. When using a crystal, you can hold it, place it around you, or tape it to a specific area or organ needing healing, or even wear it in a metal spiral around your neck. Crystals usually activate well directly on your skin. Most work through clothes however and can still be beneficial this way. Keeping crystals in your pocket can also help. This can make it easy to access too, especially for a stress relieving stone.

You will inevitably have crystals choose you. However, you will be drawn to one or more just for their shape, color, size, purpose, or properties. Once you have a crystal collection of your own, you will then have stones to choose from for a specific purpose. Even then, choosing the right one for the job can seem daunting. There are a few tips you can follow to be certain you are finding the best match.

You can ask yourself "Which crystal do I need?" and listen for the answer. Asking this removes any preconceived notions. What you may think you need to be healed isn't actually what needs healing. Your subconscious can guide you in the right direction so listening to that is one of the most efficient ways in selecting the appropriate crystal.

Read through a multitude of listings of crystal properties and subsequent conditions, such as the ones in this book or online. There are many helpful websites to sort through to help pick a particular crystal. Metaphysical stores can also help. Salespeople at them are usually there because they have unique knowledge about the usages of crystals, or they have hands-on experience in using them.

You can choose a crystal based on color and crystal system or how the crystal's shape is made up. Use your best knowledge to guide you to a crystal that's right for that moment.

Muscle testing, a form of Applied Kinesiology, AK, can also be used to help choose a crystal. Kinesiology is a study of how muscles move, voluntarily or involuntarily. It is defined as the use of muscle testing to pinpoint imbalances in the body's physical, chemical, and emotional energy. It allows a person or practitioner to evaluate energy changes and decide the exact healing needs of the body on all levels. It is commonly used in sports medicine and chiropractic practices. It can also apply to choosing and using crystals. There are simple techniques anyone can use to test the effects of the subconscious mind on the muscles.

Place a crystal anywhere on you. With your giving or dominant hand, extend your pointer finger and press down on it with your middle finger of the same hand, resisting a bit with your pointer finger. If your pointer finger holds strong, you do not need that crystal at that time. If you cannot hold strong and the hold is weak, that is the crystal to work with. You can also muscle test while standing. Raise your right arm and hand so it is parallel to the floor. Hold a crystal in your receiving or non-dominant hand. Ask a partner or other person to push down gently on your right hand with just their right or left hand. Do this before, during, and after holding the crystal in your left hand. Before holding the crystal, ask if it is needed right now. If when the other person pushes on your right hand, there is strong resistance, that is a "yes" and a good crystal to use. If the hold is weak and your arm easily goes down, that is a "no" and not a good crystal to use.

Applied Kinesiology could be used to figure out if a crystal needs clearing or not. If it contains a lot of negative energy, it will test as a "yes" when asked if it needs cleansing. You could also use Applied Kinesiology when starting a crystal collection, to muscle test "yes" or "no" if a crystal is good for you in general or not.

Use your intuition and your gut feeling when choosing a crystal too. Trust in your subconscious mind giving you clues. Trust yourself that you will use the crystal you choose in the right way that will benefit your higher self. When you do this and trust yourself, everyone benefits in the long run. This is part of the healing process and being aware we are all part of a bigger picture together.

The following catalog of crystals is only an abbreviated list of types of earth stones that can aid common ailments and disorders, as well as help to regulate balance and wellbeing. There are so many more crystals available to you than on the following pages. However, the ones listed are the core healers as well as most common to find and own. Crystals are useful to keep us balanced on a daily basis, but they can also be very beneficial in healing. The list describes the properties of each crystal, its characteristics, and how you can benefit from them. As you read through the list and each description, see which ones stand out to you. As healing usually occurs on more than one level simultaneously, you may be attracted to more than one crystal at a time.

Tips for Crystal Choosing

Ground yourself before you go or enter a crystal shop or show. Many crystals in one spot can be disorienting. If you feel dizzy or lightheaded while in a shop or at a crystal show, imagine strong roots growing from your feet into the ground. Pick up any black stone until you feel stabilized.

Asking questions at a gem show or in a metaphysical shop can help guide you in the right direction for choosing crystals, especially in the beginning of starting a collection. Shop owners, workers, and vendors can be a valuable resource. They are usually in the business because they have hands-on experience in using crystals and are knowledgeable about their healing qualities and properties. They can be a lifelong source of information and are usually more than willing to answer any questions relating to crystals and gems.

Go where you are drawn to and pay attention. If there is a particular location in a shop or gem show you are drawn to, go to it. Then see which crystal draws you to it. This helps initiate your intuitive process and the choosing of crystals.

Touch and handle the crystals. Get a feel for what their energies feel like. See how they actually make you feel when handling them. You can quickly intent them to be clear and cleansed, free of anyone else's energy, so you can get their actual vibration. If anyone in a shop or at a gem show does not let you feel or hold a stone, do not buy from them and go elsewhere.

Try to do research before going to a crystal shop or gem show. Check a seller's reputation if you can. Read reviews if they are available. Check for articles online or elsewhere.

Don't always buy the first thing you see. It is easy to be overwhelmed when you go to a store or show that has an overabundance of pretty, shiny, sparkly stones. Take your time and learn about the crystals and products available. You can even get a feel for different prices of the same stones by comparing stores or websites. Find the best price for the crystals that appeal to you most.

If you do not recognize a crystal by its name, ask if it is trademarked. If it is, ask for the generic version. You can look it up online or on your phone. You can also use an app to see if it is a trademarked crystal or a less expensive generic version. You can search under "Healing Crystals."

Crystal Catalog

Amazonite
Amazonite's healing powers help with emotional issues, physical ailments, in energy healing, and chakra balancing. Its light green, blue-green or aquamarine color works with the heart and throat chakras. In this way, it is a loving communication crystal. It is often called the Stone of Truth and Stone of Courage, allowing those who use it to bravely speak and live their authentic self. Amazonite is thought to be a calming, balancing stone. Its appearance can be either natural and tumbled or smooth and polished. Amazonite helps communicate your true thoughts and feelings without too much emotion. When you keep Amazonite near or wear it as jewelry, it can enable you to see things from a different perspective, thus allowing one to be objective. This crystal can help balance one's own inner turmoil. Amazonite also helps with forgiveness, peace and understanding, integrity, prosperity, protection, and loving one's self and others unconditionally.

Amber
Amber is not technically a crystal but has such healing properties that it is used extensively in the naturopath and metaphysical world. It has an affiliation with both the sun and the earth with its golden color. It is also connected to insects and nature that may become eternally suspended in its hardened sap. Amber is best known to relieve inflammation and the pain associated with it. It can appear natural or cut and is characteristically golden, brown, honey colored. Amber is good for the solar plexus chakra. It helps with creating positive energy, self-esteem, increasing life force, and averting others' energy.

Amethyst
Amethyst is a form of quartz most commonly purple. It has strong healing powers and is especially useful in providing pain relief. You can place an amethyst crystal directly on a part of your body in pain and it will gently draw it out while releasing any stuck energy. In this way, it is very effective in relieving tension headaches and migraines by placing directly on your forehead or sinuses. Amethyst crystals help with intuition and insight, connecting to higher self and the Divine, insomnia, stress, anxiety, safe travel, nightmares, and addiction. It is associated with the third eye and crown chakras. Its shape can appear natural, in points, clusters, geodes, tumbled and polished, or cut. Amethyst is a wonderfully versatile stone.

Ametrine
Ametrine is a beautiful crystal with clear purple and yellow colorings. It has the ability to combine and amplify the properties of both amethyst and citrine crystals as they naturally form in this one crystal. It is highly effective at increasing prosperity, abundance, psychic communication, aura cleansing, transmuting negativity, positive energy flow, balancing opposite energy characteristics, and promoting spiritual dreaming, and balancing of spirit with human energies. Ametrine is associated with the solar plexus chakra as well as the third eye and crown chakra. It appears naturally, in points, clusters, tumbled and polished, or cut. You can place ametrine on the solar plexus region, third eye chakra, near the crown of your head, or head of your bed when working with it. Wearing an ametrine necklace will help motivate and balance the

flow of the energy from the solar plexus through the crown chakras.

Apache Tears
The legend of Apache Tears is a sacred one. Anyone with this healing stone should be aware of its history. In the 1870s an Apache tribe hid on a ridge in Arizona from US Cavalry they supposedly stole cattle and supplies from. Their land had been under siege for a long time and they were being attacked. 50 of 75 Apache died under a quick surprise attack on the cliff. The other 25 Apache warriors chose to jump off rather than be killed by the white man. Apache women and family of those who died gathered below and cried for a moon. It is said their tears fell onto white sand, turning to black obsidian stones that held their tears. Anyone with an Apache Tear stone does not need to cry for the Apache Women have done it for them and the grief is no more. Apache Tears are actually obsidian stones from volcanic glass, usually round or oval in shape, varying in color from dark gray to deep black. These stones are extremely effective in helping to overcome grief, sadness, or dark emotions. They are beneficial to the root chakra, thus a balancing stone. It is believed if you wear or carry Apache Tear stones when dealing with the death of a loved one, you can use them as worry stones to stop grief from becoming overwhelming.

Apatite
Apatite is a beautiful blue-green stone associated with deep spiritual wisdom and truth. It is a soft crystal that can be brittle. It should be stored separately and carefully away from other crystals. Apatite is an amplifying crystal that can aid in focusing on goals, eliminating negativity, raising energetic vibrations, connecting to the Divine, enhancing intuition, and increasing truth and motivation. It also works with decreasing social anxiety and self-consciousness. The root, solar plexus, heart, throat, third eye, and crown chakras are the chakras associated with apatite. It appears in a natural state, as points, tumbled and polished, or cut.

Aquamarine
Aquamarine is a manifestation stone with a brilliant yet calming blue-green color. It can appear natural or pointed, tumbled and polished, or cut. The chakras related to it are the heart, throat, and third eye. This crystal can help with aligning and balancing all of the chakras, soothing anxiety, decreasing phobias, assisting with

manifestation, courage, protection, self-expression, and spiritual truth.

Aventurine
Aventurine is created by a mixture of quartz and other minerals which lend to its coloring. They can be blue, green, red, orange, yellow or white, but green is the most common color. Since green is associated with healing in general and the heart chakra, green Aventurine is said to be the ultimate healing stone while also promoting prosperity. It can enable you to live by the desires of your own heart. It can also help get rid of illness or disease tied to old emotions. This allows anyone with the stone to break free from old habits and get to the underlying reason for the disease. It can help with conditions of the heart and blood pressure, as well as relieve manic type stress or overproduction of adrenaline due to chronic tension. Its appearance can be natural, pointed, tumbled and polished, or cut. Other chakras associated with the other colors of Aventurine are red for root, orange for sacral, yellow for solar plexus, blue for throat and third eye, white for crown.

Bloodstone
Bloodstone gets its name from the opaque green appearance with lines of blood red jasper Bloodstone, also known as Heliotrope, is a master healer for the body as it relieves chronic conditions such as fatigue and with revitalizing effects on a person's immune system. It can help with auto-immune diseases such as thyroiditis and rheumatoid arthritis. Bloodstone is also a strong detoxifier. It cleanses the blood and lymph to remove waste and toxins from blood-rich organs and body tissues. It can be placed in the bath to increase blood flow and circulation. Bloodstone aligns with the heart, root, and lower chakras. It can have a raw cut appearance or tumbled and polished.

Blue Lace Agate
Blue lace agate is a nurturing crystal with a gentle, cooling energy. It is a powerful throat cleanser and healer, thus benefits the throat chakra and thyroid and parathyroid glands. It aids in opening lines of communication and activating that which has previously been held back. It is a gentle stone that allows built up energy to rise to the surface slowly to finally be released and let go. It stabilizes heat

from a fever, inflammation, and infection, while its calming energy promotes peace of mind. Agate is a very holistic healer that works on balancing all levels, including physical, emotional, mental, and spiritual. It helps to relieve tension in the neck and shoulders and chest and lung congestion which can be associated with grief. Agate is good for relieving arthritis, asthma, bones and circulation issues. It appears natural, tumbled and polished, or cut.

Bronzite
Bronzite is a brown, usually speckled and tumbled stone associated with all the chakras. It is a protective, activating, grounding crystal. It can help with figuring out what it is you want to achieve in your life, promotes certainty and control, calmness, enhances creativity and forward thinking. It allows you to think objectively and see the bigger picture. Bronzite can help alleviate anxiety associated with starting something new or being in a new situation such as a social one. It can dispel negative energy, ease stress, warm the extremities, aid in digestion, supports kidney function, balance the body's pH levels, and enhances the assimilation of iron, making it a good stone for anemia.

Calcite
Calcite comes in a rainbow of colors, each with specific properties associated with the chakras with which they align. It is an excellent manifestation stone as it naturally helps in achieving desires. It is also an amplifying crystal. It helps with cleansing, grounding, inner peace, speaking your truth, integrity, abundance, unconditional love, self-esteem, intuition, personal will, communicating with a higher power, and spiritual growth. The different colors aid in corresponding chakras are as follows: red, black or gray with the root chakra; orange or peach, sacral; green or pink, heart; purple, third eye; honey or yellow, solar plexus; blue, throat; white, crown. Create a relaxing and peaceful environment by placing different colored calcite stones around a room such as bedroom, bathroom, or living room. Calcites appear naturally, tumbled and polished, or cut.

Carnelian
Carnelian is associated with boldness, courage, life, and vitality. It is a very energetic crystal. You would not want to keep it near your bedside table or wherever you rest. Do keep it on your desk or

workspace to increase energy throughout the day. Its brownish red to red-orange coloring is associated with the root and sacral chakras. These chakras have to do with creativity, physical energy, safety in ourselves and with others, fertility/sexuality, and happiness. It can be used to improve strength, sense of self, and humility. It can help you set proper boundaries. Carnelian has been used to help vocalists as well as public speakers increase courage and bring strength to the voice. Its shape can be natural, tumbled and polished, or cut.

Chalcedony
Chalcedony is a form of quartz that gets its color from mineral occlusions. Agates are a form of chalcedony, as is carnelian. However, when discussing healing crystals, chalcedony typically refers to a creamy blue variety of the stone. Known as the Speaker's Stone, it helps you speak your truth with fact. Chalcedony also helps with manifestation, creativity, promoting peace, lessening self-doubt, and balancing emotions. It is associated with the throat chakra and communication. It is an amplifying crystal. Place chalcedony close to your lips, tongue, or mouth before public speaking to help you speak truthfully and well. Chalcedony appears naturally, as geodes, tumbled and polished, or cut. They are very useful in necklaces and earrings, wearing directly on the throat chakra, or in a chest pocket close to it.

Citrine
Citrine is a powerful golden-yellow and clear crystal associated with the solar plexus chakra. It appears naturally, in clusters, tumbled and polished, or cut. If placed in the back left corner of your home or business, it is thought to bring prosperity. It also helps with self-esteem, creativity, thinking clearly, manifestations, asserting personal will, and bringing forth new beginnings. It dispels negativity while increasing positive feelings. It is a good stone for depression, self-doubt, anger, and mood swings. It can bring you happiness, strength, and success.

Clear Quartz
Clear quartz is considered by many to be the most versatile and powerful of the master healing stones. It works through any and all conditions. If you are beginning a crystal collection, clear quartz is a wonderful first choice. It contains the full spectrum of visible light

and links the physical body with emotions, the mind, and spirit. Clear quartz is a terrific conductor and increaser of energy. It can strengthen any crystal's power just by being near it. It also clears all other crystals while being self-cleansing. It helps with balance, protection, cleansing, purification, healing on all levels, amplifying energy and thought, connecting to higher consciousness and the Divine, and improving concentration. It is an excellent overall healing and clearing stone and for using in crystal grids. This crystal uniquely attunes itself to your individual needs and adjusts its healing energy accordingly. It is mostly associated with the crown chakra for its effectiveness in meditation and connecting to your higher self, but it can benefit all chakras equally. It is a clear to milky white crystal appearing naturally, polished, cut, in points, geodes, or clusters.

Danburite
Danburite comes in multiple colors that affect different chakras. However, all colors are high vibration stones associated with spiritual enlightenment and connection to a higher power. It is also a cleansing and clearing stone that can help to heal deep emotional pain and wounds. Danburite appears naturally or tumbled and polished as clear, gray, or green. Green danburite is associated with the heart chakra, clear and gray with the crown chakra. It is a crystal that helps with intuition, deep emotional healing, compassion and unconditional love, connecting the upper chakras heart through crown, easing transitions, calming, stress relief, purifying the aura, and cleansing. Danburite is an excellent meditation stone when you wish to connect with your higher power. Hold it in either hand as you meditate. You can place danburite on the heart or crown chakra directly, in a pocket during stressful times, around the home to promote healing energy throughout.

Emerald
Emerald is actually a form of a mineral called beryl. Other beryls include aquamarine and morganite. Emerald is often cut and polished and made into jewelry as it is well-known. With its characteristic green color, emerald is a classic heart chakra stone that promotes love and compassion. It helps with prosperity, unconditional love, compassion, romance, kindness, forgiveness, manifestation, increasing spiritual awareness, serenity,

experiencing Divine love, protection, and healing trauma. Emerald can be placed directly on the heart chakra, worn as jewelry or specifically as a ring on the commitment finger. They are often given as a promise or engagement stone. Emerald is a hard stone but has a lot of inclusions so can break easily.

Epidote
Epidote is a protective stone primarily associated with the heart chakra and love. It can help improve interpersonal relationships, creating a balance between partners, and enhancing love and personal growth. It also amplifies the energy of other stones. Epidote helps with prosperity, love, connection with nature, optimism, grounding, clearing energetic blockages, strengthening, and stimulating healing. Its green color connects it to the heart chakra and issues relating to love. You can place Epidote directly on the heart chakra, hold in your hand after meditation for grounding, and next to any other stone you wish to increase the effectiveness of. If you live in the city or haven't been outdoors in a while, you can meditate with Epidote to connect to the natural world.

Fluorite
Fluorite is a soft mineral crystal that can chip easily. It should be used and stored very carefully. Fluorite can range in coloration from light green to deep purple all in one stone. For this reason, it is often called rainbow fluorite. Fluorite helps with calming and balancing energies and emotions. It is a good connector of body, mind, and spirit as well as with assisting in communication with higher planes and the Divine, intuition, enhancing creativity, peace, and wellbeing. It can be a gentle healer and is often used by natural practitioners to encourage slow but steady self-healing. It is associated with the heart, throat, third eye, and crown chakras.

Fuschite
Fuschite is a sparkling green silicate mineral embedded with mica. It can also often have ruby embedded in it. It is a protective stone and a classic healer's stone that can help with physical, energetic, and emotional healing. Fuschite is a soft stone that must be stored carefully and away from other crystals because of this. It is associated with the heart chakra. It helps with healing on all levels — physical, emotional, mental, and spiritual, rejuvenation,

balance, prosperity, love, intensifying energy with other crystals. It can be placed on the heart chakra, if embedded with ruby, it can be placed on the root chakra and heart chakra, or worn as a necklace or bracelet.

Garnet

Garnets are commonly a red stone called pyrope everyone is familiar with. They can also be yellow to orange and brown and called spessartine garnet, and green garnets are called tsavorite garnets. Garnets are a protection, manifestation, and amplifier of energy crystal. They also boost energy, help with transitions, overcoming trauma, and getting rid of limiting ideas and beliefs. They are good for career success and moving forward, getting out of the past. If you are going through a lot of changes or a transition, wear or carry garnet to help ease the shift. In this way, garnet can be a very overall useful crystal while healing. Wearing garnets in rings or bracelets is very popular and beneficial. Garnet appears naturally, in points, clusters, tumbled and polished, or cut.

Hematite

Hematite is a shiny, black pearlescent stone used for absorbing negative energy. It is a protective, grounding, balancing, detoxifying crystal. It is strongly associated with the root chakra but can also benefit the solar plexus chakra. A lot of jewelry is made of hematite. Wearing it can help us feel grounded or connected to the earth so it can be good in stressful situations. It helps the mind focus, stimulates concentration, memory, and original thought. It can also help us release old thoughts or feelings without realizing it for our greater good. Hematite is the mineral form of iron oxide thus aids in all blood disorders, restoring and regulating blood supply. It can be natural, polished, cut, or in rings. Hematite absorbs a lot of negative energy so is often over-worked. It can break easily because of this.

Howlite

Howlite is a white to light grey colored stone with dark grey to black lines in it. It is a crown chakra stone that helps in connecting to higher truth, linking users of the stone to the Divine. It also aids in calming anxiety, reducing stress, and easing intense negative emotions such as anger and rage. It appears natural, tumbled or polished, carved, and cut. Howlite is a soft stone easily carved into jewelry, benefiting the crown chakra by wearing earrings or a necklace close to it. The jewelry can have a calming effect during high stress or tense situations.

Jade

Jade has been used since ancient times, often carved into jewelry or other statues and artifacts. Most people recognize green jade but it may also be white or even orange. It appears naturally you can hang, tumbled or polished, and carved. Since jade has been of value and is extremely popular in many cultures for so many centuries, there are a lot of imitations. True jade should have irregularities under close inspection and should be looked for. Jade helps with protection, easing guilt, disrupting negative thought patterns, safe travel, reducing excessive wanting of power, strengthening life force energies, increasing trust, and promoting love of all kind. Jade can be worn as jewelry or in a pocket on any of the corresponding chakras. Chakras Jade is associated with are red, black, or gray jade with the root chakra; orange, sacral; yellow, solar plexus; green, heart; blue, throat; purple, third eye; white, crown chakra.

Jasper

Jasper is a cosmically colorful stone. There are multiple opaque colors and varieties of Jasper, which is actually a combination of quartz or chalcedony and other minerals. Different varieties have varying properties. In general, however, Jasper is a manifestation stone that absorbs excess energies to help with energetic balance. It can appear naturally, tumbled and polished, carved, or cut. Jasper is an absorbing crystal rock. It is associated with the following chakras according to corresponding colors: Red or black, root; orange, sacral; yellow or brown, solar plexus; green, heart; blue, throat or third eye. It helps with manifestation, grounding, stability, balancing excess energies associated with addiction, and obsessive-compulsive behavior. You can hold jasper after meditation for grounding. It can be worn on any of the chakras, as jewelry, or in a pocket.

Kyanite

While blue is the most common color of kyanite, it also comes in yellow, green, black, and orange. It is a brittle stone that is often blade shaped which makes it a good worry stone for rubbing your thumb across. Kyanite never needs cleansing because it does not hold on to energy. It just facilitates energy's movement. This is also why neither absorption nor amplification is noted for this crystal. Kyanite helps with creating pathways from one thing to another, clearing blockages, getting you out of rut, initiating communication, loyalty and fairness, memory recall, and grounding. It appears as natural, in blades, tumbled and polished, carved, and cut. Chakras associated with corresponding colors of kyanite are black or gray, root chakra; orange, sacral; yellow, solar plexus; green, heart; blue, throat or third eye; white, crown chakra. You can place this crystal on any of the corresponding chakras, in a pocket, or in your hand as a worry stone. You can also use kyanite between other crystals in a grid to facilitate energy flow from one crystal to the next.

Labradorite
Labradorite is a magical crystal that can enhance intuition, psychic, and mystical abilities by raising consciousness and dissolving illusions. It will clear your aura and close it for protection. It is a very spiritual healing stone, stress reliever, and can help lower blood pressure. It harmonizes all of the subtle outside bodies with the physical body. Labradorite is an opalescent stone with a gleaming blue or gray base. When it is not cut or polished, it looks like a regular rough rock. It assuredly aligns with the crown chakra as well as throat and third eye.

Lapis Lazuli
Lapis lazuli isn't technically a crystal, because it doesn't have a crystalline structure. Rather, it is a metamorphic rock. However, it has been recognized for centuries as a semiprecious stone having magical powers. The sarcophagus of King Tutankhamen is decorated with lapis lazuli, as are many other ancient artifacts. Lapis lazuli helps with communication of all types, particularly written, learning, encouraging honesty and speaking one's truth, harmony, and improving performance. It is a performer's stone. Wear it for auditions or public speaking engagements to help provide a perfect performance.

Larimar
Larimar is a calming, tranquil stone that forms in lava. It is also known as the Atlantis Stone or the Dolphin Stone found only in the

Dominican Republic. It is the blue version of the stone pectolite and can be white, light to deep blue, green blue and have a milky or translucent appearance to it, reminiscent of the Caribbean waters it is found in. It is thought to be a remnant from Atlantis and to have the ability to help in communicating with dolphins. It appears natural, in blades, tumbled or polished, and carved. It is an absorbing stone that works well with clear quartz and selenite. Larimar helps with many healings including relaxation, calming and soothing, promoting peace and serenity, clarifying dream meanings, assisting in resolving trauma, and giving voice to wisdom. It is associated with the throat and third eye chakra. You can place it on the throat chakra, next to your bed, or taped under the head of your bed to assist in its usages. Wear larimar as a necklace when it is important to speak your truth calmly and wisely.

Lodestone
Lodestone, also called magnetite, is a black magnetic stone made from iron oxide and is very amplifying. You can find it with small pieces of iron stuck to it from magnetism. If you do find it this way, be sure to store it away from other crystals so you can retain the small pieces of iron with it. Lodestone helps with grounding, protection, and attracting what you create. You can place it near the root chakra, in a bracelet. It is a very strong stone and should probably be stored in a protective container even when being used. It is associated with the root chakra. It can be found naturally, natural with iron stuck to it, or tumbled and polished.

Malachite
Malachite is a beautiful deep green color with bands of lighter and darker green through it. It is a stone of the heart, nature, prosperity, and healing. It absorbs energy and is associated with the heart chakra. Malachite helps with absorbing negative energy, guarding against energetic and physical pollution, protecting against accidents, and relieving fears associated with travel. Malachite is believed to offer protection during air travel. Carry a small piece in a carry-on handbag when you fly. You can place malachite on or near the heart chakra, as a necklace or bracelet.

Moonstone

Moonstone is a variety of feldspar characterized by its milky white color with an opalescent sheen. It is a good stone for new beginnings as well as connecting to higher realms, Divinity, and intuition. It provides protection while traveling by water or by night. It aligns with the third eye and crown chakra. Moonstone can provide calmness by soothing emotional instability and stress. It appears naturally or tumbled and polished or cut. It is associated with the third eye and crown chakras.

Obsidian
Obsidian is a type of volcanic glass but has many healing qualities. It is usually shiny black but can also have specks of white and be known also as snowflake obsidian. Obsidian is a root chakra stone that is very grounding and protective. It helps to protect against negativity and is good for clearing your aura. It is also helpful in releasing anger and resentment. If you are feeling foggy or energetically stuck, hold a piece of obsidian in your receiving, dominant hand, while breathing evenly and deeply.

Onyx
Onyx is a variety of chalcedony with parallel bands in the stone. It is a black, protective, and grounding stone that can also aid in manifestation and it can help balance excessive sexual desire. Onyx absorbs energy and is associated with the root chakra. You can place it on or near the root chakra or in a pair of a pants pocket. Onyx helps with grounding, improving harmony in intimate relationships, improving self-control, calming worry and tension, and soothing nightmares. To use onyx efficiently, put it on your bedside table or taped to a headboard to help balance intimate relationships.

Opal
Opals are highly valued as a gemstone and a healing stone. They have a beautiful, soft rainbow, luminescent quality to them. However, because opals do not have a crystalline structure, they are technically not regarded as crystals. Opals are soft with a high water content, which makes them particularly delicate. They can be colorless, white, and yellow, violet, red, pink, orange, green, blue, and black. Root chakra is related to red or black opals, sacral relates to orange, solar plexus on yellow, the heart chakra on green or pink, throat on blue, violet the third eye, the crown and higher

chakras on colorless or white. You should never clean an opal in water or with chemicals, including opal jewelry pieces. They are natural, tumbled and polished, or cut. They have amplifying energy qualities so they will help increase the power of other crystals. They help with creativity, dreams, connection to the Divine and higher self, facilitating the flow of transformation, assisting in moving easily through obstacles, improving memory and inspiration. You can place opals near the head of your bed for meditation and dreaming, on or near any chakra, and as a jewelry of any type. It is considered good luck to receive an opal piece of jewelry from someone else. Opal is very popular in jewelry. It is important to store opals carefully, away from other crystals to prevent damage as they are so soft.

Peridot
Peridot has a beautiful green color that makes it very popular and highly valued as a gemstone. It is also known as olivine or chrysolite. It is a stone of unconditional love, compassion, forgiveness, and other heart associated experiences and emotions. It is also a cleansing and clearing stone. Peridot appears naturally, tumbled or polished, and cut. It is an amplifying crystal associated with the heart chakra. It helps with promoting positivity, forgiveness, all types of love, prosperity, luck, healing emotional trauma, lessening ego, aura cleansing, and balancing all the chakras. You can carry or wear peridot when you feel like you need a little extra luck or feelings of love. It is a very popular gemstone for jewelry pieces. Wear it on or near your heart chakra as a necklace, or as a bracelet or ring on your commitment finger. Periodot works well with clear quartz, rose quartz, and smoky quartz.

Rhodochrosite
Rhodochrosite is a vibrant, banded pink stone. The lighter pink varieties can be often confused with rose quartz. Because of the color similarities, it does have some of the similar metaphysical properties of rose quartz. In general, however, you can tell it is rhodochrosite instead of rose quartz by its intense, deep pink color and the white bands running through it. It does appear in its natural state, tumbled and polished, or cut. The deep pink varieties can be associated with the root chakra. The lighter pink crystals are associated with the heart chakra. Rhodochrosite helps with

unconditional love, compassion, kindness, calming, grounding, self-compassion, forgiveness, and aura cleansing. If you are struggling with self-compassion or self-love issues, hold rhodochrosite in your receiving, non-dominant hand as you state firmly, "I love myself unconditionally." You can also place it on or near your root or heart chakra, wear as a necklace or bracelet, or as a ring on your commitment finger. It works well with rose quartz and clear quartz and it is an amplifying crystal.

Rose Quartz
The crystal of unconditional love, compassion, and kindness. It exudes forgiveness, self-love and healing, and overall feelings of joy. It helps in feeling connected to others with peace and calmness. Although green is usually associated with the heart chakra, rose quartz is definitely a heart chakra stone. It is a wonderful stone for self-forgiveness or self-healing, break up, betrayal, and handling emotions with losing a family or a loved one. It appears naturally as a pale, clear pink stone tumbled and polished, cut, in points, or clusters.

Ruby
Ruby is a vibrant red, precious gemstone. Rubies and sapphires are forms of corundum, a valued mineral. Along with finding ruby crystals by themselves, you can also find them embedded in fuchsite or zoisite. Rubies found this way can be more affordable yet still contain all the properties of a single ruby. It is a crystal associated with the root and heart chakras. Ruby helps with all types of love, opening the heart, expressing love, compassion, trust, courage, forgiveness, grounding, clearing blocked energies and emotions, and connecting to spiritual and Divine love. If you feel stuck in any emotion, wear ruby jewelry or carry a gem with you or in a pocket to help you break free of the emotion. It can be worn as any jewelry such as necklace, bracelet, or ring on your commitment finger. Place it on or near your root or heart chakra for effectiveness as well. It is an amplifying stone that works with sapphire and rose quartz. Ruby can appear naturally, tumbled and polished, or cut.

Sapphire
Similarly to rubies, sapphire is a form of the valued mineral corundum. Most people think of sapphires being only blue, but this gemstone also comes in a variety of colors including orange, yellow,

and pink. The popular deep blue sapphire is associated with the third eye or throat chakra; orange with sacral; yellow with solar plexus; and pink with the third eye chakra. It is a stone for protection and manifestation. Sapphire helps with self-expression, communication, speaking personal truth, loyalty, surrendering of personal will to Divine will, and sleep issues. It works well with ruby. Sapphire is particularly powerful when used with some type of vocal meditations such as mantra meditations. It can be placed on or near the appropriate chakra, especially the throat chakra, as a necklace or earrings, or near the head of your bed for insomnia.

Selenite
A variety of gypsum, selenite is a very soft crystal. Because of this, it is easy to carve and you will often find it carved into interesting shapes, towers, and wands. It is primarily a protective stone and is a soft, pearly white. It is also a crystal that does not absorb or store energy so it does not need cleansing. It serves as a cleansing stone for other crystals. It is also an amplifying stone associated with the third eye and crown chakra. It appears naturally, carved, cut or tumbled, and polished. Selenite helps with protecting against negativity, cleansing negative energy, forgiveness, cleansing other crystals, cleansing the aura, and connection with intuition and the Divine. You can place it on or near the third eye or crown chakra. It works well with all other crystals. Due to selenite's softness, it can get damaged easily and should be stored separately from other crystals. Never expose it to water or salt.

Sodalite
Sodalite is a natural amplifier that balances energies if you have too much of one and not enough of another. It can be deep blue to light blue, with white and black. It eliminates confusion and unites logic with intuition, enabling you to find your inner truth. It is helpful in overcoming repeated patterns, phobias, and panic attacks. It can help in group situations by encouraging trust and everyone to speak their true selves. Sodalite resonates with the throat and third eye chakras. It can also be useful in absorbing electromagnetic smog, radiation damage, and emanations from electronics. It can help to keep sodalite at your workplace to help dispel. It appears naturally, tumbled and polished, carved, or cut.

Tanzanite

Tanzanite can help release things that no longer serve you. It can also help clear energetic blockages and get rid of unwanted energy. This gem is named after where it was discovered, Tanzania. It is a violet-blue stone, thus associated with the throat, third eye, and even crown chakra. It is an amplifying crystal that helps with clearing away unwanted energy and things that don't serve you, aiding in self-discovery and discovery of your true spiritual nature, promoting connection to higher self and to the Divine, and integrating third eye and crown chakras. It appears natural, tumbled and polished, carved, or cut. Place it on or near the throat, third eye, or crown chakra, wear as earrings, or a necklace. Tanzanite can help you discover and clarify your own spiritual beliefs. To help with this, hold it in your receiving, non-dominant hand during meditation or a prayer or affirmation. It works well with clear quartz and celestite.

Tiger's Eye
Tiger's Eye is a manifestation stone and can help issues with self-esteem or self-worth. It has a rich layering of yellow and brown that shimmers in the light. Tiger's eye can also be blue or red. It is a protective stone that promotes balance and connection to the earth. It relates to the root, solar plexus, and throat chakras. It helps with self-expression, self-love, self-criticism, and manifesting goals. It increases willpower, emotional stability, and psychic abilities. Place on the third eye during meditation to connect to higher realms and Divinity. Tiger's eye appears natural, tumbled and polished, carved, or cut. It is very popular in wearing jewelry such as earrings, bracelets, and necklaces.

Topaz
Topaz is an exceptionally clear gemstone that can help you cleanse energies and release things that no longer serve you. It can also help to align and balance energies. Golden topaz is the most commonly known form of the crystal, but other colors can occur as well including blue, colorless, green, peach, pink, red, and yellow. Red topaz relates to the root chakra, peach on sacral, green on heart, yellow or gold on solar plexus, pink on third eye, blue on throat, and clear or colorless on crown chakra. Topaz appears naturally, in clusters, tumbled and polished, carved, or cut. It is an amplifying crystal that works well with tanzanite and celestite. It helps with self-expression, self-worth, self-esteem, self-definition,

self-love, self-criticism, self-concept, manifesting creative vision, and manifesting goals. You can place topaz on or near the appropriate chakra you are working with, as any type of jewelry, around the perimeter, or in the corners of any room that you want cleared of negative energy. Hold or wear topaz when you state your affirmations or as you work on any creative projects.

Tourmaline (Including Black)

Tourmaline is a powerful mental healer. It helps to balance both right and left hemispheres of the brain so it can be very beneficial for those dealing with dyslexia, paranoia, hand-eye coordination, and speech. It is a protection stone and is used to bring about a feeling of overall wellbeing. Tourmaline is excellent in releasing stagnant energy to remove blockages. Natural tourmaline wands can be held over chakras to address what needs to be cleared for healing. This will open, balance, and connect all of the chakras together. This can help in spinal adjustments and balancing of yin and yang. Tourmaline appears in many different colors. Which color it is will benefit the corresponding chakra. Red and black tourmaline will help the root chakra, green, pink and watermelon the heart chakra, yellow the solar plexus, and orange the sacral chakra. Natural tourmaline is very popular as is any type of jewelry pieces containing its natural shape. It can also appear tumbled and polished, carved, or cut.

Turquoise

Turquoise has historical significance for many nations, aboriginal tribes, kings, warriors, and shamans. It is a sacred stone of deep healing, power, luck, and protection. It is believed to hold the powers of the heavens balanced with the powers of the earth. It is very popular in jewelry. It relates to the throat chakra, giving voice to creative ideas and personal truth. Turquoise absorbs excessive energy and is a calming and harmonizing stone. Its variation of light blue to deep blue-green turquoise appears naturally, in points or tumbled, and polished.

Zircon

Zircon is a naturally occurring mineral that protects and attracts. It is usually blue or yellow and appears naturally, tumbled and polished, carved, or cut. It is an amplifying crystal that works well with clear quartz and aquamarine. Yellow zircon is associated with the solar plexus chakra and blue zircon with the throat or third eye chakra. It helps with self-love, increasing motivation and enthusiasm for things you may not normally be excited about, creating joy, spiritual growth, connection to the Divine and intuition. You can place zircon on or near the appropriate chakra, as any type of jewelry, especially a necklace or bracelet, at your desk at work or home for when you have tasks that underwhelm you.

Crystal Pairing

Some crystals pair well with others, making them better than the sum of their parts. Crystals that pair well have complementary energies that can really help direct their properties and healing energies. Almost any crystal is amplified when paired with clear quartz. Some other pairings of crystals are described below.

Smoky quartz + Apache tears
This is a powerful combination for people who are grieving. Apache tears help process grief to move forward, while smoky quartz turns negative energy to positive.

Amethyst + Labradorite
This pairing can help you have a more restful night's sleep. Amethyst is a perfect calming stone for insomnia, while labradorite calms nightmares and supports good dreams.

Black Tourmaline + Clear Quartz
This combination balances masculine and feminine energies and can help aid in the free flow of balanced energy.

Citrine + Black Tourmaline
This can help you feel grounded in prosperity. Citrine is a stone of prosperity while black tourmaline is grounding but also blocks negative energy which can help remove thoughts that prevent prosperity.

Rose Quartz + Ruby or Garnet
This pairing is excellent for relationships. Rose quartz is the crystal of unconditional love and supports all kinds of it, as does ruby and garnet. They are also grounding stones which can help keep you

grounded while experiencing love and keeping you from losing yourself too much in love.

Crystal Color Guide

Black Crystals
Black crystals absorb light. They are known to show the hidden potential of any situation. Black is grounding and manifesting. It can hold energies safely hidden yet accessible for exploration. Black crystals can have a purifying effect as well. Some black crystals are apache tears, black calcite, hematite, black jade, black jasper, black kyanite, lodestone, obsidian, onyx, black opal, and black tourmaline.

Blue Crystals
Blue crystals are associated with the throat, communication, self-expression, and standing up for yourself. Blue can help in feeling calm and self-assured. Some blue crystals are blue lace agate, blue apatite, aquamarine, blue kyanite, labradorite, lapis lazuli, larimar, sapphire, sodalite, tanzanite, blue tiger's eye, turquoise, blue aventurine, blue calcite, blue chalcedony, and blue fluorite.

Brown Crystals
Brown is associated with the earth, trees, and nature. Brown crystals are known to help with grounding, nurturing, and stabilizing energies. They can help exude warmth, comfort, security, clarity, and balance. Brown agate, brown apatite, amber, bronzite, tiger's eye, and jasper are just a few brown crystals.

Gray Crystals
Gray crystals can be very grounding, protective, and deflective. They will dispel negativity back out into the universe. Gray stones can be helpful in meditation and cleansing. It is also good for overall balancing. Some black crystals include black or gray agate, Botswana agate, gray aventurine, and smoky quartz.

Green Crystals
Green crystals are associated with the heart. They encourage personal space and growth while supporting relationships and balance emotions. Green is also linked to relieving anxiety, calming, good luck, and prosperity. Some green crystals include

moss agate, amazonite, green aventurine, green calcite, emerald, epidote, green fluorite, fuchsite, tsavorite garnet, green jade, malachite, moldavite, peridot, green tourmaline, and turquoise.

Orange/Peach Crystals
Orange crystals energize, focus, and allow creativity to flow. It increases motivation, enthusiasm, and basic energy. It can be a warming color as if being the kindling of a fire to get one moving. Orange crystals can benefit the flow of blood in the body supporting organs and tissues. Some orange crystals are orange apatite, orange aventurine, carnelian, hessonite garnet, peach moonstone, fire opal, and padparadscha sapphire.

Red Crystals
Red crystals activate, stimulate, and energize. Associated with the root chakra, red crystals embody practical, everyday survival skills, safety, and security. Red stones are also associated with protection, movement, and motivation. Some red crystals include red agate, red calcite, red garnet, red jade, red Jasper, ruby, and red tiger's eye.

Yellow/Gold Crystals
Yellow crystals relate to the body's nervous, immune, and digestive systems. Stress, fear, contentment, and happiness are all linked to this color. It is also a clearing and focus stone. Some yellow crystals are yellow agate, amber, yellow apatite, yellow aventurine, yellow calcite, citrine, yellow danburite, yellow fluorite, yellow jade, yellow kyanite, yellow tiger's eye, and topaz.

Pink Crystals
Pink crystals have a calming, nurturing, reassuring effect. They have a gentle and subtle way of bringing about a resolution in a compassionate way. They bring sensitivity to daily situations. It will be stated many times that pink is the color of unconditional love. It can also bring to fruition unexpressed feelings of emotion that have been blocking someone from personal growth. Some pink crystals are pink apatite, pink calcite, pink danburite, pink fluorite, rhodochrosite, rose quartz, and pink tourmaline.

Purple Crystals
Purple or violet is associated with intuition, divinity, imagination,

inspiration, and empathy. Purple stones help to rebalance even the most extreme out of balance systems of the body. They are good stress relieving and overall healing stones. The can also be calming, promote lucid dreams, and clarity. Some purple or violet stones are purple agate, amethyst, purple calcite, purple fluorite, and lavender jade.

White/Clear Crystals
White represents clarity, cleansing, and purification. It reflects what is already visible. White and clear are universal energy stones that amplify all other stones, strengthen, and balance. White is also good for healing, manifesting, and during meditation. Some white or clear crystals are white agate, white calcite, danburite, colorless fluorite, howlite, white jade, moonstone, opal, clear quartz, and selenite.

Multicolored Crystals
Multicolored crystals are balancing, grounding, deepen intuition, and promote feelings of love. Multicolored crystals include banded agate, ametrine, rainbow fluorite, and watermelon tourmaline.

CHAPTER 2
Crystals And Healing

Crystals have a long history of healing on many levels. For centuries, societies have valued crystals for their brilliance as precious and semiprecious gemstones as well as for their unique vibrational energies within each crystal that can help facilitate healing for the body, mind, and spirit. Cultures throughout history, including ancient Roman, Greek, Egyptian, and Asian, used crystals for their healing properties. Sacred texts included information about crystal healing, people buried the dead with significant stones, warriors and royalty wore crystals on different parts of their body and made use of talismans and amulets for good luck and protection. Ancient acupuncture needles were tipped with crystals to enhance healing. We find ourselves today utilizing similar techniques involving crystals and healing stones.

History

For a long time, gems, minerals, and crystals have been utilized to achieve physical, emotional, and spiritual wellbeing. Nearly every ancient civilization as described above has used crystals in healing. The history of crystals and healing goes far and wide.

Since the Stone Age, Jade is one of the first mined stones in China. There is a prehistoric monument built on 3,200 BC in Ireland that makes it even older than the pyramids of Egypt and the Stonehenge which is called Newgrange. There is a tomb where the front entrance was built using white quartz cobblestone. Over thousands of years ago, amber beads were found in Britain.

Crystals were a power source in ancient civilizations of Lemuria and Atlantis. The people of Atlantis created patterns with strong energy resources to serve multiple purposes including healing. This is similar to crystal grids we still create and use today.

Ancient Egyptians used many different crystals for a multitude of purposes. Quartz crystals or other gems were placed on the dead's forehead at a funeral. It was believed the energy of the stone would guide the person in the afterlife. Dancers wore crystals, especially carnelian or ruby to appear attractive and support their personal strength. Those of royalty used lapis lazuli which is crushed and placed on the eyes to enhance awareness such as Cleopatra. To promote enlightenment and support the third eye chakra, Pharaohs placed amethysts on their third eye. Clear quartz, carnelian, emerald gems, ruby, turquoise, and lapis lazuli are used for cosmetics and jewelry. For the prevention of wrinkles, Egyptians thought of the use of powdered rose quartz on the face. As for the Priestesses and Priests of Egypt who are also known as healers, they have worn multiple crystals on their bodies. They believed that the gemstones renew their energy and then transmute to those with illness or who needed healing energy.

Mayans used green jade for funeral masks, especially among rulers. They would be buried with the masks believing those in the underworld would recognize them as leaders and treat them well and help them in the underworld. Incans had a belief that the blood of their ancestral rulers is in rhodochrosite. Obsidian weapons were created by the Aztec warriors and used for their strength and grounding energy.

In ancient Chinese culture, green jade was also of high value. The Chinese believed the energy of this crystal promoted prosperity and love. Small and large statues alike have been and continue to be made to symbolize the power of this ancient stone. It reflects the symbol of status, spirituality, health and clarity, and overall good luck.

Greek soldiers would crush hematite that contains iron on them during battle. They thought the energy will give protection as opposed to their opponents. To protect them in battle, as well as to promote health and attraction of good things, Romans wore crystal amulets and talismans. To work against drunkenness, both the Romans and the Greeks used amethyst crystal. This stone was also often used to carve wine goblets.

The healing properties of crystal were documented on Vedas, which is a sacred text in Hinduism. The Kalpa tree which is considered in India as a legendary tree is supposed to be made up of precious stones like topaz, diamond, tiger's eye, ruby, green zircon, coral, emerald, and sapphire.

Virgin Mary, mother to Jesus was symbolized by lapis lazuli in Christianity times. A sapphire from the 12th century is used for the cardinal's ring today.

In Renaissance Europe, healing stones, along with herbal remedies, were used to aid in healing the sick.

For Australia and its native inhabitants, crystals and gemstones have always been given great importance. The commonest is the quartz crystal. It is thought to help connect to the spirits of family and friends who have passed on. A cave that is also believed to house a giant rock quartz crystal is found under the Ayers Rock, Uluru.

In the 1980s, a New Age dawned, creating a resurgence of crystal use, both practical and continued use for healing. Crystal healing continues to grow in popularity today. People, practitioners, and modern healers look back to the historical uses of crystals, gems, and stones and realize their beneficial powers are still the same today. Crystals, including quartz, are even used in a multitude of technological devices such as watches, radios, appliances, computers, and televisions. Western medicine is opening to the effectiveness of alternative therapies such as crystal healing.

Everything is made up of energy. Science has proven all things in the universe have their own frequency and vibration, including crystals. Famous scientists such as Nikola Tesla proved how certain forms of energy can affect the vibrational characteristics of other forms of energy. If you have ever felt the energy sucked right out of you from being around someone who is negative, or felt extremely happy around someone who is upbeat, this is what it feels like to be aligned or entrained by others' energy fields. This can apply to crystals as well, as they too have energy levels. The vibrational energy within crystals affects the energy fields all around them, including the human energy field. How this helps in healing is that crystals usually have a higher vibrational frequency than subtle human body fields. If we use crystals on or around our energy field, we can then take on that higher vibration of the crystal. We will start to feel lighter, brighter, on a higher frequency than before we began to work with crystals. Crystals do not actually do the healing themselves. They vibrate a certain energy that your body aligns with and you do the healing by taking in that energy. Our bodies then naturally take that higher energy and adjust to that for whatever needs necessary at the moment, instead of any negative or heavier energy that may be causing a blockage or disease. Vibrating at a higher rate is helpful to humans because it helps us advance spiritually and move in more positive directions physically, mentally, and emotionally. We learn to heal from within, naturally. This type of healing occurs gently and non-invasively yet is very self-empowering.

Healing must take place on all levels to fully initiate and complete the healing circle. It is not enough to treat any disease or illness only on the physical level as this would only treat the symptoms. This is the common western way of medical treatment. The root of the disease must be found and treated on the soul or spiritual level in order to completely heal with permanent results. Many natural healers believe we are here on earth for soul growth. This occurs through our body's natural healing abilities and powers. Crystal healing can be viewed as certainly promoting this type of development on the physical, emotional, mental, and spiritual levels. Practitioners of natural healing are re-discovering this ancient healing modality.

Crystals are natural elements that come from the earth. They can help us feel grounded. They can also help us connect to our energetic selves, the subtle energy bodies existing outside our physical one. This includes our aura, etheric body or biomagnetic sheath, as well as our higher self and Divinity. This helps us keep balance with spirit and our physical, emotional, and mental wellbeing. Humans exist only with all of these levels. Crystals support this existence in a positive way. When choosing a crystal to work with, let its color, feel, vibration, all come into play. Let it resonate without judgment. Sometimes you will just know when a crystal looks or feels right.

Holistic Healing

One way to use crystals in healing on all Physical, Emotional, Mental, Spiritual (PEMS) levels is through meditation. This will be discussed more specifically in Chapter 7. When we meditate, we are focusing on the present very intently. When we introduce the healing work of a crystal into this practice, we enhance the benefits greatly! Meditating allows us to be still, present, repeat a positive affirmation. This intention or mantra connects us to our higher selves and a higher vibration. Since crystals generally have higher vibrations, they are a natural enhancement to meditation practice. When we focus our intentions while gazing at or holding a specific crystal, this increases the power of the energy and intention. You may not feel something right away. Be patient, open-minded, and keep trying.

A thoughtfully considered intention is the starting point for healing with crystals. Specific intentions instilled into daily thought patterns also become part of its energy. We always have free will to choose our thoughts as each day brings forth new challenges and wonderful beginnings. Healing crystals help us focus our intention, quiet our mind, and reconnect to the universally healing vibrations of the Earth.

Thoughts create vibrations throughout the universe, which makes setting intentions a powerful way to achieve happiness and wellbeing. Having a clear purpose provides us with insight into our dreams, aspirations, and values. It also helps us to be in the present instead of being caught in negative thought patterns. We can also get stuck in past patterns that have never or no longer serve us in any way positively. Crystals can help alleviate these doubts. Intentions are like magnets by attracting what can make them come true. Creating an intention starts by setting goals that align with your values, aspiration, and purpose.

Healing the body
Your body is the physical part of you. Crystals can help balance bodily energies and facilitate physical change. This could include relieving headaches, exhaustion, fatigue, joint, or muscle pain. Crystals can even help with such physical ailments as seasonal allergies, sore throats, and fevers. They should, however, never substitute care from a qualified healthcare provider.

Healing the mind
Your mind is both physical and nonphysical. The physical aspects

of your mind include the brain and nervous system. The nonphysical aspects include emotions, thoughts, and dreams. The vibration in crystals can help balance energies of the mind to bring about healing. Conditions that can be eased might include emotional issues, stress, anxiety, insomnia, nightmares, depression, and grief.

Healing your spirit
Your spirit is purely a nonphysical part of you. Crystals can assist in balancing spiritual energies such as unconditional love, forgiveness, compassion, and belief systems. They can also facilitate communication with your higher self and a higher power.

Health benefits
When crystals are carried, worn, held, or even just gazed at or placed in a meaningful area, they have an added benefit to our subtle energies surrounding our physical body.
Chakras linked the subtle bodies to the physical body or centers that mediate and circulate energy. Using crystals in our daily lives this way can help create balance, stability, peace, and joy.

Increase energy
Many specific crystals can be used to increase energy. Red and orange ones are excellent for overcoming energy depletion. They not only boost energy but they also help to get positive thoughts flowing again while getting rid of negativity. From long ago to now, it is said to be beneficial to wear a red crystal or amulet to help purify the blood and allow it to flow freely. When blood flows clear and free, our life force or Qi is strong! Vitality is strong and we feel driven, have a purpose.

Crystals which are red and orange are commonly known to give motivation and energy. Orange carnelian, red jasper, ruby, and bloodstone are fine examples of crystals that are associated with stimulation while providing balance. Carnelian can be carried for an instant pick me up. Simply holding it for a few minutes can improve your energy levels. Red Jasper can be used longer term, holding a long storage of energy when needed. It can help to place this on any lower chakras when you need a boost of lasting energy or have been exhausted over time.

Clear quartz is a master energizer for the aura or biomagnetic sheath. Energizing your aura has an overall beneficial effect on your energy level in general, but it also makes your physical body feel more energetic. Placing a clear quartz crystal over your body, just below your navel for ten to fifteen minutes can help you feel recharged and ready for anything.

Clear the Mind
Crystals are powerful in stimulating a lethargic mind and promotes calmness as well. Crystal can assist in boosting a person's creativity, clarity, and concentration. They help raise human vibration thus bringing focus to your mind. Crystals to use for mind calming and clearing are clear quartz, amethyst, sodalite, bloodstone, and carnelian.

Clear quartz placed above or around the head and crown chakra will provide your body with clearing energy and allow it to get back to its most perfect state of balance. Calming amethyst relaxes your mind and improves your memory, creating focus and concentration. Carnelian can be very activating, letting the mind sharply focus, and dismiss mental fogginess. Sodalite also has a strong effect on the mind. It can eliminate mental confusion and encourage intuitive perception and reasonable thought. This opens the mind to see things in a different manner and to receive useful new information. Bloodstone can be an excellent tonic crystal to relieve an overactive mind. It reduces mental confusion while increasing alertness. It helps in adapting to changing or stressful situations, maintaining mental stability. This helps in clear decision-making. It can be beneficial to keep a bloodstone in your pocket during any type of test or exam, to help focus on a solution rather than a problem.

Creativity
By uniting the right and left hemispheres of your brain, the capacity to solve problems and creativity can be expanded. The right side is more intuitive, creative, and willing to take risks. The left side of the brain is analytical, logical, and fact-based. Crystals can bridge the gap between the two and channel their powers. Crystals are able to assist and help when you feel burned out and your creative paths feel stuck. Red and orange crystals such as carnelian, red or even yellow Jasper are warming and stimulating

stones. They can be used to stimulate creativity and boost self-esteem with their vibrant colors. You will be able to reach your goals and confidently move forward as they increase passion and motivation. Carnelian, in particular, is considered a strong action stone.

Red or yellow Jasper helps you realize a problem assertively. They combine organization (think compartmentalization) with imagination. Red Jasper, in particular, can bring forth conflict before it becomes too overwhelming. It allows you to investigate new coping strategies and provides useful insight into the most difficult situations. Both red and yellow Jasper increases creativity.

Healing sessions
Crystal healing therapy has been used for over 5,000 years but still continues today, especially in Ayurvedic Medicine from India and Traditional Chinese Medicine or TCM. Practitioners have studied past uses of the therapy to become knowledgeable about the techniques in order to apply them to modern illnesses and disease.

This book will help you collect and work with crystals on your own. However, it is important to know how a healing session with a practitioner may be, or if you would like to emulate your own healing session in the comfort of your own home. Healers who use crystals believe the stones work as conduits to attract positive energy into the body while drawing negative energy away from it. Neither the practitioner nor the crystals are doing the actual healing. It is up to the person receiving it to be open to this natural modality in order to allow the healing to occur within them. It has been discussed previously how this can help keep all levels of energy balanced, from the physical, emotional, mental, and spiritual aspects. Indeed crystal healing is a gentle yet powerful way to heal!

One way a crystal healer may perform a session is to have you first fill out an informational form regarding past and current issues and background. They may have you sit or lie comfortably on a therapy table or even on the floor. Your chakras will be assessed to see where attention is needed. Appropriate crystals will be used to open, cleanse, and balance the major chakras. Usually, a specific crystal layout will be determined for individual needs and placed on and around the body. They will be activated to their fullest healing potential to promote healing and restore balance. There may be soothing music, sound therapy, and essential oils used. The receiver should be deeply relaxed during the session and rejuvenated afterward. Anything that is felt after a session is deemed appropriate as we all react differently to healing. You may feel tired or anxious as you release some no longer needed energy. Overall, you should have a complete feeling of wellbeing. Never does crystal therapy replace medical attention from a traditional medical doctor, nor does it claim to cure any illness.

What to Expect
When energy healing work is done, the energy will align with your highest and greatest good. Sometimes the change you think you need or want is not what best serves you. Get rid of any expectation of the result and allow what serves you to come forth. When we set expectations and stick to them, we limit ourselves and results. What we imagine is usually smaller than what the universe makes available to us. Sometimes what serves our greatest good doesn't appear as we think it should.

Try to remove "should" and "could" from your vocabulary and accept what the energy brings. Sometimes changes are subtle and take a while to occur. Sometimes they are immediate and very obvious. Oftentimes, when major healing occurs, a shift in our reality can throw us completely off balance. Understand the need for change but allow yourself to let go of any expectations of how and what change should happen. Set your intention, do the work, remove judgment and expectation, and be open. The energy will always serve your greater good.

Crystals and the Moon
A new and a full moon are very sacred times full of energy. The full moon reflects the outcome of both your physical work and your energetic manifestations. To utilize this energetic, sacred time to your advantage, a full or new moon ritual is a powerful way to harness the energy and to magnify it positively to benefit your life and higher self. Whether you choose to celebrate the full or new moon with an elaborate ritual, a brief meditation or any other personal technique, introducing healing crystals into this practice

will increase and strengthen your manifestation abilities. Working with crystals in this way strengthens them for that moon cycle, as well as the one immediately following.

There are particular crystals that will work most effectively during the full or new moon phase. The ones you pick for use are usually uniquely personal choices based on what you relate to the best. You can very clearly state intentions between the phases of the moon. The new moon is actually a wonderfully magical time to set intentions. By the time the full moon has arrived, it is believed your intentions set will come to fruition. When the full moon does arrive, it is good to reflect on any gifts received and express gratitude. This is often a time for deep introspection. What can you do to better yourself, your life, grow physically, mentally, and spiritually? The energy of the full moon is always positive. It is thought to be feminine, goddess-like. This means it relates to the psychic, mysterious, softer yet cooler aspect of our selves. The moon is feminine yin and dark, to the masculine yang and light of the sun.

Using crystals and their unique powers during the phases of the moon can increase what you create to be even more abundant. If you are satisfied with your status quo and ask for that to stay the same, use this energetic time with your crystals to be grateful and expand your gratitude for what you have. Always live in gratitude. With the next moon phase, you can state a new intention including any growth you may have experienced. Let go of whatever you need to let go of and let the powers of the crystals and moon expand the positive aspects of the whole experience.

When working with different phases of the moon, your genuine intention and working with that particular moon phase is more relevant than the specific crystals you choose to work with. There are a number of crystals that have vibrational frequencies that align with the moon in general, no matter what phase it is in at that particular time.

Even though the moon really represents feminine energy, it does embody both yin and yang, like our own bodies. The moon is balanced in itself. The full moon is thought to be masculine, yang energy, a time for action and completion. The intentions or seeds we plant at the time of the new moon are now in full swing and must be acted upon. The new moon is more introspective, about going within. It is feminine, yin energy, a time to gratefully express desired intentions. New moon energy requires more thoughtful action with our minds and spirit. We can meditate quietly yet be acutely aware of any messages we receive in order to help us set objectives.

Selenite

Selenite is a beautiful, soft white crystal that can be iridescent and reminiscent of the moon and its glow. This crystal can be beneficial for letting go or for setting forth action. It is a highly protective and amplifying crystal. This makes it quite perfect for setting intentions during phases of the moon. It is very unique and powerful in that it does not need to be cleansed as it does not absorb or store energy. It serves as a clearing stone for other crystals because of this quality. It readily protects against negativity. Selenite also helps with clearing your aura, increasing intuition, and connecting with your higher self and divinity. Selenite is a good crystal to work with when wishing to work with forgiveness and the moon phases. During the full moon, selenite can be receptive of its abundantly available bounty and clear blockages to help you let go of anything that no longer serves you. It will rejuvenate you and recharge your energy field and chakras, to help you step into the next moon phase with your full potential.

Moonstone

Any type or color of moonstone is terrific for working with lunar energy at any moon phase. Its basic coloring is a milky grey, peach or white with an opalescent sheen. It is known for its protectiveness, connecting to higher realms, divinity, and intuition. Moonstone is also helpful during water or night time travel. These characteristics make it a perfect crystal to use in working with the phases of the moon.

Labradorite

Labradorite is another wonderful choice to work with moon energy. It is a protective crystal associated with magic. It can help open your third eye chakra, thus allow you to be receptive to receive from higher realms and your higher self. It is beneficial to increasing intuition. It reduces negativity and dispels illusion. This can help in setting realistic yet mystical intentions during the moon phases.

Usage

There are a number of different ways to use any of the above crystals during new or full moon phases. You can place the crystal under your pillow during the night of a full or new moon. This can help release the power of the moon in your dreams and cause you to have very vivid dreams with intuitive messages. You can also place a crystal or group of crystals in the full moonlight for charging. Clearly state the intention you wish these stones to amplify. Ask that they carry that energy into the next moon phases. On the day of a full or new moon, carry a crystal of your choice with you. It will serve as a reminder of your intentions, work to be done, letting go, as you are in tune with that powerful moon phase throughout the day. During a new or full moon ritual or meditation, keep a crystal of choice near you or in your hands. This will enhance the moon's powerful energy of this phase and allow you to go deeper into your practice.

Grounding

When working with the powerful phases of the moon, it is easy to become overwhelmed or imbalanced. To help with this, it is important to have a grounding crystal readily available. Good grounding stones are smoky quartz, black tourmaline, and hematite.

CHAPTER 3
Creating Crystal Grids

A crystal grid is the formation of different crystals with the intention of creating powerful energy focused on a specific intent. Grids can be simple or complex. A crystal grid is the combined energy of the crystals you use, the layout you create, and the intention you set. You should intent what you need, not necessarily what you think you want. Once you decide which crystals you would like to use in your grid, you can choose or create a shape. You can certainly make your grid in any shape and include any extras such as tree branches or bark, leaves, flowers, candles, etc., but some find using basic sacred geometric shapes enhance the power of the grid. Spirals represent the pathway to consciousness. Circles signify continual rebirth, unity, and growth. The infinity symbol represents endlessness and dates back to 1655. Squares represent earthly elements. Triangles or pyramids are connected to divinity and represent the connection between body, mind, and spirit.

To use a grid, create it anywhere it will be most beneficial such as under your bed or on your desk or sacred space. You will be able to set the intent and keep the grid there over time. Write an intention on a piece of paper to include under the center crystal. This should be an intent we truly need rather than just a want. The universe will only give us what we are ready to handle.

To arrange your grid, there should be a focus stone in the center or middle of the grid. This is the primary energy you are trying to attain. The surrounding stones enhance the energy, allowing it to move outward from the focus. Outer stones can either be the source of intention for the primary energy, or they can be a perimeter stone to keep the energy within the grid.

Choose your crystals based on specific need, your intuition, as well as what you have readily available to you. Clear the crystals and space you will create your grid by burning sage, incense, or singing bowls. You can also clear crystals using water, moonlight, or by burying in the earth for the amount of time that feels right. Be aware of the crystal's properties when clearing them. Some do not like water or to be in the ground very long.

Put your intention you wrote on a piece of paper in the center of the grid under the center crystal point. You may state your intention out loud or silently. Take a few deep breaths before-hand and be aware of slowing down, mindful of your breath and clearing your mind. Allow your intention to resonate within you and your crystals and grid. Place the rest of the crystals in whatever shape you feel drawn to. Using a crystal quartz or whatever point you choose, start to activate your grid. You can go from the inside out or outside in. Touch each crystal with your starter point and create an invisible line connecting each crystal to each other, keeping in mind your true intention. When finished touching each crystal point to point, take a few more deep breaths. Thank the universe and Divine for allowing your intentions to be heard. With gratitude, keep your grid up for at least 48 hours or more or whatever time frame feels right for you.

Grid for abuse
Create a crystal grid that helps with three major issues that often may arise from abuse — security, self-esteem, and personal strength. Use a triangle grid that balances body, mind, and spirit. Place the grid anywhere where you usually are such as near the bed and desk. Cleanse the crystals about once a month. Any size or shape of stone will work as long as it feels right to you.

Use black tourmaline as the main focus stone for safety, security, and absorbing negative energy. The intention stones could be citrine for self-esteem and power, rose quartz for self-love, carnelian for personal power and activation. Perimeter stones should be clear quartz to enhance all the other stones.

Anger release grid
Use a basic circular grid for unity and oneness. The stones in this grid are designed to do two things — absorb the anger and increase compassion. Place it anywhere you spend a lot of time or under your bed. Cleanse the stones, particularly the focus stone every few days. Any shape or form of stone will work here.

Courage grid

Amazonite is a good crystal to use to promote courage. Create a square courage grid using aquamarine and citrine above and below with amazonite as the focus or center stone and quartz points as perimeter stones to direct and amplify the energy. Place the courage grid anywhere you spend a lot of time and can reflect upon.

Intuition/Psychic grid
Make a third eye grid with amethyst and clear quartz to stimulate your intuition and psychic abilities. You can create the grid as an actual eye shape with amethyst in the center. Lay it out on your bedside table, state your question or intention before you go to sleep, then sleep on it. The amethyst and clear quartz will help the answer come to you as you are asleep.

Forgiveness grid
Using a spiral shape with Selenite as the center focus stone and clear quartz as all other points on the grid, create a forgiveness grid. Place it where you can meditate on it easily and comfortably. Sit or lie near the grid and visualize the person you wish to forgive. Imagine both of you connected together energetically as physical ties between you. Then imagine cutting those ties as you repeat a mantra such as, "I release you." Once the ties are cut, visualize the person you need to forgive surrounded in white light. This can be a very powerful release and may cause strong emotions to flow. Allow them to be released from you. Forgiveness is not always about the other person but rather allowing yourself to forgive and move on. It is not always easy. State your forgiveness intention clearly and truthfully and amazing letting go will occur.

Gratitude grid
Living with gratitude can be such a wonderful, humbling experience. It allows you to align with who you truly are and what really matters in life. A gratitude grid can help amplify all the goodness that surrounds us as humans. Create a heart-shaped grid where you can easily and comfortably meditate. Use rose quartz as the center focus stone, preferably heart-shaped if you have it! Clear quartz should be the amplifying perimeter stones as the outline of the heart. Sit near the grid and close your eyes. Visualize gratitude flowing through your body and into your heart and imagine your heart delivering gratitude throughout your entire body. Allow the gratitude to flow through and around you. When you live with

gratitude, real change can occur for you.

Grief grid
Grief is the natural feeling of loss and is necessary to experience in order to move forward. If we get stuck in grief at any point, crystal healing can help facilitate removing of blockages to pass through the sadness and again experience joy. A grief grid can help speed the process along if we are stuck for too long. Make a stage of grief grid and place it somewhere you spend a lot of time.

Place the stones in a spiral with an Apache tear as the center stone with the following stones spiraling outward — hematite for anger, rainbow fluorite for denial, blue kyanite for bargaining, smoky quartz for depression, and amethyst for acceptance. There really isn't a focus stone or perimeter stone as each stone in the grief grid helps you manage one stage of grief at a time. Working with this grid helps you feel love again, release, and heal pain.

Peace grid
There is a Serenity Prayer that creates a path to peace — changing what you can control and letting go of what you cannot, and understanding the difference between the two. A peace grid can help you feel peace in even the most challenging of times because it helps you let go and overcome the urge to control. It helps us experience inner peace and wisdom.

Shape a circle grid for oneness and unity with turquoise as the center focus stone representing inner peace. The first circle around the turquoise should be aquamarine for letting go and another circle after that with amethyst to represent good judgment.

Regret grid
Regret is a strong emotion that can keep us focused on negative past circumstances instead of the current, more positive present conditions we are living in the here and now. It can be a big cause of situational disease or long-term illness by holding on to past regret. Self-forgiveness is crucial in overcoming regret. A grid to release regret using crystals can be very beneficial.

To create a grid for releasing regret, place it on a flat surface in which you usually stay. Use a triangle shape to connect body, mind, and spirit. The main center focus stone should be a smoky quartz to release old belief systems and transform negative to positive. The middle intention stones should be aquamarine which helps release old patterns. The perimeter stones of protection should be black tourmaline which absorbs negativity. It can help to repeat the mantra "I separate and forgive myself from my regrets of the past," while confirming your intention in a grid to release regret.

Rejection grid

As will be stated in further chapters, we have no control over whether somebody wants us, likes us, or chooses us, but that doesn't stop it from hurting when rejection does occur. To heal the pain from rejection, you must return to a place of self-love. Rose quartz is extremely effective for this. It is the stone for unconditional love and will bring you back to that space. Rhodonite is also a good stone for dealing with loss and rejection. It is often used to prevent injury and loss, thus can be seen as a protection and insurance type crystal. Any pink, green, or vibrantly colored orange or even yellow crystal can help with the lower chakras and heart chakra. When these are open, balanced, and functioning optimally, you will feel safe, grounded, protected, yet have a strong sense of self and self-worth. These qualities will help you feel safe from rejection and have the courage to keep opportunities available. Carnelian is a bright orange crystal that aids in overcoming abuse of any kind in order to trust yourself and others again. It can help dispel envy and rage. These crystals will also help in dealing with recovery from any rejection or abandonment in the future. Use a triangle shaped grid to connect body, mind, and spirit. Have the main center focus stone be rose quartz or rhodonite to accentuate self-love. Use the other crystals mentioned in a pattern you intuitively arrange. There is no right or wrong placement of the crystals. Repeat the mantra, "I trust myself and know I am always worthy of true love" while affirming your intention in a rejection grid.

Prosperity grid

Learning to be grateful for what we do have is key to feeling an abundance of prosperity. We often do not lack as much as we think we do. When we begin to focus on the positive, what we do have, instead of the negative, what we think we want, we then begin to live a light, prosperous life.

To create a prosperity grid, place it in your home's prosperity corner, or the back left corner of where you spend the most time daily. Create a square with infinity symbol in the center of it or the creation shape. The center focus stone should be citrine for prosperity. The crystals along the middle infinity symbol should be turquoise to represent luck and prosperity. The perimeter square stones should be clear quartz to amplify all the other crystals and intentions. Repeat the mantra "I am thankful I am prosperous."

Crystal grids can work wonders to fulfill positive intentions. They can help us let go and fill our daily lives with balance and fullness. You can complete a crystal grid whenever you feel the need to, but a new moon or a full moon is an excellent time energetically to do a grid. Using the powers of mother nature, where crystals originate and feel right at home in, can only enhance the healing capabilities of all crystals and stones. We are at our best when we are one with nature. Crystals let us know this whenever we allow them to help us heal. You can use any of the grids described in this chapter or feel free to create your own individualized grid and intention.

CHAPTER 4
Crystals And Chakras

Chakras are energy centers that connect your physical body to your subtle bodies that surround your physical body in your biomagnetic sheath or aura. Your chakras connect your body to the energy of your mind and spirit. Chakras distribute life force, vitality, Qi, through the physical and subtle bodies. Many energy workers, practitioners, and healers count 12 main chakras. Some count even more up to 114 of them, including major, minor, and micro chakras! Your seven main chakras, the ones focused on in this book, run along your spinal column. Each main chakra is associated with a specific color that corresponds to various energies that govern different aspects of human emotion and behavior. Imbalances in the chakras may correlate to physical, emotional, mental, or spiritual issues. Diseases and conflicts on the physical, emotional, mental, or spiritual level occur and the flow of subtle energy becomes imbalanced when chakras are blocked.

To help balance these energies, you can work with crystals by placing similarly colored ones on corresponding chakras.

Chakras create a state of harmony or disharmony depending on how well each one is functioning. Keeping them cleansed, balanced, and recharged is important for holistic healing and wellbeing. There are techniques in which crystals can help with this. If you have physical, emotional, mental, or spiritual issues connected to a specific chakra, your health and wellbeing will benefit by placing the crystal on the chakra and keeping it there for 20 minutes or longer while relaxing quietly. Certain issues correspond with the chakras and each chakra has a different color associated with it. Other energies are also associated with colors, so choosing crystals with those colors can help you work through particular issues.

Root Chakra - The first and the root chakra is located at the seat or base of your spine and vibrates red. It is the center associated with survival instincts and relates to safety and security issues as well as issues of the legs, feet, and hips. Family and tribal/community identity have to do with the root chakra. Some positive qualities associated with the root chakra are basic security, sense of one's own power, mobility, independence, and leadership. Some negative or shadow aspects of this chakra are impatience, fear, vengeance, anger, violence, overactive, manipulative. The root chakra links distinctively to the physical body.

Red is equal to grounding, passion, vitality, physical energy, and stability. Crystals good for the root chakra vibrating red are red jasper, garnet, ruby, hematite, smoky quartz, red zincite, black tourmaline, and black obsidian.

Sacral Chakra - The sacral and second chakra is located right below your navel area and vibrates orange. It is the source of creativity, personal power, prosperity, and procreation. Issues related to the sacral chakra are digestive, abdominal, lower back, and sexual organ issues. Positive aspects are assertiveness, confidence, joy, sensuality, fertility, and acceptance of sexual identity. Shadow qualities include low self-esteem, infertility, sluggishness, inferiority, arrogance, and emotional hurdles or blockages. The sacral chakra connects the physical body.

Orange is associated with self-identity, sexuality, family issues, ego, and social anxiety. Crystals that benefit the sacral chakra are orange carnelian, orange calcite, turquoise, and fluorite.

Solar Plexus Chakra - The solar plexus and third chakra are right below your sternum and above your navel, vibrates yellow, and is related to boundaries and self-esteem. Physical issues are often related to the lower mid-back, pancreas, spleen, gallbladder, and urinary system. Some positive qualities of the solar plexus chakra are organization, logic, intelligence, empathy, and good use of energy. Negative qualities include overly emotional, lethargic, poor use of energy, cynical, emotional baggage, energy leakage, and taking on other's feelings and problems. The solar plexus chakra is linked to the emotional level.

Yellow relates to self-worth, self-esteem, self-love, and identity. Yellow jasper, citrine, amber, and golden calcite are good crystals for this chakra.

Heart Chakra - The heart and fourth chakra is located in the center of your chest and vibrates green related to compassion, unconditional love, kindness, nurturing, accepting, generosity, and forgiveness. Shadow qualities include jealousy, possessiveness, unable to demonstrate love, disconnected from feelings, insecure, and resistant to change. Issues associated with the heart chakra are physical ones relating to ribs, lungs, and heart. Grief can take a toll on the heart chakra. This chakra links to the emotional level.

Green is associated with love, finances, wealth, forgiveness, and compassion. Crystals that benefit the heart chakra are rose quartz, watermelon tourmaline, green aventurine, and jade.

Throat Chakra - The throat and fifth chakra is in the center of your throat and vibrates blue. It is related to speaking your truth and letting go of personal will to allow in Divine guidance. Positive attributes are being loyal, receptive, a good communicator, and idealistic. Shadow qualities are being unable to speak about thoughts or feelings, being stuck, inflexible, and disloyal. Physical issues include thyroid, throat, and mouth. The throat chakra links the emotional to the mental level.

Blue exudes truth, wisdom, loyalty, and listening. Crystals that help the throat chakra are sodalite, blue calcite, blue chalcedony, blue calcite, amazonite, blue turquoise, and aquamarine.

Third Eye Chakra - The sixth chakra or known as the third eye or brow chakra sits directly in the center of your forehead. This chakra vibrates indigo and corresponds to intuition and intellect. Positive qualities consist of being intuitive, perceptive, visionary, and in the present. Negative qualities are being fearful, attached to the past, superstitious, and overwhelmed with the thoughts of others. Physical issues include eyes, ears, head, and brain. The third eye chakra is linked to the mental level.

Indigo represents spirituality, psychic power, and intuition. Beneficial crystals include lapis lazuli, azurite, tanzanite, and sodalite.

Crown Chakra - The seventh chakra or the crown chakra sits at the top of your head. It vibrates violet purple. The crown chakra corresponds with your higher self and Divinity. Positive qualities include being mystical, creative, and humanitarian. Negative aspects are controlling, illusory, arrogant, and overly-imaginative. Systemic issues and musculoskeletal issues are related to the crown chakra. It links to the spiritual level.

Purple is associated with universal consciousness, energy, perfection, and enlightenment. Crystals to use with your crown chakra include amethyst, quartz crystal, white topaz, selenite, and Herkimer diamond.

Cleansing and Recharging Chakras with Crystals

Intuitive healers can see or feel healthy spinning chakras as colorful, bright light wheels. They spin vibrantly and completely. When they see gray, dull, or black sections, or unsteady spinning of chakra wheels, this signifies imbalance or physical, emotional, mental, or spiritual disease. When using crystals to heal yourself, it isn't even necessary to be able to see the chakras spinning or not. A crystal will attune to any imbalance, bring re-energize the chakra and bring it back to harmony. It is beneficial to do a whole chakras cleanse for a full adjustment. You could cleanse just one or two if you identify with an illness associated with that particular chakra such those described earlier.

Full Chakra Cleanse
For a full chakra cleanse, balance and recharge, you can follow these steps, using the appropriate crystals:

Lie down in a comfortable position. As you place each crystal as described below, imagine an energy and light that is radiating from the crystal for a couple of minutes.
You should be mindful that the chakra's spin is regulated and it is in the process of being cleansed.

On the earth chakra, put the smoky quartz slightly below and between your feet.
On the root chakra, put the red jasper.
On the sacral chakra, put the orange carnelian.
On the solar plexus chakra, put the yellow jasper.

On the heart chakra, put a green aventurine.
On the throat chakra, put the blue lace agate.
On the brow or third eye chakra, put a sodalite.
On the crown chakra, put an amethyst.

Now, slowly turn your focus on the soles of your feet up to the body's middle part. Feel how more balanced and harmonized each chakra has become.

Relax, taking deep breaths downward in the abdomen then hold and count to seven before exhaling. When you inhale and hold off for a while, feel the crystal's energy re-energizing your chakras. You should be able to experience the chakras radiating vibrantly through you from there.

If you are done and you are ready, collect the crystals and you should start on the crown chakra. Be aware of a grounding cord anchoring you to the earth and to your physical body as you are reaching the earth chakra.

After using the crystals, you should cleanse them.

Activating Higher Chakras
Include all crystals as described for the full chakra cleanse layout. In addition, you will be using bloodstone, rose quartz, labradorite, and clear quartz. You may need some assistance laying out all of the crystals on and around you.

Hold all 12 crystals in your hands for a few minutes, visualizing them bathed in bright white light. Lay out each crystal as described for Full Chakra Cleanse. In addition to the eight crystals in a full chakra cleanse, for activating higher chakras, you will need to:

Place bloodstone about 30 cm or 12 inches below your feet.
Place rose quartz three fingers width above your heart.
Place labradorite 15 cm or six inches above your head.
Place clear quartz 30 cm or 12 inches above your crown.

With all 12 crystals in place, draw your attention down to the bloodstone and be mindful of the higher earth chakra opening. Feel how it pulls refined earth energies in and radiates them up to the smoky quartz and through your whole body. Be aware of your connection to the earth's biomagnetic sheath or aura. Feel yourself aligning to the faster and lighter vibration that it carries and how it connects to the lower chakras.

Take your attention up to the rose quartz. Feel how the higher heart chakra opens and expands, receiving and radiating unconditional love as it activates your innate compassion and connection with others. Feel how this chakra connects to the throat chakra so you can communicate love out to the world.

Finally, take your attention up to the clear quartz above your head. Be aware of its connection to higher spiritual guidance. Feel how the energy flows down into the labradorite, activating its hidden awareness and soul memory. Recognize that you are a spiritual being on a human journey!

When the activation is finished, slowly remove the crystals starting with the highest crown chakra, working down to the earth chakra. When you reach the earth chakra, again be mindful of the grounding cord linking your feet to this chakra, grounding you within your physical body to the earth. After you pick up the bloodstone from the higher earth chakra, stand up and feel your feet firmly on the ground. Repeat this higher chakra exercise daily until activation is complete.

In addition to chakra cleansing and activation with crystals, many people wear crystal jewelry corresponding to the main chakras connected to the physical body. You can wear the rainbow of chakra related colors or one of the colors corresponding to a chakra that needs extra support. For example, wear a red Jasper bracelet to support your root chakra. Wear a green aventurine necklace to help activate your heart chakra.

Crystals can be very powerful healing tools in cleansing and activating chakras.

CHAPTER 5
Crystals In Reiki

Reiki is a great, holistic procedure used to relieve stress and develop good overall feelings of wellbeing. It is also known to promote relaxation. It can also be an extraordinary healing modality. Even though each experience will be uniquely felt, most people report feeling extremely safe, warm, radiant, and filled with peace and calm. Some have even left a session completely rid of their disease or concern they came in with.

Thoughts create vibrations within the universe. This makes setting intentions a powerful instrument in achieving feelings of joy and wellbeing. Intentions are like magnets. They can attract what will make them come true, as in the law of attraction. Setting healing intentions with the use of crystals is even more powerful. Crystals vibrate with universal bright light. Having them absorb and work with positive human intentions adds to their usefulness and make them all the more powerful. Reiki, or spiritually guided life force energy, allows a body to learn to heal naturally. Combined with crystal use, these two gentle healing modalities enhance health and wellbeing on all levels powerfully. Reiki and crystal healing allow the physical body to be balanced and healthy by touching the subtle bodies. Healing then occurs on the physical, emotional, mental, and spiritual level.

Reiki is a non-invasive and gentle healing modality that enhances the body's natural healing abilities by utilizing universal life energy. Reiki is derived from two words – Rei or the Higher Power, and Ki or Life Force Energy. A session of Reiki, along with the healing power of crystals, results in an amazing, mutual healing experience. Energy blockages and stagnation are cleared easily with this potent pairing. The receiver will feel lighter, refreshed, centered, and relaxed.

A Reiki crystal healing session is similar to a traditional Reiki session, with the addition of carefully chosen crystals. The client lies with his clothes on and comfortably on a treatment table. The hands of the Reiki practitioner are placed and moved over the client's body by either very lightly touching or just above. This placement and movement of hands allows the Reiki energy to flow in and around the client's body. In a Reiki crystal session, precise crystals are placed on the body, usually on or around a chakra center. The addition of the crystals to the Reiki session enhances and amplifies the healing power of the Reiki energy. The practitioner becomes a mode of transportation for Reiki energy to flow through, to be received by the client where it is needed most. Crystals can help speed up the healing process of a Reiki session.

Before any Reiki session with crystals, the healing room or area should be cleared energetically. This can be done using clear quartz points or really any crystal that feels right. You or the practitioner can channel Reiki energy, positive intention, through the crystals or Reiki symbols to clear the room and protect it.

When a client arrives for a session for the first time, they fill out a health background questionnaire. This helps the practitioner figure out precisely the issues of concern that need to be addressed for that session. Crystals are carefully chosen and placed on and around the client. Some crystals may be chosen to help a client who may feel particularly anxious or nervous about the session. They may be placed under the client. A full body Reiki treatment is conducted with the crystals in place. All of this is done peacefully and gently. They may be re-arranged during a session, according to the practitioner's intuition, spiritual, or Reiki guidance. The session ends with the removal of the crystals and checking of client's chakras for optimal balance and function. Gratitude should be expressed to the spiritual energies as well as to the crystals. Information is shared, questions asked, and good energy felt from combined Reiki and crystal earth elements. The client may receive a Crystal Prescription on how to use prescribed crystals for further healing at home.

Reiki is truly a special healing. Crystals certainly enhance this unique experience.

CHAPTER 6
Clearing And Protection With Crystals

It has been stated before and will be again, when you feel that you want to wear or have a particular crystal, subconsciously, you can be expressing a need for its protective vibrations. Vibrations of crystals are great for counteracting all kinds of negative energy. Negative energies are lightly repelled, excess energies are alleviated, and toxicity is absorbed, thus providing harmony in the home, office, or any surroundings. They also create harmony within the self. Where would we be without these light energy workers?

Crystal Protection

There is an overabundance of negative energy out there in the world. Several crystals are extremely efficient in protecting against someone with negative intentions toward you, or from those who drain energy away from you. Many crystals also dispel other people's negative attitudes or emotions such as jealousy and envy that may harmfully affect you. Those who are sensitive very often feel the pull if anyone is drawing on their energy. Placing yellow jasper over your solar plexus can protect you against this. If you are a main attraction for ill-wishing, wear amethyst or labradorite around your neck for protection.

Energy vampirism happens when someone feeds off your own energy. A soft kind of this vampirism can happen through the spleen. If anyone is strongly attached to you or is vigorously draining your energy, you may feel fatigued or have a pain below your left armpit area when in contact with a particular person. Green aventurine crystal will protect your spleen and rejuvenate your energy. You can also use a spleen protection pyramid to protect your energy.

Spleen
To perform a spleen protection pyramid, sit comfortably. Draw a large triangle just below your left armpit toward your navel then around your waist, to the opposite point near your spine using

green aventurine. Finally, bring the crystal back to where you have started. Visualize the triangle you have drawn surrounding your spleen as a pyramid. Now, at about a hand's width beneath the armpit, put the green aventurine for about 20 minutes to renew and heal the spleen.

Car

A smoky quartz crystal can be programmed and placed in your car to keep it and you safe at all times. Hold the smoky quartz in your hands while visualizing it surrounded by light. Ask it to protect you, your passengers, and your car all the time. You can also use black tourmaline and program that for protection in your car, to absorb and deflect negative energy. Rose quartz can also help keep passengers and other drivers happy and peaceful. It will keep road rage at bay too. If you have any of these crystals with a point in it, face the point outward to ensure a circle of protection around and inside the car. Amethyst can also be used for its protective and calming qualities. Since cars travel and different passengers can come and go, it is wise to cleanse and rejuvenate any crystals used in your car for protection. It will help to keep them positively charged and vibrating healthily to clear and cleanse them on a regular basis.

Home

Crystals are brilliant and beautiful objects which cannot just beautify your home but also have a very useful holistic purpose. Crystals can assist in keeping the home vibrations and energy vibrant and harmonious. They have the ability to protect your home against electromagnetic pollutions or environmental pollution such as those from microwaves, radio waves, radar, and cellular devices. They can also protect against noisy neighbors. It is important to regularly cleanse the crystals in your home.

Amethyst is one of the super protector stones. It brings a high spiritual vibration into your home. It also guards against psychic attack and negativity, environmental pollution, and ill-wishing. Bloodstone usually works on the physical body, but it also has a strong ability to block out unwanted influences to the home. Place a bloodstone at each corner of your house to keep you and your home protected.

Orange carnelian kept near the front door will attract an abundance of positive realities to your home. Rose quartz placed near an outside wall facing neighbors will guarantee peace and tranquility from them and bring harmony to both homes. It is particularly useful if you have noisy, inconsiderate neighbors as it promotes consideration for others and encourages them to be quiet and peaceful. Rose quartz is a beautiful stone that will always clear negative energy while replacing it with love.

Smoky quartz is a good stone to dispel negative energy from electrical wires, phone towers, nuclear power sources, smog, and x-rays. It is also a good stone to have around if anyone in the house is experiencing depression or has a negative attitude. It will absorb the negativity and emit higher frequency vibes.

Sodalite absorbs the discharge of high-frequency communication antennas, infrared, microwaves, and radar. It also blocks out subtle emanations from your home computer or excessive static electricity. Place sodalite in any room that needs negativity absorbed.

Work
Crystals can be subtle tools for enhancing your workplace and for enabling peaceful coexistence among colleagues. Place one on your desk as a paperweight, on plants, on a windowsill or floor, or on desktop or laptop. Small crystals are as powerful as those larger ones. The whole room can be energized by a small orange carnelian.

Blue lace agate efficiently restores peace and harmony if there is conflict within your working environment. Green aventurine promotes sympathetic leadership and is effective at absorbing environmental pollution and for creating prosperity. It defuses negative situations and turns them into something positive. You can place green aventurine at each corner of your desk or in the desk drawers if you have a co-worker who steals your energy. Labradorite, orange carnelian, smoky quartz, and sodalite are all other good crystals to energize a workplace. Orange carnelian helps to get things done as quickly as possible while being as successful as possible. Smoky quartz can help protect against other's stress and frustration. It also lifts communication problems. You can keep one near your work phone. Sodalite is especially helpful in keeping a group of dynamic people working harmoniously. It creates a basis of trust and solidarity of purpose. Sodalite has the ability to bring things into the open in a non-judgmental manner which can be useful in any workplace.

Electrical equipment has subtle discharges which may really affect your aura surrounding the body. Cell phones, handheld devices, and laptops all create gaps within the biomagnetic sheath around the head and neck and lower chakras. You can place or tape a green aventurine to your phone, computer, or device to block the harmful emanations and revitalize your aura with this crystal. It is an excellent neutralizing stone for all electromagnetic pollution sources. Amethyst, bloodstone, clear quartz, red jasper, rose quartz, green aventurine, smoky quartz, sodalite, and yellow jasper all help block environmental and electromagnetic stress. You can place any of these crystals on the equipment or wear one around your neck.

Strengthening Your Aura

As discussed earlier, your aura is also known as your etheric body or biomagnetic shield. It is a subtle energy field that surrounds your physical body. It is made up of several layers spread out. The outermost layer relates to the spirit, the next layer the mind, the next to emotion, and the one closest to the physical body relates to the physical level of being. Many believe they can sense or even see auras as a white glow or a swirling rainbow of colors. If there are dark or cloudy patches within an aura, that indicates an imbalance or presence of disease or illness. Keeping your biomagnetic sheath as healthy and balanced as possible is an effective defense against illness and guarantees your wellbeing on all levels.

Clear quartz is the main appropriate crystal for strengthening your aura and smoky quartz for cleansing it and getting rid of negative energies. You can train yourself to feel how far your aura extends and to check for weak spots. An energy intuitive healer can sense the state of others' auras. They will use crystals to help keep it clear and strong.

To clear your aura with added benefit of crystals, sit down quietly in a comfortable position. Place smoky quartz at your feet. Place red jasper beneath you and as close to your perineum as possible. Hold labradorite in your left hand. Close your eyes, breathe gently, focusing your attention into your right hand. Extend your right arm out fully with your palm facing your body, or hold clear quartz in this hand. Move your hand slowly toward your body. At some point, your hand will start to tingle and you will be aware of your subtle energy field. This may take some practice. Note how far this field extends from your body. Move your hand with crystal around to see if you can detect any cold or weak spots. If you do, leave the crystal over that spot for a few moments.

With clear quartz, comb your body from the top of your head, working down the front middle of your body to your feet first, then the outside of your body on each side. Finally, run clear quartz as much as you can down your back. Repeat the combing with the Labradorite in your left hand. Place your clear quartz in front of your solar plexus for a few minutes. This will energize your aura. Remember to cleanse the crystals after use.

CHAPTER 7
Using Crystals For Holistic Living

Crystal Prescriptions and Everyday Use

In the natural healing world, among practitioners and healers, crystals can be "prescribed" for specific healing purposes. They can relate to a particular condition or moreover, issues that can very often be perceived as being true. If we work toward correcting an issue, we can reach a state of homeostasis or balance. This allows us to be balanced on all levels, emotional, physical, mental, and spiritual. When we are balanced, energy flows unobstructed and we feel well, happy. If we get stuck, whether emotionally, physically, mentally, or spiritually, energy gets stuck and can manifest as discomfort, disease, a state of illness, and we feel unbalanced and unhappy. Crystals can be a powerful tool to overcome such blockages as grief, stress, rejection, etc. Crystal prescriptions can also help in connecting to our higher selves and divinity. This will bring about clarity, a sense of a bigger picture, and calm spirituality.

Crystals do not have to be used only in a strict healing environment such as a treatment room or during any type of session. Their benefits can be enjoyed on a daily basis, in simple everyday actions. They can help dispel negativity or enhance a state of balance. As always, they reiterate that we are spiritual beings on a human journey. Crystals are here to provide us with added physical, emotional, mental, and spiritual support as needed.

In this chapter, you will find crystal prescriptions, as well as exercises to practice using crystals in everyday life situations. They can be used to help alleviate stress, get back to a state of balance on all levels, or to connect to higher realms and divinity for our greater good. We *can* bring spirituality to our daily lives. Crystals certainly help us connect to our higher selves and enhance spirituality.

Rejection, Loss, or Abandonment
Everyone has felt a rejection of some kind sometime throughout

life, whether it was a rejection in a personal relationship or from something else such as a job. We make ourselves available by putting ourselves out there. This is especially true today with so much social media. Whenever we do this, we subject ourselves to any type of "rejection." It is going to happen no matter what and will happen over and over. We cannot control it. What we can control is how we handle or react to the rejection. What you do not want to happen is have fear take over so much so that you do not try new things for fear of further rejection. We have no control over whether somebody wants us, likes us, or chooses us, but that doesn't stop it from hurting when rejection does occur. To heal the pain from rejection, you must return to a place of self-love.

Prescription #1: Rose quartz is extremely effective for this. It is the stone for unconditional love and will bring you back to that space. Wear rose quartz jewelry after hurting from the sting of rejection. Visualize unconditional love flowing from the rose quartz throughout your entire body.

Prescription #2: Yellow tiger's eye can help with self-expression, nurturing and self-motivation. Rejection can hit us right at the core. This can affect our solar plexus chakra and self-image or self-worth. Keeping this chakra strong can help to overcome past rejection and keep from feeling pain of any future rejection. When self-worth is strong, you are less likely to feel pain and loss when you are rejected. To utilize yellow tiger's eye, place the crystal on your solar plexus region while lying down comfortably on your back. Visualize its energy flowing through you and strengthening your sense of self-worth.

Prescription #3: Hematite is a wonderful grounding stone that can help with feelings of safety and security. Overcoming fear of rejection has to do with overcoming fear in general. Fear is an emotion that originates at the root chakra, relating to safety and security. Meditate with a hematite crystal in your receiving, non-dominant hand. Repeat the mantra, "Even when I am afraid, I take risks that serve my highest and greatest good." As you do this, visualize your fear of rejection as a black cloud flowing from your body and into the hematite stone. Cleanse the hematite after the meditation.

Courage

Courage is not about not being afraid. It is about doing what you know to be the right thing for you even though you are afraid. Courage is a trait that originates from the solar plexus chakra, so this is where to focus on crystal use.

Prescription #1: Use citrine as an amplifying crystal with its golden yellow coloring vibrating at the frequency of the solar plexus chakra. In these ways, citrine is a powerful stone of courage. When you feel you need courage, hold a piece of citrine in your receiving or non-dominant hand. Repeat the mantra, "I have the courage to do what I know serves my highest and greatest good."

Prescription #2: Aquamarine is known as one of the stones of courage, so it is a wonderful crystal to carry with you or wear as jewelry when you feel you need a boost of courage. When you know you are going to have to do something out of your comfort zone, adorn yourself with an aquamarine bracelet, necklace, or ring. Call on its energy to bring you courage. Repeat the above mantra. Be grateful for the support of courage. You can also create a courage grid described in the grids section of this book.

Happiness

Happiness is definitely a choice. Sometimes though, when we get overwhelmed by the stress and repetitiveness of our day to day lives, we forget that in order to create happiness or joy, we only have to choose it! The following crystal prescriptions can help you remember to choose happiness regardless of the external situations of your life.

Prescription #1: Amber can be the ultimate stone for happiness. It has a beautiful golden color and a natural warmth that radiates when next to your skin. Wearing amber jewelry can help you vibrate with this happiness energy. It can also serve as a visual reminder to choose to be happy. This can be a life game changer, to follow this advice each day. Hold the amber jewelry in your receiving, non-dominant hand, repeating the mantra, "I choose joy and happiness in every moment!" before putting it on.

Prescription #2: Smoky quartz is a beautiful crystal for transmuting negative energy into positive energy. If you are going through a difficult or stressful time finding it difficult to feel happy, meditate while holding a piece of smoky quartz in each hand. Visualize your negative emotions flowing through your body and into your giving or dominant hand, and into the quartz you are holding. See the quartz change the negative emotion to happiness. Visualize the happiness flowing from the quartz in your giving, dominant hand into the quartz in your receiving, non-dominant hand, up to your arm into your heart, which then pumps it throughout your entire body and being. Feel and delight in pure joy.

Prescription #3: Use citrine to help you be one who spreads happiness and cheer! Before you interact with others, hold a piece of citrine in your giving, dominant hand and repeat the mantra, "Wherever I go and whomever I encounter, I spread happiness." Place the crystal in a pocket and go out into the world. You can also charge small pieces of citrine in this manner and give them to people as gifts, to bring happiness to others.

Inner Peace
All peace, whether it's personal peace, peace within relationships, peace within societies, or world peace, start with inner peace. By being calm no matter what storm is raging outside, you set the vibrational example for others. As others find peace through your example, they spread it as well. It is possible to be in this place of peace, even when the world seems at its darkest. Retreating to your peaceful place can help you weather even the most difficult times.

Prescription #1: Larimar, with its dreamy blue exterior, is a beautiful stone of peace and calm. Use larimar as a gazing crystal. Set it about a foot away from your eyes and gaze at it as you repeat the mantra, "Regardless of what it is happening around me, I am at peace."

Prescription #2: Blue calcite is another peaceful stone. It can help bring you peace even in the most stressful times such as when adrenaline peaks and you experience the fight or flight response. Keep a piece of blue calcite with you and hold it in your receiving, non-dominant hand when you need peace. Visualize the calm blue energy going into your hand through the crystal and flowing throughout your entire body.

Love

We all have love in our lives even when we do not realize it. We are all unconditionally loved by the Divine, Spirit, Universe. Sometimes we feel lonely if our romantic situation is not ideal or we do not have a partner to share in things with. When we experience relationship problems, we fear we may lose love. This is never the case as we are never without love. Like happiness, we must choose to feel love.

Prescription #1: Rose quartz is one of the most common crystals to use for all kinds of unconditional love. If you are seeking romantic love or partnership, meditate with a rose quartz held against your heart chakra. Visualize the energy of love coming out from your heart, passing through the crystal, and expanding into the universe in a way that is magnetic and will attract love. As you do, repeat the mantra, "As I give love to others, so do I receive love in gratitude."

Prescription #2: If you are experiencing difficulty within any type of relationship, peridot can be a very useful crystal to release anger and hurt feelings. It brings loving, healing energy to the relationship. Lie comfortably with a peridot at your heart chakra. Visualize the person with whom you are experiencing difficulty. See a green light extending from your heart, through the peridot, and into the heart of the other person in the relationship you are trying to heal. Repeat this mantra, "I allow love to heal the pain we have caused one another."

Prescription #3: If you feel a lack of trust in a relationship you are in, and that is causing a blockage to love, try working with pink tourmaline which can help build trust. Hold the tourmaline in your giving, dominant hand. Visualize its energy surrounding both of you and feel the love.

Self-Confidence

A lot of issues are caused by not having confidence and low self-esteem. It can be hard to balance the energies of having enough self-confidence to succeed and having too much or too little to either be arrogant or feel unworthy of deserving accomplishments. It can help to think of a mantra such as "I accept myself unconditionally."

Prescription #1: Yellow tiger's eye again is helpful in building self-confidence while absorbing any excess that could cause self-centeredness or arrogance. Meditate while holding a piece of yellow tiger's eye to your solar plexus region with your giving or dominant hand. Repeat the mantra "I accept myself exactly as I am."

Prescription #2: Citrine is a brilliant crystal that amplifies and strengthens the solar plexus chakra, thus self-confidence and self-worth. Hold citrine in your receiving or non-dominant hand as you meditate while speaking the mantra. Visualize the golden light from the citrine surrounding you completely and flowing through you as self-confidence. Be forgiving and accepting of yourself just as you are. You are completely perfect and worthy of success and happiness no matter what others perceive.

Prescription #3: Amber supports solar plexus chakra energies and projects its own confident warmth. Wear amber jewelry to help keep energies of self-confidence balanced. Wearing a necklace or bracelet is the perfect location for the amber. Amber helps in feelings of security and belonging. It will open you up to accepting yourself for who you are and feel safe in your own self.

Trust
Trust occurs only with feelings of safety and security. Many people struggle with trust issues. Something from our childhood can bring back feelings of mistrust. Those who have experienced mild or significant physical, emotional and mental traumas struggle with trust occasionally. Some struggle on a daily basis. It is necessary to recognize the ways in which we are safe and secure, in order to establish feelings of trust once again. Crystals can be very helpful with this. A mantra to say is "I trust in the compassion and generosity of the universe. I am safe."

Prescription #1: Garnet is a good crystal choice to help establish and keep balanced root chakra energies. These aid in keeping us grounded, feeling safe, and secure. Sit or lie comfortably and place the garnet near your root chakra. Close your eyes if that feels safe to you. Breathe deeply and repeat the mantra above.

Prescription #2: Many of us can lack trust in ourselves. We break our own promises and that can lead to a lack of trust of self. Lack of integrity is a sacral chakra issue. Carnelian is a wonderful crystal choice to balance this chakra. Lie comfortably and place the carnelian on your sacral chakra area. Repeat the mantra "I trust myself because I keep my word to myself."

Prescription #3: Many people feel they cannot trust the world or the universe even. They may feel life, in general, is unsafe and act and react according to this. To help with this, amethyst is a good crystal to help with connecting to higher self and divinity. Listening to Divine guidance leads to greater trust in the universe. Place an amethyst on your third eye chakra. Meditate as you repeat the mantra above.

Relieve stress
Stress can show up as physical, mental, or even emotional and really affects the human body. When you are stressed, especially chronically, the adrenal glands that are located above the kidneys go into "fight or flight" mode, causing an overproduction of adrenaline in the body. This increases cortisol and causes your body to react in multiple negative ways. Symptoms of stress include headaches, bloating, aches and pains, depression, fatigue, restlessness, ulcers, and even auto-immune diseases just to name a few. If excess adrenaline and cortisol are not removed from your body, it can feel impossible to relax or sleep. Lying or sitting quietly for 20 minutes helps to release stress with an appropriate crystal. Also, you can wear and carry one whenever you feel the need to relax and recharge.

These gems may also provide great assistance when you are suffering from any number of forms of stress. In today's fast-paced, electronic-based world, it is no wonder stress, which can lead to anxiety, is one of the most common discomforts people complain about. Managing stress is essential for overall health and balance. Gratefully, crystals can help.

Crystals to Use for Relieving Stress

Green Aventurine and Rose Quartz are both good at helping to prevent over-production of adrenaline and reduce the feeling of restlessness. Green aventurine helps mental stress and rose quartz aids in emotional stress, but they both work together to support each other and enhance their effectiveness. Place or tape rose quartz on your left kidney and green aventurine on your right kidney, just above your waist and on either side of your spine. Leave on for about 20 minutes to significantly reduce adrenaline over-production.

Amethyst is a wonderful crystal to use if you are feeling stressed, especially if experiencing tension headaches. Put the amethyst on the center of your forehead or at the back of your skull and lie still, counting to six while breathing in slowly. Hold your breath for six seconds and then breath out for seven seconds. Do this for fifteen to twenty minutes to feel completely relaxed. Amethyst can be extremely calming. It attracts positive energy while getting rid of negative energy. When you are feeling especially stressed out, you may try placing it under your pillow at night.

Bloodstone is an excellent stone to keep your mind calm and focused during times of mental stress, supporting the immune system as well.

Clear quartz and labradorite are both good stones to help you maneuver through emotional stress. Labradorite will gently bring up suppressed emotions that may be contributing to disease. Clear quartz will energize and recharge if stress is causing you to feel exhausted.

Rose quartz is a calming stone that supports during emotional trauma, giving you reassurance and helping you to accept necessary change. It lends itself to feelings of unconditional love which can help relieve stress.

Smoky quartz helps relieve stress, especially if caused by harmful environmental energies. It is also a very stabilizing stone. It can help you regain balance after being thrown into fight or flight mode due to stress. It helps to keep you calm under overwhelming situations and protects against environmental stress. Keep smoky quartz with you whenever you feel stressed or anxious. Hold it while breathing in and out slowly, until you feel calm and stable.

Yellow Jasper is an excellent crystal if you feel you need support or nurturing during stressful times. It brings about tranquility and can give you the added strength to overcome difficulties.

Anxiety
Anxiety can be an occasional thing such as common worrying, or it can be a chronic or even debilitating condition. If left untreated, stress and anxiety can lead to a whole host of other diseases including heart disease. There are many types of anxiety such as social anxiety, phobias, obsessive-compulsive disorders, and general anxiety. The prescriptions here are for persistent anxiety as opposed to short-term stress, which is covered in other prescriptions. Anxiety is a condition of excessive energy, so you should work with opaque stones that absorb, soothe, and calm.

Prescription #1: Amber can help support you when you are feeling anxious. For social anxiety, wear amber as a necklace, bracelet, or ring, or carry a piece carefully wrapped, in a pocket as you go into socially intense situations. In these situations, amber will help ease your anxiety. Hold a piece of amber in your receiving, non-dominant hand and note the warmth of it. Visualize a yellow light connection from your solar plexus to the solar plexus of other people in the room. Breathe deeply as long as you need, until the anxiety passes.
Prescription #2: Sodalite has a calming blue color and can be seen as the perfect anti-anxiety crystal. It balances energies while connecting to intuition and spirituality. Hold a piece of sodalite in your giving, dominant hand. Sit calmly and relaxed. Close your eyes if that feels safe to you. Visualize your anxiety flowing through you into your dominant arm, into your hand, and into the sodalite. As you visualize, repeat the mantra, "I am peace." Do this at least once a day and cleanse the sodalite daily.

Prescription #3: Anxiety is common in the evening when we are trying to rest or go to sleep. When our bodies are ready for sleep, our mind can go into overdrive and cause anxiety-induced insomnia. If your anxiety arises when trying to sleep, try this two-part remedy. Add four to five drops of lavender essential oil in a bathtub filled with warm water. If it is warmer months and you have it, place actual lavender stems and leaves from the plant. Soak for ten to twelve minutes. As you lie still and your anxieties rise to the top, watch them drift away and repeat the mantra or word, "calm." Sit in the tub as it drains and visualize your worries draining with the water. When the water is completely drained and your anxieties with it, get out and gently dry off. Then crawl into bed with a piece of amethyst taped underneath the head of your bed or on your bedside table or both. Again, as anxieties arise, visualize them as clouds that drift harmlessly out of your head and into the universe. Repeat the mantra or any calming phrase you resonate with.

Balance
When we are out of balance in any way, it can make it seem like our whole life is spiraling out of control. Lack of balance manifests in many ways, such as poor work to life balance, excessive focus on body, mind, or spirit at the expense of others, or too much stress without enough relaxation just to name a few. The first step is recognizing you are out of balance in some way. Next, you can use these prescriptions and the healing power of crystals as you seek to get back to a state of balance or homeostasis.

Prescription #1: Rainbow fluorite with its large array of colors can help balance energies. Wear rainbow fluorite as jewelry when you feel out of balance. It will help balance and stabilize all energies and aid in connecting mind, body, and spirit. It is a very harmonizing crystal. A few times a day, especially upon waking and when going to bed, hold a piece of fluorite in your receiving or non-dominant hand, and repeat the mantra, "I am balanced in all things."

Prescription #2: Use turquoise as a stone of harmony that can help balance your energies and bring you back to a centered place of calm peace. Wear turquoise jewelry as a great way to enjoy this crystal as you seek balance. Be sure to clear the turquoise every few days to retain its harmonic power.

Prescription #3: Black tourmaline and clear quartz work in harmony to create balanced energy throughout your system. They are grounding, cleansing, and overall healing stones. Lie on the floor or on a comfortable bed or sofa. Place a piece of black tourmaline near your root chakra and a piece of quartz near your crown chakra. Close your eyes if this feels safe to you. Visualize energy flowing from root to crown and back. Repeat the mantra if it feels right. Feel the working healing energy bringing you back to complete balance.

Boundaries

Creating and keeping healthy boundaries is something many people have difficulty with. Maintaining these boundaries, however, is essential for mental, spiritual, emotional, and physical health. Having firm boundaries in place protects your sense of self while still allowing you to interact with others in ways that are kind and compassionate, both to you and to another. Boundaries shouldn't be so strict that they do not allow for loving action when it is required. Therefore, they need to be firm but flexible, and ultimately, self-loving.

Prescription #1: Yellow kyanite has two properties that make it a great stone for setting boundaries. First, it's a part of the triclinic crystal system, which is a boundary or perimeter stone. Second, it supports the solar plexus chakra, which is where the energy of a healthy sense of self and boundaries exists. As you meditate, hold a piece of yellow kyanite in your giving, or dominant hand and repeat the mantra, "My boundaries are firm but flexible enough to allow for love." Do this for five to ten minutes, or until you feel your boundaries are firmly in place.

Prescription #2: Turquoise, another triclinic crystal, is an excellent boundary setter. Wearing turquoise jewelry of any kind is strongly recommended. Put a piece of turquoise jewelry on in the morning. Repeat the mantra, "My boundaries are firm but flexible enough to allow for love," as you visualize energy expanding from the turquoise and surrounding you.

Prescription #3: Labradorite helps you find empowerment and connects you to your intuition, which helps you have the strength to set healthy boundaries. It is also a stone associated with the throat chakra, which can help you speak your own truth, something necessary for giving voice to your boundaries. When someone asks you to do something, take a moment and pause. Hold a piece of labradorite in your hand and ask yourself, "Is this something that is within my own personal boundaries to do?" See what answer comes to you. It is okay to say no if you feel it is beyond your personal boundaries.

Compassion

Compassion, whether for ourselves or others, is one of the most important qualities you can foster. Sometimes it can be difficult to feel compassion, including self-compassion. It is an essential high vibration quality that allows us to experience ourselves and others, as Divine.

Prescription #1: Compassion is an emotion that comes from your spirit and from your heart. Because the desire is to amplify compassion, using an amplifying crystal can help you grow and nurture this important quality. Rose quartz is one of the highest vibrational stones for cultivating compassion and as a hexagonal system stone, it is also a natural amplifier. For self-compassion, hold the rose quartz stone in your receiving or non-dominant hand and hold it at your heart. For compassion for others, hold the rose quartz in your giving or dominant hand and hold it at your heart. Close your eyes if that is comfortable for you. Repeat the mantra, "Everything and everyone I see before me, I see with compassionate eyes." Feel compassion moving through you.

Prescription #2: Sometimes it can be difficult to experience compassion until you release judgment. Aquamarine is another hexagonal, amplifying stone that can help you let go. When you notice that judgment about yourself or another is blocking compassion, hold the aquamarine in your giving or dominant hand and visualize releasing judgment. As you hold the stone, repeat this mantra, "I release judgment. I allow compassion."

Prescription #3: Peridot is another crystal of the heart, a stone of compassion. Its bright green clarity can help in promoting healing of the heart to feel compassion regularly. It will also help with letting go in order to make room for compassion and love of all types. Lie comfortably on your back and place a peridot on your heart chakra. Notice the beating of your heart. Close your eyes if that feels safe to you. Visualize someone or something for whom you have tremendous compassion for. Pull that feeling of love and compassion into your heart and feel it filling your body with every beat of your heart, moving through all your blood vessels into every part of your body. Feel love and compassion expanding beyond you and into the world, out into the universe even. Do this for as long as you feel comfortable and like.

Crystals for Your Spirit and Connecting with Divinity

Crystals are full of spiritual energy and light as earth elements, vibrating brilliantly and strongly. They can definitely provide support to the spirit in opening intuition. Quartzes and labradorite are high-vibration crystals that work to ground spiritual energy into the physical body. They also provide great insight.

Hold one of the following five intuition crystals at your third eye whenever you need spiritual guidance or support.

Labradorite works in two ways to enhance intuition. First, it brings messages from the unconscious mind to the surface and helps to intuitively understand them. Second, it accesses other lives and other realms, bringing intuitive wisdom to the forefront. Labradorite is especially useful to get to the heart of matters and to understand the actual motivation behind other people's thoughts and actions.

Sodalite unites logic with intuition. It initiates spiritual awareness and brings information from the higher mind to the everyday mind. This stone stimulates the pineal gland, directly correlated to your third eye and third eye chakra, thus deepens spiritual perception.

Clear quartz can behave like a database. It stores information and is a spiritual library just waiting to be accessed. This stone enhances intuition and psychic abilities. It has been used since the beginning of time as a scrying stone to transport into the future or past.

Amethyst is one of the great heighteners of intuition and spiritual awareness. The calming energies of amethyst take you to a different plane. It is an excellent crystal for gazing into as a scrying tool and can be placed on the third eye to access it.

Smoky quartz brings higher spiritual energies down to earth. It can be used as scrying stone to initiate intuition and stay focused in it.

This can be achieved by holding the smoky quartz and gaze into its depths, allowing your eyes to go out of focus. This is very similar to meditation. Notice what comes into your mind. Don't judge it and just let it go.

Connecting with the Divine
Connecting to Divine energies and the spiritual realm often happens when meditating. With the assistance of crystals, you can be connected to Divine energy all of the time. Consciously connecting to Divine energy and then directing it into your crystal allows you to always be linked to Divine universal light.

Labradorite again comes into play when raising spiritual vibration and connecting to divinity. It is a highly mystical stone, raising your consciousness to the highest possible level so that you can make contact with the Divine. It then connects the energies into your body and grounds it there. It takes esoteric knowledge to nourish your soul.

Rose quartz is the stone of unconditional love. It takes you into the heart of the Divine light. It helps you realize that you are a spiritual being whose true being is Divine. This enhances overall spiritual awareness.

Blue lace agate is a spiritually uplifting stone. It can take you on a cosmic journey to your Divine home. It can help to place under your pillow or near your bed while sleeping, to travel in your dream state.

Clear quartz carries the vibration of Divine light. Just by holding clear quartz above your head for a few minutes, you can experience a flood of spiritual energy that connects you directly with the Divine.

Travel spiritual waves
Holding blue lace agate, be aware of the gentle arcs that flow over its surface. These are the waves in the sea of spirit to which all beings belong. Trace these curves with your eyes, letting them go a little out of focus. Travel the waves until you reach your spiritual home. Bring the stone to your throat and anchor the connection there.

Anchoring divine light
Holding labradorite and gazing into its depths, be aware that the blue flashes you see are the light of the Divine anchored into your crystal. Know that whenever you hold this crystal, you will have an immediate connection to the Divine. Place this crystal to your forehead and absorb the diving light into your whole being.

Attuning to unconditional love
Holding rose quartz, allow yourself to feel the unconditional love radiating out from its serene center. This is the love that is at the heart of the universe and which moves through all things. Place the stone over your heart and allow your heart to absorb this unconditional, Divine love, feeling it rush through your whole being.

Crystal programming
Crystals are programmable. They will still work even if not programmed, but when they are, it is like bringing a laser beam focus to them. It sets a clear intention for a very specific purpose, a need, or desire. The crystal will then help in any way they can to achieve this intention. They will be super focused. It is best to program a crystal to go along with their natural properties. Program a stress relieving crystal to help alleviate stress. Program a crystal that helps with digestion to aid in digestive issues. To do this, for a few moments, hold your crystal in your hands, imagining that it is surrounded by light. Affirm the intention that should be brought to you by the crystal. Again, only if you are comfortable in doing so, you may program your crystals. It can make them even more focused and powerful, but they will not lose any qualities by not programming.

Healing dreams
You can program your crystal to help aid in healing dreams. Hold your stone of choice in your hands and imagine it bathed in white, healing light. State your intention that your crystal will bring you a healing dream that you will remember and understand when you awaken. Then place the crystal under your pillow before you go to sleep. Keep a pen and paper or a dream journal by your bed to write down your dream.

Some helpful crystals for dreaming are red and yellow jasper. They assist in recalling significant dreams. Jasper helps the subconscious mind to communicate with the conscious mind in the dream state. Bloodstone stimulates vivid dreaming. Amethyst makes intuitive dreams and journeys out of the body easier and helps you in understanding your dreams. An amethyst under your pillow protects against nightmares and ensures sweet dreams.

Dream Healer
A simple yet effective visualization before going to sleep can put you in contact with the dream healer. Begin by sitting or lying down comfortably. Holding an amethyst in your hands to enhance your visualization abilities, rest quietly and close your eyes. Breathe slowly and evenly, focusing your attention deep within yourself. Without opening your eyes, raise them to be looking at your third eye in the center of your forehead. Imagine this eye-opening and revealing a peaceful, beautiful place in which you can enter into. If this is especially hard at first, place the amethyst on your third eye to stimulate its opening.

Spend a few moments going around in and enjoying this beautiful place, however it is you are picturing it. There is no right or wrong type of place. As you explore, you will become aware of a figure joining you. This figure is the dream healer. It is not necessarily human. Explain to the dream healer exactly what kind of healing you need, whether it is physical, emotional, mental, or spiritual. If you do not know the source of your disease, then ask the dream healer to assess and give the correct type of healing. Request that tonight, you will receive healing, and that upon waking, you will recall your dream clearly and know exactly what it means.

When you go to bed, place your amethyst under your pillow. Confirm to yourself that you will be meeting the dream healer and that you will remember your dream. When you wake up, write the dream and any thoughts on it in your dream journal.

Crystal meditation
Meditation is anything that focuses your mind on the present moment. A mantra is any word or phrase that focuses you on an intention or affirmation. Together with the use of powerful yet subtle crystal power, meditation can transform and heal.

Meditation is one of the simplest ways to connect with the healing power of crystals. Each crystal will feel different so keep experimenting and be grateful and patient.

Meditation rests an overactive mind and puts you in touch with your spirituality. It can greatly turn off the "fight or flight" response you may be experiencing from stress or anxiety. Gazing into the center of a clear crystal enables you to quickly enter a meditative state. Crystals have a natural likeness to meditation as they calm your mind and allow it to be open to receive spiritual energy. Your brain waves change according to levels of consciousness. When we are in an altered state of higher consciousness such as during meditation, our alpha brain waves are dominant. During everyday awareness, we emit beta brain waves. Holding a smoky quartz crystal can help move between beta brain waves and alpha brain waves. Smoky quartz is also a calming of the mind crystal. It is an excellent stone choice for meditation.

Sodalite is useful to activate higher awareness and stimulates spirituality, allowing meditation to go to a deeper level.

Crystals and meditation go hand in hand. There is a ritual you can perform to help meditate using crystals. Settle yourself in a quiet, peaceful area where you know you will not be disturbed. Focus on your breathing gently and evenly. As you inhale, imagine great peace and allow your body to relax and soften. As you exhale, let go of any tension or thoughts and anxieties. Allow your body and your mind to settle into a still place. Using your crystal toolkit, but not yet using labradorite, make a crystal chakra circle around yourself starting at the brown of smoky quartz through red, orange, and yellow to green and blue, then into purple amethyst and clear quartz. Focus on each crystal for a few moments before touching it to your third eye and then placing it back in the circle.

Hold labradorite in your hands and turn it until it catches the light, to then gaze into its enigmatic depths. Breathe more deeply, into your belly, consciously grounding yourself with spiritual energy. Close your eyes. Allow all thoughts or sounds to drift right past you and be aware only of the crystal in your hands, its energy, and the insight it brings to you.

After 10 to 20 minutes, gather up your crystals and place them to one side. Holding smoky quartz, stand up and feel your feet firmly on the ground. Be mindful of the grounding cord that goes from your feet deep into the earth to hold you gently in your physical body. Be grateful for your spiritual being in human experience. Thank your higher self and any spiritual energy felt during meditating.

Protection against electromagnetic field or EMF

All electronics emit an electromagnetic field. We are bombarded by electronics with widespread cell phone use, handheld devices, laptops, computers, speakers, microwaves, etc. These emissions cause negative effects on our physical, emotional, and mental wellbeing. Crystals help dispel these negative forces. A powerful shield against EMF is the crystal Shungite. It helps to absorb negative pollutants, toxins, and energy. It is a very powerful crystal with strong effects on the body. It can soothe anxiety and increase the detoxification process. Try placing shungite near your computer or wi-fi hub while you work, on your cell phone, or you can wear the crystal to shield you.

Cultivate love and revitalize your sex life

Rose quartz is a stone of unconditional love as mentioned many times here. This beautiful gem revitalizes and heals the energy of the heart and heart chakra. It emanates love and compassion vibrations. It is nurturing as well as supportive while giving a person to feel the most potent energy of the universe — love! It will encourage you to practice more self-love and will also bring love. Many healers will say this is the secret to finding true love. Rose quartz can help heal old wounds to forgive past loves while releasing any lingering negative emotions. If you are single and looking for a compatible, loving mate, near your bedside or wherever you spend a lot of time in a relaxed state, you may place two rose quartz crystals.

Sexuality and sexual activity is linked to the lower chakras. When these chakras are clear and working properly, libido is able to flow freely. Crystals energize these points as well as those of the emotional body so love can be given and received without restraint. Your sex life can be regenerated if you and your partner utilize some of these lower chakra enhancing crystals.

Red Jasper is an excellent crystal for stimulating your libido and prolonging sexual pleasure. This stone cleanses and energizes the base or root chakra. Orange carnelian is a recharging crystal. It energizes the sacral chakra, helps to overcome impotence or low libido, and restores vitality to the female reproductive organs. Smoky quartz helps you to accept that you are in a physical body with normal and natural sexual desires. It clears the lower chakras so that your passion can flow unobstructed. Rose quartz opens your heart chakra and restores love and trust between you and your partner. It enables you to love yourself in order to receive love from someone else. This stone also increases fertility.

Activating and care of crystals

In order for crystals to work for you, they must be cleansed, activated, and attuned to your particular frequency. This helps to get rid of any vibrations they may have picked up on before getting to you. Crystals should be cleared and cleansed often, especially after a healing session.

Clearing or cleansing of crystals

There are a few ways to clear crystals. One of them is to keep them under running water for a few minutes, to then place them in the sun for a few hours. If the sun is not out, envision a white light that radiates down in your crystals. You can also place crystal quartz near any other crystal you wish to clear. You may burn sage or a smudge-stick around the crystals you wish to clear. Even burying crystals in the earth or placing in the moonlight will clear a crystal appropriately. You can also use sound. The vibrations of a pure sound such as a bell, gong, tuning fork, or singing bowl can be used to energetically clean a crystal. It is always important to cleanse your crystals before and after a healing session.

To activate your crystals, hold them in your hands. With your eyes shut, concentrate on the crystals and see them surrounded by healing, white light. Ask that they be attuned to your own unique frequency and that they will be activated to act as healers at any level you may need now or anytime in the future. Ask that the crystals be blessed by the highest energies in the universe and be dedicated to your self-healing and the environment around you.

The best way to store your healing stones is individually wrapped in a cloth bag. A plastic bin with individual compartments as used for beads or crafts can be used for smaller crystals. If they are kept out in the daily environment, they can and will absorb negative energy and need to be cleansed or cleared more often. You should also keep crystals and stones dust and dirt free by wiping them with only a soft cloth. You can also wear stones or keep them in your pocket until ready to use.

Practical use of crystals
You can use crystals in so many ways as described here in this book. Healing sessions and meditation are two very common methods, but others exist as well. There are suggestions in the specific crystals and conditions sections of this book so you will know how to use them, but the tips below are very practical suggestions for applied use.

Crystal elixirs - Place clean, cleared crystals in a bowl of spring or purified water in the sunshine for two hours. Remove the crystals then and drink the water as needed. You can also create a crystal spray by placing crystals in spring or purified water, again with a specific intent for the crystal. Keep it in the sun or moonlight for up to five hours or even overnight. Remove the crystals, place the charged water in a darkened spray bottle with about a teaspoon of brandy or vinegar as a preservative. Spritz the spray as needed, on or around yourself, your home, your car, pets, etc.

Secure a piece of fluorite to the bottom of your work chair to help you stay focused.

Carry carnelian in a pants pocket or wear it as a bracelet when you need a boost of creativity.

Wear rose quartz so it hangs over your heart center when you are expecting or involved in a romantic activity.

Drop water safe crystals in your bathwater. Remove them before draining the tub.

Wear happy and energetic amber to give you a positive boost.

Sprinkle positive energy crystals such as smoky quartz or crystals that absorb negative energy such as black tourmaline, around the perimeter of your house to keep negativity at bay. You can use inexpensive crystal chips or beads for this.

Sacred Space
Sacred spaces are peaceful, welcoming environments that create a clean, free-flowing energy space. They are often seen in yoga and meditation practices or studios. They can also be seen in a practitioner's offices such as a chiropractor, massage therapist, or energy worker. You can create an altar or sacred space in your home. Using crystals in these calming spaces adds a beautiful piece of earth energy surrounded by peace, unconditional love, and acceptance. The addition and use of crystals in a sacred space can serve as a reminder to reconnect with your intention each time you revisit the space.

Amethyst is a very useful, popular crystal for sacred spaces. It emits positive energy and nurtures a deeper state of meditation and connecting to your higher self and divinity. Crystal points can also help set an intention in your space, especially on or near an altar. Write your intention on a piece of paper and place a crystal point on top of it. The point amplifies the intention into the universe.

Carry crystals
Once you set an intention or program a crystal, you can carry it with you to remind yourself of that intention. The more direct contact you have with a crystal, the more aware you'll be of its energy. You will be able to easily access it whenever you need to feel grounded, center yourself or bring your attention back to the intention you are working toward.

Crystals and yoga
Placing crystals on your yoga mat can increase the power of asanas and any intention set forth during meditation during your practice. You can even place crystals on your body during yoga to encourage a deeper state of healing.

Home décor
Crystals large and small help to add to home décor beauty. They can help achieve positive feng shui and dispel negative energy

while emitting positive vibes. They look beautiful and like pieces of art as well. They can be a perfect addition to any room while serving a specific purpose. The placement of crystals in areas of the home was discussed earlier. So while beautifying a space, they can also be powerful catalysts for positive energy in your home.

Home spa treatment
Placing crystals in and around your home, self-care treatments can enhance healing and add a calming aspect to your routine. Place only strong crystals able to withstand warm water into your bath or around your shower or bathtub. You can soak with the crystals in a bath or hot tub or in water in the sink you plan to wash your face with. The crystal energy will have peaceful and restorative effects on your at home spa day. Crystals in your bathroom and any room or area you get ready in at the beginning or end of the day can help you feel relaxed and prepared for that time of the day.

CHAPTER 8
Crystals For Disorders, Specific Ailments, And Systems

In addition to the previously mentioned disorders, diseases, and illnesses, the following specific conditions can benefit from regular crystal therapy. Crystal use never claims to cure any ailment. Crystal therapy is only ever meant to complement any other treatment and never meant to cure nor prescribe. Seek proper medical attention for any illness.

Aches and pains
Aragonite, blue lace agate, celestite, charoite, chrysocolla, clear quartz, lapis lazuli, and malachite all help with relieving general aches and pains.

Addiction
Amethyst is helpful in overcoming addictions or overindulgences of any kind. It has a calming effect.

ADD/ADHD
Fluorite, crystal and lithium quartz, lepidolite, petalite, and stilbite help to balance energies associated with ADD and ADHD.

AIDS/HIV
Carnelian, clear quartz, lapis lazuli, and malachite help in dealing with symptoms of HIV AIDS.

Allergies
Green aventurine, zircon, and aquamarine help with allergies and allergy symptoms.

Alzheimer's
Rose quartz is a good crystal to help reduce the confusion of Alzheimer's and senile dementia.

Anger
Carnelian, amethyst, rose quartz, peridot, and muscovite help with

anger issues and to release restricted negativity that causes deep-rooted anger.

Anxiety/Panic Attacks
Sodalite calms anxiety attacks. Keep it in your pocket and hold it over your chest at the first sign of an attack. Breathe slowly and deeply while counting to seven, hold your breath for a count of six, and then exhale for a count of five. Rose quartz can also help relieve anxiety and prevent panic attacks.

Arthritis
Blue lace agate and orange carnelian are useful in easing the pain of arthritis.

Autism
Amethyst, blue lace agate, sodalite, charoite, lapis lazuli, and clear quartz all help with autism imbalances.

Auto-immune Disorders
Aquamarine, red aventurine, carnelian, and turquoise are good for relieving auto-immune disorder symptoms.

Bacterial Infections
Bloodstone is effective in clearing bacterial infections. Place over the thymus gland for optimal results.

Back Pain
Hematite, lapis lazuli, orange carnelian, fluorite, and smoky quartz can help alleviate back pain, including lower back issues.

Bladder Issues
Use bloodstone crystal for clearing of blood, kidneys, and blockages in general and to aid in bladder issues. It also helps to soothe inflammation and irritation in and around the bladder.

Blood Pressure, High
Sodalite, Green Aventurine, bloodstone, and labradorite are helpful to relieve high blood pressure.

Blood Pressure, Low
Rose quartz is a good crystal to help with low blood pressure issues.

Blood Problems
Orange carnelian, red jasper, and bloodstone are useful for blood issues such as anemia.

Bones
Orange carnelian, howlite, and fluorite are all good choices in working with bone issues.

Brain Health
Amethyst, aventurine, Botswana agate, and lapis lazuli help with overall brain health.

Breast Health
Amazonite, lapis lazuli, moonstone, peridot, rainbow moonstone, and milky/snow quartz are all good choice crystals to balance breast and chest health.

Bruises
Amethyst and rose quartz help with healing bruises quickly.

Chemotherapy
Smoky quartz can help clear and alleviate the negative effects of chemotherapy.

Childbirth and Labor Pains
Amethyst, bloodstone, lapis lazuli, and tiger iron help in labor pain and childbirth.

Chronic Fatigue
Carnelian, citrine, chalcedony, Jasper, and tourmaline aid in relieving chronic fatigue syndrome.

Cholesterol
Fluorite and green aventurine help the body rid of the negative effects of high cholesterol.

Circulation
Bloodstone and red jasper help with poor circulation.

Claustrophobia

Green aventurine helps with claustrophobia.

Colds
Bloodstone helps clear blockages associated with the common cold, especially if placed over the thymus gland. Citrine, amber, and aventurine can also help.

Constipation
Malachite, citrine, and apatite help with constipation and digestive issues related to it.

Cramps
Smoky quartz can help relieve all types of cramps.

Depression
Amethyst, orange carnelian, and smoky quartz are good crystals in dealing with depression. Amethyst is a powerful calming stone, orange carnelian can activate a sense of security, and smoky quartz is a gentle yet effective mood enhancer. All of these crystals stabilize your energies enabling them to function harmoniously.

Diabetes
Citrine, red jasper, sodalite, emerald, and malachite all help in aiding diabetes.

Digestion
Sodalite, yellow jasper, citrine, and apatite all aid with digestive issues.

Ear Issues
Amethyst, amber, tourmaline, snowflake obsidian, and clear quartz point all help in dealing with issues related to ears.

Eating Disorders
Citrine, amber, tiger's eye, and yellow jasper are beneficial for those struggling with eating disorders.

Endocrine System
Amethyst helps with endocrine imbalances.
Energy
Orange, red carnelian, and red jasper benefit energy depletion or

fatigue.

Eye Issues
Blue lace agate, green aventurine, and labradorite can be helpful with eye problems.

Fever
Hematite, peridot, sodalite, and blue lace agate all help relieve symptoms of fever.

Flu
Bloodstone, carnelian, citrine, amber, and aventurine all help alleviate flu symptoms.

Headache
Selenite, amethyst, quartz, and lapis lazuli are good for headaches, including migraines.

Hormone imbalance
Placing an amethyst over your pituitary gland can help with hormonal imbalance.

Immune System
Blue lace agate, green aventurine, bloodstone, amethyst, amber, and fluorite all aid in immune system disorders.

Insomnia
Amethyst, sodalite, and bloodstone are crystals of choice to alleviate insomnia. Place one or all of these stones under your pillow or near your bed and positively intent or program them to help you sleep well. They will calm and stabilize your body, mind, and spirit for a sound sleep.

Joint Pain and Arthritis
Blue lace agate, apatite, bloodstone, copper, fluorite, and hematite are all excellent at aiding in alleviating inflammation, assists in bone, teeth, and cell regeneration, increasing blood flow and circulation, and absorbing of calcium. Blue lace agate is known to remove blockages within the nervous system that can lead to physical pain in muscles and joints. Place this healing crystal in your bath water for 15 to 20 minutes.

Learning Challenges
Clear quartz, amethyst, rose quartz, citrine, aventurine, and carnelian help in aiding those struggling with learning challenges.

Leukemia
Bloodstone, peridot, alexandrite, and smoky quartz are helpful for those dealing with leukemia issues.

Lupus
Bloodstone, amber, fluorite, and hematite are all detoxifying, immune system boosting, and healing crystals helpful in relieving negative effects of lupus.

Lymphatic System
Blue lace agate, sodalite, bloodstone, and rose quartz help enhance and clear the lymphatic system.

Menstrual Disorders
Citrine, moonstone, labradorite, and amethyst help in pre and menstrual symptoms.

Metabolic System
Amethyst, sodalite, orange carnelian, bloodstone, and labradorite help to keep the metabolic system in balance.

Mid-life Crisis
Rose quartz is helpful to maneuver through a mid-life crisis, enabling you to get your life back on track.

Neurosis
Green aventurine is beneficial in severe neurosis. It helps to understand the underlying reason behind the condition.

Nervous System
Blue lace agate, rose quartz, and amethyst benefits the nervous system.

Phobias
Sodalite is an excellent crystal choice to help you overcome your phobias. Green aventurine specifically overcomes claustrophobia.

Skeletal System
Blue lace agate, howlite, fluorite, and apatite are all good crystal choices for general bone growth and health. Even lapis lazuli can help strengthen the skeletal structure.

Sleep Disorders
Crystals to help relieve sleep troubles include amethyst, clear quartz, labradorite, rose quartz, black tourmaline, and angelite.

Sore Throat
Amber, aquamarine, blue lace agate, and sodalite help relieve a sore throat.

Stress
Amethyst, clear quartz, moonstone, rose quartz, tourmaline, howlite, sodalite, and labradorite are wonderful crystals to help alleviate all kinds of stress.

Transition
Amethyst, garnet, malachite, labradorite, rose quartz, and clear quartz help aid in transition or change of any kind, including crossing over.

Varicose Veins
Adding bloodstone to bath water can help relieve varicose veins.

Wrinkles
Rose quartz will help increase self-love and get rid of the negative effects of wrinkles.

CONCLUSION

Thank you so much for making it through to the end of this book. I hope it was informative and able to provide you with many of the tools you may need as you begin your Crystal Healing journey. The next step is to try some of the techniques described here, to practice in your own life. Find out what works best for you and what feels right. Remember to keep an open mind. Know that healing can be a slow and steady process. Follow your intuition using information in this book to help you start a useful and meaningful crystal collection. Crystals can be subtle yet powerful. If a particular stone resonates with you when you see or hold it, do not disregard that. It is telling you to listen to what your body, mind, and spirit are saying and that you may need it for support.

You can lead the balanced life you desire, filled with positive energy! It is possible to release unwanted negativity. Let go of what is no longer needed. Forgive yourself and others and behold your true being. Live the life that is meant for You! Crystals and their healing powers can allow you to follow this holistic approach toward your mind, body, and spirit.

Finally, if you enjoyed this book, please take the time to rate it on Amazon. Your honest review would be greatly appreciated. Thank you!

DESCRIPTION

Discover the gentle, non-invasive healing power of crystals! Learn about and use these natural earth element stones that connect us to our higher selves and higher beings, in order to activate our inner healing abilities. *Healing Crystals* will allow you to become knowledgeable in many aspects regarding the healing power of crystals. You will be able to recognize their healing qualities in order to improve all areas of your life holistically, in powerful ways. You will be able to reference this book every day. These are a few of the Crystal Healing techniques you will read about to incorporate into your daily life:

- History, properties, meaning, and purpose of popular healing crystals
- Crystal grids at home, at work, on the go, wherever you are
- Colors of crystals and how they relate to corresponding chakras
- Chakra balancing using crystals for everyday centeredness
- Aura clearing, cleansing, and protecting using crystals
- Using crystals in relaxation, meditation, healing, and positive affirmation
- Crystals as powerful healers — how they aid in specific ailments such as depression, exhaustion, grief, joint pain, and more
- Crystals for balancing the body, mind, and spirit holistically
- Crystals in Reiki — positive intent, connecting to higher self and Divinity for the greater good
- Crystal prescriptions

Crystals can be subtle yet powerful in their healing work. While they may not initiate change overnight, with continual use, keeping an open mind and believing in their healing properties, they can help us overcome emotional blockages that may be causing physical ailments that could last a lifetime. This is the amazing power of crystals. They can quickly alleviate a tension headache but also support us through our life's journeys and soul's lessons. This can result in a long-lasting improvement on any number of conditions and ailments. Crystals can also benefit us in our daily lives to help us cultivate our own courage, true voice, compassion for self and others.

CRYSTALS BEGINNER'S GUIDE TO CRYSTAL HEALING

How to Heal the Human Energy Field Through the Power of Crystals and Healing Stones

Crystal Lee

© Copyright 2018 by Crystal Lee - All rights reserved.

The following eBook is reproduced below with the goal of providing information that is as accurate and reliable as possible. Regardless, purchasing this eBook can be seen as consent to the fact that both the publisher and the author of this book are in no way experts on the topics discussed within and that any recommendations or suggestions that are made herein are for entertainment purposes only. Professionals should be consulted as needed prior to undertaking any of the action endorsed herein.

This declaration is deemed fair and valid by both the American Bar Association and the Committee of Publishers Association and is legally binding throughout the United States.

Furthermore, the transmission, duplication, or reproduction of any of the following work including specific information will be considered an illegal act irrespective of if it is done electronically or in print. This extends to creating a secondary or tertiary copy of the work or a recorded copy and is only allowed with the express written consent from the Publisher. All additional right reserved.

The information in the following pages is broadly considered a truthful and accurate account of facts and as such, any inattention, use, or misuse of the information in question by the reader will render any resulting actions solely under their purview. There are no scenarios in which the publisher or the original author of this work can be in any fashion deemed liable for any hardship or damages that may befall them after undertaking information described herein.

Additionally, the information in the following pages is intended only for informational purposes and should thus be thought of as universal. As befitting its nature, it is presented without assurance regarding its prolonged validity or interim quality. Trademarks that are mentioned are done without written consent and can in no way be considered an endorsement from the trademark holder.

INTRODUCTION

For thousands of years, crystals have become a significant part of healing. Whether it is for emotional, mental, or physical recovery, people have recognized the power hidden inside these beautiful gems. But for a time, the practice was relegated to the mysteries of the dark spirits. It was something that was tantamount to striking a deal with the devil to even be seen using crystals and for that reason, for a number of generations, the practice of crystal healing was looked down upon.

But today, in our modern world of technology, this art is experiencing a rebirth. No one can deny any longer the vibrations hidden inside each of these ancient stones and the power that they have over many people. Their ability to channel both the emotional and spiritual energy they possess and direct it to areas where it can cause true positive change is starting to be accepted again.

Every day, crystals are being used in a variety of ways from making a connection to your inner spiritual being to helping people through their emotional struggles. They have found a new life again.

Many who are unfamiliar with crystals, fail to realize that we are not just physical beings. There is a very powerful connection between every element that exists inside all of us. Crystals are simply a tool that can be used to connect all the different parts of our beings (the physical, mental, emotional, and spiritual) together, and as it does, it can have a powerful effect on every aspect of our lives.

The problem is that few understand when these elements of our whole being are out of balance, things can go terribly wrong. We tend to spend too much time dwelling with our mental thoughts, to the point of losing touch with the rest of who we are. As a result of this imbalance, we struggle with illnesses, depression, and even struggle physically. We find ourselves lost and alone in a world full of people. Relationships begin to suffer, we lose our jobs, and we fail to achieve our true purpose in life.

Today's world, full of all the modern conveniences we can imagine, places a lot of stress on the mental and physical bodies. Nearly everything we do is out of balance. Our lives are hectic and as a result, we make sacrifices of the things we know, deep down, that we should hold dear to us. It starts with little things but in time, it builds up to those big things that we can no longer ignore. In the end, we walk around like empty shells unable to find joy in anything. And if the problem is left unaddressed for too long, it will start to affect us physically. That's usually the time when we start to realize something has gone wrong, but in our innocence of the deeper things of life, we are unable to really identify it.

The answer may not be as aloof as you think. Turning to crystals to help you find yourself, regain mastery over your own life, and heal the inner person may be the very thing you've been searching for. In this book, we will guide you to understand how crystals can work and the benefits you can gain from them. You'll learn...

- What crystals really are and the power they possess
- The source of its energy
- The history of crystal healing
- How you can benefit from using crystals to heal
- What are chakras and how crystals can help you connect to them
- Why you need crystal grids and how to create one
- Why everyone should learn something about crystals
- How to use crystals to heal what ails you
- And so much more

You can consider this book your guide to a whole new world. One that puts the power of your life back into your hands. You can use it like a map that will lead you to a bigger, better, happier, and healthier self that you won't ever want to neglect again.

CHAPTER 1
What Are Crystals?

We'll start our journey by coming to understand what crystals are from a scientific perspective. To the average person, a crystal is nothing more than a pretty rock. Likely that makes you wonder just how an inanimate object like a rock is going to help you heal. This is a normal reaction by most people and is probably one of the main reasons why so many are reluctant to recognize the healing powers hidden inside each one of these precious gems.

Yes, it is true that crystals are on the surface just another type of stone, but each one is unique and you won't find any other stone with the kind of properties it possesses. Every crystal has its own energetic properties that can be channeled in all sorts of directions. These beautiful rock formations can be used in thousands of different ways, many of which go far beyond mere decoration.

This is not just some spiritistic hype that only those with blind faith might believe. Few people realize that the world's first radios were only able to transmit their signals with the aid of crystals. It is a scientific fact that we will discuss throughout the following pages of this book. While people see first their natural beauty and want to put them in the same company as they would diamonds and rubies, looking beyond the surface will reveal so much more.

What are Crystals and Where Do They Come From

In scientific terms, crystals are simply a grouping of molecules and atoms. While they are hardened like a stone, each crystal has its own unique characteristics. First, they are formed from a variety of different natural materials on earth. Some are made from salt, and others come from other elements found in the natural world. Gemologists and geologists have a unique definition of a crystal. They describe it as a solid object with atoms that are organized in a repeating lattice pattern. While there are several different crystal patterns, we're only going to focus on those that can be used for healing. These are sometimes described as gemstones, minerals, or rocks.

Minerals: Not all minerals can be classified as crystals, but those that are, have a highly organized structure that is formed by the special way the atoms interlock together. As they grow, the variations of temperature and chemical composition that occurs underneath the crust of the earth throughout the eons of time, it takes for them to form to give them their distinctive properties.

Rocks: Rocks are stones that have been formed from several different minerals, but all rocks can be considered as crystals.

Gemstones: These are those rocks that have been cut and polished so that they are more attractive to the human eye. There are two classifications of gemstones — precious, such as diamonds or rubies, and semiprecious such as garnets and quartz.

They come in all shapes and sizes, each having its own set of unique characteristics. The base material the crystal emerges from determines how it will be formed. For example, crystals made from salt will form cube-like shapes, while snowflakes or ice crystals will form into lattices.

The process they go through when forming is referred to as crystallization. They naturally form in nature all around us. When hot liquid (like magma) cools and then hardens, the molecules in the liquid start to bond together in order to create stability. As they do this, they create a uniform pattern that repeats over and over again until they form a crystal. Other types of crystals are formed when water evaporates from a mixture. This is how salt crystals are created.

You can actually see this with your own eyes. If you want to try a little experiment, take a teaspoon of table salt and put it into regular tap water and let it sit for 24 hours. When you check it again, you will see how the cube crystals have begun to form. These are created because as the water evaporates, the salt atoms are pulled closer together. As more water evaporates, the atoms will continue to pull together until they create a cluster. Eventually, you'll be able to see the cluster with the naked eye in the form of salt crystals.

You will notice that each crystal has its own distinctive shape, which develops based on the type of molecules and atoms at its base. It doesn't matter if the crystal is large or small, if it has the same base molecules and atoms, it will have the same shape.

Of course, not all crystals are formed so quickly, but they are all formed in the same way. Some like salt can be formed in a matter of days, but others, like those that are carbon-based, may take thousands of years to develop.

Natural crystals that have been formed within the earth's crust, often take millions of years to develop. However, today there are many crystals that are now being developed in laboratories. This is because a true crystal is extremely rare to find these days, but if you do have the privilege to own one, you will have in your possession an extremely powerful tool with the ability to do wonderful things.

Many people will sell you crystals, but they are not naturally formed. Natural crystals will always have some type of imperfection that can be spotted if you examine them closely. Those made in the laboratory will be perfect, absent of any flaws. Natural crystals can be dyed a different color or altered in some other way, but a laboratory made crystal can't be changed.

Another important difference is in the cost and the practicality of it. While a man-made crystal will have some level of energy, it will be far less than those that have been carefully made in the bowels of the earth for thousands of years. So, while they may be less expensive, you won't get the same results you get with natural crystals when you use them.

The Power Inside the Crystal

You've probably already experienced the power and vibration in a room without even realizing it. It's that feeling you get when you're in a room full of happy people, everyone smiling, laughing, and enjoying themselves. Then without any explanation, another person enters the room and the entire atmosphere changes. There seems to have been a sudden drain of energy, just by that person's presence.

This is called the Law of Vibration and it shows that everything we see, touch, feel, hear, etc. is made up of energy, even our physical bodies. From the scientific perspective, there is a little difference between you and the furniture in your room. Everything is the product of energy. This energy is constantly in motion, the only difference is that all of it runs on different vibrations. Those that share the same energy and vibrations are considered the same.

As these energies vibrate, we develop thoughts, feelings, emotions, and are spurred on to take different actions, which can have an effect on the vibrations in some form. When we feel down and depressed, our vibrations are low and sluggish, but when we feel up and happy, our vibrations are faster, run at a higher frequency, and produce more energy.

We may not be aware that we emit these types of energies, but as we go about our day, we instinctively respond to those energies that are emanating all around us, and people are also responding to the energy we are putting out. So, if you start your day in a bad mood or on a low vibration, chances are the people around you will respond accordingly. You'll attract the same type of negative energy to you and it will be difficult to move out of that low frequency if you are not aware of it.

The good news is that it doesn't have to be that way. You do have the ability to change it in much the same way as if you wanted to change what you were wearing that day. It all starts with changing the way you think. Once you change your thought process, you'll change your energy. This is the basics of the Law of Attraction. As a result of this change, you will be able to attract a different sort of people to you, those with a faster vibration than what you've normally been pulling in.

It is that energy that exists in all things that has the power to heal whatever it is that ails us. This is not something new or mystic but is at the core of many scientific discoveries. It is the kind of evidence that is used to back up physical theories for more than a century. Albert Einstein's theory of relativity is based on this very knowledge. It is the basis for nuclear power and will be the foundation of many new discoveries to come.

We might be inclined to believe that this energy only exists in living things, but we would be wrong. Even inanimate objects like crystals have their own form of energy and vibrations, and it is when these two connect (humans and crystals) that we begin to see amazing things happen.

Once we understand that all things vibrate, everything starts to become clear. While humans may not be able to automatically sense or identify those vibrations, they are there. In humans, the energy may present itself in three different ways — through chakras, meridians, and auras.

Chakras are the primary energy centers in every human body. Each person has seven different chakras that can be found in specific areas. It can be associated with color and a number of other qualities.

- The first chakra is found at the base of the tailbone
- The second chakra or the sacral is found near the belly button
- The third chakra or the solar plexus sits at the base of the sternum
- The fourth chakra, the heart, sits right in the center of the chest
- The fifth chakra or the throat is found right above the Adam's apple
- The sixth chakra or the third eye sits directly in the center of the forehead
- And the seventh chakra or the crown can be found at the very top of the head

If you could visualize these chakras, you could draw a line directly from the first chakra at the base of the tailbone and draw it in a straight line all the way up through all of the other six, ending at the seventh chakra at the crown of the head.

Meridians are the paths of energy that are running through the body. Auras are the energy fields that are surrounding the body. These auras help us to identify energy in ourselves and in others. They work a little like special cameras for us.

Similar to human bodies, crystals also have their own vibrations and auras, and when the two forms of energy connect, crystal energy can have some sort of effect on our own vibrations. They can be used to help to modify or adjust our energy and as a result, bring about a certain element of healing. In other words, they can change how our energy vibrates.

Now that people are recognizing this internal energy and its effects on the human body, more people are exploring ways to tap into it. Besides through crystals, you might find other treatments once scoffed at becoming increasingly popular. Reflexology and Reiki are just two examples. In the following pages, we're going to show you several ways to use crystals to change your energy and vibrations.

Benefits of Using Crystals

There are many different ways you can benefit from using crystals. Many have found that they help them mentally, emotionally, spiritually, and physically. Some have found practical use when they are used in conjunction with traditional Western style medicine. If they are having a physical problem, they have found that using the crystals will lessen the discomfort they may be feeling or help to relieve the suffering altogether. But aside from easing physical ailments, there are other ways that crystals can be used to your benefit.

- They help you connect to your inner consciousness. They can help you to focus on that inner voice that is constantly running in your head.

- They can assist you psychologically so you can take more positive action in redirecting your life.

- They can clear away any emotional blockages that are getting in your way.

- They help clear away negative energy and thought patterns.

- And they can help you to tap into your more creative side.

We can understand how this is done by understanding the physics of human beings. While we are all made up of vibrating energy, our vibrations are not constant. When we are happy, our vibrations are usually much faster than when we are depressed. Our vibrations change from one day to the next, and even from one situation to another. We're kind of all over the place. When we get close to someone with a low vibration, our vibration usually comes down too. The same is true when we are in the same vicinity as those with a high vibration. We feel good and we pick up on their emotions.

With crystals, it's different. These stones do not have emotions and feelings in the same sense that humans do. Therefore, their vibrations are always constant. They never change, and so they can provide us with a stabilizing effect that is hard for us to achieve on our own.

There are no set rules for how to use crystals. Some people benefit from their energy just by holding them in their hands. Others will keep them close by, in their office, pockets, handbags, etc. Others sleep with them under their pillow or they lie down and place them directly on one of their chakras.

While there are no specific guidelines for how to tap into crystal energy, you do have to have your mind in the right place to gain the most benefit. But when the world is crowding in on you from all sides, it can be difficult to channel your mind in the right direction. Many who use crystals recommend meditation to help you. This is not something that can be done once in a while. To get the best results, one needs to make a daily practice of meditation for at least 10 to 20 minutes. It will help you to focus long enough to decide on the direction you want to go and what steps you want to take.

This can be a challenge in the beginning, but those who make a habit of it, usually find that in time, they can learn to push out all of their worries and stresses and eventually tap into that inner voice in their head. One of the easiest forms of meditation today is practicing mindfulness. It doesn't require any position to take, nor do you have to worry about chanting any expressions or performing any rituals. Through mindfulness, you simply start to observe your thoughts as a neutral person, looking at them without judgment.

By doing this, you separate yourself from your thoughts and eventually, you will learn to think more clearly. In time, you will feel as though you are a completely separate entity from your thoughts. Then you will be able to connect to your internal energy and channel crystal energy in the right direction.

Other forms of meditation you can adopt are guided imagery, mantra chanting, repetitive movement, and affirmations. Find the type of meditation that works best for you and before long, you'll be able to tap into your energy field and gain the most benefits out of crystal energy.

CHAPTER 2
Crystal Energy – Where Does It Come From?

One of the most common questions asked of beginners is where does the crystal get its energy? Because these gems have been around for thousands of years, there is no real definitive answer to that question. Crystals form in the bowels of the earth, far from human eyes, so much of what we have learned about them is based on a theory first, and then from experience later.

We know that the discovery of their energy happened thousands of years ago, but here is what we have come to learn so far.

Color: You can gauge the energy found in a crystal by its color. When people are drawn to a certain color stone, it is usually the energy that they are attracted to. Different colors have different meanings, which may relate to the elements that form the crystals.

As we learn more about chakras in a later chapter, you'll realize that they too have a deep connection. Crystals help to bring the body's energy into balance through the chakras or the aura. Those crystals that have a combination of different colors also contain additional energy flows and chakras. As you learn more about these energies, you'll begin to understand more about the different colors and what they actually mean.

Shape and Form: Crystals take on all sorts of shapes and sizes. We can learn a lot about the power of crystals from their shape. The concept is related to Sacred Geometry and shapes, similar to the colors of a crystal, will have different meanings associated with them.

For example, crystals with a spiky exterior are more defensive, so they are often selected for protection. Crystals with a round stone are considered to be more feminine, and so are used to ground a person or to bring peace.

But these are not the only considerations when it comes to crystals. You might also look at how the light affects it. If it is transparent, it tends to hold more energy, but if it is reflective, as in a more earthy stone, it is more likely going to be used for grounding.

While many people are not consciously aware of the energy emanating from a crystal, it does exist and it can affect us in many ways. There are some people, however, that tend to be more sensitive to this energy than others. Throughout history, you've probably heard of a long list of those who have been able to not just identify the power of a crystal but have in some ways been able to harness it. Shamans, healers, or those who are believed to possess a unique wisdom or understanding have been able to tap into these stones. Wherever you find yourself lost somewhere on this spectrum, one thing is certain, the power of these crystals cannot be denied, nor can they be ignored. When you are able to connect with this type of energy, you will instinctively know how it will help you.

In today's modern age, we tend to scoff at historical proofs as being primitive and insignificant. It is true, that we live in a fast-paced information age, and with our progressive knowledge of science, we have come to understand much more than our ancestors. Historical records abound that relate to how these gems were used throughout our past.

No doubt, we can learn a lot about the power of these little gems, however, we live in very different times. We cannot rely entirely on historical records to guide us in the proper way to harness crystal energy. Historical documents were often based on superstitions and myths. Today, we can understand the science of these things a lot better. Even now, we are discovering more crystals and minerals every day. We now have scientific evidence of their internal power and have a much better understanding of how to use it. By combining what we have learned from the past with our new understanding, we can use these crystals much more effectively in a lot more ways than we might have otherwise suspected. We can eliminate the mystic superstitions of the past and learn how to use them in a way that will be of benefit to even more people in the world, without fear.

The Power of the Crystal

We've already come to understand that the power of crystals can help with emotional, mental, physical, and spiritual problems. There are a thousand ways to use them in each of these areas. Some people use them exclusively for the treatment of what ails them, while others have found better success in using them in conjunction with other forms of therapy, or as an accompaniment to traditional Western medicine.

You might use it to help with a migraine or you might choose to use them to help with the physical healing of an injury of some type. Some might use them to help put their minds at ease, and still others may use them to help release their creative mind. When it comes to how you use the power of the crystal, the possibilities may be endless.

Enhance Intuition: Like all other creatures, we have a strong instinctive nature. Humans though are naturally intuitive about many things. But in our busy lives, we are often flooded with a myriad of minutia that over time can crowd out your natural intuitiveness. Using crystals to help you bring all of that back, can help you to listen to that inner voice again.

Improve Concentration: It is easy to get distracted in the hectic world we live in. You may find yourself struggling to get out of a rut you've gotten yourself into. Constant distractions can keep you from moving forward. Using crystals along with medication, visualization exercises, and affirmation can make a huge difference.

Break Free from Emotional Baggage: We all carry around suitcases full of emotional baggage. Past traumas and uncomfortable experiences seem to follow us wherever we go. Often, these can get in the way of our ability to move on in our lives. Once you are able to harness the power of crystals, you will clear out much of the baggage that is haunting you and find yourself in a whole new space in your life.

Removing Negative Energy: We've already learned that everything in existence has an energy that influences other things around them. If you find yourself living in a cycle of negative energy, crystals can quickly free your mind and leave you open so more positive forces can find you.

Stimulate Creativity: Our brains are mighty instruments. However, our society has made many of us believe that we don't need to tap into all of our natural resources. We live in a highly analytical world where facts and figures have become more important than creativity. However, when you cannot tap into your creative side, you lose out on many things. Crystals can help you to channel their energy in a way that will allow you to handle your problems in a more creative manner.

Over thousands of years, the power held within crystals has been able to harness the elements found in the earth, the oceans, the sun, the moon, and the stars, and pass them onto us. However, to tap into these powerful resources, you need to come into direct contact with them. However, once you do, you'll find yourself on a journey full of new ways to change your world for the better.

The History of Crystal Healing

The practice of healing crystals has likely been around since the dawn of humanity. While we don't have records that date back that far, we do know that for thousands of years, they have been used for all sorts of things. Many have used them in amulets, as talismans, and other protective ways to ward off evil spirits.

Absence of specific records in recorded history, archaeological digs, and the study of artifacts have revealed how these gems have been used over the years. Here is what we know for sure.

- Approximately 30,000 years ago, amulets were used in what is now part of Great Britain. These were made from Baltic amber, which is located many miles from the location where they were found. This is an indication that for the people of the time to carry them such a long distance, that they were highly valued and likely considered a cherished possession.

- Approximately 12,000 years ago, beads, bracelets, and necklaces were uncovered in several gravesites in the regions of Belgium and Switzerland, indicating that they were likely used to ward off spirits.

- Archaeologists discovered the first recorded use of crystals was in Ancient Sumatra (approximate 1400AD). The records show that the crystals were used in a number of magic formulas, helping us to understand that they recognized the power contained in these stones.

- The Ancient Egyptians used lapis lazuli, carnelian, turquoise, quartz, and emeralds in amulets they wore for their health and protection.

- The Ancient Greeks gave many of the crystals we use today their names. In fact, the word crystal comes from the Greek word for ice. The Greeks actually believed that quartz was water that had been frozen so solidly that it would never thaw again. They wore amethysts as a measure to prevent drunkenness and hangovers, and because of its red color, the name hematite comes from the word blood and was worn by Greek soldiers before a battle in hopes that they would become invincible.

- In Ancient China, jade was the preferred healing stone. Even today, this gem is still very highly valued. Throughout their history, it has been used for kidney ailments and to bring good luck.

- Even during the Renaissance period of history (around 11th century AD), crystal use was combined with herbal remedies to heal all sorts of illnesses.

- During the 1600s, physicians in Germany declared that the power of the gemstone was directly related to the presence of angels, both good and bad.

No doubt there are countless more cases we can find throughout history. While the stones may have received a bad reputation for a time, their rebirth, coupled with modern science, has allowed it to regain its former popularity. Today, however, its use has been adapted to suit our new knowledge of the properties, so we have a much clearer idea of just how to tap into its power and channel that to do even more than anyone else could have possibly done in our history.

CHAPTER 3
Benefits Of Healing With Crystals

It is without question that crystals have these healing powers. Whether we are aware of them or not, the beauty and power of them are widely recognized. You may not be a healer or a shaman, but you too can tap into the power behind these gems and use them in many ways that will benefit you. While we discussed some of the most basic uses for crystals in the last chapter, let's look a little more deeply into what their powers can do here.

Red Crystals

A good example of how color can influence your results is clear by what you can do with red crystals. Long known as a means of activating and energizing, red crystals are associated with your most basic of survival skills. A ruby, one of the most beautiful red crystals, works with the energy of the heart, giving you energy and balance.

Historically, rubies are a representation of royalty and wealth. The color range of rubies can vary from a light pink to a deep red. It is most often connected with the root chakra, but it can also be used to give you the energy you lack. Anyone feeling down or low either emotionally or physically will likely discover that they are losing energy through their aura. Rubies are often used to repair such leaks and to bring more balance to the body so that all energy flows freely.

Red crystals also protect you from psychic attacks, nurture your emotional health, enhance lucid dreaming, stimulates creativity, and gives you spiritual wisdom.

On the other end of the red spectrum, pink crystals can help you to find a resolution to certain problems. It brings emotion and sensitivity to your daily actions. A commonly used crystal, rose quartz, has a very calming effect, but at the same time, it releases many unexpressed emotions that may be buried underneath the surface, inhibiting you from personal growth.

Orange Crystals

Orange crystals work well by combining energizing elements with your ability to focus. This opens the door and allows for more creative skills to emerge. A popular orange crystal is a carnelian, which brings a sense of warmth to its user. It can boost your motivation, stimulate energy, and enhance enthusiasm.

When using carnelian, you will be able to recognize your self-worth, which will naturally help you to heal in a wide range of ways. On a physical level, it can help the body to absorb more vitamins and minerals and ensure that there is enough blood flow to the organs and tissues.

Yellow Crystals

Yellow crystals work well in improving the function of the nervous, digestive, and immune systems. They can ease stress, fear, and anxiety and give you a sense of contentment at the same time. A favorite yellow crystal is an amber, which has been very beneficial in helping the body to heal itself. Citrine quartz, if it is a bright, clear yellow, works well to clear the mind allowing you to focus better. Iron pyrite (sometimes referred to as "fool's gold") cleanses and strengthens the digestive system and leaves you with a sense of calm.

Green Crystals

Green crystals heal the heart, both physically and emotionally. They keep your emotions in balance and move you to build positive relationships. The green aventurine crystal makes it easy for you to express your feelings and can help to relieve anxiety, which will naturally have a positive physical effect as well. Malachite helps you to uncover hidden feelings, so you can break free from unwanted negative behavior patterns. Amazonite heals issues with the throat and the lungs, the bloodstone, and enhances blood circulation to the heart.

Light Blue

Light blue crystals are more often associated with communication and connect to all of the five senses. Its primary focus is on improving the way you talk to yourself. It improves your thought patterns and edifies how you express yourself. The aquamarine crystal promotes better communication, stronger courage, and more confidence. You'll be better able to stand your ground against a formidable foe, and you'll be prepared to speak your mind clearly.

Celestite is better suited for enhancing your inner spirituality. Turquoise helps eliminate much of your negative energy and the electromagnetic smog that exudes from the environment. This will allow for clearer thinking, leaving you with calmer nerves, especially when having to speak publicly.

Indigo

Indigo is often associated with your "third eye." It enhances your perception and intuition. That coupled with an improved understanding and a deep sense of calm can be achieved by working with indigo. The azurite crystal frees up those long-term blocks in communication and will aid in revealing whatever it is that is getting in the way of us reaching our full potential. In addition, you can look forward to a better memory too.

Violet

These tap into your creative side, improving your imagination, and whatever it is that inspires you. You get the empathy you need to feel more connected with others and it can help to rebalance your body, pulling you away from emotional extremes. Amethyst, one of the most practical of the violet crystals, can be used in a wide range of applications. Used with meditation, it gives you a sense of quietness and helps to clear the mind. It paves the way for lucid dreaming and serves as a block against computer and electromagnetic stresses you may not be aware of. This gives you an improved mental clarity, so you can be much more efficient at what you need to do.

White

Clear stones (or white stones) allow you to reflect all the other energies that surround you. It is directly related to your abilities in clarity, cleansing, and purification. A clear quartz, for example, can give your energy levels a boost, channel exterior energies to you, help to absorb, store, amplify, balance, and even focus on other energies. This aids your ability to heal, meditate, and manifest your individual qualities.

The moonstone has a soft luminescence about it that is perfect for helping to ease tensions that result from emotional disturbances. It can help to improve digestive issues or anywhere else where your body's fluids may be out of balance.

Black

The black stones work the opposite of the white. Black stones will reveal to you the hidden potentials of the circumstances that surround you. They help to manifest and give you a solid perspective of a situation. Because they can absorb light, they hold all of the energies inside. It requires patience to use a black stone. They help you to ground yourself and serve as an anchor so that you can function normally. In time, you will uncover many different hidden aspects of your life so that you can deal with them more effectively. In that respect, black stones have more of a purifying role than anything else.

The smoky quartz is a protective stone that is able to help dissolve any negative states that surround you. Using it will help you to attain a deeper level of who you really are inside and then allow you to cleanse and balance your beings. It is for this reason that many black stones can be very practical to use when practicing meditation.

There are many more ways you can benefit from the use of crystals. As you can see from the above examples, they all have different ways to help you heal. It is not like a medication prescribed by a doctor that only has one purpose. Crystals can be used in a wide range of areas and you're not limited to a single one. As you grow in your knowledge of these gems, you'll come to a much better understanding of how you can use them to your advantage.

Eliminates Negative Energy

All of us have good days and bad days from time to time. But when you find that you're in a constant spiral of negativity, it can be a difficult struggle to break free. No human action taken in this world happens if it hasn't been thought about first. Every action appears first as a thought, then an emotion, before it actually happens, so to eliminate the negative energy that you're struggling with, you first must harness those negative thoughts.

We all understand the power of negative people. If you don't do something to stop the spiraling effect, then chances are, you'll end up in a cyclone of bad feelings, which will eventually disrupt your mental and physical abilities, taking it down the tubes with you. But all of this is not so easily done.

First, you must surround yourself with positive energy, but that's not always possible. For this kind of help, it is best to use crystals. After you've done everything you can physically to resolve or change your situation, you can turn to crystals to help to neutralize this negativity. There are several different crystals that can do this quite effectively.

Probably the most powerful of these is the Black Tourmaline crystal. It is the go-to piece that many people rely on. Simply by placing in nearby while you're in a negative situation can help to cut down on a great deal of the dark energy flooding your environment. It is very effective at blocking electromagnetic fields that are in the air from all of the electronic devices we have come to depend on.

Black Tourmaline, however, can be quite a formidable piece of stone. While a larger stone may be your favored piece, carrying it around with you can be cumbersome. Instead, many people choose to have amulets, bracelets, and pendants made from it so that it is more practical and less obvious to others. It works by putting an invisible protective shield around you that can block a lot of that negative energy from getting in your way.

Another similar stone used to eliminate negative energy is the black obsidian. This stone is extremely powerful and may not be a good option for regular use. Many crystal users actually prefer the gentleness of the black tourmaline over the black obsidian for that purpose.

Smoky quartz can also be effective in protecting you from negative energy. In addition to keeping the negative energy from overwhelming you, it is also a great way to detox you from the inside out. Any negative thoughts that are hovering just below the surface can easily begin to fester and foster new negativity in your life without you realizing it. The longer it goes undetected, the deeper and denser it gets, until it begins to manifest itself in some physical way (headaches, stomach aches, colds, flu, etc.)

A good defense mechanism is to have a combination of both stones working together. You can have them made into a nice bracelet or pendant that you can wear at all times. Some even take them along in a little pouch that they can keep in their backpack or purse.

To further enhance your forcing out of negativity, you can use your crystals along with essential oils. Sage, orange, and tangerine scents are very effective at lifting a positive mood. It can be very difficult to stay in a negative frame of mind when you are surrounded by the scent of citrus in the air. It can quickly change the mood of any number of bad situations.

Other very effective options for pushing out negativity are bergamot and ylang-ylang. So whether you choose to use black tourmaline, black obsidian, or smoky quartz, the next time you need to neutralize the negativity infiltrating your space, choose one, a combination, or a mix of the stone with essential oils, and you should see an almost immediate effect.

Reenergize Mind and Body

As we've already explained, crystals, like everything else, are infused with a constantly vibrating energy. This energy flows through every cell in our bodies. But in addition to this energy, our cells also contain very specific energy patterns. When we are under stress, we tend to take up unhealthy habits that can lead to illnesses and other physical problems. When this happens, the energy that flows within you can be interrupted or at the very least compromised.

In using crystals to help reenergize the mind and body, we need to understand our body composition better. Since we are all composed of around 70% water, we can use this knowledge to help us to heal correctly.

This type of healing can be done in many ways. Since each crystal is composed of natural minerals found in the earth, and our bodies are mostly comprised of the most precious liquid found on the earth, by simply holding a crystal in our hands, we can allow its energy to connect with the water in our bodies and make it possible to infuse ourselves with more energy.

Many people like to say a chant, a mantra, or some type of phrase to activate the power of the mind to work with the crystals. While there are many books that will provide you with a chant or phrase to use in these instances, the best results come from words that have been specifically tailored to your personal circumstances. For example, you might want to say something like:

"I feel energized in my heart, mind, and soul. Every day, my body will achieve its optimum health no matter what the circumstances."

You can hold a crystal stone in your hand or you can simply touch a necklace made with the stone. As you say it, your energies will be transferred to the necklace or stone. Once done, take the necklace and drape it around a glass of water and wait until the water is energized from the stone. Some like to take the water and place it outside in the direct sunlight and wait for at least 4 hours before drinking it. In this way, you begin to slowly reprogram your mind and body.

Other ways to reenergize your mind and body with crystals is to try a few techniques with different stones.

Turquoise: The beautiful blue of the turquoise usually has a little black flowing through it. These stones are most effective in diffusing depression, fears, anxiety, and even physical exhaustion. If you're practicing meditation, turquoise can help to bring you balance and restore positive thoughts to your mind.

Amethyst: If you've lost your energy because of stress, an amethyst can be very powerful in restoring energy balance back in your life. Especially if you're going through the loss of a loved one, a divorce, or insomnia.

The lavender amethyst helps to keep the hormones in balance, stimulate the immune system, and gives your metabolism a boost all at the same time. It's is great for relieving stress and even some physical problems you might suffer as a result of that stress (headaches).

Blue Topaz: Helps to keep the fifth Chakra in balance. When this is in balance, you will have better communication skills, feel happier, and will naturally be drawn to things that will bring you success. It is a powerful stone that is strong enough to strengthen your nerves, improve your digestion, and reenergize the whole body at the same time.

Other stones that are effective in reenergizing the body are rubies, amazonite, citrine, rose quartz, crystal quartz, onyx, and moonstone.

Feel More Relaxed and Centered

There are also many calming crystals you can use to help you relieve chronic stress. When your stress and anxiety levels get out of control, rather than turning to traditional medicine, think of using crystals as your first go-to treatment. They work just as well as deep breathing exercises can when infusing oxygen to the brain.

Start by taking the time to meditate on a regular basis. This helps to open the door to an inner peace and give you a mental refuge from the world. Since there are so many crystals that can help to calm and center you, we suggest that you start by experimenting with several of them until you find the one that 'talks to you' in a way that you understand. Once you find the one that fits you personally, start incorporating it into your meditation practice.

As a beginner, here are a few you can start off with.
- Blue Lace Agate
- Lepidolite

- Amethyst
- Angelite
- Flourite
- Black Tourmaline

The Blue Lace Agate, for example, has a beautiful periwinkle color that has a very calming vibration that can bring you peace of mind. Holding it daily can calm your nerves and lower your anxiety. If you tend to have frequent anxiety, try wearing it as a bracelet or carrying one around in your pocket.

Lepidolite is partially composed of naturally occurring lithium, which is often used as an anti-anxiety medication. Jet stones fight against negative emotions like grief and stress and work like a suit of armor, protecting you from many of the external things that can negatively impact your mind, body, and spirit.

As you continue on in your study of crystals, you will find there are many that have a calming effect that can help to ease your anxiety. Experiment with several of them and choose those that speak to you. You may be a beginner when it comes to using crystals, but you were born with an internal intuition that will help you decide if you allow it to guide you. If you find that you can touch, feel, and get an effect from any one of the crystals you try, you should be well on your way down the path to true crystal healing.

CHAPTER 4
Crystals And Chakras

It's true that you can do a lot with crystals without any knowledge of your chakras and how they work. However, if you're really serious about learning how to use crystals to your advantage, you should know at least a little about chakras. It can only help to enhance your healing and bring you more powerful effects.

The 7 Chakras in the Body

Chakras make up the key energy centers of the body. We already talked about each of these centers:

- The first chakra sits at the base of the tailbone
- The second chakra sits near the navel
- The third chakra sits at the base of the sternum
- The fourth chakra sits right in the middle of the chest
- The fifth chakra sits in the throat directly above the Adam's apple
- The sixth chakra sits in the center of the forehead, between the eyes
- The seventh chakra sits at the very top of the crown of the head

These are the body's main chakras, but they are not all of them. Your chakras are located throughout the body, however, these are the primary ones and a good place for a beginner to get started.

Energy flows in and out of your body through chakras, but at times, the flow of energy can become blocked through one or more of these chakras, giving you an unbalanced flow of energy. These blockages can be a direct result of trauma, illness, or lifestyle practices you may have. You may not be aware that your chakra is blocked, but there will be evidence of it if you know what to look for.

For example, you may begin to have emotional problems, an unexplained physical pain, or a health issue that doesn't seem to want to go away, no matter what you do. When the root chakra is blocked, you may start to experience lower back pain. If the heart chakra is blocked, you may develop heart problems or find yourself stuck in an emotional downfall.

Each of the chakras has its own corresponding color, which directly correlates to the frequency of vibration of its energy. So if you are working with both crystals and chakras together, make sure you choose the colors that best match the chakra you are trying to heal.

Why They Work

With both major and minor chakras, if it is not working properly or if it has become blocked, our overall health and well-being will begin to suffer. Generally, if you are feeling physically, emotionally, or psychologically off balance, you can be pretty sure that something is wrong with one of your chakras. If you are feeling down, it could be the result of not getting enough energy to support your needs. If you are blocking negative feelings, you may be unconsciously interfering with a healthy flow of energy.

On the other hand, if you are working hard on balancing your emotional, mental, physical, and spiritual health, you can better accomplish your goals by balancing the flow of energy through your chakras. The trick is to know how to tap into that chakra when needed.

One way to make this work is by regularly practicing yoga. If you've ever practiced yoga, then you know how one simple movement can clear your head of all sorts of clutter, physically and emotionally. This is because that move opened up the pathways to that chakra. The more you understand the unique properties of chakras, the easier it will be to see exactly how they work.

The Root Chakra or the Muladhara: This chakra is related to your survival and the ability to feel safe and secure. Located right at the base of the spine, its associated color is red. Because it is the lowest of the major chakras, it sits closest to the earth. In order to maintain a healthy Muladhara, you need to perform exercises that are closely related to the earth like dancing, jogging, and jumping. The combination of those movements with the crystals will help to put your mind at ease. Once you begin to see the world as a safe place, the chakra will open up to a flood of energetic vibrations.

The Sacral Chakra or the Svadhistana: The second chakra is closely related to your sensuality, sexuality, and your internal desire for pleasure. It is located right in the lower abdomen and its associated color is orange. Exercises that work well with your Svadhistana are belly dancing and yoga. It also helps to be involved in a loving partnership to enhance its effects on your energy flow. When the energy flows freely through this chakra, you are better able to live your dreams and do whatever is necessary to make them your reality.

Solar Plexus Chakra or Manipura: The Manipura's associated color is yellow and it is directly connected to your view of your power in the world. When you have an overbearing personality, out of sync with the other chakras in your body, you can develop some very negative tendencies like obsessive-compulsive disorders (OCD) for example. However, if your energy flow through this region is healthy, you will feel more empowered and you'll have better control over these types of disorders.

Heart Chakra or Anahata: With the associated color of green, this chakra is directly connected to your feelings of love and compassion. It's also associated with the natural element of air. When you have healthy relationships with family, friends, even animals, your heart energy flows freely. Even when you have that spiritual connection with nature and its beauty, the energy from this chakra can be very strong. It allows you to not only give love when you feel it but to accept it as well.

Throat Chakra or Vishuddha: This chakra has an energy that flows through your words. It is the energy of communication. Its associated color is blue. When the energy flows freely through this region, you can speak with confidence, asking for what you need without reservation. It also reflects your truth. Exercises that build up this chakra are singing, chanting, and breathing.

The Third Eye Chakra or the Ajna: The Third Eye's natural color is indigo. It is the gateway of the energy that controls your insight, intuition, and awareness. Situated right between the eyebrows, exercises that work best with Ajna are meditation and visualization, which can aid in the healthy flow of energy in this region.

The Crown Chakra or the Sahasrara: This chakra energizes your spiritual connection. Its associated color is violet. It supports unity, blissfulness, and the knowledge that you own. This chakra allows you to be consciously aware of elements in your life and allow you to be at peace with them.

If you're planning to use crystals along with your chakras, to get the best effect and better energy flow from each one, use the exercises suggested with each one. As you can see, understanding the chakras can help in breathing new energy into your body. It is best to start with your base chakra, seeing and using the associated colors to get your energies flowing in an uninterrupted and healthy way.

Some people prefer to start off with meditation to get their minds focused on the purpose with each session. It is one of the best means of helping your body's energy to flow the way it was originally designed to do.

Chakra Connections

Each chakra has a unique mode of expression and will show you a different picture of life. At times, your work with chakras will involve more than yourself. When making a chakra connection with another person (as in a relationship), you communicate by sending your energy from you to the other person and vice versa.

If you are sending energy from the right side of your body, they should be receiving it on their left side. In such cases, the flow in both of your bodies remains balanced. However, this kind of energy transmission is not always necessary, nor is it always possible. If either one of you has a blockage in one or more of your chakras, the communication you are sending can be blocked as well. There are several steps you can take to correct this situation.

When you use crystals to heal a chakra, everything will begin to work correctly. These chakras are found in a straight line that runs right up the center of the body. To make the best use of your crystals, place it right where the chakra is located. There are specific healing crystals that work well with connecting to the natural properties of the chakra. They can amplify the energy that is flowing through the region, open it, or even heal it. So try to find the crystal that works best with the chakra you're trying to help.

The Root: Its primary color is red but grey and black are also closely associated with it. Look for stones of these colors like bloodstone, garnet, onyx, ruby, and red jasper.

The Navel: It has an orange color so crystals that work best with it are carnelian, goldstone, orange zincite, or tangerine quartz.

The Solar Plexus: Look for stones that match its yellow color like citrine, sapphire, picture jasper, yellow calcite, and yellow sapphire.

The Heart: It can be green or pink so crystals like green calcite, pink morganite, rose quartz, and green tourmaline works best.

The Throat: Use blue crystals like turquoise or aqua. You can use any shade of blue, but try to choose the lighter shades like blue lace agate, aquamarine, and angelite.

The Brow: The colors to look for here are indigo and any of the darker blue shades like lapis lazuli, sodalite, and the hawk's eye.

The Crown: A violet or purple color crystal that can radiate out its clear or white color. Look for stones like amethyst and clear quartz.

Balancing Chakras

It is important to choose a crystal that will vibrate at the same frequency as the chakra. This will help to clear the blockage and restore the flow of energy through the body. It works well to heal a wide range of spiritual, emotional, mental, and physical challenges that may have developed as a result of the blockage.

To use the crystals properly, take the following steps:

- Lie on your back with eyes closed.
- Place the crystal on the blocked chakra.
- With eyes closed, visualize the color of the chakra and imagine the energy as it flows free of interruptions.
- Each chakra will yield different results to help you to know when you have freed the blockage.

First Chakra: Allows you to connect to your emotions, feel more secure and safe, and have a sense of belonging in your community.

Second Chakra: Will give you a stronger sense of personal power, sexuality, and tap into your creative side.

Third Chakra: Improved self-esteem, a sense of prosperity, better self-identity, and a stronger sense of morals.

Fourth Chakra: You will have more emotional balance, you'll love easier, be more forgiving, and more compassionate.

Fifth Chakra: Better self-expression, communicate with others more easily, be more honest, and have a stronger sense of integrity.

Sixth Chakra: A heightened sense of intuition, better insight, stronger beliefs and attitudes, and you'll have a clearer mind than before.

Seventh Chakra: A stronger connection to the spiritual world, a heightened consciousness, and a feeling that you are connected to the universe, a sense of oneness with other things outside of yourself.

This type of crystal energy, when used in the right way can have a major impact on every aspect of your life. If you allow it, it can take you on a spiritual journey that will help you to move beyond the physical and become a part of the bigger picture of life. In order for all of this to happen, you have to approach your work with crystals with the right intentions.

This is not a practice that can no longer be relegated to the mystic world. Science has zeroed in on the power of crystals and has used it to their advantage. How it works can best be explained by IBM scientist, Marcel Vogel. He observed crystals growing under a microscope and made an intriguing observation. As he watched, he noticed that they took on the shape of whatever he was thinking about. This was the first significant realization that crystals were transmitting energy to the human mind and was receiving energy from humans.

Even Albert Einstein recognized the vibrations of everything that exists in our world. Just like you can't see sound waves, your thoughts emit vibrations that impact other things in your life. Therefore, with crystals to enhance our feelings, emotions, and thoughts, amplifying them in the right way, we can have the ability to change our lives and transform them into something that can keep us in balance, so we can literally embrace life and the abundance of opportunities they have for us.

CHAPTER 5
Crystal Grids

Now that you understand the fundamentals of crystals and chakras and how they work, we can go on to applying this information with crystal grids. To put it simply, a crystal grid is a method of working with crystals that involves creating very specific arrangements of different geometric shapes or patterns. These patterns usually include some type of sacred geometry in their form.

When used properly, these grids can amplify the power of the crystals even more. While it is possible to get good results from the use of a single crystal, when you use a grid, it can only enhance the results and give its energy a significant boost.

To create your own crystal grid, you first need to establish a foundation or a base to work with. The shape you use can be printed on a piece of fabric or a paper. Some have engraved wooden boards that they can lay out to place their crystals on. In some cases, you can even obtain a template to show you exactly where to place your crystals for the best effect.

Why You Need Them

You can use a crystal grid for many different reasons. Some people use them primarily for spiritual connections, but they can also be used for healing, to provide protection, to find love, to achieve prosperity, or any other number of things.

When you use the crystal grid, the collection of crystals all working together has an increased power that works alongside the sacred geometry to harness extra energy to work on your behalf. They also serve as a solid anchor when you need them.

As you can probably imagine, there are many ways to create a crystal grid, each with its own unique benefits to you. While there may be many reasons to justify using a grid, we can break them down into four different categories.

Crystal Energy: Because of their unique structure, crystals work really well when used in certain patterns. The crystal grid helps to harness even more of their properties to give you added support in accomplishing your goal.

It is important to choose those crystals that have the very properties you're searching for. To achieve your intended purpose, you may have to think beyond the obvious though. If for example, you are looking to improve your chances of success, then you would obviously choose crystals that will help you to achieve that goal, but you could also include crystals with related properties like determination, prosperity, and self-confidence to support it. Together, the power of all of these elements can help to direct their energy in the right direction for you.

Sacred Geometry: There is a form of metaphysical science that supports the belief that certain patterns that are found in nature are actually a fingerprint for understanding the universe and how everything in it actually works. These shapes are referred to as sacred geometry and they represent the actual framework of all creation.

Each of these shapes has their own use and form of energy. While not every crystal grid uses sacred geometry, when it does, it makes the entire grid far more powerful than one that does not. When using sacred geometry, choose your grids very carefully to ensure that the power you will receive will be directed towards your actual purpose.

Using sacred geometry also is beneficial in helping you to transmit your energies out of the grid into the rest of the universe so that the results can be manifested. You can also channel that energy inward to heal your broken aura to improve yourself when needed. The point is that while crystals have their own unique powers that can help you, using them with specific chakras within a grid can enhance their power even more. If you use a crystal grid with sacred geometry, you get the most intense power possible in the metaphysical world.

Numerology: Crystal grids used with the ancient spiritual science of numerology is very similar to sacred geometry. By selecting the number of crystals based on their symbolic meaning and energy as it relates to the grid, you can connect to support your purpose and better connect to their energy. Not only does this amplify the energy emanating from them, but it channels it better to focus on a very specific task.

Your Intention: Don't forget the power and the energy that is generated by your own thoughts. When you can transmit that information to crystals, especially when they have been carefully placed on a grid, this is when they really work their best. You can program your crystals with your thoughts and dreams. The grid will store them and broadcast them out into the universe for as long as you need them to.

These grids can become powerful tools in your hands and are extremely effective. However, in order for you to get the best results, you must follow through on any intentions you transmit to them. Their power is a source of energy and motivation, but you will not receive rewards for anything that you don't wish to work on. They can only connect to something that is real within you and broadcast that intention around the clock for as long as you need them to in order to effect the change that you need.

Helps to Harness Power

It is not enough that you are able to amplify the power of the crystals in a grid. While all that additional energy can be a huge benefit to you, you need to harness it and direct its energies in a way that it will truly heal your chakras in a more focused manner.

When you start your grid by selecting only those crystals that will enhance and push your intentions out into the universe, in such a way that their energies become complements of each other, the solution to your problem often becomes very clear. As a result of harnessing this plethora of power, you will no longer need to worry about a conflict of energies or if the crystals have been arranged in a manner that might even restrict their powers. Rather, this harnessed energy can be channeled in any direction you wish it.

In essence, using crystal grids in the right way can literally put the power of the universe into your hands.

How to Create a Crystal Grid

To get started, it is important that you carefully select the crystals you plan to use on the grid. There are many different ways to choose the stones, but most experts believe that the stone actually chooses you rather than the other way around. Remember, you are tapping into the powers of the universe and connecting them to the energies inside of you. This is not a decision that is made purely in your head, you will have to involve your own intuition along with your logic in making this decision.

When you go shopping for your new crystals, walk around the room and casually observe each crystal there. Study its shape, color, and patterns carefully and wait for one of them to pull you in. Because each crystal has its own unique vibration, when one connects with you, you will notice it if you are paying attention.

Choosing the right stone requires patience and a quiet mind. When a particular stone pulls you in, maybe by the intricacy of its pattern, its color, or its shape, pick it up. Hold it in your hand and think about your purpose. If it is the right stone for you, you should begin to feel sensations in your hand. Some report that they feel a warmth come over them, others say it is cold. Other possible sensations you might feel are soft pulsations, a sense of calm and tranquility. All of these are signs that the stone you're holding is the one that is calling to you.

Therefore, choosing the stone requires knowing your intent before you begin. It doesn't really matter what your intention is, you will be much more successful in using crystals if you have it clearly in mind. Your thoughts have their own vibrations that emanate throughout the universe. This means that one of the most valuable tools you'll have at your disposal is your own mind. This will provide you with insight and help you to live better in the present.

Your intentions or purpose works like a magnet, attracting what will make them come true. Preparing your mind to choose a crystal is an extremely important step that helps crystals to align themselves to your values and purpose of life.

- First, decide what is most important to you.

- Explore different areas of your life that you feel need improvement.
- Be very specific in clarifying your needs and when you want to see them come true.
- Write them down in the present tense.

Once you have your intention clearly written down in front of you, they begin to take on a physical life of their own. They are now starting to become real and as a result, will help guide you to the right crystals.

Cleanse and charge your crystals: Because of their highly energetic properties, crystals will react to any energy pattern they come in contact with. By the time you get your crystal home, it has probably been touched by hundreds of different hands. So one of the first things you need to do is cleanse the crystal and then do a weekly cleaning afterward.

There are several different ways you can cleanse your crystals. Here are a few suggestions:

- Soak them in salt water. Let them remain submerged in the salt water solution for a minimum of one hour. Make sure you use Himalayan pink salt rather than regular table salt for the best effect. Do not use this method of cleaning for porous stones like rose and gypsum as the saltwater could cause damage. You also want to avoid using salt water on magnetic stones like lodestone. The salt could cause portions of the stone to rust.

- You can also smoke them by burning a small bundle of sage, cedar, lavender, or sweetgrass. Set fire to these dried plants and then once they begin to produce smoke, extinguish the flame. Hold the crystals in the tendril of smoke to cleanse them. You can use only one of these herbs or all four if you like. If you don't have those herbs, then consider using incense instead.

- If you practice some type of special healing skills like Reiki, you can use your own energy to cleanse them.

Be careful. Crystals are amazing pieces of nature, they will never lose their energy. Even if by chance, you should break one, the source of its energy is still there. The only real way to bring about the demise of a crystal is to not clean it. As it comes in contact with more and more people, it will begin to take on the energy of everyone who touched it, for the good or for the bad. Without cleaning it on a regular basis, you're leaving yourself vulnerable to possible negative energies flowing in and out of you.

Once your crystals have been properly cleaned, they need to be charged or programmed. This restores it back to its natural condition, so they can continue along using their energy on your behalf. Every time you cleanse your crystals, they also need to be charged.

This involves putting your own personal intentions into them. In other words, you need to give your crystals a job to do. It is up to you to transmit your thoughts, intentions, and purposes to the crystals. This is important as you will inevitably have times when you will be vibrating at a very low frequency. Those are the times when you will be feeling down, depressed, and unfulfilled in some way. When that happens, your intentions can easily evaporate. However, if your intentions have been transmitted to the crystal, when you reconnect with it, your purpose can be restored and you can more quickly get back on the right track.

Programming your crystal is relatively simple. After cleaning, take the crystal and hold it in both hands, close your eyes, and take three deep, slow breaths in and out. Meditate on your faith, the Earth, and all those things that make you happy, give you contentment and satisfaction in life. These thoughts will take your body to a higher vibration, which is the frequency that is more connected to a spiritual or religious belief. The belief in something that has a power that is far greater than anything you can produce on your own. For some people, this spiritual vibration is more of a scientific connection. Whatever it is for you, it is up to you to tap into this vibration. When you do, ask the crystal to clear itself of all unwanted energies or previous programming it may have once held, so it will be clear of everything but what you put into it.

However you choose to say it, verbalize your intent. Speaking out loud, you might say something like the following words. *"I am requesting that the highest vibrations found in love and light join with my highest vibrations and work together to clear away any unwanted energy or any previous programming it may have received. I order this crystal to hold my intentions of ...."*

You can complete the phrase by adding three very specific intentions of your own for the crystal to follow through with. You can give it any intentions you want. You finish the programming by saying "thank you" three times. By offering thanks three times, it is your way of emphasizing that what you want to achieve is in fact, possible in the universe.

The Elements of a Crystal Grid

Once your crystals have been cleansed and programmed, you are ready to start forming your grid. While each grid is unique to you and your purpose, there are some very basic elements that you must have for it to work properly. When all of these elements are combined, the grid can produce a powerful but synergistic blend of energies. Knowing which crystals can be used and where they can be placed on the pattern requires some level of understanding about crystal energy as well as the universal patterns of life. As you create your grid, you must make sure that it has these components:

The Path: the direction of how the energy will flow inside the grid

The Design: An energy path that will work with the objective or purpose of the grid

The Visuals: These would include a balance of the designs and colors, any words or images that will enhance the aesthetic of the grid and give you the desired feeling when you are in contact with it.

The Elements: The actual crystals you will be using on the grid. These include the Focus Stone, Way Stones, Spirit Stones, Desire Stones, and Perimeter Stones. We'll discuss each of these a little later in this chapter.

The Wand: The tool you use in order to activate the grid.

The Path: The path is based on a pretty basic principle. It is the direction you want the energy to follow throughout the grid. A well-designed path will have a clearly laid out direction for the energy to follow so that it can be concentrated and directed towards one single point on the grid.

The Design: The design or the layout for the grid can take on a number of possible shapes and forms. While you are free to create a design at random, the most effective grids rely on sacred geometry and use only those forms you can actually find in nature. We could dedicate an entire book to each of these shapes and what they mean, but you can easily access information about many of these online and find a sacred geometrical shape that will match your purpose. These can be downloaded and printed out and used as a base pattern for your grid whenever you need them.

However, as a beginner, you can start with some of the most commonly used designs to create your grid.

- **The Circle:** Represents completeness, divine will, unity, purposeful action, singularity, inclusion and/or new beginnings.
- **The Vesica Piscis** (*which looks like two circles intertwined*): Represents bringing together opposites. It can be used to bridge misunderstandings, join the spirit and the body together, or to unite a number of things that have been divided. It is also used to heal emotional wounds.

- **Tripod of Life** (*which looks like three circles intertwined, two on the top and one underneath*): Represents balance in life. It centers, unites, and stabilizes groups of three elements. The mind, body, and spirit for example, or the past, present, and future.

- **Seed of Life** (*appears with multiple circles intertwined and held within one larger circle*): Represents the completion of a task or the achievement of a specific goal. It can also reflect harmony, balance, sincerity, and truth. In essence, it is a sacred geometrical shape that can be used for a wide number of things.

The Visuals: Once you have chosen your design, the next step is to enhance the aesthetics of your grid by adding visuals to it. While the design we spoke about above is one area of aesthetics, you can also add other visuals to emphasize your purpose or intent.

For example, you might want to consider using the colors of the crystals to help form more aesthetically pleasing patterns or add color to your grid in some other way that connects to your intention. Many people add color in the form of flowers, pictures, colored text, candles, etc. This added color is not limited to the crystal stones and can come from anywhere.

You can also create a vision board and place your grid on top of it. A common practice is to use images that relate closely to your purpose or vision. These could include health and wellness, wealth and prosperity, career fulfillment, close and loving relationships, etc.

Affirmations: Affirmations are powerful tools you can use at any time, but combining them with a crystal grid can make them even more powerful. By writing down an affirmation that specifically relates to the purpose of the grid, you draw the attention of the powers that exist in the physical realm to your purpose and can receive the support through the energies in the grid.

The Elements: When it comes time to actually start putting the grid together, you need to make sure that you have very specific elements in place. Each crystal will have its own purpose. You will need to have a focus stone, way stones, spirit stones, and desire stones. All of these will fit inside a series of stones called the perimeter.

Make sure that the crystals you select are chosen based on their ability to amplify and focus the energy in the direction of your purpose or intention. Which crystals you choose will depend on the elements of each crystal itself. Your decision could be based on the color, its power of influence, or its shape.

- **The Focus Stone:** Every grid needs to have a center crystal referred to as the Focus Stone, which works like an anchor for the entire grid, then you must choose several other stones to work with that one. The purpose of the focus stone is to gather energy from the other surrounding stones, from the universe, and then channel it back into the grid. This creates a downward flow of coherent energy. Any energy that emanates from the Focus Stone will be modified and reshaped by the power produced from the crystal grid.

- **The Way Stones:** The Way Stones are placed around the Focus Stone and laid out on a specific path. They work to modify the energies that emanate from the Focus Stone and then amplify and modify any energy that is coming into the grid from outside.

- **The Desire Stones:** These are placed on the outermost section of the grid and signify your desires, goals, or purposes that you want to achieve. They can also gather energy, especially from areas that have been channeled and modified by the Focus and Way stones. You could consider these stones as a means of fine-tuning the energies channeled from the other crystals. Select your desire stones in the same way as you would your Way Stones. Look at their color rays and the energy lattice. These are usually the same stones you would select to use outside of the grid. You know, the ones you carry with you throughout the day to help you achieve a specific goal. However, you can considerably amplify their power by using them in a crystal grid.

- **The Path:** This is the path of energy that flows through the grid. Its purpose is to channel the energy from the Focus Stone to the Way Stones and then on to the Desire Stones. It's a representation of the journey you must take in order to achieve the object or action of your desire. The path will be directed by the shape of the grid, so you can enhance its specific powers and meanings. There are many directions the path must take. Some will go in a very familiar direction like in a circle, square, or a triangle. Others will take on more complex directions like hexagons, pentagons or even spirals. Do a little added research to determine which path will work best for your purpose. Rarely will you find one that leads you in a straight line. There are many others besides the one mentioned here, that are very useful and can add even more power to your crystal grid.

When creating a crystal grid, it is best to first visualize yourself engaging in your desired activity. If you are building a grid that will help you to become more profitable, you might visualize yourself with the money or the material things you are trying to attain. If your goal is to find love in your life, visualize yourself in a happy family environment.

Let's Lay It All Out

Just as important as all of the elements of your crystal grid, is the location you place the grid. You will need to find a location where it won't be disturbed while it does its work. Keep it in a place away from kids, animals, and anything else that could somehow accidentally alter its shape once it's been set up.

Start with a small piece of paper and write down your intention. Make sure that your words are very specific because this will help you to make a better choice on which crystals are needed in the grid. While there are no right answers for which stones to choose, always go for the ones that are calling or speaking to you.

Next, cleanse the space where the grid will be by burning palo santo or sage. The smoke will purify the area before you begin laying everything out.

Take the paper that you wrote your intentions on, fold it and place it in the center of the grid.

Take several deep breaths while you have your intentions clearly in mind. State those intentions out loud. Then start to create your grid.

Begin by forming the outside first and move towards the center. It is important for you to keep focusing on your purpose while you place each stone in place.

Finally, place your Focus Stone on top of the paper with your intentions written on it.

Congratulations! Your crystal grid is finally finished. Now it's time to activate it!

The Wand: To activate the grid, use a quartz crystal point, which is a special crystal with a pencil-like point on the end that radiates pure white light into your grid. These are some of the most powerful crystals you can find for focusing on and amplifying your purpose.

With your point, connect each crystal in the grid by drawing an invisible and unbroken line to each of them. Start with the outside crystals and don't stop until you connect every one of them to the center Focus Stone. After they are all connected, your grid is fully activated. It is important that you keep your grid until your intention has been fulfilled.

Once you have achieved your purpose, you might want to keep it up a little longer to show your thanks and appreciation for the help, but eventually, you'll want to make other grids and your focus will end up being directed to other places. You are now ready to move on to other things in the world of crystals.

CHAPTER 6
Why You Should Learn/Practice Crystal Healing

If you're not entirely convinced of the power of crystals, you tend to be more cynical about their worth. There are a few points you should be aware of. Most people who fall into this category tend to be those that are still of the mind that crystal healing should be relegated to the old school of thought associating it with magic, mysticism, and even a fragment left over from the hippie era of the 1960s. While that was the way it once was viewed, because of new science, we can now give it a more prominent and proven role in our lives.

Rather than thinking of it as a connection to the spirit world, think of it merely as a means of bringing our lives in tune with the more abstract aspects of our universe. Since we already know that everything in the universe is in a constantly vibrating state, including us humans, it is only logical to see that things will work better with fewer problems if those vibrations are in harmony with each other.

Your relationship with your crystals is a highly personal one and if you use them as tools to bring you that harmony, you will find a new approach to solving any personal, financial, physical, emotional, or psychological issues you face.

When we say that everything in the universe is vibrating at a different frequency, we mean everything. You may be one person, but you are made up of different parts. Your organs, chakras, and your thoughts are all vibrating differently as well. In essence, your body is a symphony of vibrations that you are trying to get to work together to create the rhythm of your life. Crystals have a unique way of making this happen. By embracing their unique and clear vibrations, they can work to harmonize your life in much the same way as a piano tuner tunes the different keys on the piano. They can recalibrate all of your vibrations, so they blend much better together. This will help you to be more balanced emotionally, physically, mentally, and spiritually.

While you may be drawn to crystals for their unique color or intricate patterns, in time, you will learn that much more was involved in your choice. As you connect and learn more about your crystal, you will learn about its specific purpose and energy and you'll discover that it wasn't you that chose it, but that it chose you. These stones bring about a certain type of balance that is difficult to achieve in any other way in the world.

Later, we'll discuss some of the most prominent stones and how they can benefit you personally. As you learn more about the properties of different crystals, you'll find that you will be a better gauge of what will work right for you and why.

It's Effects on the Body

Even now, in the face of modern science, medical professionals are beginning to see that crystal healing is a perfect complementary form of treatment. When used in this way, they help many to understand why they are so important. Here are some facts that we must keep in mind.

1. Our human body is merely a collection of different energy fields with their own energy centers or chakras. While it may feel solid to us, parts of our body are made up of light and liquid. Each of these parts is vibrating at a different frequency.

2. Crystals have their own vibrations, which can have a direct effect on the flow of energy that surrounds our body. Surrounding our body are electromagnetic fields that we refer to as our aura. In addition to this aura are the seven major chakras, which have a direct effect on the different areas in our physical body. Our external aura is an outward reflection of the health of our physical body and the flow of energy through our chakras. If our aura is bright, it means that the energy flowing through our chakras is strong and uninterrupted. On the other hand, if our aura is dim, it means that we have some sort of blockage that needs to be cleared.

This is why many people have been able to successfully treat even severe cases of depression with crystal therapy. Through this type of therapy, it was observed that the aura was dimmed or otherwise damaged. On further examination, these were patients that had a) undergone some type of trauma that caused an energy imbalance, b) underwent chemotherapy, or c) had been given a drug of some type to deal with extreme pain. In all of these cases, recovery from the physical damage done could take an extremely long time with traditional western treatment and medication. In the meantime, the patient often struggles with a loss of vitality and maybe even an inability to cope with everyday life. However, with crystal therapy, these imbalances have the potential of improving much faster and in a more natural way.

It is the subtle vibrations that each of these crystals has that makes this type of healing possible. They have a way of re-energizing the body's energy fields. When you use the right crystal for your specific needs, amazing things can happen. The more you learn about these beautiful gems, the sooner the healing process can begin. When you know intuitively how to find a blockage and which crystal to choose to free it, then you will feel more grounded and that's when you will receive the maximum benefits their healing energies can provide. As a result, you will be able to relax, easing up on all the stress in your life.

The Effects of Crystals on Emotions

It has often been reported that simply by placing crystals around you, can bring a great deal of comfort to an individual. When you are struggling with emotional issues, it is often because of being out of balance. By wearing crystals as jewelry or carrying them around with you every day, they can flood you with a continuous calming effect that you can't get from medication and all without those nasty side effects. They can be safely used in conjunction with a number of psychotherapeutic approaches without any negative consequences.

As crystals work on your imbalance, they can have a powerful impact on emotional healing. Whether you're suffering from extreme stress, anxiety, or some other negative emotions, you will find that there are certain crystals that will help you to cope better.

For example, many people use blue lace agate, jet, or black tourmaline to relieve anxiety and stress. Even for emotional trauma like coping with a breakup or a problem in their love life, they turn to rose quartz, lapis lazuli, or rhodonite.

When you are struggling with an extreme loss as in the case of the death of a loved one, you can also find comfort in amethyst, carnelian, or moonstones.

Anyone struggling with an extreme emotional issue should always consult with their doctor first. However, by working with crystals in tandem with your medical doctor, you can greatly enhance your recovery and heal yourself by balancing your energies. In many cases, this can be done through crystal therapy without the use of medications, which often work in ways that can be more harmful than good.

The Effects of Crystals on the Mind

Anyone who has struggled with negative thoughts knows that clearing the mind is not easy. However, crystal healing for mental clarity can be very effective in helping you to focus and push out all the negative mind chatter so you can get back to a more positive mental process. This is possible because of the multifarious powers that are held within each crystal. Whether you're trying to focus on something specific or you're trying to tap into your creative processes, there is a crystal that can help you through the process.

With accessing the energy in the crown chakra, you can activate your mental process and receive more mental clarity. While there are many crystals that can help you achieve this mental clarity, there are several that are much more powerful and can yield some pretty impressive results.

Amazonite: This stone is very effective for dealing with problems of absent-mindedness. Often this problem is the result of not being able to filter out things that are not important from your mind. Using amazonite in your presence can help you to have better communication and sensitivity in your thinking patterns. It also brings a calmer energy level that can prevent you from saying things without thinking and thus end up expressing thoughts you really didn't mean.

Malachite: This stone is very helpful for keeping your mental focus in check when life gets out of control. Often when things get hectic, you develop a negative cloud over you that can quickly force you to lose control. Malachite can help you to make the right decisions and focus more on the positive side of things rather than allowing your mind to drift off into a deep mental downward spiral. It can amplify your positive energy that can transform your mind into a more productive direction.

Clear Quartz: When you program clear quartz, it can hold any type of energy you need. It works best for those who find it difficult to concentrate on any one thing and helps them to take the kind of action that will allow their dreams to unfold. It forces you to repeat your resolutions again and again until you achieve your goals.

Hematite: If you're having trouble staying grounded mentally, Hematite can help you to get a more stable hold on your life. Regular meditation with this stone will help to put your mind back on the right track. You will be able to eliminate many of the wayward thoughts that overwhelm you, get rid of the negativity that is controlling you, and dispel the bad energy that may be surrounding you. As a result, you'll be more grounded and focused, so you can continue on your mental journey in a more positive direction.

Smoky Quartz: Smoky quartz is great for helping you to practice mindfulness. They work best when you take them out into the natural world helping you to focus on what's more important. As you let your mind absorb the energy of the smoky quartz, you'll be able to meditate better. You will be able to develop a positive train of thought and maintain it for a longer period of time. You'll also be able to avoid mental thoughts that are illogical and can lead to undue stress when you find yourself overwhelmed. In the end, you'll have a clearer mind that will allow you to focus on what's important and gloss over insignificant thoughts or those that bog you down in negativity.

It is recommended that you meditate on crystals for a minimum of three minutes or more every morning and then go about your day. These stones help you to be more consciously aware of everything you come in contact with throughout the day and allows you to find some positive contribution to give to them. Always keep in mind that you should be thankful for every moment you have and use them as tools. If everyone were to tap into the power of these gemstones, it would not only improve their lives, but it can be of incredible benefit to everyone around them as well.

CHAPTER 7
Healing Fundamentals

It is always important to remember that crystals possess a special kind of power. One that they harvested from the bowels of earth and time. Their unique energetic vibrations will have a direct impact on how you feel, think, and reason. So no matter what your intention, what you hope to accomplish, or whether you use a grid, a single crystal, or some other method, always select those stones that have properties that match your goals.

Choosing the right stone is one of the most important steps in crystal healing. Chances are, the first stones you choose will be based on their visual appeal. We can grow to understand that if you are being pulled towards that stone, it may not be solely based on your aesthetic preferences. While it may seem that way, you may subconsciously have connected to that stone's energy and recognize that it is the one that can provide you with what you need.

There are some people that are extremely sensitive to these vibrations of energy, but most are not. Still, as you get more in touch with a particular stone, even those who are not particularly sensitive to the vibrations will begin to notice small changes. So don't assume that because you are not highly sensitive to a particular stone, that it is not having some sort of effect on you. If you're unsure if a stone is working for you or not, try to exercise patience and recognize that the energy is there, and it is at work even if you don't see the results right away.

Keeping these thoughts in mind is extremely important for a beginner to crystal healing. It is easy to allow the naysayers of the world to dissuade you from this practice. The power in crystals is as real as your own willpower. All over the natural world, we respect the power of things we don't physically feel. The power of gravity, the electromagnetic waves, the mysterious force that moves the waves of the ocean. All of these things exert power and can affect us without us ever realizing it. The same is true of the crystals that come from the earth. Once you understand this basic fundamental, you are ready to embrace the power of crystals with an open mind and allow it to do its work on you. You are ready to establish your intentions.

Another important fundamental is your intention. Regardless of whether you're planning on using a single crystal or a grid, your purpose is the most important element in your healing process. Here, you must be completely honest with yourself, otherwise, your own inner desires will be working contrary to what you program your crystals to do. Some of the most common intentions for crystal healing are:

- Grounding yourself mentally, emotionally, or spiritually
- Finding love or repairing a damaged relationship
- Manifesting your dreams
- Healing old hurts and wounds
- Spiritual growth
- Practicing forgiveness or letting go of past wrongs
- Fertility, expanding your family

As you grow in your crystal healing knowledge, you'll likely find many more intentions that you can have and you will find the right stone for every one of them. However, honesty is the most important aspect of identifying these intentions and accessing their power.

For beginners, it might be best to start simply and grow from there. Most new ones start with three stones that have high vibrations to help you clear away your negative energies. Once these are cleared, you'll find it much easier to uncover more detailed intentions that you never knew you had.

Common starter stones are a piece of quartz to uplift and clear away negative energy that may be blocking you, obsidian to help you get grounded and activate your root chakra, and a blue kyanite to help you to open up and tune into all of your chakras so everything within you starts to work in better harmony.

Once you've got those fundamentals in order, you can move on to more specific approaches to crystal healing.

Chakra Healing

Every one of your chakras has a direct connection to specific colors, foods, sounds, smells, and crystals. Without even realizing it, many people are walking around in this chaotic world with our chakras unbalanced. This is pretty easy to do. Because our own personal energy field can be knocked off kilter by just about anything.

The good news is that it can be just as easily put back in place by using chakra healing crystals. When you use colored chakra crystals, you will get very specific vibrations that will help you to maintain balance and be able to cleanse your chakras at the same time. However, if you want to heal your chakras individually, here are a few suggestions that can put you on the right path and help you to choose the best crystal.

Healing the Root Chakra: Located right at the base of the spine, red-colored crystals work best on the root chakra. Look for crystals like smoky quartz, red garnet, hematite, red jasper, and black onyx. These will give you a solid grounding, a sense of security, and confidence to follow through on your goals.

Healing the Sacral Chakra: Located in the lower part of the abdomen, this chakra is best healed with orange-colored crystals. Your sacral chakra is out of balance when you are having problems with your sexuality, creativity, or personal power. Start off with crystals like amber, carnelian, goldstone, orange calcite or tiger's Eye.

Healing the Solar Plexus Chakra: Located right behind the navel, this chakra is the center of your breathing and is best healed with yellow-colored crystals. When the Solar Plexus is in balance you have more courage, honor, empathy, and a stronger connection with others. Look for stones like citrine, pyrite, rutilated quartz, and yellow jade.

Healing the Heart Chakra: Located in the center of the chest, the heart chakra has a powerful connection to the colors pink and green. When it is in balance you allow your heart to dictate the way you live. If it is blocked, you can open it with amazonite, aventurine, chrysoprase, emerald, green calcite, and rose quartz.

Healing the Throat Chakra: Located right about your collarbone in your throat, this chakra enhances your ability to communicate. It relies heavily on truthfulness and honesty in all things. It responds well to blue colored crystals like apatite, angelite, aquamarine, kyanite, and sodalite.

Healing the Third Eye Chakra: Located right in the middle of the forehead right between the eyebrows, your third eye enhances your intuition, guidance, and self-realization. It responds well to the color purple so choose stones of amethyst, angelite, charoite, flourite, and iolite.

Healing the Crown Chakra: Located right at the top of your head, this chakra is very good at distributing energy throughout the body. It is more closely connected to your spirituality, meditation, and helps you to think deeply about matters. It responds well to the color white so look for stones like amethyst, blue lace agate, ametrine, clear quartz, and lepidolite.

As you can probably tell, some of the crystals mentioned here can be used for more than one chakra, so don't feel like they can't be used for other intentions once your original purpose has been fulfilled. However, just by matching the color of the crystal with the chakra you want to unblock you can open yourself up to a whole new world of positive experiences.

Energy Healing

Every part of your body has its own energy vibration. Every stone has its own energy vibration. The goal of crystal healing is to match the stone to the energy source that you are lacking so it can infuse more energy where you need it most. In the above section, we spoke about which chakras help you in what areas and which stones will yield the best results. Once you've chosen your stone, then you have to know how to use them in the right way.

There are more than a few ways to work with crystals, but here are just a few basic steps that will apply in nearly every situation.

Use the crystal while meditating: Meditation and crystal healing are natural partners. It is a means of combining the energy of the crystal with the mind, body, and spirit all at the same time. When you meditate, hold the crystal in both hands, close your eyes, and focus only on your breathing. As you do, you will notice that your body will feel like it is being pulled down to the earth. Don't worry about this, it is the crystal working to ground you. The longer you meditate, the lighter you should begin to feel.

For beginners, you may not feel anything the first few times you try it. There are some crystals that just doesn't have a strong enough vibration to give you the sensations you're looking for, but that doesn't mean they are not working. Each crystal will feel different to you, so be patient. If after a time, you still do not feel the changes you're looking for, try a different crystal. The key is to be patient and to be open enough to allow the power of the crystal to come in.

Crystal Grids: One of the best ways to restore energy to the body is through a crystal grid. When using your grid, always choose those stones that are closely aligned with your intentions and use a grid along with sacred geometry. The power of the crystals working together will help to manifest your intentions to the universe and draw in the energy you seek.

Some people also like to incorporate a bit of Feng Shui in their crystal grids to help them to choose the right colors and location to place the grid in order to get the best results.

Designate a crystal space: By designating a space for your crystals, you can attract more energy to you. This is a common practice that is often used in yoga and meditation. When your crystals have a permanent home where they can be displayed in all their glory, they can serve as a constant reminder to you to connect with your intention frequently. Any time you enter into your inner sanctum, just the vision of their calming display not only will add a touch of beauty to your life but an inner peace along with it.

One of the most popular crystals for a sacred space of this nature is the amethyst. It sends out a constant stream of positive energy and helps you to achieve a deeper state of meditation. You can also place crystal points in your space to strengthen your intention and amplify your goals.

Wear or carry your crystals: Many people have smaller crystals that they carry around with them wherever they go. Smaller crystals allow you to have more contact with them as you can touch them whenever you need to. You can have them made on a keychain, carry them in your pocket or in your handbag so that you have access to it whenever you want. It can serve as a reminder that you have an ultimate purpose that you are working towards and keep you from getting distracted.

Position crystals on your body: Placing crystals on your body will give you a completely different effect than you get by simply holding them in your hand. If you're trying to heal a specific chakra, place the crystal directly on the chakra. It will stir up the energy emanating from that chakra and draw out the emotions that you need to address in order to heal.

Combine crystals with yoga practice: Another very effective way of using crystals is to place them around your yoga mat while you practice your positions. This will help you to achieve a more tranquil state of mind and encourage an even deeper state of healing while meditating.

Use them as decorations: In addition to their healing properties, crystals also create a nice aesthetic addition to your home décor. Larger crystals especially those that make for great conversation pieces can do quite well in shifting the energy in your space to a more positive one. For example, a large piece of amethyst can create positive vibes and push out any negative energy that may enter the room, making for a consistently peaceful environment.

Use crystals in your bath: We all know just how soothing a soak in a hot bath can be. Using crystals and essential oils can only enhance those benefits even more. Let them soak in the water with you so that they can restore any energy you've lost after a long stressful day. If you don't have time to soak in a bath, then soak your crystals in warm water before you wash your face, to give you a little bit of peace and calm before you start your day.

Reiki Healing

Reiki Healing is an alternative form of energy healing that comes from Japan. It involves transferring universal energy from one person to the next. Unlike with crystal energy, it is the transferring of this energy through the laying on of hands and can be used to treat a wide number of psychological and emotional states of mind. While there is not a lot of research done to date on Reiki, many believe that it can be used to relieve pain and treat a number of other physical ailments.

The word "Reiki" literally can be translated to mean "mysterious atmosphere" and it is most commonly used to target the energy fields that surround the body. In the case of physical pain, the idea is that when there is an injury of some kind, the energy can get stuck in that place and eventually stagnate to the point that there is not just physical pain but emotional pain as well.

Reiki can be used to unblock the energy that flows through that injured area. Like every other form of energy healing, Reiki works on improving the flow of energy in the body's aura, so that you are better able to relax, reduce the pain, and escalate the healing process.

To enhance the benefits of Reiki healing, using them together with crystals will help to improve the recovery process even faster.

There are several different ways you can use Reiki in this way. Some Reiki Masters prefer to use the Tibetan Master symbol, which can be drawn over the crystal. The user then repeats the name of the symbol three times in order to activate it. Then in their mind, they visualize the symbol as it passes right through the crystal, cleaning away any negative energy as it does.

If you're inclined to work with symbols like this, then you can practice programming the crystal to go a step further and physically heal and give you grounding at the same time. For a more physical healing, you can use the Cho-Ku-Rei symbol to help you. If the healing is more of an emotional nature, then use the Se-He-Ki to give you more stability.

Reiki can also be used in a more intuitive way. By drawing the Reiki down from the Crown Chakra all the way to the arms crossing it over into the hands, you can ask the crystal to help heal any individual you have in mind. Simply focus your mind on that person and ask the crystal to work its magic.

Reiki Kotodama: For those who have advanced enough to get past using symbols, you can graduate to using Reiki Kotodama. This is the process of chanting specific sacred sounds in order to evoke a change in the energy and vibrations of the crystals. As you chant, the crystals you hold in your hand will start to vibrate differently, which can not only affect you but also the environment. The Kotodama is an ancient Japanese form of chanting that teaches that every vowel chanted has its own mystical powers and vibrations. So when you connect with the crystal using these chants, the crystal will emit a very specific form of energy that can alter the person, object, or the surrounding environment in the way it is intended.

Spiritual Healing

More and more people are accepting the fact that there is a spiritual being inside of them. In fact, there is a direct connection between one's spirituality and their physical health. Using crystals can help you to connect better to the spiritual person buried deep inside of you. Anyone who is interested in tapping into the spiritual gifts we all possess, then crystals are the way to access them.

There are many crystals that can aid you on your spiritual journey. Since crystals are gaining in popularity now, they can easily be obtained without having to spend a lot of time searching them out. Because of this, more people are using them now and getting in touch with their more spiritual side.

If you are unfamiliar with the connection between spirituality and physical health, then you're likely not sure what kind of healing these can provide. Many people suffer from emotional issues and how they can be healed through their own spirituality. However, using heart chakra stones can be a good way to get started and learn at the same time.

Whether you're trying to heal a broken heart, nurture an inner child, or deal with some other issue, it is just a matter of choosing the right crystals to work with. Many metaphysical healers are now using crystals in their practices to aid people to find their spiritual path. They not only create a connection to all of the beings inside of you (physical, emotional, spiritual), but they also are very effective in easing many of the health issues that people may face.

Anyone who wants to benefit in a spiritual way can do so with the right stones. For spiritual healing, start with a piece of green fuchsite. Take it to your healing space and start with a meditation practice while holding it. It will help you to open up to others in your life and give you the freedom to live your own life the way you want.

Meditation is the secret to making this type of healing work. Regardless of the type of meditation you use, it can open up your chakras in a way that allows you to get into contact with your higher spiritual being.

For beginners, learning how to meditate is not always easy so it is probably best to start with short sessions that can grow in length over time. While there are many variations of meditation, if you follow the basics, you can get started pretty quickly. After you've mastered these skills, you can then move on to other meditation techniques that you can apply. If one meditation form doesn't work for you, keep searching, you'll find one that matches you perfectly.

- Find a location where you can sit comfortably. Some people like to sit on the floor while others prefer to sit on a chair. Your position should be a place where you can sit upright, but still have a relaxed position. You want to be reasonably comfortable but not too comfortable.

- If you like, you can put on some music, but make sure that it is more relaxing. You might even want to purchase a little meditation mood music to help you get your mind in the right place.

- Close your eyes and start taking in slow, deep breaths, concentrating on the flow of air going in and out. This will help you to relax even more. Notice how your body feels more relaxed after each breath.

- As you continue this slow, rhythmic breathing, allow your consciousness to start focusing on your toes.
- Tense your toes and then your legs, then release the tension and fall into a relaxed position again. Feel the tension as it leaves your body, making you feel even more relaxed.
- Continue this exercise, tensing and relaxing each part of the body until you get up to the top of your head.
- Imagine a light hovering just above it.
- Focus on that light and allow it to travel down into your body.
- As it travels, allow the tension to be released from each part of the body the light touches.
- Allow the light to go down and stop at your third eye, then down your throat, and keep doing this through all of your chakras.
- Finally, allow the light to leave your body through your root chakra and enter back into the earth pulling you along with it. This will ground you and your energy to the earth, letting you connect to the natural elements that surround you.
- Allow the light to grow outwards creating a bubble of light that surrounds you.
- Stay within this light for as long as you want.
- Take the time to sit in this relaxed state and let your mind drift and soak in all of its spiritual essences allowing it to flood your entire body.

Regular practice of this type of meditation, especially done while holding crystals in your hands will help to clear away any disharmony inside of you. When you have drunk your fill of this light, say a quiet "Thank you" to the spirit, allow the light to go from you and embrace in the excess energy you have acquired.

This type of meditation is very easy to do. You don't need to memorize any special chants or use any unique equipment or tools. All you need is your body and a few crystals to hold and you're all set.

To do this, though, you need to have some grounding crystals. This will help you to connect better with the light and help you to ground yourself more easily to nature. The best crystals for this are the smoky quartz, black obsidian, shamanite, black calcite, and black tourmaline. Connecting to your spiritual self can be extremely rewarding as long as you choose the right crystals to work with. Start simply and grow with the process as you gain more knowledge and you'll be well on your way to making a spiritual connection that will take you into a whole new realm of what's possible.

CHAPTER 8
How To Choose The Right Crystals

There are many different ways to choose crystals. We've already discussed the fact that the crystals are actually the ones making the choice in your partnership, but it is still your responsibility to know when they are calling to you.

In order to choose correctly, you need to be very familiar with the condition you are trying to heal. Knowing your intention will help steer you in the right direction and allow the crystal to be able to pick up on your vibes.

You can also choose your crystals by the way they appear to you. Crystals usually first draw people in because of their intrinsic natural beauty and striking colors. It is only after this initial pull that you begin to notice the other features of a true crystal.

Sometimes crystals find their way to you through no act of your own. You may receive one as a gift or you may discover one someplace near your home.

However way the crystal comes into your possession, follow your intuition. It is the best way to know for sure if the crystal is the right fit for your purposes. You may not realize it, but you already are gifted with the natural instinct to make this choice.

When you are drawn to a particular crystal, allow it to pull you in. Pick it up and hold it in the palm of your hand. Close your eyes and focus all of your energy on feeling the vibration and allow it to connect with your own inner vibrations. As you hold it, don't be surprised if you start to see images in your mind's eye. You may see a splash of color if you are strongly connected to it. If the crystal is not the right crystal for you, you will know it. You'll have a strong sense that something is not adding up or you won't be able to connect with its vibrations.

There is a unique kind of mystery that surrounds crystals that you have chosen. We recognize their energy, but often do not understand it fully. It is said that crystals will only remain with you as long as you need their energy. Many people usually report that their crystals have suddenly disappeared after they have fulfilled their purpose. It is like they have returned back to the earth from where they have come. So don't be surprised to find your crystal missing after you've used it for a while. This is a good sign that you've healed and your purpose is fulfilled, or that you now have a new purpose that another crystal may be better suited for.

Where to Buy Crystals

There are three ways to buy your crystals. Many people choose to buy them through online sites as they can be much cheaper than walking into a brick and mortar shop to purchase some rare form brought in from some distant region of the world.

However, buying online has its own drawbacks. One of the most important keys to choosing the right crystal is making a physical connection with it. Buying them online prevents you from doing this. In addition, there is no way you can determine the true authenticity of a stone without having the chance to examine it carefully.

This does not mean that all online dealers are deceptive. There are many dealers that produce crystals of a very high quality from online shops, and there are many individuals who are extremely intuitive and can choose a perfect crystal match just from looking at an image on their computer screen. In time, you will gain that kind of skill and talent, but for purchasing your first crystal, it is probably best to take a more tactile approach to select one that will work well for you.

Another way to purchase crystals is to visit events and shows. In fact, this is an excellent way to find unique crystals that have unusual shapes and patterns. When buying these types of crystals, keep in mind that you will be purchasing something that may have been handled by hundreds or even thousands of people before it finds its way to you. This can affect the kind of energy they emit so you may need to spend a little more time connecting with it before you make a decision.

Finally, you can purchase them through a brick and mortar shop.

There are many specialty shops that deliver high-quality crystals on a more personal level. These are probably the best option for the beginner as the owners or workers in these shops have specialized knowledge that can help to guide you in making the right choice. They also allow you to closely inspect the stones and spend more time with it, so you can be sure that you're choosing the best one for you.

Choosing Crystal Shapes

You also want to pay close attention to the shape of the crystal you choose. While the healing properties within the crystal will remain constant regardless of the shape, the experience you have when connecting with it may differ because of it. There are many facets of crystal shapes you should be aware of that will help you to decide exactly which shape will work best for your needs.

The Point: Crystal points are those crystals that have intense energy and can channel or amplify it in many ways. You can use a crystal point to focus the energy inward when the point is facing you or outward by focusing it away. Points are one of the best starter crystals because their energy can be easily harnessed and directed to where you want it to go.

The Cube: Crystal cubes are often used when working with the root chakra. It is an excellent grounding stone that can bring in a powerful sense of calm to your environment. Cubes can also help you to create a protective grid surrounding your environment by placing one in each corner of your space.

The Pyramid: The pyramid is considered to be one of the sacred shapes used throughout many ancient civilizations. When you want to send out a concentrated beam of energy into the universe or make your intentions manifest, you would use the crystal pyramid by setting it on top of the paper you have written them on.

The Heart: The heart-shaped crystal is used as a reminder that you need to continue to use the healing properties and keep them close. People work with them as a form of spiritual nourishment that will help them to always give and accept energy sent out to them.

The Harmonizer: These cylinder-shaped crystals help you with meditation and make it easier for you to enter a more spiritually stimulated space. They also help with giving you a better sense of mental and physical balance.

The Cluster: Crystal clusters are some of the most beautiful creations found in nature. A cluster occurs only when you have many points that develop within the same matrix. Clusters generally vibrate at a higher energy so having one in your sacred space will keep your energy levels high, so you have more power to work with.

Tumbled Stones: These stones can be used in a variety of ways. Those that are small with smooth surfaces can be carried in your pocket or purse. They are perfect pieces to make into jewelry and they are ideal of use in a crystal grid. They also make great starter stones because they are easy to use and draw energy from.

What to Look For

Knowing exactly what to look for in a crystal is extremely important as it is the one decision that will start you on your journey to balancing your energy and healing yourself. When it comes to buying these little gems, you want to be absolutely sure that you're getting the kind of quality you need. If you are intuitive enough to pick out a quality piece of crystal, you've saved yourself from a whole lot of headaches.

You can also look at the color of the crystal. There is no doubt that each color has its own healing properties. For a detailed list of each color and their healing properties, you can refer to a crystal directory. These have a color and an image of each crystal categorized by its healing properties. However, below is a list of the most common colors and what they can do.

Black: Power, protection, and mystery. Black obsidian, black tourmaline, hematite, jet, and onyx are the most common black crystals used.

Blue: Tranquility and emotional healing. Angelite, aquamarine, apatite, blue lace agate, azurite, blue chalcedony, celestine, and chrysocolla.

Brown: Absorb negative energy and harness the healing powers of the earth. Smoky quartz, brown jasper, bronzite, tiger's eye, and petrified wood.

Yellow/Gold: From the color of the sun, these stones give optimism and joy. Amber, citrine, golden topaz, yellow tiger's eye, pyrite, and yellow jasper.

Green: Activates the heart chakra and provides an emotional balance. Brings good fortune and prosperity. Aventurine, emerald, green fluorite, jade, and malachite.

Orange: Arouse passion in the spirit. Captures the spirit and energy from the sun. aragonite, calcite, copper, carnelian, and sunstone.

Pink: Love and compassion, heart energizers, and opens up the heart. Pink tourmaline, pink sapphire, rose quartz, and lepidolite.

Grey: Reflects the moonlight and the expanse of the universe. Provides protective shield. Hematite and moonstone.

Purple: Gives enlightenment and intuition. They keep emotions balanced and provide relaxing and soothing vibes. They can also amplify the energy, especially when used with the heart chakra. Amethyst and charoite.

Red: Infuses passion and has a grounding energy that supports the root chakra. Garnet, ruby, and red tiger's eye.

White: Represents purity and transformation. Excellent healing tools when used with other healing grids. Clear quartz and selenite.

You can also look for stones based on the chakra you want to heal.

Crown Chakra: Selenite and clear quartz

The Third Eye: Lapis lazuli, sodalite, and fluorite

The Throat Chakra: Aquamarine, angelite, blue apatite, sodalite

The Heart Chakra: Aventurine and rhodonite

Solar Plexus Chakra: Pyrite, rutilated quartz, citrine, and yellow jasper

Sacral Chakra: Carnelian, orange calcite, tiger's eye, and sunstone.

Root Chakra: Black onyx, red garnet, red jasper, hematite, and smoky quartz.

There are many ways to look for the right crystal for you. If you're still not sure, don't be shy about asking the shopkeeper to assist you. They work with these stones every day and have a highly trained intuitiveness that helps them match you with the right crystal.

What to Avoid

Buying crystals can be a little scary at first. You walk into a nice little shop and you may see hundreds of crystals on display. Unlike heading into your local supermarket where all produce is placed together and the deli counter has all the cuts you want, crystal shop owners do not have such a regimented way to display their wares. It is left entirely up to the individual owners so what may work for you in one shop may not be the same at the next shop.

This makes it hard to walk into the store and quickly find exactly what you're looking for. So don't hesitate to browse and ask questions. Still, while crystal healing is a noble occupation, it doesn't mean that all the shop owners are equally as noble. There are some major pitfalls you will want to be aware of.

Natural or Manmade: Now that modern science has been able to imitate the creation of a crystal in the laboratory, synthetic crystals should cost far less than natural ones. Examine the crystal closely looking for flaws. If it seems too perfect with no flaws, it's a good chance it is manmade and it won't bring you the same kind of power that comes from those crystals that have been shaped by millions of years in the earth.

Labels: You also want to keep a close eye out for stones with a trademark name or that comes with an excessively high price tag. Any name that is trademarked may be the same quality as one that is not, but they will cost a great deal more.

Check for Alternations: Some crystals may have been altered from their natural state. This may also alter the effectiveness of the crystal. Some shop owners may change the appearance of a crystal so that it looks more like another crystal. They may dye it, heat it, or coat it so that it appears to be another stone with completely different properties.

There are many ways you can "fake" a crystal. It may have started out as a partially real crystal but when you coat the exterior or combine it with a synthetic, like what is often done with opals and turquoise, you may find yourself buying mostly glass. Rubies are another crystal that is often altered in some way.

To determine if it's a fake, you can ask the seller, but if it is, he's not likely going to tell you. However, there are a few other steps you can take to be sure.
1. Check the base for any signs of mounting, glue, or paint.
2. Look for uneven coloring or shades not normally found in nature.
3. Look into the glass for signs of air bubbles
4. Look for flaws. All naturally occurring crystals have flaws. If it looks too perfect, chances are, it is.

While there may be many crystals that can be altered in some form, there are some common crystals that you should be watchful of. Since finding authentic turquoise is rare, it can be quite expensive. Sellers will usually make a synthetic stone that is made from dyed resin or ceramic. They may also substitute it with howlite, which has veins that are very similar to turquoise veins. You can identify fake turquoise quite easily. First, its blue color will appear to be unnatural and there will be brown lines running through it.

Another crystal to be cautious of is citrine. Most of what you will see in a crystal shop is not authentic citrine, but in fact, amethyst which has been heat-treated until it turns to the desired yellow color. The heat will actually change the properties of the stone, so it is always important to get some sort of authentication before you make a purchase.

CHAPTER 9
Crystals And What Ails You

At the core of every crystal healing is the desire to infuse your life with something that will bring about a positive change. However, there are thousands of ways you can accomplish that with crystals, so before you can decide on which form of crystal healing you want, you need to carefully examine and get a more precise idea of what type of remedy you need.

The remedies that follow are not meant as a cure-all for the issues they address but are only given as a possible alternative form of treatment to consider. Your particular issues may be successfully dealt with using these methods or you may opt to use them in conjunction with a medical and psychological treatment at the same time. However, using crystals, whether alone or alongside other traditional forms of treatment, can add a powerful element to your life, so they are definitely worth giving them some serious consideration.

Abandonment

There are many people who may not even realize that they have issues with feelings of abandonment. These can stem from a loss that happened years earlier and may not even seem related to the challenges that they face today. Suffering from a past break-up or even a loss of a loved one can leave them feeling empty and alone.

Using a chant or a mantra to remind you that finding unconditional love is something that is found when one first loves themselves. Chanting along with crystals can edify you both spiritually and emotionally and give you the kind of support you need when things are the most difficult.

One crystal that works well with Abandonment issues is the rose quartz. When using it along with deep meditation and visualization, you will gradually begin to feel its warm effects.
- Hold the rose quartz in your hands.

- Visualize yourself enveloped in its warm, pink light while focusing on your breathing.
- Continue this visualization for a minimum of 10 minutes and maintain it until you start to feel a calming sense of peace.

You can expand this form of healing even further by setting up a crystal grid and placing it close to where you work or sleep. Use the rose quartz as the center stone and place a square of apache tears, amazonite, carnelian, and garnet around it. Each of these stones will bring a different element to your healing.

Rose quartz will bring unconditional love
Apache tears will help to release the grief
Amazonite will heal the emotional pain
Carnelian will empower you
And Garnet will give you a stronger sense of belonging

Together, these stones can offer the kind of healing that will rejuvenate you and put you on a more stable grounding.

A second way to heal abandonment issues is by combining rose quartz with citrine & obsidian chakra work. Start by lying on your back in a comfortable position. Place the rose quartz on your heart chakra. Then place the citrine crystal on your solar plexus chakra and the obsidian on your root chakra.

Close your eyes and start to breathe deeply, repeating the following chant until you start to feel a calming sense of peace.

Affirmation: *I give myself unconditional love and will accept unconditional love from the universe.*

When dealing with abandonment issues, it helps to uncover why you are having these negative feelings. If you're not really sure of the reason behind it, start with some mindfulness practice. It will help you to uncover your true source of the problem so that you can target your healing more accurately.

Abuse

The psychological damage that results from abuse can be astronomical, and its effects can negatively impact your life for years, leaving many scars. Struggling to overcome this damage on your own can sometimes seem impossible.

Each type of abuse can have its own unique signature in the different chakras. A person dealing with sexual abuse may have a blockage in their root chakra, while someone dealing with abuse from their parents may have a blockage in their solar plexus or sacral chakras. Because abuse can be so varied, it might be best to seek out psychological counseling and use the crystal healing treatments as an additional support to help you heal faster from the trauma.

Affirmation: *I release the pain and hurt from my past in exchange for a more positive and loving future.*

The Meditation: Start by closing your eyes and allowing the pain and suffering you felt in the past to come in. Take notice of where you feel that pain. Take a few deep inhalations and start to visualize the light from the crystal entering your body through your breath. Allow it to fill you up and flow to where you feel the pain. As you exhale, repeat the affirmation. Continue in this exercise until you start to feel a sense of calm come over you.

Depending on how severe your trauma has been, you may not feel results right away. If you don't feel anything during the first few sessions, continue the exercise for at least ten minutes and repeat it regularly until you start to sense the positive energy entering you.

Garnet: As you go through your meditation, you can use the garnet on your root chakra. It will help you to release all the pain of your past and reclaim your own power. As a support to the meditation, you can also keep a garnet with you wherever you go, to keep a cloud of calm positive energy around you at all times.

Abuse can affect several chakras at the same time, so always place the crystals on the damaged chakras to help clear away any energy blocks. Below are some suggestions, but feel free to use any crystals that will help heal the pain in any of your blocked chakras.

Garnet: root chakra
Carnelian: sacral chakra
Yellow tiger's eye: solar plexus chakra
Rose quartz: heart chakra
Lapis lazuli: throat chakra

It is important to understand that rather than trying to suppress the pain you feel from the abuse, these treatments work better if you acknowledge them. Suppressing pain can often make it worse by forcing it deeper down into your soul making it even harder to recover. When you recognize that you have pain, it is the first step in letting it go, so you can move on with your life.

Acceptance

Sometimes our struggles are because we can't let go of regrets or painful past memories. We spend all of our days reliving things that can't be changed or consumed with excessive worry about the future. This often keeps us from living in the present moment, the only time period that we have control over.

When difficult things arise, we need to learn how to accept those things. If this has not been your habit, it can be difficult to do. It means surrendering to what has happened and no longer allowing it to have control over us. For many, that is a huge change in their thinking.

Affirmation: *I accept things as they are and release from my hold anything that is not in my power to change.*

Meditation:
- Find a comfortable sitting position
- Close your eyes and focus on your feelings
- Take note of where in your body the pain presents itself
- Repeat the affirmation
- Visualize the pain as a black mass
- Take note of the white light that enters your body as you breathe

- Watch the light cause the mass to slowly begin to dissolve
- Exhale slowly, letting the dissolution leave your body with each exhale
- Continue this practice for a least ten minutes or until you begin to feel a sense of calm.

Crystals: There are several crystals that will enhance the effects of the meditation to help you let go of this negativity that consumes you.

Apatite: This is the stone of acceptance. Keep it close to your heart. You can wear it as a necklace or a pendant around your neck.

Apache tears: These small stones help bring relief from disappointment and make it easier for you to accept things that make you uncomfortable. Hold them in your hand as you repeat the Serenity Prayer.

God grant me the serenity to accept the things I cannot change, the courage to change the things I can, and the wisdom to know the difference.

Part of the reason people struggle with letting go is society's idea that to surrender means that you are weak, but in reality, it is a sign of true strength. Allowing yourself to accept that some things are completely out of your control can empower you to take positive steps towards those things you can handle, giving you better prospects of a brighter future.

Addiction

Addiction does not always have to be to some illegal substance or alcohol. You can be addicted to your favorite food, an activity or sport, or something else entirely. The problem with addiction is that once it gets out of control, it can disrupt your life in some very extreme ways. One way to treat this type of addiction is with psychological therapy. However, crystals can help you on a higher plane by giving you spiritual grounding and emotional stability that will empower you so you can resist the constant pull of your addiction.

Affirmation: *I am free of my desires for _____ and I set them free, releasing me from their hold.*
Meditation: When you are addicted, you have an imbalance in all of your chakras. Practicing meditation with crystals placed on all of your chakras is a great way to restore balance. You can work with one chakra at a time or you can choose to work with them one by one. The two main chakras you should start with are the sacral chakra and the throat chakra. These two are directly linked to your willpower and can help you gain better control of your addiction.

- Lie in a comfortable position
- Close your eyes and concentrate on your breathing
- Place crystals on one or all of your chakras
- As you exhale on each breath, repeat the serenity prayer out loud
- Continue with this exercise for at least 10 minutes or until you can feel the energy of the crystals empower you.

Labradorite: Carry it with you or wear it throughout your day. Make sure it is close to you when your cravings are the strongest. Labradorite helps to detoxify your body and free you from the effects of your addition.

You can also sleep with it underneath your pillow. You must clean your labradorite daily, so it is free from the energy that is commonly associated with addiction.

Amethyst: Sometimes referred to as the sober stone. You can wear it as jewelry or carry it around with you as you go about your daily routine. It can be especially helpful when you find you are going through withdrawal symptoms.

You can also create a crystal grid using the sacred geometry that gives you more power. These will only reinforce the therapy you're likely already getting to deal with your addiction issues.

It is important to understand that addiction usually is triggered by underlying issues from your past that hasn't been addressed yet. Often, the addiction is not the real problem but only a symptom for something else in your past. As you work through crystal healing your addictions, consider also doing a deep introspective study to see if you can uncover the true source of your addiction.

Anger

There is both good anger and bad anger. It is a perfectly normal emotion when it is controlled. Healthy anger can enter our body, express itself, and quickly dissipate without leaving any harm behind. However, when we are demonstrating an unhealthy form of this emotion, it can turn ugly very quickly. Unresolved anger can slowly fester like an open wound and turn into resentment, causing a domino effect that will lead to other problems in your life. Learning how to let go of your anger will help you to move on to a more positive a healthy emotional life.

Affirmation: *I breathe in the peace that surrounds me and releases the anger in return.*

Meditation:
- Find a comfortable sitting position
- Place both hands over the solar plexus chakra
- Breathe in slowly
- As you inhale, visualize the peace filling you up and flowing throughout your body.
- Say the affirmation as you slowly exhale
- Imagine your anger leaving you through your nose
- Repeat this exercise for at least 10 minutes or until you feel the peace enter into you

Anxiety

Anxiety is another very normal emotion that we all feel. Under normal circumstances, your anxiety can be heightened at times and then can stabilize allowing you to continue on living the best life you can. However, when a person is found to be in a heightened state of anxiety, it can cause both physical and emotional damage.

Anxiety has many faces, it doesn't always appear the same in every situation, nor in every person. Extreme anxiety can present itself as phobias, obsessive-compulsive disorder, or PTSD. Milder cases could be seen as a social phobia, nervousness, and avoidance techniques. Anxiety is closely connected to the root chakra as it relates to a strong sense of security, so crystal therapy with this chakra can help to ease some of the pressures and make you feel more confident.

Affirmation: *I relax in infinite serenity.*

Meditation:
- Find a comfortable sitting position
- Hold your crystal in your hands
- Close your eyes and take deep breaths
- With each inhale, visualize the peace entering your body with it
- Repeat the affirmation
- As you exhale, visualize the anxiety leaving with each breath
- Repeat for at least 10 minutes or until you feel the anxiety begin to subside

Crystals

Blue lace agate: Its peaceful blue color has a calming effect. Wear it or carry it with you, especially when you are expecting to be in stressful situations.

Lapis lazuli & and clear quartz grid: Here is where a grid can be extremely helpful. With a circular grid, use a large lapis lazuli for its focus stone. Around it, place eight clear quartz points in a circle. Make sure to turn the quartz points away from the lapis lazuli so that they are directed outward. This will amplify the calming qualities in the environment, giving you a strong sense of peace.

Black tourmaline: Carry it around with you when you are feeling anxious. This is a grounding stone that will absorb much of your negativity.

Boundaries

Setting boundaries can be difficult for some people. To be able to do this, one needs to understand their own limitations. With this understanding, they can then help others to understand how they should be treated.

At times, setting boundaries is hard because we all want people to like us. It can be difficult to think that you are going against the grain and so we are reluctant to demand the respect we know we deserve, creating an internal conflict within us.

Affirmation: *I can assert my wishes in kindness, confidence, and compassion.*

Meditation: Your solar plexus chakra is at the very heart of your self-identity. Without balance in this area, it can be difficult to know how to set boundaries. Your throat chakra is where you communicate those boundaries, so you need to activate both of these chakras in your meditation practice.
- Lie down on your back
- Close your eyes and concentrate on your solar plexus chakra
- Inhale deeply
- Ask "what are my boundaries"
- Lie still, breathing normally while you meditate on this question
- Keep your focus on your solar plexus
- Slowly slide your hand up your midline and let it rest on your throat chakra
- Repeat the same affirmation 10 times or until your boundaries are revealed to you

Crystals: As you are trying to determine your boundaries, place a citrine crystal underneath your pillow. Repeat the same question as you are drifting off to sleep so that it can help you to understand. When you wake the next morning, write down what was revealed for you. Repeat this process every night for a week and your boundaries will then become clear.

After you have identified your boundaries, you can use a rose quartz to give you compassion and sodalite to help you with communicating these to others. Carrying these two crystals around with you will help you to better assert yourself in a kind and compassionate way whenever you need to.

Centering

The act of calming the mind, body, and spirit can aid you in many ways. When a person is centered, they are not just calm and relaxed, but they are also more alert. This makes it easy for the energy to flow in and out of them and allows them to tap into their own creativity. Centered people are more in tune with their feelings and have a strong intuition that can help them to communicate better with the spirit world.

Affirmation: *I relax my body, mind, and spirit so I can find my center.*

Meditation:
- Find a comfortable sitting position
- Sit with your eyes closed
- Breathe in deeply
- As you breathe, take notice of how the breathing is relaxing you
- Focus your mind on your center (this is the point between your solar plexus and sacral chakras)
- Concentrate on this area as you let the breathing bring you to a calmer state

Crystals: Blue lace agate is an excellent calming crystal that can help you find your center. Hold the stone in one hand while you are meditating. Breathe in deeply and let its calm cover you. You can also make it a habit of carrying the blue lace agate stone with you wherever you go. Pull it out whenever you find you are feeling a little off center, so it can help you to find your way.

Clear quartz is a crystal you can reach for at the start of every day. This one can also be used during meditation.
- Sit in a comfortable position
- Hold a piece of clear quartz in your non-dominant hand
- Close your eyes and take in 10 deep breaths
- Focus on your core
- Feel the energy from the crystal enter your body

- It will naturally gravitate towards your center

Change

Whether you are accepting or giving change, it can be very difficult to handle. This is likely because we instinctively fear the unknown. However, life would never exist without change so being able to accept it and adapt to it is crucial to our survival.

Affirmation for Accepting Change: *I am thankful for the changes I have experienced because they give me the power to grow.*

Affirmation for Creating Change: *I am motivated to make the necessary changes in my life because I know I need them to grow.*

Meditation:
- Find a quiet place and sit in a comfortable position
- Close your eyes
- Place both of your hands over your heart chakra
- Take a few deep breaths
- Visualize the fluid white energy floating down through your crown chakra and flooding your body
- Let it fill up your arms and hands before going into the heart chakra
- Repeat the affirmation for at least 10 minutes or until you feel the peace and comfort to accept the change.

Crystals: When you are going through a period of extreme change, carry a piece of watermelon tourmaline with you. It will give you the kind of calmness you need to be able to accept and understand the new situation.

The prehnite & clear quartz grid can also be very effective. Use the prehnite as your Focus stone and three clear quartz points form a triangle around it. Make sure the points are facing outward away from the center of the grid. The points will help to amplify the power of the prehnite and bring you the kind of strength you need to accept what's coming.

There may be times when you are reluctant to accept the change in your life and continue on doing the same routine even though it is not working for you. It can be difficult to take the necessary steps that will move you in the right direction. Your comfort zone is where you live and you can't seem to move from it. In such cases, your meditation will take on a different kind of tone.

- Find a comfortable sitting position
- Sit with your eyes closed and your body relaxed
- Relax your mind
- Visualize where you feel you need to make changes in your life
- Allow yourself to go through the change in your mind's eye
- Follow through on your mental actions until the change comes to a logical conclusion
- Reward yourself with joy and positive energy from making the change
- Repeat the chat for nine more times. (In Numerology, nine is the number for completion)

Crystals: Blue or green aventurine. These opportunity stones are open to change. Start by sleeping with this stone under your pillow to work on your subconscious mind while you sleep. It will subtly awaken your desire for change.

Blue kyanite is used to break free from many old habits that may cause you to get into a rut. When meditating, hold the blue kyanite in your non-dominant hand. As you take each breath, repeat the chant for bringing change into your life, and as you exhale, release those old habits into the universe.

Start trying to think of change in a different way. Instead of thinking of it as something you have no choice over, reframe your thinking to accept that change as another way of introducing new opportunities into your life.

Cleansing

Cleansing is another element of life that can make people uncomfortable. When you cleanse, you push out your negativity and make room for more positive vibes to enter your world. Cleansing does not limit itself to a spiritual cleanse, you can also apply this when you move into a new home, enter a new relationship, or embrace a whole new space in your life. Cleansing crystals can also be used when you are trying to push out negativity from something bad that might have happened (a fight with a loved one, a serious illness, or a tragedy of some sort).

Affirmation: *This space is filled with the light of love*

Meditation:
- Position yourself in a seating position in the center of the space you want to be cleansed
- Close your eyes and breathe normally
- Visualize the white light descending from above and enveloping you
- Allow the light to push out all energy in the space
- Repeat the chat for ten full minutes or until you sense that the space has been cleansed

Crystals: When cleansing a physical space, place a clear quartz cluster in the center of the area. You can also place smaller pieces of it around the perimeter of the room. Stand in the center with your eyes closed. From this position, start your meditation practice.
Black tourmaline can be used after smudging. Smudging is when you light a bunch of sage, cedar, sweetgrass, or lavender. Once it is lit, blow out the flame and let the smoke tendrils waft in the air. Moving in a clockwise direction, carry the smoking herbs around the perimeter of the room and wave it around every entrance. Visualize the white light entering the room and repeat the affirmation again.

Once you have completed the smudging around the entire space, take four pieces of black tourmaline and place one in each of the four corners of the space to ward off any new negative energy that may enter the room later.

For emotional cleansing, you need to enter a physical cleaning first by bathing. Using some simple techniques, you can remove any type of lingering negativity, so you can feel a new spirit enter you. One should go through cleansing anytime they have gone through a difficult negative period or when you feel like you need to be refreshed for some reason.

Affirmation: *I am filling myself with pure cleaning white light*

Meditation:
- Sit in a comfortable position
- Close your eyes
- Visualize the white light entering your body from above
- Allow it to travel down through you passing through each chakra until it touches the earth
- Repeat this meditation practice for about 10 minutes anytime you feel the need for emotional cleansing

Crystals: Start by dissolving a quarter cup of Himalayan Pink Salt in the bathtub. Sit in the tub and let your body relax. Drop a clear quartz crystal and a smoky quartz crystal into the water. Sit back and soak for at least 10 minutes. Keep your eyes closed, repeating the affirmation the whole time. Remove the crystals from the water and let it drain out. Stay in the tub until all the water is gone. Cleanse the crystals afterward, before leaving the tub.

With selenite, you can boost the cleansing effects of your meditation practice. Hold the selenite in your non-dominant hand or place it on your crown chakra. Place another piece on the root chakra so that the energy can run through all of your chakras, cleansing them as it goes.

To cleanse your aura, use bloodstone. Hold the crystal in your non-dominant hand and close your eyes. Visualize the energy in the form of white light emanating from the stone and flowing into your body and then allow it to spread outwards until it consumes your aura.

Communication

It is important to be able to communicate effectively. It is an essential ingredient in any healthy relationship. Good communication skills can boost your career, cement your marriage, and help forge lasting bonds that will stick with you for the rest of your life. Your throat chakra is the energy source that powers your communication ability. If you are struggling with poor communication skills, then using meditation and crystals can help you to change.

Affirmation: *I can speak the truth both clearly and calmly*

Meditation: One of the most effective crystals used for communication is the amethyst. It works with the crown chakra to guide and inspire you in your words and how you deliver them. The lapis lazuli works well with your throat chakra, enabling you to be able to speak clearly.

While meditating, sit in a comfortable position with your eyes closed. Place the amethyst on your crown chakra and a lapis lazuli over your throat chakra. Repeat the affirmation for at least ten minutes or until you no longer feel the need to.

Crystals

Other crystals that work well with your communication skills are the rose quartz and sodalite. These work well when you're seeking to improve communication in a personal relationship. Lie on your back and hold a rose quartz over your heart chakra. Place a sodalite stone on your throat chakra. Close your eyes and repeat the chant, "I communicate with love" for ten minutes.

Aquamarine is the best crystal for when you are out and about. It comes in handy whenever you are in a situation where your communication is important. If you wear it as a pendant around your neck or in some form of jewelry, it will always be there, so you can access its energy anytime you need it. Use it on job interviews, or whenever you must have an important conversation with someone.

Keep in mind that communication is not just about knowing what you have to say. A good communicator is also a good listener. If you rearrange the letters in the word listen, you can get the word silent as well. Crystals can help you to know when to be silent and let the other person speak. It will help you to avoid any miscommunication that could lead you down a negative path.

Compassion

Compassion is a powerful emotion that springs from the heart chakra. With compassion, you are able to show deep feelings for others, demonstrate kindness and offer assistance when it is needed. Sometimes it may be difficult to show compassion, especially when it is needed by those close to you. However, the benefits of healing can definitely be enhanced if you know how to show a little compassion in your life.

Affirmation: *The energy of the Divine God lives within me and I recognize its power*

Meditation:
- Find a comfortable place to sit
- Sit with your eyes closed
- Visualize the person that you want to show compassion to
- Repeat the affirmation
- See the white light emanating from your heart
- Watch as it enters the heart of the other person
- Allow the light to envelop both of you completely
- Continue to do this for a minimum of ten minutes

Crystals: Rose quartz works well with your heart chakra. Hold a piece in your non-dominant hand while pressing lightly against your heart chakra. Position your other hand out in front of you with your palm facing up. Close your eyes and visualize the energy emanating from the crystal and filling up your heart chakra. Let it flow out from your dominant hand and spread out into the universe until it finds the person you want to share your compassion with. Continue this meditation for at least ten minutes.

You can also use celestite when you need compassion in a relationship. Carry a small piece of it around with you when you are planning to spend time with anyone you are involved with. It will help you to develop more compassion for that person.

Confusion

We can easily slip into emotional, mental, or spiritual confusion from time to time. Sometimes, it is the result of a physical incident, and other times, it stems from some psychological impact we might have encountered. Whatever the source, confusion can prevent you from growing and progressing as a person. When that happens, you need to find clarity to counteract the chaotic energy caused by the confusion. This will free you up so that you can get back on track with your life and become more productive.

Affirmation: *I can see my life and the choices I've made clearly and can now move forward with self-confidence*

Meditation: To break free from confusion, you need to receive direction from the higher spiritual powers. Only then can you bring about the kind of clarity that will clear away the fog.
- Find a nice, comfortable place to sit
- Close your eyes and breathe normally
- Visualize the pure white light of clarity floating above your crown chakra
- Observe as the light enters your body through the crown and drifts down to the third eye
- Focus on the third eye
- Repeat the affirmation for at least ten minutes or until your confusion fades

Crystals: Ametrine is very effective in clearing away confusion. It works along with the third eye giving you more insight into any situation. It also can be used with your solar plexus, infusing you with more confidence. Carry it around with you wherever you go and when you start to sense the confusion begin to set in, hold it in your hand and with eyes closed, repeat the affirmation ten times or until you start to feel the confusion fade away.

Selenite crystals have a very high-frequency vibration, which can be used to connect you to the wisdom of a higher power. If you are feeling confused, find a quiet place to sit for a few minutes, hold a piece of it in your hand with your eyes closed. Take a few deep breaths and repeat the affirmation. It will help to clear your head and relieve you of the stress that may be causing your confusion.

Contentment

It is not always easy to find contentment in life. It is a feeling you only get when you are happy and at peace with your own personal circumstances. Being content is not a matter of the life you lead, but rather it's a conscious choice to be at peace with whatever situation you are in. So it can be achieved even if you're living a life of distress and chaos.

Affirmation: *I am content and at peace in all circumstances*

Meditation: One way to experience true contentment is to visualize it first through meditation. Your mind might conjure up all sorts of images that trigger the feeling of contentment, a blade of grass yielding to a soft breeze. The kind that will bend but will not break when it is faced with the pressures of the wind. When the wind abates, it will go back to standing upright, facing the sun.

To create these visual images, meditation is often necessary.
- Find a quiet place to sit
- Breathe normally
- Repeat the affirmation as you visualize your image of contentment
- See the blade of grass bending but not breaking
- Watch as it stands tall again in your mind's eye
- Continue with this visualization exercise for at least ten minutes

Crystals: You can enhance your visualization exercises by adding crystals to it. The amethyst is a stone that can be used for a wide range of purposes. Wear it as jewelry or carry it around with you. Hold it in your hand while you visualize the imagery that will instill contentment into your life.

Green aventurine works with your heart chakra, can give you a solid piece of tranquility.
- Lie on the floor and hold the green aventurine on your heart chakra
- Close your eyes and repeat the mantra for at least 10 minutes

You can also use rose quartz, the crystal of unconditional love. Carry a piece of it around with you so you can have it whenever you need it. Keep one in a nearby location so that you can touch it whenever you need to find solace in a particular situation.

Creativity

We are naturally creative beings. This quality exists in all of us and it is passed down from one generation to the next without effort. However, in today's world where creativity is not highly valued, we can seem to lose connection with our own intuitive creative talents. When creativity is lost, it is usually because of a blockage in our sacral chakra. Learning to meditate with crystals can help us to reconnect with this inner quality buried deep inside of us.

Affirmation: *I thank the universe for the unlimited supply of creativity it has given me*

Meditation:
- Find a quiet place to sit comfortably
- Hold a carnelian crystal in your hands
- Close your eyes
- Focus all of your attention on the sacral chakra
- Take a deep inhale
- Visualize your creativity as it flows in from the universe and enters your sacral chakra
- Exhale and feel the creativity flow out of your sacral chakra and spread throughout your entire body
- Continue breathing normally
- As you breathe through this exercise, repeat the affirmation 10 times or to the point where you feel an inner sense of peace and calm.

Crystals: One crystal that taps into creativity quite well is ametrine. It is actually a blend of two different crystals together – the amethyst and citrine. In order to stimulate more creativity in your life, tape the ametrine to the bottom of your chair or place it under your pillow while you sleep.

Water sapphire, another creativity booster, can stir up more inspiration. Wear it as a piece of jewelry or carry it around with you whenever you feel you're going to need a little more inspiration in your life.

If you are a person that makes a living from your creativity, place a bowl of these beads on your desk. They can work to stir up your creative juices throughout the day, keeping your spirit open to receive new and fresh ideas.

As you can see, the list of crystals and the problems they can solve can be quite extensive. We are unable to include all of them within the confines of this book. However, it is clear that you can resolve many of these common problems that all of us have with crystals. In the following chapter, we'll list some of the basic properties of many crystals and give you a general idea of how to use them.

Learning about crystals can require a lifetime of study, but this book and the crystals listed in them is a good place to start. From there, you can research them in more detail on your own.

CHAPTER 10
What Crystal For What?

In this chapter, we'll discuss some of the most commonly used crystals and give you enough information about them, so they will be familiar enough to use them on your own. Each listing will include the crystal origin, its color, and its primary uses. In addition, we'll include which chakras it is best associated with if you plan to use it when working with other crystals, on a grid, or some other form of meditation practice.

Agate

A translucent blend of quartz and chalcedony. It comes in a variety of colors and shapes including round, polished, rough, and slabs. Many agates you find in shops have been dyed to deepen the color in order to enhance its characteristics.

Naturally found in regions of Australia, Brazil, the Czech Republic, India, Mexico, Morocco, and parts of the United States.

Colors: Black, blue, brown, gray, pink, purple, red, yellow, and white
Uses: Emotional balance, yin and yang, calmness, self-confidence, enhance focus and concentration, and heals resentment and bitterness
Chakra: Heart and root
Placement: Place on top of the chakra, hold it in hands, wear as jewelry, carry with you

Blue Lace Agate

Has distinctive gray and white veins running through it. This hard crystal has a light translucent quality and a very polished shine.

Naturally found in parts of South Africa, Australia, and Brazil

Colors: Sky blue, violet-blue with white and gray veins
Uses: Calmness, truthfulness, aids in public speaking, tranquility,

reduces deep negative emotions, and assists in communication with spiritual beings.
Chakra: Third eye and throat
Placement: Place the stone on the chakra, hold in your non-dominant hand when seeking calmness, hold in your dominant hand when you need to speak honestly, wear as jewelry, carry with you, or place on a lectern when speaking in public. You can also place it around any room you regularly meditate in.

Moss Agate

This stone is usually the color of moss. The translucent color can vary from a very faint green to a deep green. It has flecks of black, brown, gray, and white.

Naturally found in Australia, Brazil, Czech Republic, India, Mexico, Morocco, and the United States

Color: Green
Uses: encourages appreciation of nature, enhances gardening skills, new beginnings, prosperity, and love for everyone.
Chakra: Heart
Placement: Place on the heart chakra, hold in hands, carry with you, place in your garden

Alexandrite

The color of the Alexandrite can range from a bluish green to a green or a purple. The color will change depending on how it is positioned or how the light hits it. It is a very rare stone and is highly desirable. Most alexandrite you find today is synthetically made from Austrian crystals, which have no healing properties.

Naturally found in Brazil, Russia, and Sri Lanka

Colors: Green to bluish green changing to a deep purple or a raspberry
Uses: Improves self-esteem, deepens positive emotions, promotes confidence, optimism, joy, and luck. It also aids in improved intuition and in a stronger connection with the inner person.
Chakra: heart, third eye, crown

Placement: Place over the chakra, wear it as jewelry, hold in your non-dominant hand, or carry it with you.

Amazonite

From the feldspar family, amazonite sports a range of blue-green and turquoise colors. It has a slight iridescent luster and is relatively soft for a stone. Because of its soft texture, it can be scratched or suffer from dings. It is best to carry it in a protective cloth wrapping to preserve its surface. Never use water or salt to clean this crystal as it could cause permanent damage.

Naturally found in Australia, Brazil, Canada, Namibia, Russia, the United States, and Zimbabwe

Colors: Green and aqua
Uses: Protection from electromagnetic waves, calms and soothes, encourages peacefulness, stress reliever, balances the yin and yang, opens the heart, and embraces love. It also enhances your intuition.
Chakra: heart and throat
Placement: Place on the chakra, use with the third eye for intuition, hold in non-dominant hand for peace, hold in dominant hand for stress, carry it with you or wear as jewelry.

Amber

Technically not a crystal but a fossilized tree resin. It can be found in many places around the world, but the best amber is located in the Baltic region. It has many small impurities like bubbles, small pieces of matter, and even insects that have been trapped inside. Never clean amber with water or salt to prevent damaging its delicate exterior.

Located in the Dominican Republic, Germany, Great Britain, Italy, Poland, Romania, and Russia

Colors: Golden yellow, deep honey brown
Uses: Pain reliever, erase negativity, cleanses auras and chakras, cleanses negative energy from your surroundings, boosts memory, fosters peace, and encourages trust.
Chakra: Solar plexus and throat

Placement: Wear as jewelry, carry it with you, hold in non-dominant hand to attract positive energy

Amethyst

A form of quartz crystal, amethyst can be used for a wide variety of things.

Naturally found in countries like Brazil, Canada, East Africa, Great Britain, India, Mexico, Russia, Sri Lanka, and the United States

Colors: Purple
Uses: Intuition and spiritual insight, aids with sobriety, and heals insomnia. It encourages a restful sleep and enhances psychic abilities, connects to the spirit realm, and to your inner spiritual self.
Chakra: Third eye and the crown
Placement: Place directly on the chakra, wear as jewelry, carry with you, hold in non-dominant hand for receiving, place underneath the pillow when sleeping, or leave it in your meditation room.

Bloodstone

Often used to purify the blood and help heal blood disorders. It is usually green with small red flecks interspersed throughout.

Naturally found in places like Australia, Brazil, China, India, and Russia

Colors: Green with red spots
Uses: Aids in grounding, opens up the heart, and encourages developing a stronger personal power, boosts courage, aids in breaking free from fear, and gives you a stronger strength of mind.
Chakra: Root and heart
Placement: Place directly on the chakra, hold in non-dominant hand for more courage, hold in dominant hand for fear, carry with you, wear as jewelry.

Carnelian

This translucent stone can range in color from a pale orange to a deeper orange-red with inclusions of brown, white, or yellow inside. The spiderweb carnelian has many threadlike bands of white running all the way through it.

Naturally found in areas of the Czech Republic, Great Britain, Iceland, India, Peru, and Romania

Colors: Orange, Brownish orange, and red-orange
Uses: Security and safety, courage, energy, willpower, determination, overcoming abuse, and increased vitality.
Chakra: Root and sacral
Placement: Place directly on the chakra, carry with you, wear it in a small pouch tied around your waist, place next to your bed, keep in the refrigerator or in cupboards.

Desert Rose

This is actually a gypsum stone that can be found in a sandy color with little bands of white. It is rounded with multilayered petals, so it is sometimes referred to as a selenite rose. Because it is primarily made of gypsum, it can be very soft or brittle. Never use water or salt to cleanse it as it can be easily damaged.

Naturally found in places like Austria, France, Germany, Great Britain, Greece, Poland, Russia, and in parts of the United States

Colors: Sandy with white
Uses: Communication with higher beings, focusing the mind, acceptance, calmness, comfort, and cleaning out negative energy.
Chakra: Third eye and the crown
Placement: Place directly on the chakra or hold in your hand during meditation. You can also place pieces of it around your meditation area.

Emerald

This familiar bright green stone is transparent and translucent. In its natural state, it can be found with a rough surface or as a cloudy crystal.

Normally found in countries like Austria, Brazil, Egypt, India, Tanzania, and Zimbabwe

Colors: Green
Uses: Success in romance, faithfulness, unity in relationships, positivity, releasing negativity, and for receiving more wisdom.
Chakra: Heart
Placement: Place directly on top of the chakra, wear as jewelry, or carry with you

Fuchsite

This beautiful green stone has a rough exterior with a slight sparkle when it catches the light. When polished, the color can range from a soft light green all the way up to a deep green with tiny bits of rub inside.

Normally found in places like Brazil, India, and Russia

Colors: Light to very dark green
Uses: Used for enhanced intuition, resolving power struggles, better understanding, feelings of self-worth
Chakra: Heart
Placement: Place directly on the chakra, hold in non-dominant hand when seeking medical intuition, carry with you, wear as jewelry, place in your meditation space, or in a sickroom next to the bed or under a pillow.

Garnet

Garnets come in a wide range of colors, but the most popular choice is red. These help with safety issues and give you a sense of security. Green garnets are used primarily for prosperity and love. Yellow and gold ones boost your self-esteem. Orange garnets help to strength your self-identity and find your place within a particular group.

This crystal has a transparent and translucent appearance and can be distinguished by its deep rich colors.

Garnets are found in almost every place on the planet

Colors: brown, gold, green, orange, red, and yellow
Uses: Cleanses chakras, grounding, promotes passion and love, cleanses negative energies, and can be used to boost the energies emanating from other crystals.
Placement: Place directly on the chakra for cleansing, hold in hands, wear as jewelry, and you can keep it in your meditation area.

Howlite

This beautiful white stone has black bands that sometimes are dyed to a deep turquoise. It is often used as a less expensive alternative for turquoise or lapis lazuli. If you are shopping for either of those two stones, make sure it's not howlite dyed to look like one of them because the properties and characteristics of howlite are very different.

Howlite is only found in the regions of the United States

Colors: White
Uses: Connects to a higher consciousness, balances chakras, insomnia, and patience.
Chakra: Crown
Placement: Place the stone directly on the crown chakra, hold in hands, keep under your pillow or on a night table, or keep in your meditation room

Iron Pyrite

Sometimes referred to as Fool's gold because of its gold-like appearance. Iron Pyrite does not hold the same value as true gold, but you will find soft gold flecks embedded inside the darker stone. It has an opaque quality with a beautiful shiny golden luster.

Normally located in Canada, Chile, Great Britain, Peru, and the United States.

Colors: Gold
Uses: Success in business, prosperity, good fortune, and willpower
Chakra: Solar Plexus
Placement: Place directly on the chakra, carry with you, use in a

prosperity corner of the house, place where you keep your cash, keep on your desk at work.

Jade

While jade is most often found in a watery green color, it can also be found in black, purple, red, and white. It is commonly used to improve relationships, help in a decision-making process, and aid in the discovery of inner peace. Its texture is smooth and translucent with a creamy essence to it. Never use water or salt to cleanse jade as it could damage it beyond repair.

Normally Jade is found in certain regions in China, Italy, the Middle East, Russia, and the United States

Colors: Black, green, orange, purple, and white
Uses: Good luck, peace, self-definition, self-knowledge, insight, and guidance
Chakra: works well with all chakras depending on the color you use
Placement: Place directly on the chakra, wear as jewelry, carry with you, hold in hands during meditation, or keep in a meditation room.

Kyanite

This is a silicate mineral with veins of white or gray running through it. It has a rough texture and looks more like a long slab with blades. Polished kyanite is smooth and has a soft luster with swirling bands of white and/or gray. It can be transparent or opaque. Do not cleanse with water or salt so you can preserve its delicate appearance.

Kyanite can only be found in remote regions of Brazil.

Color: Green
Uses: Release negative energy, balance, alignment with all chakras, comprehension, and discernment
Chakra: Heart and the third eye
Placement: Place directly on the chakra, wear as jewelry, carry with you, place in an area that needs to be energized or cleansed.

Lodestone

This naturally magnetic stone is made from black iron oxide. When you examine it, you will notice tiny pieces of magnetic materials that have been attracted to it, giving it a bit of a fuzzy appearance. Always keep your lodestone in a plastic container to keep from drawing in the smaller metal bits. You'll find it is extremely heavy for a stone of its size.

Normally, Lodestone is found in regions of Austria, Central America, Finland, India, Italy, and North America

Colors: Black
Uses: Grounding, to align chakras, and magnify the Law of Attraction
Chakra: Root
Placement: Place near the chakra, carry it with you, or hold it in your hands

Muscovite

Formed from mica, this stone has unique formations that appear to be similar to flakes of slabs from a larger stone. It has a pearlescent and multicolor luster. It holds the same type of energy across all colors of muscovite crystals. It can be very brittle, so always take special care when using or storing it. Never use water or salt to cleanse it because it can erode very quickly.

Normally found in remote regions of Austria, Brazil, Czech Republic, Russia, Switzerland, and the United States

Colors: Gray, green, pink, gold and red
Uses: Connection to higher beings, connections to inner self, guidance and insight, and intuition
Chakra: Third eye and the crown
Placement: Place directly on the chakra, hold gently in hands, keep in meditation area, or put next to your bed for guidance while dreaming.

Obsidian

Obsidian is made from volcanic glass. This lustrous stone can be either smooth or have rough, craggy edges. It comes in a number of different colors, but the most demanded color is black.

It is found in many places around the earth.

Colors: Black, black and white, blue, green, and red
Uses: Grounding, clearing the root chakra, absorbs negativity, coping with grief, strength and energy, emotional protection, and spiritual connections.
Chakra: Root and heart
Placement: Place directly on the chakra, hold in hands, carry with you, place in a room to absorb negative energy, keep a meditation area calm and peaceful.

Peridot

This clear stone comes in varying shades of green. Some will have small black or brown flecks inside. You will often find it cut and polished and used as jewelry.

Normally found in remote areas of Brazil, the Canary Islands, Egypt, Ireland, Russia, and Sri Lanka

Colors: Varying shades of green from a light olive color to a bright apple green
Uses: Opens up the heart chakra, love, emotional trauma, understanding of relationships, protection, cleanses all of your energies (auras, chakras, and meridians).
Chakra: Heart and solar plexus
Placement: Place directly on the chakra, wear as jewelry, carry with you, hold in non-dominant hand, keep in your meditation room. Keep this stone close to you when you are working to build or repair a relationship.

Quartz

Quartz comes in several different colors: clear, rose, rutilated, and smoky. The clear quartz is usually transparent and/or translucent. It is usually found in clusters, geodes, points, or double terminated points. You can buy either polished or rough quartz. The vibration of quartz is quite high and because of this, it is often called upon as a master healer because it can work on almost any condition.

Quartz can be found in every part of the world.

Colors: the clear quartz can be clear or milky white, the rose is a pink color, rutilated can be either clear or smoky with long brown or reddish strands running through it. The term rutilated means that it has fine little needles of titanium dioxide running through it. Smoky quartz has a beautiful brown smoky color.
Uses: Used by shamans in their work, enhances psychic energy, aids in connecting with higher spiritual beings, builds trust in a higher power, cleanses and detoxes energies. It can amplify energy, clean spaces of negative energy, a master healer, cleanses and charges other crystals, and provide protection.
Chakra: Works on all chakras depending on the color. Rose – the root and the heart, rutilated and smoky – solar plexus and the crown. The clear quartz will work with all chakras, especially the crown.
Placement: Place directly on the chakra, carry with you, wear as jewelry, hold in hands during meditation, keep in the meditation area

Rhodochrosite

This beautiful pink stone is banded with white or black strands throughout. It is partially translucent and very soft, so you should always exercise care when using it. Avoid using water or salt with this crystal as it can be damaged.

Normally found in the regions of Argentina, Russia, South Africa, the United States, and Uruguay

Colors: Varying from a light pink to a deeper orange-pink
Uses: Unconditional love, heals a broken heart, resolves emotional issues, love, self-worth, and helps you to forget past hurts
Chakra: Root and heart
Placement: Place directly on the chakra, carry with you, can be placed on any area of the body where your emotional pain is affecting you physically

Sodalite

Very similar in appearance to the lapis lazuli but with a much lighter color. Sodalite usually appears in a denim blue shade with black and/or white spots.

Normally found in the countries of Brazil, Canada, France, Greenland, Myanmar, Romania, Russia, and the United States.

Color: Blue
Uses: Truth and integrity, better communication, intuition, and enhances psychic abilities
Chakra: Throat and third eye
Placement: Place directly on the chakra, hold in the non-dominant hand, wear as jewelry, or keep it in your workspace to enhance creativity

Topaz

This transparent blue (or sometimes yellow) crystal has many facets. It is often used as jewelry even by those who are not into crystal healing. When it has been cut and polished, it is very clear. It can be cut to an extremely small size. The blue topaz helps with communication whether it is internal connections with your inner being, external connections with others, or connecting to a higher being. The yellow topaz enhances self-esteem and guides you in setting boundaries.

Normally found in the countries of Africa, Australia, India, Mexico, Pakistan, and the United States

Colors: Blue or yellow
Uses: Forgiveness, truth and integrity, enhanced communication, fine-tuning thoughts, recharge your energy, empathy, abundance, and joy.
Chakra: Third eye, throat (blue), solar plexus (yellow)
Placement: Place directly on the chakra, wear it as jewelry, carry with you, or keep in your meditation room.

Unakite

This mossy green stone has large spots of pink and peach dispersed through it. You can even see tiny flecks of gold embedded inside. It is a unique type of jasper and can be found either rough, tumbled, or polished.

Mostly found in remote regions of South Africa and the United States.

Uses: Emotional balance, for better sleep, addictions, and boosts willpower
Chakra: Solar plexus and heart
Placement: Place directly on chakras, keep underneath your pillow, on a night table, hold in hands during meditation, or carry with you.

Vanadinite

This stone is formed by the oxidation of mineral ore that contains lead. It can be a yellow, orange, or red color with clear crystals seen in boxy clusters. These stones are usually very small and transparent.

Usually found in regions of Morocco and the United States

Colors: Orange, red, yellow
Uses: Creativity, motivation, mental stimulation, energizing, and moves to action
Chakra: Sacral
Placement: Place directly on the chakra, tape to the bottom of a chair, place in the workspace, under mattress or pillow, on the night table.

Zircon

This stone is often confused with the cubic zirconium. However, zircon is a naturally occurring mineral while the cubic zirconia is purely synthetic. Zircon has many metaphysical properties and can come in a number of different colors including blue, brown, clear, red, or yellow.

It is usually found in countries like Australia, Cambodia, Canada, the Middle East, Myanmar, Sri Lanka, and Tanzania

Colors: Blue and yellow. Comes in other colors but the other colors are usually the result of heat treating.
Uses: Self-love, spiritual growth, communication, amplifies energy from a higher being, aids in intuition.
Chakra: Crown, third eye, throat
Placement: Place directly on the chakra, use while meditating, keep in meditation space, wear as jewelry, carry with you

There is no space or time to list all of the crystals that are available to you. No doubt there are thousands to choose from, but we have just worked to give you a little taste of what's in store. In time, your knowledge of crystals will continue to grow, but for now, it is important to start experimenting with the ones listed here. Soon, you'll be ready to venture out into a broader landscape and put all of your newfound knowledge to the test.

CONCLUSION

Now that you have found a better understanding of crystals and the many ways you can use them, you are probably anxious to get started. It is amazing to learn just how these beautiful little gems will affect the body and the mind.

Don't worry too much about getting all the details right. There are a lot of them, and for a time, you'll have to refer back to these pages for clarification. Intuitively, you already know what to do, just learn how to trust yourself. Your mind is a creation from the Divine God of the universe and He wants you to be pulled towards him.

This is the point where most people start their journey, how about you? I promise you, it will be a ride to be remembered, no matter what happens.

Hopefully, you found this information both informative and humbling. It is amazing how many secrets are hidden within arm's reach. Once you tap into all that energy floating around there, you'll be well on your way to a future of wonders.

DESCRIPTION

Anyone ready to make some serious changes in their lives, this book is for you. When life throws us lemons, we can fight back with crystals. Learn how to reclaim your life with the power of these beautiful gems.

Whether you're just trying to get your feet firmly planted on the ground, or you're dealing with deeper psychological challenges, you'll get the basics for beginners who wish to explore the world of crystals. Here in these pages, you'll learn...

- What exactly are crystals
- How to tap into crystal energy
- You and your chakras
- How to make a crystal grid
- The fundamentals of healing with crystals
- Tips on finding the right crystals for you
- And much, much more.

You'll learn basic properties of crystals and how to take advantage of them, and be all the better for it.

If you're looking for another way to fulfill your life, then this is the book you've been searching for. If you listen closely, you might even hear it calling to you. So, why not answer it and download this book today.

CRYSTALS FOR BEGINNERS

Discover the Healing Powers of Crystals and Healing Stones

Crystal Lee

"Copyright 2018 by Crystal Lee-All rights reserved. No part of this book may be reproduced or transmitted in any form or by any means, electronic or mechanical, including photocopying, recording or by any information storage and retrieval system without written permission of the publisher, except for the inclusion of brief quotations in a review.

INTRODUCTION

Congratulations on downloading *Crystals for Beginners* and thank you for doing so. This is a beginner's book for those wanting to begin or expand their knowledge of crystals and their unique healing properties. There are a lot of ways to improve your health and peace of mind these days, crystal healing is an extremely relaxing and educational way to do so.

There is a deep profound link between body, mind, and spirit. Disruptions affect all aspects of life, including relationships, career, hobbies, emotions, and even physical health. Sometimes we overreact or have no idea how to explain the way we're feeling. Crystal healing covers the concept that you can find balance to your emotional state with therapies that exists beyond pharmaceuticals. These therapies can provide maximum benefit for you and your mind and can be a lot less expensive than other treatments.

The following chapters of this book will cover basic approaches and ideal ways to bring positive energy into your life using crystals, energy healing, self-awareness, and the knowledge that connects these to our essential being. They will also discuss healthy ways of releasing energy, chakra balancing, the importance of understanding/practicing crystals medicine, and everything you need to know about the benefits stones provide for the human condition. There is a lot to learn about crystals and how they can interact with your body.

There are plenty of books on this subject on the market, thanks again for choosing *Crystals for beginners*. I hope that the information provided in this book will help you develop how to ignite your spirituality and improve your quality of life, as well as help you get a better understanding of your spiritual being and how crystals can bring many benefits to your life, please enjoy!

CHAPTER 1
The History Of Healing Stones

What are crystals? Crystals are natural elements that originally come from the earth. They are formed through a solidification process of chemicals and have an internal arrangement of atoms and molecules that are regularly repeating. A true crystal has an organized formation of unit cells that form a unique lattice pattern called a crystal system. These lattices appear within healing stones.

Healing stones are proven to of been around since the late 19th and early 20th centuries. Throughout history, ancient cultures around the world have too aligned, clear and reinvented their energy, spirit, and overall health using healing crystals and stones. Stones of all type have become again more popular since the '80s; there has lately been a rise in interest in the healing properties and powers that exist beyond medical drugs. They are mainly used for a source of spiritual healing and as a conduit of personal cleansing. Healing stones are one of the most common yet not often discussed holistic therapies that exist. The Philosophy on modern Crystal healing is based on traditional concepts adopted from Asian cultures, the most notable-the Chinese concept of life-energy (chi or qi).

Ancient
Crystals are millions of years old pieces of rock formed in the earliest part of the formation of the earth. The oldest crystal ever discovered is called Zircon and dates back to 4.4 billion years.

Ancient Samaria
Historical reference shows that around the 4th millennium B.C. crystals were used. The Sumerians believed that every crystal was linked to the energy of the planets and therefore used the crystals in magic formulas. They would also use certain stones for cosmetic purposes, such as eyeshadow, lipstick, and contour, just as we do now. All of which was documented in an ancient text.

30,000 Years Ago
Some of the oldest amulets in Britain made from Baltic Amber date

back to about 30 000 years ago. A gem belonged to Timur Lenk in the 1300s and was named after he died. He is best known as the Islamic conqueror of Eastern and Central Asia. Timur Ruby's 361 carat is an impressive red gem. The distance to Britain that the crystal traveled shows its importance and value to the people of that time.

Names and dates carved on the stone show that it belonged to five Indian rulers later on. One of them was Shah Jehan, the Taj Mahal builder. In Britain, amulets were primarily used to show wealth, power, and high status. The Timur Ruby was one of the treasures brought to England from India in 1850.

Paleolithic Era

In the grave sights around Belgium and Switzerland, jet beads, bracelets, and necklaces were discovered. Other crystals and stones had mainly been used in the manufacturing of everyday functional tools. Such as fire flint, hunting arrowheads, housing parts, axes, wheels, and spears.

Ancient India

In ancient Ayurvedic documents such as the Hindu Vedas, the use of healing crystals was well documented. The people of India especially loved diamonds, which they believed to have great strength and endurance to withstand adversity. They liked Sapphire for clarity and balance of mind, as well as Jasper for harmony and the sex life.

Ancient Egypt

Egyptians have been referred to in history as one of the first people to decorate themselves with crystals to prevent disease and negative energy. The crystals would be used for decoration, religious purposes, good luck charms and more. It was strongly believed that the Egyptians were very spiritually enveloped in the stones, they connected certain stones with specific gods and used the crystals in burials, which they thought would help the deceased to find their way into the afterlife.

Ancient Greece

Most names we give to crystals are originally from the Greek language. Surprising enough, the Greek word " Krystillos," which translates to Ice, comes from the word crystal. Greek culture worshipped Athena, the god of war. Before a battle, soldiers crushed hematite up and rubbed it on themselves believing it to make them "invincible."

Jewelry was also very popular in ancient Greece, the earliest necklaces come from 1,500 BC incorporating mainly Emeralds, Rubies, Sapphires, Pearls, and Carnelians. The Greeks believed that amethyst had many powers, including protection against intoxication. The word " amethyst" is derived from the Greek word " amethyst."

Native Americans

In both North and South America, Native Americans believed heavily in the healing powers of crystals. For them, Turquoise was the most sacred of all crystals, used primarily for personal protection, but also for spiritual and emotional healing. Of course, the diverse northern and southern cultures have practiced numerous unique crystal healing techniques.

North America – For Mayans, one of the most famous civilizations in ancient North

America – the fire opal and Jade were considered to be very valuable and important in Mayan culture. It is also related to breath. The Aztec civilization also used healing crystals. These civilizations were one of North America 's first ancient cultures to use crystals to cure physical diseases and emotional imbalances.

South America – Although there is little information about the use of Norte Chico crystals, there are countless references to the use of crystals as jewelry by Norte Chico's leaders. The Inca civilization used a wide variety of crystals to heal. Incas used large amounts of quartz and jade for healing.

Ancient China

Jade was the favored healing stone of ancient Chinese people and has been mined in China since the Stone Age. In fact, most of the major gemstones/healing crystals were originally mined in China.

Renaissance

Mystical healers started to learn how to draw and use the energy of crystals for a variety of health conditions. Literature has described how healing crystals were used in medicine and some famous authors, including Binghen, Saxo, and Mandeville, often mentioned that the benefits of crystals became much more powerful when used in conjunction with herbal healing practices. During this period, crystals were regarded as endowed with 'virtues' that could easily be destroyed. Some mystics believed that even if there was original sin, some gemstones could lose their virtue. Others believed that a virtue inherent in crystals could be lost if it was misused or if it was handled by someone with bad intentions.

In this light, crystals were used with utmost caution and care in the Renaissance. Before their powers were harnessed, stones were cleaned, consecrated, and sanctified– a practice reflected in the cleaning and programming process of crystals before use.

Some crystals in the period of renaissance were particularly valuable. A gem in the possession of Henry III was allegedly stolen by his chief justiciar. The gem was said to have been given to the King of Wales – Henry's enemy. This angered Henry, and the justiciar was branded a criminal since the gem he has stolen was considered most powerful, capable of making its wearer invincible.

Mythology

Amazing enough crystals and gems, rare and beautiful played an important role in ancient mythology. People used them in the hope of transmitting some of the properties of the crystals they used: strength, beauty, magic power, etc.

Crystals in Technology Past

Military radios – in World War II, the military used quartz oscillators to control the frequency of two-way radio transmissions, the oscillators were highly precise but difficult to mass-produce.

Consumer electronics – electronic manufacturers use electronic-grade manufactured quartz in computer circuits, cell phones, and similar equipment. CNet even reports that quartz in its natural form and other piezoelectric crystals were used in their raw form to manufacture an experimental rudimentary computer that transmitted or received signals such as randomized sound or light

Watches – due to the precision of quartz oscillators, they are used in watches, which require precision in timekeeping. Only a tiny piece of quartz is used, according to the watch company, but it oscillates so precisely that it can be accurate to a few seconds per year.

Holy Texts and the Energy Connection

Holy, religious books from various cultures discuss the importance of life force (energy) in the spiritual, emotional, and physical health of humankind.

In the Bible, it says, "that energy is God's energy, any energy deep within you, God himself willing and working at what will give him the most pleasure. (Philippians 2:13) In the Gospel of John, Jesus heals the sick using the energy of God and prayer."

The Hindu Vidas speak of prana, the life force that flows through all living things. According to the Yajur Veda, "there are 11 in the vital energy (prana) existing by their own virtue (ear, skin, eye, tongue, nose, speech, hands, legs, two organs of excretion, and mind.)" These are body parts of volition and perception, not reality.

Buddha also noted energy in defining Seven Factors of enlightenment: mindfulness, investigation of the dharma (cosmic laws), energy, joy, relaxation, and tranquility, concentration and equanimity.

Those who follow Kabbalah, the mystical branch of Judaism, study the Zohar, a collection of comments that reveal the Torah's spiritual essence. The Zohar notes that when the Tora portion is known as "Pinchas" is read aloud once each year during the Sabbath, those who listen with an open heart and remorse for prior misdeeds (even without any knowledge of Hebrew) may experience a great, healing light.

Crystals in Technology Today

One of the most intriguing and extraordinary features of certain crystals is that they produce a permeable electric charge. This is known as the piezoelectric effect and was discovered by Pierre and Jacques Curie in the early 19th century. Eventually, with the development of technology and science, it was possible to put this discovery to use.

Crystals transmit a piezoelectric charge that impacts the biomagnetic fields of the body. Crystals reflect and withdraw light rays like infrared and ultraviolet rays, which are both used to repair and sanitize the body. Crystals also have the power to carry information. Even from a scientific perspective, it seems possible natural crystals can influence physical functioning.

Pyroelectric effect: pyroelectric crystals such as tourmaline generate electrical current when heated or cooled, according to scientists, many applications exist for pyroelectricity, for example, power conversion and infrared detection, among others.

Piezoelectric effect: the piezoelectric effect occurs when no conducting crystals generate an electrical charge when put under mechanical stress. Quartz is one crystal that demonstrates piezoelectricity, which makes it popular for use in devices like radios, watches, and other digital integrated circuits.

It would be very hard to imagine life without crystals since they play a vital role in electronics and optical industries. It is safe to say technological development without crystals would not be possible.

Examples of Modern Science with Crystals

Solar cells – powering instruments from calculators to place vehicles.

Transistors – based on the same types of materials and crystals as solar cells. Transistors can negate electron flow, and amplify radio signals, as well as act as a digital switch.

Liquid Crystals – wrist watches, some types of clocks and pocket calculators.

Protein Structures – crystals help solve different protein structures, which is extremely useful in biochemistry.

Pencils – graphite is a type of crystal.

Computer Chips – silicones form the basis for all microelectronics, such as computer chips.

Optical Equipment – some optical equipment is made from crystals.

CD's and DVD's – crystalline solids in them enable us to write and store information on them.

Myths about Crystals

Myth #1: It's all in my head.
The crystals work is designed to take you out of your head and make you feel like it. Crystals do not require rationalization or explanation; they give you the opportunity to experience them. If you're worried its all in your head, stop thinking and experience the sensations the crystals provide. You can rationalize it later.

Myth #2: If crystals can help, they can hard.
Crystals vibrate with energy that can entrain to your energy. Intention and mindset play big roles in this. If you expect crystals to harm you, that may wind up being your exact experience, this- this is true of anything. Your beliefs always play an important role in your results and experience, whether you use crystals or placebo or medication. In general, if you approach the crystals with the intention of shifting vibration for your highest and greatest good, it is highly unlikely you will be hurt in any way.

Myth #3: I have to be spiritual or new age to use crystals.
To use crystals, you don't have to be New Age, spiritual or religious, nor do they run counter to any religion or spirituality, all you need is an open mind and a sincere desire for change that serves your highest and greatest good.

Myth #4: I don't need to cleanse my crystals.
Since crystals tend to absorb energy, it is important to clean them so that unwanted energy is removed. If you use them consistently, energy can build up and you will have to clean up more frequently if the energy is negative.

Myth #5: expensive crystals are more powerful.
Quartz is one of the most common and inexpensive crystals, it's also one of the most powerful. The amount of money you spend on crystals really doesn't have anything to do with how effective it is. What matters is how a crystal affects your energy, and some of the least expensive crystals may be exactly what you need.

Crystal Remedies for Certain Emotions

When you are dealing with mental, emotional, or spiritual issues, you may find remedies in this chapter quite helpful.

Abandonment – There may be feelings of abandonment resulting from a recent breakup, loss of family members or somebody important to you. You can feel lost, alone, empty. Use this mantra to remember that you are the real source of unconditional love.

"I give myself unconditional love and receive unconditional love from the universe."

Meditation – Meditate using this manta and while holding a rose quartz crystal, the stone of unconditional love. Picture yourself in a very happy, loving state of mind. Continue until you feel peace.

Stones that help feeling abandonment:
- Amazonite for healing emotional pain.
- Garnet for healing issues of belonging.
- Carnelian for self-empowerment.

Abuse – Whether emotional, physical, or mental, this can leave lasting scars. Many people carry the effects of abuse with them, essentially sometimes becoming their own tormentor long after the abuse has ceased. If you are experiencing current abuse, seeking professional help is an important first step.

"I release the pain of my past for a more positive and loving future."

Meditation – Close your eyes and allow yourself to feel the grief and pain. Take note of where you feel the pain, then use breathing exercises to release the pain. Exhale and repeat the mantra until you feel peace.

Stones that help with abuse:
- Garnet for a sense of belonging and identity.
- Carnelian for personal power.
- Yellow tigers eye for self-esteem.
- Rose Quartz for unconditional love.

Addiction – Whether you are addicted to an activity, an idea, a person, or even a substance, addiction can quickly throw you and your life completely out of balance. Supporting yourself spiritually and emotionally can help ease that process.

"I am free of my desire for _____. I release it, and it releases me."

Meditation – Addiction can make you very off balanced, so meditating on the mantra while lying with stones can be helpful to restore your balance. Focus on your sacral and throat chakra for they deal with willpower.

Stones that help with addiction:
- Labradorite for detoxification.
- Amethyst for its sober properties.

Anger – A natural and acceptable emotion that everybody has. When we allow ourselves to fully experience anger, it can easily pass through our body's and dissipate. However, sometimes we get stuck in anger until it hardens into resentment. Know that holding onto anger only harms you.

"I breathe in peace. I release anger."

Meditation – Place both hands over your solar plexus chakra, repeat your mantra, and picture energy flowing out of your body through your nose.

Stones that help with anger:
- Carnelian for a calm and grounded feeling.
- Amber to absorb negativity.
- Black tourmaline for positive energy flow.

Anxiety – While it is natural to feel anxious from time to time, persistent anxiety can keep you from living your best life. Anxiety can take many forms such as Phobias and social anxiety. Anxiety resides in the Root Chakra.

"I relax into infinite serenity."

Meditation – Sit quietly while holding a stone that relates to the Root Chakra. Visualize peace flowing inside of you and say the mantra.

Stones that help with anxiety:
- Blue lace agate for reflective calming properties.
- Lapis lazuli for grounding and relief.
- Black Tourmaline for absorbing negative energy.

Accepting Change – Most people find change difficult because of the fear of the unknown and getting too comfortable. Change is a necessary and natural part of life; you cannot grow without it.

"I am grateful for the change in my life because it serves as a source of positive empowerment."

Meditation – Breathe deeply while visualizing pure white energy flowing throughout you, repeat mantra at the same time.

Stones that help accepting change:
- Watermelon Tourmaline for clarity to your situation.
- Prehnite to amplify inner strength and accepting new circumstances.

Compassion – Intricately linked to unconditional love, which is connected to the Heart Chakra. It enables you to feel deeply for another and act toward them with kindness and care.

"The spark of divinity in me recognizes the spark of divinity in you."

Meditation – Sit or lie with your eyes closed and visualize the person for whom you want to cultivate compassion for. Repeat mantra while visualizing pure energy coming from your heart.

Stones that help with compassion:
- Rose Quarts for loving energy.
- Celestite for healing relationships.

Confidence – Comes from the Solar Plexus chakra, where you foster your sense of personal identity and self-esteem to grow more confident, pay close attention to these two chakras, learning who you are and then living that truth with integrity.

"I exude confidence because I know I am living my truth."

Meditation – Visualize yourself going about your day with the confidence that you are living within your integrity. Repeat mantra and try to be detailed in the visualization.

Stones that help with confidence:
- Moonstone for boosting confidence.
- Hematite for building confidence.

Depression – Depression can affect your mind, body, spirit, and cause lingering physical pain and ennui that keeps us from living a vibrant, joyful, and productive life.

"I seek out and enjoy all the pleasure and happiness available to me in my daily life."

Meditation – Speak your mantra loud and add, "I am grateful for" to the end and state, what you are grateful for.

Stones that help with depression
- Amber for spiritual healing.
- Smoky Quartz for absorbing bad energy.

Eating Disorders – They appear to be about food but they tend to have emotional, spiritual, and physical roots. It is important you seek professional help as well if you have an eating disorder.

"my body, mind, and spirit are beautiful, and I bless myself with unconditional love."

Meditation – Any time you feel compulsive eating disorder behaviors stop for a moment, close your eyes, and take big, deep, and long breath. Repeat mantra.
Stones for eating disorders:
Rose Quartz for unconditional self-love
Carnelian for self-acceptance and motivation

Emotional Balance – maintain emotion balance can help you stay steady throughout the day which allows you to think clearly, access your creativity, experience gratitude, and enjoy your life.

"I allow my emotions to serve as opportunities for growth, and then I return to my center."

Meditation – Daily mindfulness meditation can help your overall balance of emotions, when thoughts come up, simply allow them to pass by quickly.

Stones that help with emotional balance:
- Garnet for emotional foundation
- Malachite for rebalancing

Rainbow Fluorite for balancing all of the chakras

Achieving Goals – Setting and achieving goals is an important part of your life path. While walking a straight line to a goal may seem ideal, sometimes the detours on the way to our goals offer the most valuable lessons and insights.

"Anything blocking my path to my goals dissolves at this moment."

Meditation – Speak the mantra and visualize yourself living your life when you have achieved your goals. What will life look like? Visualize and repeat.

Stones that help to achieve goals:
- Carnelian for goal-oriented action
- Clear Quartz for manifestation.

Grounding – Grounding keeps us connected to the earth, which is our source of support and strength. You should ground yourself whenever you feel out of sorts, it can keep you focused and centered.

"I honor the jewel with the lotus bloom."

Meditation – Sit comfortably whole holding grounding stones and repeat the mantra.

Stones that help grounding:
- Lodestone for grounding visualization
- Black Tourmaline for connection to the earth
- Obsidian for self-love and reflection

Indecisiveness – Life would be so much easier if you could make instant decisions every moment of the day, but some decisions are more difficult to make.
"I am in tune with what I need, and trust my intuition to guide me to the right choices."

Meditation-Focus your attention to your third eye chakra, and consider the decisions you need to make and repeat the mantra.

Stones that help with indecisiveness:
- Amethyst for paying attention
- Ametrine for intuitive problem solving

Insomnia – Many things can come from this sleep disorder insomnia such as stress, physical pain, inconsistent sleep patterns, and environmental issues.

"I release the stress of my day and drift off into a deep, refreshing sleep."

Meditation – At bedtime, use progressive relaxation and mindfulness to clear your mind of stressful thoughts and promote relaxation and restfulness in your body. Use visual meditation to help you drift off.

Stones that help insomnia:
- Amethyst for relaxation and tranquility
- Moonstone for sleep aid

Laziness – Sometimes we form a lack of initiative, as a reaction of doing things we have to do but don't want to do.

"I am energized to take action to make things happen in my life."

Meditation – Repeat this mantra to yourself, visualize yourself taking action on things you have resisted, allowing the visualization to carry through to the results of having taken action.

Stones that help with laziness:
- Calcite for overcoming inactions
- Rainbow fluorite for focusing your energy

Obsession – Obsessive thought arrives from anxiety while compulsion is a repetitive behavior that helps relieve some anxiety.

"I embrace the uncertainty of life, and choose to live peacefully within it."

Meditation – A problem that arises from obsession, compulsion is when your brain gets stuck in a thought loop.

Stones that help with obsession:
- Ametrine for controlling thoughts and emotions
- Herkimer diamond to relieve stress
- Citrine for visualizing energy
- Amethyst for tranquility and peace of mind.

CHAPTER 2
Chakras

Chakras are seven energy sites in the body which help to regulate all of its systems, from immune function to the organ system and emotions. They are directly associated with the nine endocrine glands. Each chakra is specifically placed throughout your body, and every chakra has its own frequency of vibration, color, and governs processes that make you human. Crystals are directly associated with our Chakras and can be extremely beneficial to our health when used correctly.

Chakras have the ability to close, therefore allowing the inward and outward flow of energy. There are two major energy flows that contribute to your chakras ' balance. An upward flow from the magnetic field of the earth and a downward flow from a universal energy that incorporates all. It is said that these two currents balance the entire system.

Before you dive deep into the meaning of chakras you must understand one thing: You are energy. All living things are created by and compromised by energy. Optimally, the function of your energy centers keeps you psychologically, emotionally, physically and spiritually balanced inside.

Chakra Imbalance
How do you identify a Chakra blockage?
Understanding what your chakras are and what they're for should help make it easier for you to determine whether they're under attack.
There are specific ways to identify each chakra:

Blockages to the Root Chakra: When you are feeling stuck in a situation, a sense of sluggishness, persistent problems that plague different areas of your life (financial, job, long-term, relationships), a feeling of abandonment by family and friends; a feeling of just barely getting by in life with a foreseeable end, or a feeling of lack of control over your body, your fitness, and your health.

Blockages to the Sacral Chakra: When you are having difficulties expressing yourself sexually, fear of exploring your sexual facet, challenges tapping into your sensual side, moving from relationship to relationship, struggling to feel comfortable in your own body, and the inability to believe that others might feel attracted to you as you are.

Blockages to the Solar Plexus Chakra: When you have a feeling of powerlessness over your situation, giving others power over yourself in order to maintain peace in your relationships, difficulty acting on your aspirations and goals since you feel too weak to act on them, and difficulty expressing yourself in front of a crowd or audience.

Blockages to the Heart Chakra: When you are constantly pleasing others in order to attain a feeling of being loved, excessively guarding your heart to the point of refusing to let other people in, holding on to your feelings of anger and disappointment when others around you fail to meet your expectations of them, and challenges in giving too much compassion or too little.

Blockages to the Throat Chakra: When you have developed a fear of telling others what you think or feel, allowing other people and conforming to the majority in order to avoid bringing your uniqueness to light, and feelings of frustration because no one seems to understand how you feel or what you think.

Blockages to the Third Eye Chakra: When you have feelings of disconnectedness with your intuition or weakness, difficulty or inability of making decisions for yourself without sound evidence and information to guide you to the right choice, feelings of frustration at frequently making mistakes with decisions that involve the future.

Blockages to the Crown Chakra: When you have feelings of loneliness, insignificance, and meaninglessness, a strong attachment or affinity with material possessions, a lack of guidance from any higher being, and a general feeling of not being able to maximize the capabilities of your cognition.

A Chakra Imbalance Can Affect
How much power flows through the systems of the chakras.
When energy is blocked or closed, chakras are ineffective.
Chakras are overactive if the flow of energy is increased excessively and not properly regulated.

Chakra Balancing
The process to restore the harmonious energy flow through the chakra system. Whenever a chakra is blocked, underactive, or overactive, it can make you off balance. You see, your body wants a strong balance in your chakras. They may actually have negative effects on the person if they are underactive or overactive and may be counterproductive to the energy body and chakra healing process.

What to Expect When the Chakras Are Functioning Properly
Balance, Equilibrium.
Distinction between the different energy and frequency quality of each chakra.
Appropriate polarity and direction.

Chakra Cleansing
The whole blockage and/or negativity must be removed in order to restore the positive balance to the energy center involved. Energy healing is the most common method for balancing chakras, which can include:
Tai Chi
Conscious breathing exercises
Reiki
Chakra meditation
Yoga
Aromatherapy
Music
Positive affirmations

The Seven Chakras
Crown Chakra (Brahmarandra) – Pink for spirituality.
Located at the top of your head.
Representation: Associated with issues involving poor, shallow

relationships, difficulties exploring new experiences and places, repressed emotions, weak connection with spirituality, and the ego.

Third eye Chakra (Sahasrara) – Dark blue for awareness.
Located between your eyebrows.
<u>Representation</u>: Associated with issues involving sleep, mood, feelings of paranoia, depression, and anxiety. And relates to your intuition, imagination, and cognitive abilities.

Throat Chakra (Vishuddhi) – Light blue for communication.
Right in-between your collar bones.
<u>Representation</u>: Associated with issues involving the inability to express feelings and personal truth to oneself, and dealing with other people's deception.

Heart Chakra (Anahata) – Green for love and healing.
Located right over your heart.
<u>Representation</u>: Associated with issues involving relationships, emotions, peace, and threats to our emotions.

Solar Plexus Chakra (Manipuraka) – Yellow for wisdom and power.
Located from the center of your belly button to the center of your chest.
<u>Representation</u>: Associated with issues involving personal preconceptions, public relations, and self-value. As well as self-confidence, self-esteem, and self-worth.

Sacral Chakra (Swadhisthana) – Orange for sexuality and creativity.
Located right below the belly button.
<u>Representation</u>: Associated with issues involving the pleasure response, the feeling of abundance and well-being. As well as creativity and your ability to adapt.

Root Chakra (Muladhara) – Red for basic and trust.
Located at the very base of your spine.
<u>Representation</u>: Associated with issues involving survival such as the basic biological needs and financial concerns. As well as proving you with a foundation that should make you feel grounded.

Healing the Aura

The Aura is a multi-layered energy field covering the human body. It appears to form a shape around the physical body and project colors. Some people are said to be able to see the Aura, others cannot. Auras are believed to be caused by the vibrations that surround every material object. Light energy is drawn into this kind of egg that acts as a prism and transforms light into its elements of color.

Aura Layers – They are seven major aura layers with an interconnected relationship between the aura layers and the body's seven main chakras:

The Etheric layer – It is an indicator of a strong weakened physical health; it is primarily linked to the root/base chakra and is the auric layer that is most easily seen. It can also be seen around plants, trees, and animals. Good health is depicted by a uniform bright band of light surrounding and contouring the human body. Poor health is indicated by a bulge in the physical layer near the affected area. It looks a bit like lumps and bumps. Most hereditary disorders and old injuries can also be located in the physical layer

The Emotional body – This layer is beyond the etheric field and ranges from 1 to 3 inches. It acts as a storage of thoughts and feelings and our personal relationships. It is linked strongly to the sacral chakra and contains bright energy blobs and healthy colors. These primary colors are emitted in the same way that the emotions change in a 'mood' ring.

The Mental body – This layer is beyond the emotional body and extends away from the body. It shows a person's thoughts and attitudes and refers to mental activity. Not only does it radiate energy from the environment. This body connects to the plexus chakra of energy.

The Astral body – Lies beyond the mind. It is associated with our relationships with people around us and closely linked to the chakra of the heart. It's the connection between the spiritual world and the physical world. Information about past and present life is contained in this layer because it stores good and bad experiences and life lessons.

The Casual Body – Lies beyond the astral field. It displays a person's ability on the conscious or intellectual level. It is associated with the power of the self-expression and connected to the throat chakra.

The Celestial Body – It is linked to universal wisdom and the sense of awareness of the self of life. Also connected to the Third-eye chakra. It is the layer through which you can experience spiritual ecstasy and the ways of religious ceremony.

The Ketheric Body – Vibrates at the highest frequency and is most difficult to fully understand. This is where we experience divine wisdom and our oneness with the universe around us.

Aura Colors

The most common colors seen around people and their different meanings are listed below, depending on your health, mood and spiritual connection.

Maroon: daily vocation, ambition, life work.

Dark red: hate, anger, passion, violence.

Bright Red: life, passion, vitality, energy.

Orange: artistry, vitality, creativity, ambition.

Orange-red: energy, sexuality.

Yellow: happiness, optimism, purity.

Pink: pregnancy, unconditional love, love, femininity.

Green: intellect, jealousy, nature connection.

Dirty Green: illness, spite, envy, jealousy.

Blue: higher connection, spiritual feelings, teacher.

Purple: deep spiritual interests, ideals.

Grey: tiredness, illness, lack of spiritual connection.

Brown: Usually indicate lethargy and an indication of physical problems about to manifest.

Black: Extreme illness, addictions, close to death. It is often seen on those who are either victims of abuse or who are substance abusers.

Silver: angels, unconditional love, strong connection to a higher power, master qualities.

Gold: purity, connection to a higher power.

Energy Impurities in the Aura

Aura impurities are energy areas in the aura that are not required for the regular, healthy energy functioning of the field. They can be described as areas of unwanted stagnant energy build up in the aura, energies that block or inhibit the free tide of energy in the field of energy.

They are often found in and directly above the body's surface, in contact with the body, usually around the head, face, neck, shoulder, chest, and abdomen. The removal of these unhealthy energy sources also helps to treat and prevent physical illness.

Cleaning the Aura

The aura energy can be felt most easily in your hands and fingers. To feel the aura, run your hands vigorously for about one minute and hold your hands a little apart, palms facing each other. You will feel a heat pass between your hands. Take one hand and run it, palm down, along with the front of your body, without actually touching your body. You will feel a similar heat. This energy can be used for the physical body's protection. Surround yourself with a white light shower with a strong, golden shell.

CHAPTER 3
Negative Energy Cleansing

Why cleanse your house and body? There are basic principles governing how energy flows, we are all made up of energy and you as a human being are perfectly able to understand and work with it. Every day you come across opportunities to absorb bad energy. The more familiar you become with your NEA the more familiar you will become with conscious ways to release the energy. Negative Energy Absorption (NEA) is an actually serious condition that occurs with every human being on a daily basis. It is when a person absorbs either subconsciously or consciously, unhealthy and negative energy. It is heavily related to our own vibrational frequencies; you can catch a bad vibe very easily. While you intake negativity energy, you also intake positive and healthy energy. So the outcomes aren't all bad, there often is a balance. But when there isn't? What do you do?

How to detect negative energy. Without attention and constant care, things naturally move from order to disorder unless we put things way were they belong. You definitely don't have to be a master healer to notice if the energy around you is a little bit off. Simply take a second to really take in the vibe around you and decide how to go about your cleanse.

Removing negative energy from your body and home. Sometimes we say that we have to talk a break or go for a walk to clear our heads. If you've ever felt that way, you have recognized that your mental energy body was blocked and needed to be cleansed. Clearing your energy body is just like that. You consciously examine what is residing within you. Then you can decide what you want to keep and cultivate and what you want to release based on your free will. Our energy bodies could look like a hoarder's house, so full that it is hard to move around and be organized. This is why clearing takes a little more effort and time when you first begin to work.

How often should you cleanse? Negative energy cleansing is not something we do just once, it is an ongoing activity. A lot of people in this age are not educated in good energy maintenance, as we walk through our days we are bombarded with other people's energy in the form of thoughts or emotions.

In What Ways Can You Cleanse?

Sage has been considered a sacred plant for thousands of years. This multipurpose plant was used for cleansing, healing, ritual ceremonies, and even smoked. Today practitioners continue to use sage to help restore one's basic health. It is said to neutralize your energy field. Adding Frankincense, Palo Santo wood, or Copal incense works wonderfully to balance out the intensity of the sage. Aromatherapy has holistic benefits that can help heal or lift your spirits. Practicing Yoga helps you exercise your soul with mantras, movements, and breathing exercises. Establish meditation practice, it helps reset, rest, and recharge your mind, soul, and body. Prioritize self-help such as eating habits, exercise, healthy sleeping patterns, and doing things you genuinely enjoy. Explore holistic health because you can always dig deeper into remedies that just might speak to your soul or be exactly what you need. And last but not least believe in the unexplainable because sometimes trying to analyze things that don't have a direct answer can be unhealthy and especially tiring.

Movement-Based Techniques
Movement is a great and easy way to move energy around or get rid of lingering negative energy. Movement can be subtle and vigorous.

Mountain Pose – Yoga's mountain pose might seem like more of a non-movement activity. However, the act of assuming and holding the pose includes subtle but important movement. You stand with your intention. Make sure to keep your back straight, air flowing, and muscles tightened.

Walking – When done with intention, walking is a wonderful practice. With each step of your walk, you should feel the energy that you are focusing on the break-up and begin to move down to your feet. Walk until you feel clearer than before. While walking, try to maintain a strong, aligned posture because it is really good for removing intense and negative energy when done right. Pay attention to what your body is doing while you're walking. Our bodies are a great source of wisdom and can tell us a lot about our energy body. Bring attention to the areas and see if there is energy that needs work or cleansing.

Dancing – Dancing is a natural energy mover. There are various kinds of dancing, as well as reasons and venues where people go just to dance. Even going to a concert or party and getting your blood pumping can be apart of spiritual energy cleansing practice. Any kind of dancing can be apart of energy maintenance.

Setting your intention before dancing is something a lot of people like to do. Dancing is primal for us and we have to learn to trust our body. Sometimes these less consciously controlled methods are great choices, especially when you aren't really sure what is wrong or where it is wrong.

Yin Yoga – Westerners often engage in activities like tai chi and yoga for physical benefits. However, these practices are deeply rooted in energy work. In their entirety, they are clear, contain, and activate. When practiced mindfully, they are awesome for aura cleansing and energy health. Yin Yoga focuses on holding passive poses for long periods, generally from one to five for beginners. These long poses can physically tend beyond our larger, more visible anatomy and treat to the deeper anatomy. Yin Yoga is helpful for releasing because so many of the poses create free space for energy to flow in the body. The principle of this technique is, "as above, so below".

When we move our physical bodies, we move our energy. Stagnation is extremely prolonged and inappropriate stillness. Anxiety is intensely vibrating energy; your body can help maintain the appropriate vibration for you in almost any circumstance. Keep stagnant energy and anxiety out of your life and make sure to keep your energy clear and flowing by moving your body properly.

Sound – using sound is an easy way to move your energy around by raising vibration, creating space, and breaking up stagnant energy. While this technique is mostly used for physical spaces or while doing energy work for others, you can also use it on yourself. Remember, intention always matters. Traditional methods of using sounds to get rid of negative energy include rattles, drums, gongs, bells, singing bowls, and clapping. You can also use singing and chanting, but those are often found more of use for energy cultivation. Common sound techniques incorporate movement and follow with breathing out the activated energy and consciously breathing in a light vibration such as peace or grace.

Water-Based Techniques

Water is a refreshing and wonderful tool for cleansing and clearing. Water can be used in creative visualization as well, when actual water isn't handy or when you want to get deeper into it.

Washing – The easiest technique of all is to wash your hands or face with plain water, sometimes that isn't enough, so a bath or a shower is better. This refreshes the brain and senses.

Infusions – Adding essential oils to your bath is a common infusion water technique. Placing a crystal in some water and letting it sit for a couple of days can infuse the water with the qualities of the crystals and thereby assist with your clearing work. Salt is a great natural cleanser; you can add it into your water to boost its clearing abilities. You can also explore solar and lunar infusions. Simply put water in a container and leave it in the sunlight or moonlight for what you feel is the right amount of time.

Fire-Based Techniques

Fire can be the most clearing ally. You can incorporate fire in your energy-cleansing work through burning things such as candles, water, through visualizations. It is so powerful that it can actually be dangerous, so always be careful and sensible.

Burning – You can easily write down the energy you want to release on a small piece of paper. Using a set of tongs, hold the paper with the tongs and light it using a long-nosed lighter or a candle. You have to make sure it burns completely, you can then bury the ashes, keep them, or throw them away.

Candle Work – Another method of fire cleansing is to burn a small candle and then try putting all of the energy you want to be released into the candle. To do this you should hold the candle in your hands, center yourself and focus on cleansing negative energy. Once you have released your energy into the candle, you then burn it until it is gone.

Visual Meditation – Visual meditation with fire is a very powerful way to incorporate this tool into your cleansing repertoire. After getting comfortable in your meditative state, practice deep inhaling for a few counts and visualize the breaths as drawing the negative energy and then releasing it.

Air-Based Techniques

Breath Work – for cleansing with air, breathe work is incredible and highly recommended. No tools are required, and it can be done from practically anywhere we are focusing on clearing negative energy, the key is to empty yourself and create space. This means that while you want to take long, slow, deep inhales, the focus is on tor exhale and the release of energy.

Organization – This air technique is especially helpful for clearing the mental energy body and for those who feel overwhelmed by their work life. While it is normal for people to be "At work" all the time, we know it isn't healthy and does not increase productivity, even if it feels like it does. Before you shut down for your weekend, try clearing your emails, your desktop, and maybe even your actual desktop. Crazy, right? The benefits are amazing, you can leave with a clear mind and come back ready for your work week. You can also do things like keep your home more organized, your phone, maybe even keep up more so with things that relate to your health.

Maintain a healthy energetic life is always a work in progress. The nice thing is that once you establish a system and practice it consistently, it eventually becomes second nature, so you can move on to the next area without feeling overwhelmed. Organization and energy clearing work wonders in both the physical and energetic worlds.

Earth-Based Techniques
Crystals – The simplest and most common practice is to carry a

crystal around with you so you can touch it whenever you need grounding or earth healing energy.

Trees – Even though it has become somewhat of a joke over the years, hugging trees or leaning against them is such a powerful way to cleanse negative energy. A tree feels so powerful and wise. No matter how chaotic or reactive the energy, I know a tree can handle it. Likewise, even just going outside and touching the ground works if you don't have access to a tree.

Pets – Holding, stroking, or playing with a pet is very calming. Interact with a pet to settle energy, calm your nerves, or brighten your mood.

Napping – This practice may not seem like energy work, but it is among the most effective technique's known: take a nap. When the energy of the mental or emotional bodies are worked up, sometimes being conscious is counterproductive. Sleeping is an effective way to give the mind and emotions space to calm down.

Spiritual-Based Techniques

Spirit-based practices are ideal for contemplative types of people or those who like a more devotional experience with their energy work. Some of the most popular spirit-driven techniques include prayer and good works.

Prayer – or communication with the Divine–can be a simple and direct method of managing energy. For those that have already had prayer practice, this is a natural and easy method. For those who do not pray, it can become a simple, quiet, and beautiful experience if it suits your belief system. In prayer, we commune with the Divine, while meditation is a way to connect with our highest inner wisdom.

Good Works – While it may seem odd to combine spirit-based approaches with mundane physical-world actions, this is a powerful technique. If you know the nature of the energy you want to clear, determine an act that counters it. While most of the practices explained above are great for in-the-moment energy experiences, this one is particularly good for chipping away at long-standing, deep-seated energy within yourself. Sometimes energy takes up residence in us and shapes our behavior in ways that are not consistent with our values. While we would like a single ritual or one healing session to solve all of our issues, that generally doesn't work because those behaviors have become habits. Even if the energy has been released from the energy body through spiritual cleansing practices and healing work, the physical body has to catch up and that takes time for the body to release old habits. Consciously training yourself ends up being a process.

Other Ways to Remove Negative Energy from Home and Body:

- Sweep and clean a lot to get rid of dust, which over time collects energy.
- Essential oils
- Workout to release toxins from the pours
- Sea salt cleanse
- Hanging out with friends

Essential Oils

Essential oils are amazing when used to relax the body and mind. They have been scientifically shown to enter the bloodstream via the lungs and absorb directly into the brain.

Energizing Oils:
- Eucalyptus, Peppermint, Grapefruit, Basil, Wild Orange, Rosemary.

Uplifting oils:
- Peppermint, Bergamot, Geranium, Melissa, Lemon, Wild Orange

Relaxing oils:
- Lavender, Ylang Ylang, Roman Chamomile, Lemon, Geranium.

Sedative oils:
- Lavender, Veviter, Ylang Ylang, Melissa, Geranium, Frankincense.

CHAPTER 4
Incorporating Crystals And Their Knowledge Into Your Daily Life

Harness the positive vibration from healing crystals:

When used properly and with deep respect, crystals can assist you to live an additionally lively and aligned life. Although they are also exceptionally powerful, they are attractive to look at and have a very special significance behind them. You can find crystals practically anywhere these days but I highly encourage visiting a small, local shop. Ask questions about the crystals to make sure they are genuine, they absorb the energy from your extraction to your hands throughout the process, so it matters.

How long does crystal healing take?
Depending on the patient and their states, crystal healing works differently. While it is advisable for other people to undergo crystal healing on a weekly basis to see pain and pressure relief, some people only have to undergo one session.

What crystals can heal
In truth, crystals don't cause direct healing. They won't cure you directly of a disease. Rather, they vibrate with energy your body occupies and then absorbs, and it is you who does the healing by drawing in that energy and communicating with the crystal. Crystals can assist with healing a lot of things, here are some examples:

Body – Your body is your physical side. Crystal can help balance body energy and make physical improvements. These could include things such as relieving low energy and exhaustion, headaches and similar physical problems.

Mind – Your mind is physical as well as immaterial. The vibration in the crystals can help balance the mind's energies to heal. Conditions that can be alleviated include stress, emotional problems, sleeplessness, nightmares, anxiety, depression, grief and lack of enthusiasm.

Spirit – your spirit is the part of you that is completely nonphysical. Crystals assist in balancing spiritual energies such as beliefs, forgiveness, compassion, and unconditional love. They can also facilitate communication with your higher self or higher power.

How to incorporate them into your everyday life
Not all crystal routines are designed for everyone, there are countless ways to work with these fascinating stones, which is why it is important to find out what works best for you. Here are a few ways.

Hold a crystal during meditation
They can give you the energy to guide you in different ways through your meditation.

Create a crystal grid
A specialized pattern of stones used by healers to combine the powers of crystals and their intellectual capacity to strengthen them. You can set your crystals on a grid and symmetrically arrange them. Choose stones that complement your intentions and then the crystals work.

Grid shapes:
Spiral – represents the path to consciousness.
Circles – representation of oneness and unity.
Squares – represent earthly elements.
Triangles – represent the connection between mind body and spirit.

Before you create a crystal grid, you need to contemplate what your intentions for making the grid are. You can either state your intention out loud while creating your grid or alternatively write it down on a piece of paper so you are focused. The intention could be anything you hope for or dream of, such as health, love, fertility, clarity, or focus.

What crystal to use? The first crystal you need to choose is the center stone, also called the master crystal. This crystal is the one that will communicate between the other crystals in the grin. It needs to hold a lot of energy, and some people prefer to use a cluster or pyramid crystals for this placement. The next crystal to choose will be what is called the "activation wand" this will be the crystal to focus your intention on. It is helpful for this crystal to be the same type of crystal as one of the others on the grid. If you want to do long distance healing, either for someone else or a place, you can write the name on a piece of paper and place it on the grid beneath the master crystal.

The rest of the crystals you choose to use will depend on the intention you are focusing on. For example, if your intention is love and romance, use the crystals that match these emotions and thoughts. Alternatively, you can use a pendulum to help you choose the right crystals or simply listen to your own intuition and pick those you feel you should choose. Some people prefer to place clear quartz on the outer points of the grid for the amplification of energy.

Where do you put your grid?
You want to place your grid in an area of your home where it won't be bothered. This could be a quiet corner of a room, or if you have a meditation setup or a sacred place in your home, these are all good places for your grid. Some even believe that placing your grid on the northern side of the room makes the energy stronger, but this is not necessary.

How do you activate the grid?
Once your grid is set up with crystals of your choice, it is time to activate the grid. Here is a guide on how to do this:

1.) Meditate or relax for 5 minutes so you can have reground yourself.
2.) Take hold of the wand, then start your intention or positive affirmation, remembering to focus strongly on what you want the outcome to be.
3.) Now take a moment to accept that your intention is true, called 'programming.'
4.) Wait for a few minutes, then put down your wand and the grid will be activated.

What to do next?
Make sure you take some time each week to sit in front of your grid and simply relax or even better meditate, still focusing on your original intention. You can leave your grid the way it is for weeks at a time, but if you feel like it is losing its strength, you can always recharge it. Simply perform a new activation to recharge the crystals and their energy.

Using crystals for stress.
When your body is experiencing high levels of stress, its natural defenses are weakened, making you more vulnerable to developing physical, mental, and emotional illnesses. Thus stress reduction plays an important role in preserving your wellness and prolonging your life.

Stress reliever crystal pattern for the chakras:
You know where the chakras are located now, so it should be easy for you to follow this method.
What you will need:
- 4 Clear Quartz
- 3 Amethyst
- 2 Black Onyx
- 1 Rose Quartz
- assume a comfortable lying position
- First, lay one Amethyst on your Third Eye Chakra. One Amethyst should be on your right-hand palm while the other should be on your left-hand palm. Its purpose is to ground and calm you. Furthermore, the positioning of these stones is essential to let the energy guide through you.
- Next place one onyx on the sole of your right foot, and another on the sole of your left. The purpose of this is to take away and release the negative energies from your body that are responsible for causing stress.
- Place the Rose Quartz on your abdomen. You need to do this to maintain a balance between the female and male energies that all of us possess. Also, place one of the clear Quartz on your abdomen just above the Rose Quartz.

- The second Quartz should be laid above your head. Place the third beside your arm on the right side. The purpose of these clear Quartz crystals is for aura detoxification and chakra cleansing.
- When you're done, you would've successfully created dual triangle energy zones with the positioning of stones.
- Relax your muscles. Close your eyes. Concentrate on your breathing.
- Remain in a meditative state for at least 10 minutes or as long as you need.
- When you are done, you can use the crystals as worry stones. Carry them with you and whenever you feel familiar symptoms of anxiety creeping up, just massage the stones to draw strength from them.

Wear a protection stone.
Crystal amulets have been used and worn for over 30,000 years. More than just accessories or bodily embellishments, amulets serve the purpose of protection, keeping its wearer safe from a variety of dangers depending on the properties of the stone used for the amulet. Back in ancient times, amulets were used as protection against witchcraft, magic spells, and other metaphysical dangers that could be used and enacted by powerful mystics. These days, however, amulets are used for more passive forms of risk, which may be present in a variety of situations. Wearing a protective amulet can keep the wearer safe against situations like these.

When you feel weak against the negative energy, find a quiet space, hold your stone and realign your focus by repeating the intention to yourself. This recharges the energy of the stone and strengthens your defense against negative vibes. The more you have contact with a crystal, the more mindful you are of its energy and healing abilities. The crystal can also be used as a reminder, of any intentions, plans, etc.

Creating a protection shield.
A protection shield can be made from anywhere and works to neutralize negative energy in a space. They work like grids, the only

difference is that they use protective stones and work off of a protective intention.

The best crystals for protection are Black Tourmaline, Black Kyanite, Black Onyx, and Pyrite because they are all known for their potent absorbing capabilities relating to their color. They are able to detect negative energy and store it away in their expansive programmable memories. These stones are also known to create protective barriers around a space, perfect for deflecting negative energies.

Placing the crystals on your body.
The placing of crystals on your body has a completely different effect than just holding them. Crystals correspond with chakras so you should keep that in mind when placing them on your body. This helps to stimulate the energy around every chakra and raises the emotions you need to heal.

Sleeping with crystals underneath your pillow.
This is highly advised if you are suffering from insomnia or night terrors. Keeping crystals underneath your pillow will enable you to feel more revitalized upon waking up. To ward of bad dreams, use hematite, ruby, or Smoky Quartz.

Place Aventurine over your heart to open the heart chakra for love. Smoky quartz to give your root chakra some grounding energy and place Quartz above your head to enlighten and guide your crown chakra.

Why do Crystals Work?
Because of the structure of a crystal, they are able to absorb, focus, and transmit subtle electromagnetic energy. This is the energy used in healing/gem therapy. Clear quartz is proven to of been on this earth since the beginning of time, ancient civilizations have used crystals as protecting talismans, peace offerings, and quite often jewelry. Quarts makes up 12 percent of the earth 's crust and is used in almost all technology. Involves timekeeping, electronics, storage of information and more. If it is possible for crystals to communicate through computer chips, then isn't it possible that this vibrational energy could be transformed in other ways? And with their connection to the earth and its life-giving elements. It

makes sense that crystals are universally healing, especially since they've made their mark in almost every civilization before us.

One of the first pieces of scientific evidence relating to the power of crystals is the work done by IBM scientist Marcel Vogel. While watching crystals grow under a microscope, he noticed that their shape took the form of whatever he thought. He assumed that these vibrations resulted from the constant assembly and disassembly of bonds between molecules. He also often tested the metaphysical power of quartz crystal and demonstrated that rocks can store ideas similar to how tapes use magnetic energy to track sound.

At every moment, we have the ability to choose our thoughts as we continue our journey, each day presents us with new challenges and wonderful beginnings. Healing crystals remind us to quiet the chatter of the mind and reconnect to the universally healing vibrations of the earth. You must be patient with crystals because just like all eons of time it took for these semi-precious stones to evolve and transform, working with the healing powers of crystals also takes time. As you deepen your knowledge and evolve, use crystals as a reminder to be grateful for the abundance of Mother Nature and the great mysteries of the universe.

Maintenance of Your Crystals

When you first get a crystal, no matter where it came from, it is always a good idea to cleanse it before use. Crystals are great at absorbing energy, which is the property used to protect you from negative influences. They can get full though, and when that happens, they must be cleansed in order to work at their maximum potential.

Cleansing the crystal
Leave it buried in sea salt overnight, on a clear and empty tabletop. The salt will absorb the impurities locked within the crystal, leaving it fresh and ready to protect you from negative energy.

Recharging the crystal
You have a few ways to go about recharging your crystal.

Direct sun or moonlight – Your first option is to leave the crystal in direct sun or moonlight, this will recharge the stones and bring them back to their original configuration.

Burying – you can also bury the stone in the ground to let it reclaim the healing powers of the earth. You can also submerge the crystals in dry brown rice or sand, they are both absorbent. It should only take a day or two to recharge crystals this way.

Meditate – You may also meditate with the crystal, directing your thoughts, needs, and desires into it with deep, forceful breaths.

Clear Quartz – One of the crystals functions is to cleanse other crystals, which gives it a unique position in your set. A clean clear quartz can be used to recharge other crystals in your arsenal as they vibrate purifying energy that neutralizes negative energy in surrounding stones.

Programming Your Crystal

To become more in-tune with your crystals energy emissions, you should spend some time getting to know them. You can program your crystals by telling them visualizations while talking to them. Many healers program their crystals to person-specific healing functions for their practices. You must ensure that your jewel is in harmony with your programming purpose.

Any type of crystal programming is a way to sort a stone's energy design. The programmed energy pattern in the jewel can be an idea, intention, sound, color, emotion, or other oscillations. These vibrations are often used to redirect the energy of your main motive. Here are the top tips that you should not miss if you need to program your crystals:

Clear your crystals – You must make them lucid, whatever kind of crystals and approaches you prefer. Sit at your altar, which is designed for you, while holding your crystals. Make sure the programming of your crystal is done with no interferences.

Hold your crystals firmly – Use your right hand to hold your crystals and to clear your unrelated ideas. Start focusing on your goal of successful crystal programming.

Focus your intention – You must concentrate on your objective while programming. This can be done by saying loud and clear illustrative words. For example, if you choose to program your crystals for good health, repeat the phrase " good health" over and over again.

Repeat your purpose verbally – Make sure you hold your crystals and repeat your goal. Never leave your crystals for programming. You should also stretch your hand over the crystals to produce more energy.

Keep holding your crystals – Repeat the steps for a few times as much as you can. Open your hand slowly when your instinct tells you that the crystals have absorbed the energies, then thank you for your crystals.

Following these procedures, your crystals are fully programmed. This process can also be used with words, tumbled rocks, polished crystals, natural crystals, and minerals.

How to Tell Apart Real and Fake

There are countless crystal shops out there that are genuinely interested in providing you with good quality crystals and there are just as many unscrupulous sellers who simply live and build on the rebirth of crystal healing. Here are some ways you can tell real crystals apart from fakes:

- **Bubbles** – Crystals are formed through a variety of processes in the presence of a number of different elements and conditions. In all cases, crystals are formed entirely solid – with no room for air to form bubbles. If you inspect your crystal up close and find bubbles it is most likely not made out of naturally occurring elements.

- **Unnatural Rich colors** – Fraudulent sellers will often exaggerate colors to make them more appealing to the eye. Remember, natural crystals are formed in the earth, typically with a range of tinged earthy tones that might dampen their otherwise vibrant colors. Crystals that are too richly hued, and seem to not have any trace of earth on their surface, is likely to be a hoax.

- **_Magnification_** – in this case of clear crystals such as quartz, you can easily check for magnification. As a general rule, crystals shouldn't' magnify any objects in their background. Therefore, if you place a questionable stone on the page of a book and the works are enlarged when you look through the crystal, its likely made of glass.

- **_Perfect Surfaces_** – while crystals can be chiseled and shaped to make them look more aesthetically pleasing, there is no such thing as a perfect crystal, as objects born raw from the earth, even with all the buffing and shaping wouldn't be able to clear away layers of impurities. Most crystals will have traces of earth, cracks, and discoloration throughout its surfaces.

The color of a crystal can actually affect how attractive it is to you, but the color also plays a role in the energetic and healing impacts of crystals. The color of the crystal comes from three things:

- How the crystal absorbs light?
- The specific minerals/chemicals the crystal contains
- Any impurities within the crystal

The Six Crystal Lattice Patterns

Hexagonal – crystals have an interior structure that resembles a 3-D hexagon. Hexagonal crystals help with manifestation.

Isometric – crystals have an interior cubic structure. These crystals can improve situations and amplify energies.

Monoclinic – these crystals have a 3-D parallelogram structure. They are protective crystals.

Orthorhombic – these crystals have a diamond-shaped crystalline pattern. They cleanse, clear, and remove blockages.

Tetragonal – these crystals have a rectangular interior structure. These crystals are attractors; they make things more attractive and they help attract things to you.

Triclinic – these crystals have an interior structure with three inclines axes. These crystals ward off unwanted energies and help retain energies you'd like to keep

The minerals and impurities impact which light wavelengths the crystal will absorb and the color that appears as a result. For example, if a crystal absorbs all of the light wavelengths, it appears black. If it doesn't absorb any light wavelengths, it appears clear. Different impurities and chemicals/minerals affect light differently.

Crystals, Gems, Minerals, or Rocks?

It may seem as though people use the terms crystal, gem, mineral, and rock interchangeably, which is common when discussing crystals. In fact, some substances that aren't crystals, such as amber (petrified tree sap), are also referred to as crystals or stones. However, here's a quick overview:

Crystal – a mineral that has a crystalline interior structure. Agate, which is a hexagonal crystal, is also a mineral and rock.

Gem – a cut and polished crystal, mineral, or rock, a cut diamond (which is mineral, crystal, and rock) is also a gem or gemstone. Amber and pearls are organic substances that are considered gemstones, but they are not crystals, minerals, or rocks.

Mineral – A naturally occurring substance with a particular chemical composition and a highly ordered structure, crystalline or not. Opal is a mineral that does not have a crystalline structure; it's a gemstone and a rock but not a true crystal.

Rock – a combination, or aggregate, of minerals. Marble, which is made up of multiple minerals, is a metamorphic rock –a rock that has been subjected to heat and pressure over time.

Crystal Shapes

Obelisks – There are four-sided pillars forming in a pyramid shape. Symbolically, an obelisk can release tension through its tip and send it into the dissipated atmosphere. It can also draw energy from the higher atmosphere and base this energy.

Pyramids – Can be used to concentrate and base energy. They can also absorb negative energy and help all of the chakras. A gemstone pyramid is also used to enhance and concentrate the inherent properties of the stone.

Spheres / Crystal Balls – symbolize the cyclical nature of life. Circles symbolize infinity because they have no beginning and no end. Spheres/balls are usually used for healing and rituals.

Tumbled Stones – It has no rough edges and is convenient for healing or grid work. In addition, they are convenient to carry.

Crystal Clusters – Brings harmony. Clusters like Quartz crystal clusters were used to meditate, heal and expand the mind to touch the spiritual world.

Different Types of Minerals

Igneous – It is formed by magma or lava cooling and solidification.

Sedimentary – formed through the accumulation of sediments of other rocks, usually in seas and oceans or in the Grand Canyon.

Metamorphic – formed when rocks were forced to change their shape and composition due to exposure to tremendous heat or pressure.

What is the different between a crystal and a mineral?

Have you ever wondered what the real difference between crystals and minerals is? Many people say that they are the same. If you think the same way, you are wrong. There are important differences between the two and you can distinguish them from person to person.

Minerals are regarded as one of the world's most important natural resources. They are found in solid chemicals and often formed through many geological processes. Most of them have a very diverse make-up compound. They are highly ordered atomic formations with explicit physical properties.

The composition of minerals varies from simple salts to complex silicates. Minerals are used differently, most of which are either grown or owned. Crystals, on the other hand, consist of ions, molecules, and atoms that are arranged in a repeated outline that recognizes all three spatial dimensions. The mineral composition varies between simple salts and complex silicates. Minerals are used differently, most of them either cultivated or owned. On the other hand, crystals consist of ions, molecules, and atoms that are arranged in a repeated outline that recognizes all three dimensions of space.

Minerals Vs. Crystals
Minerals and crystals are not only different in the manner in which they are utilized. They also differ in terms of creation. Simply put, crystals consist of several natural materials. Crystals are classified as cubic, monoclinic, orthorhombic, hexagonal and tetragonal forms. They are also used in various relaxation processes and are believed to have healing properties.

Crystals are not dark in color and have translucent features. Some of these reflect light in a variety of colors. Based on the structure and the rare characteristics of the crystals, some are cheap while others are not. In addition, minerals are divided into two groups, silicates, and non-silicates. Silicate minerals are materials which have a basic silicate mineral unit.

On the flip side, the non-silicates are divided into several categories, such as Elements, Hydroxides, Carbonates, and Sulphides. Non-silicate minerals are quite rare than many of the other type's.

What is the best crystal?
Since many types of healing crystals are present, you must choose the right one. Not all crystals are created evenly. If you want these crystals, please consult first the experts. Some healers say that some crystals have extraordinary effects on the digestive system, although some are necessary for the reproductive system to be restored.

Whatever kind of problem you may have; a similar healing crystal suits your condition. Do not forget to consider the information provided above in the event you do not know. You can also ask some friends what you need and treat your condition instantly.

Do's and Don'ts with Crystals

Do not wear crystals immediately after purchase. Make sure you follow their programming approach, which will clean them up. Cleanse may vary from running water to being soaked overnight. Always ask the seller before wearing crystals for the best way to eliminate depression and energy.

Don't be distressed if your stones fall, crack, break or get lost. Most crystal healers believe their work is done after it has been bought.

Do get your crystals into power. You can do this by asking a healer or an astrologer for help. This can help crystals or gemstones to function on their own for the user.

Always trust the feeling in your gut about crystals. If you think your favorite stones are working efficiently and ideal, get them. Leave them if you feel uncertain about them.

CHAPTER 5
Starting A Crystal Collection

Choosing a Crystal for Yourself
Make sure you are well educated on each of the crystals you collect. The best way to choose a crystal is to feel its energy. Trust your intuition and your sense of what feels right to you. Let yourself be guided to the crystal, so let it choose you.

There is a wide range of experiences that crystal shoppers report when choosing a crystal. Often, I personally feel a good vibe and a slight tingling sensation.
- Heat emitting from stone
- A dash of light from the crystal
- Cold energy
- Lightheaded sensation
- Ringing Ears
- Sudden rush of excitement

You should also take note of crystals that you feel you dislike. More often then not they represent qualities or issues you need to deal with.

Choose By Crystal System
Each crystal is part of a different crystal system with specific properties. The crystal systems include:

Hexagonal crystals, which manifest

Isometric crystals, which improve situations and amplify energies

Monoclinic crystals, which protect and safeguard

Orthorhombic crystals, which cleanse, clear, unblock, and release

Tetragonal crystals, which contain or ward off energies

Amorphous "crystals," which have differing properties.

Choosing By Color
The importance of color extends far beyond personal preference. Each color has its own vibrational energies with associated healing properties. By choosing a crystal of the crystal system that has the properties you'd like it to display along with the healing principles of the color, you can select crystals quite specifically for certain conditions.

Choose By How They Make You Feel
When you choose a crystal, you should hold it in your hand and see how it makes you feel. Note whether or not they make you feel comfortable or uncomfortable if they feel heavy or light, and if you feel other sensations. You should feel a pleasant feeling.

Pairing Crystals
Like wine and cheese, some crystals pair well to make them better than the sum of their parts. Crystals that pair well have complementary energies that can really help focus energy. For example, the energy of any crystal is amplified when paired with clear quartz. Here are some other pairings that work well:

Smoky Quartz and Apache Tears – a powerful combination for people who are grieving.
Amethyst and Labradorite – can help you get a more restful nights' sleep.
Citrine and Black Tourmaline – can help ground you in prosperity.
Rose Quartz and Ruby or Garnet – excellent for pairing relationships
Black Tourmaline and Clear Quartz – help facilitate the free flow of balanced energy.

Choose By Using a Dowsing Rod
considered to be a more advanced process, but beginners can effectively learn how to use one in order to discover the best stones for their initial practice. Keep in mind though that pendulum dowsing might require a higher level of intuition.

As one of the oldest forms of divination, pendulum dowsing allows us to discover the energy of crystals, guiding us towards the one that is most attuned to our spirit. Of course in the process of finding a pendulum, it is important that you find the right one for you to help guarantee a seamless and effective experience.

To choose a pendulum, observe a selection of them. Your spirit will know what is best for you and will gravitate you towards the right one without you having to exert any cognitive effort. Once you have a pendulum, you can start using it to choose crystals, ask it questions, or it can assist you in making decisions that result in a yes or no answer.

Steps in using a pendulum dowser for crystal selection:
Clear your mind – Before starting any of kind of process with crystals, it's important that your mind is clear from possible distractions. Take a few minutes to focus on your breathing and set your mind to the goal of the dowsing experience.

Practice Your Pendulum
Different pendulums vibrate with different intensity and quality. So what feels like a 'yes' with one pendulum, might feel completely different with another. To attune to your specific pendulum, hold it in your hand and close your eyes. Ask it a question to which you know the answer will be yes. Once you've felt the vibrations of a yes answer, ask it a question whose answer would be no. you should be able to sense a change in the vibration of your pendulum. In doing this, you develop a deeper sense of your pendulum, thus allowing you to better understand where it wants to guide you.

Choose your crystals – When using a pendulum dowser to select crystals, simply hold the pendulum over the crystal, or over an image of the crystal if you're buying it online, and ask it a question referring to the crystal. Try not to make suggestions in your mind to influence the answer of the pendulum as this could interfere with its true recommending. Try to maintain an open mind.

Where to Shop
There are many sources where you can purchase stones –both in brick-and-mortar stores and online. Many towns and cities have retail crystal outlets. These may be listed as metaphysical bookshops, crystal stores, or New Age shops. With knowledgeable

staff, most will let you handle the crystals before you purchase. You can also find traveling mineral or gem shows are a great place to purchase crystals and can't be beaten for selection or price. Although these usually need to be planned for in advance. You can even buy crystals online when making a purchase ensure that you're working with a reliable seller. You may want to use your pendulum when ordering crystals online.

Crystal Starter Kit

Clear Quartz – if you don't know which crystal to use, start with clear quartz; it works with every type of energy.

Smoky Quartz – is the crystals a lot of people use because it's a manifestation stone that converts negative energy into positive.

Citrine – promotes self-esteem and prosperity

Rose Quartz – supports all types of love, including unconditional and romantic love.

Amethyst – helps you tune into intuition and guidance from higher realms, as well as the power of your dreams

Black Tourmaline – is a grounding stone that is protective and that keeps negativity at bay.

Rainbow Fluorite – deepens intuition, promotes love, and facilitates clear communication.

Carnelian – helps you set appropriate boundaries, have integrity, and be creative.

Hematite – is protective, grounding, and centering and can also attract energies you'd like into your life.

Turquoise – promotes good luck, prosperity, and personal power.

Sacred Geometry of Cut Stones

You can find crystals cut into many different shapes, including spheres and polyhedrons, which have varying properties. Working with stones cut into these shapes will impart the properties of both the crystal and the sacred shape.

Dodecahedron – the dodecahedron is associated with the element of the Ethereal realm and connects you to intuition and higher realms.

Hexahedron – the hexahedron, or cube, represents the element of earth. It is grounding and stable.

Icosahedron – the icosahedron is linked to the element of water. It connects you to change and flow.

Merkaba – the Merkaba is a 3-D star. It contains all five of the above polyhedrons within it and therefore combines all the effects of each. It is also associated with the energy of sacred truth and eternal wisdom.

Octahedron – the octahedron represents the element of Air and promotes compassion, kindness, forgiveness, and love.

Sphere – the sphere has the energy of completeness, wholeness, and oneness.

Tetrahedron – associated with the element of fire, a tetrahedron promotes balance, stability, and the ability to create change.

Other Names for Crystals

In recent years, some retailers have given brand names to crystals and have in some cases marked them. The reason they are typically branded is usually because it originates from a particular area on property owned by the people who brand it, but the location does not greatly affect the properties of the crystal.

- Amazon Jade is Amazonite.
- Aqua Terra Jasper is either resin or onyx.
- Atlantis Stone is Larimar.
- Azeztulite is and has the same properties as clear quartz.
- Boji stones can also be found non-branded as Kansas pop rocks.
- Healerite is generically found as Chrysolite.
- Isis Calcite is the branded form of white calcite.

- Lemurian Light Crystals are a branded form of Lemurian quartz.
- Mani Stone is black-and-white jasper.
- Master Shamanite is the same as black calcite.
- Merkabite Calcite is white Calcite
- Revelation Stone is brown or red jasper.
- Sauralite Azeztuline is quartz from New Zealand.
- Zultanite is the mineral diaspore.
- Agape Crystals are a combination of seven different crystals: clear quartz, smoky quartz, rusticated quarts, amethyst, goethite, lepidocrocite, and cacoxenite.

Crystal Safety
In general, working with crystals is relatively safe. However, some crystals contain substances (such as aluminum, copper, sulfur, fluorine, strontium, or asbestos) that are toxic to humans, so do not put them in the bathtub or make a crystal elixir with them. It's also best to wash your hands when you've finished holding them. These crystals include:
- Aquamarine (contains aluminum)
- Black Tourmaline (contains aluminum)
- Celestite (contains strontium)
- Cinnabar (contains mercury)
- Dioptase (contains copper)
- Emerald (contains aluminum)
- Fluorite (contains fluorine)
- Garnet (contains aluminum)
- Iolite (contains aluminum)
- Jade (contains asbestos)

- Kansas pop rocks (contains aluminum)
- Labradorite (contains aluminum)
- Lapis lazuli (contains pyrite, which contains sulfur)
- Malachite (contains copper)
- Moldavite (contains aluminum)
- Moonstone (contains aluminum)
- Prehnite (contains aluminum)
- Ruby (contains aluminum)
- Sapphire (contains aluminum)
- Sodalite (contains aluminum)
- Spinel (contains aluminum)
- Sugilite (contains aluminum)
- Sulfur (contains poisonous)
- Tanzanite (contains aluminum)
- Tigers eye, unpolished (contains asbestos)
- Topaz (contains aluminum)
- Tourmaline (contains aluminum)
- Turquoise (contains aluminum)
- Zircon (contains zirconium)

CHAPTER 6
Different Types Of Energy Healing

Energy Healing

Everything starts with energy. "If you want to find the secrets of the universe, think about energy, frequency, and vibration," says physicist Nikola Tesla. Energy is the one thing which can be changed but never destroyed. Energy is where the secrets of healing of crystals lie.

Indigenous cultures have had a positive influence on the health of the body for thousands of years by working with its energy fields, otherwise known as Chakras. Reiki is a Japanese tradition from the beginning of the 20th century, chakras are vividly described in ancient Hindu texts, and traditional Chinese practitioners studied meridians. Many people around the world even talk about how medical practices use the techniques related to crystals. Although almost every culture had a different idea of stimulating the ability of the body to heal itself, a positive force of good was how everyone viewed internal energy.

How it Works
Energy healing flows directly into the wavelength with the spiritual, emotional, and physical characteristics of our beings. It dispatches upsets in your flow of energy. The body stays balanced and healthy when the energy fields and flow are vibrant and equal.

Energy healing is actually based on scientific principles
As you may know, everything is constantly vibrating, always. We, humans, vibrate too. When somebody is referring to a "good vibe" they are really talking about the personal vibrational energy, the one that each and every one of us emits. Even places have vibrational frequencies. Have you ever walked into a new room and felt the energy change?

You don't have to be spiritual to benefit from energy healing
Just like you don't have to know somebody to feel like you know them. You don't need to know everything about healing energy

before you start, all you need is an open mind for the maximum benefit.

You can maintain your energetic health at home
Once you have visited an energy healer or performed an energy healing process, it is important that you keep the positive energy streaming by meditating, burning sage, taking a bath, or choosing essential oils. Even having your own crystals is always a good way to keep the good vibrations flowing.

It is always a great time to pull the crystals out or to visit an energy healer. Even if you feel anxious or drained by the day, a session will aid you to feel more balanced and relax.

Energy healing is very accessible
Healers of energy come in numerous types. They are all over the world and there are usually some in your city.

Reiki – Uses the chi energy to strengthen and help people use specific symbols and hand techniques to heal their bodies by channeling the universe's energy. Master teachers who train you for long periods of time can only teach you. Practitioners actually settle throughout the world, one fascinating thing about Reiki healing is that you don't have to be in the same place as the practitioner since the power of intention does not cause energy to flow where it is needed the most.

Acupuncture – By the insertion of needles through the skin at certain high energy points in the body, it stimulates your body's energy flow. The meridians are targeted to bring back equilibrium. It is often done to reduce chronic back pain, neck pain, and knees. Although customers also need to be in the physical presence of the needles, practitioners are very accessible. This kind of treatment stimulates the flow of the chi to equilibrate the body.

Even **Massage** is an energy healing, releasing built up tension in the muscles, encouraging the flow of deep relaxation.

More Energy Healing Techniques Are
Crystal Medicine
The use of crystals and stones to remove contaminants in the body.

These stones have specific properties that aim at various types of problems with spiritual, physical, and emotional energy. Aligning stones on the body's chakra points are what most crystal healers do, keeping in mind the symptoms reported by the person being treated.

Quantum Healing
A natural healing method combined with the body's life energy to promote optimum well-being. Quantum mechanics science is where Quantum healing is based on. It delves into how frequencies and quantum affects the body and teaches us how to control, amplify, focus, and project this energy, which emerges in a wide range of advantages with extraordinary results.

Elixirs
Elixirs are liquids, usually water, which is combined with properties of a crystal and used to allow you to drink the properties associated with the crystal It is a quick, easy method to receive a healing. You can easily make your own elixir at home.

Qigong
Qigong comes from the word "qi" meaning, "living force" or "energy," and gong means "work" or effort." Qigong cultivates and practices the breathing and meditation techniques of vital life force. Medical Qigong has two types: self-healing Qigong, in which you use Qigong exercises to prevent diseases, improve your health and treat disease, while external Qigong or qi emissions emit qi in order to cure others.

Spiritual Healing
This type of healing is a mixture of physical, medical, and non-medical, energetic interventions and mental interventions. When we are transforming the cause of illness/disease and learn to grow beyond the problem, we are then focused on healing ourselves.

In spiritual healing, we create a medicine story for ourselves that includes both a curing process and a healing destination. When embarking on a spiritual healing journey, you are to address physical, emotional, mental, and spiritual toxins. Healing the soul takes combines healing interventions for the heart, body, and mind.

Spiritual Healing Techniques

- *Exercise.* Find an exercise you enjoy and can integrate into your daily life.

- *Eat healthily.* Eat more vegetable! Learn about your diet and eat more local organics.

- *Care for your body.* Pay attention to your body, do things that help you relax or go visit a healer.

- *Sleep.* Make sure you are getting the appropriate amount of sleep. Try to hit the hay earlier, sleep deprivation can cause serious imbalances in the human body. Mentally and physically.

What kind of change can you expect?
When we do energy work, the energy always seeks to align with our highest and greatest good. Sometimes the change you think you need isn't what best serves you. Remove any expectation of the outcome and allow what serves you to arise. When we set expectations and stick to them, we limit results, because what we imagine is usually smaller than what the universe provides. And sometimes what serves our greatest good doesn't appear as we think it should. As much as you can, remove "should" and "could" from your vocabulary and accept what the energy brings.

CHAPTER 7
Types Of Healing Crystals

These are just among some of the most known and powerful healing crystals we have around today. These stones are used for a very large variety of things such as energy healing, meditation, technology, and mainly jewelry. Most people don't have time every day to engage in cleansing with crystals, therefore they wear them around their neck based upon their qualities and healing benefits.

Types of Gemstones
Precious – hard and often made into jewelry. They have a high value because they are of their scarcity, hardness, transparency, color, and brilliance.
Ex: Emerald, Pearl Sapphire.

Semi-Precious – made from a portion of mineral, more common and usually less expensive. These stones are mainly used for making jewelry.
Ex: Agate, Aventurine, Tourmaline.

Ornamental – usually extremely hard to find but not rare. They are used for ornamental value, meaning used in statues, decorations, and personal items.
Ex: Quartz, Lapis lazuli, Jade.

Charoite
The Lilac Stone

- Is always a dark shade of purple, but you will find traces of white, grey, and black on the stone, making it one of the most attractive crystals in the world.
- First discovered in Russia, along the Chara River in the 1940s.
- Excellent for making goblets, vases, or bookends.

Metaphysical Healing Properties:

- This stone can heal the body, the heart, and the spirit. It helps to remove the negativity from your life and protects you against the negative.
- Give you the emotional support you need to consolidate, reflect and re-strategize.
- Charoite will open your heart so that in your life you can clearly see and feel the love. It will break down your walls and throw your fears away.
- It can help to unleash your creativity and encourage you to live a life of truth, it can help to ensure you are working to overcome your fears and live your own life.

Physical Healing Properties:
- Has the power to transmute disease to wellness. It is effective in relieving pain, aches and can help speed up the healing process.
- Known to alleviate arthritis symptoms and to provide rapid relief for headaches, migraines, cramps and other pains and aches.
- Helps to control blood pressure and helps to treat heart-related diseases and conditions.
- Known for body detoxification, especially if you are trying to quit bad habits.

Chakra: Heart Chakra, Root Chakra.

Howlite
Stone of Eternal Wisdom

- Named after the mineralogist who first discovered it in Nova Scotia.
- Creates nodules often that look very much like cauliflower heads.

- Can be found in regions all over the world.

Metaphysical Healing Properties:
- Will give you the gift of wisdom and understanding. Can help you connect to higher realms and eliminate the veils that block the truths in your life.
- Will help you to rid yourself of stress and anxiety because it's a powerful calming stone.
- Can help you to process your emotions so that in all aspects of your life they can give you peace, happiness, and feeling of content.
- Calms your upset or worried state of mind effectively, softens or removes your aggressiveness and allows you to recognize when you are unreasonable.
- Eliminates selfishness and thoughtlessness.
- The energies in this stone can support the healing of various physical and mental states.

Physical Healing Properties:
- It can also act as a pain reliever for cramps and other forms of physical pain if you use it as a gem elixir before going to bed.
- Assistance in the treatment of anxiety disorder and other stress-related diseases has been known.
- Also good for bones and can help with bone-related illnesses or conditions, such as osteoporosis.
- Can balance your calcium levels and help to correctly distribute the nutrients you need.
- Great enhancer of memory and mood stabilizer.

Chakra: Crown Chakra.

Morganite
Stone of Strength

- The pink color of this stone is caused by the presence of magnesium in the stone, and the heat treatments that this stone undergoes enhance the colors as well.
- Discovered in California in the early 1900s.
- Also known as pink emerald.

Metaphysical Healing Properties:
- Will help you realize that your bad experiences and challenges will be the catalyst for moving forward or making that big change in your life.
- Can help you discover your own strength, courage, and it will help give you peace and confidence to just keep going.
- Will make you realize all the things and all the people you have been taking for granted, and it will teach you how you can demonstrate your gratitude for them.
- Assists in giving you peace and quiet during your busy and crazy days can also help you distress.
- Can make you more receptive to gentle and loving words and actions from other people.

Physical Healing Properties:
- Supports the heart and counter heart-related problems, illnesses, and disorders. It can help with heart palpitations.
- Can be used for treating tuberculosis, emphysema, and asthma as well.
- Beneficial for people who suffer from vertigo and is known to help with larynx, thyroid, and tongue problems, too.
- Can assist in clearing the lungs and relieving any kind of stress-related illnesses.

Chakra: Heart Chakra.

Variscite
The True Worry Stone

- Often referred to as Utah-lite for the reason that it is commonly found in Utah, USA.

Metaphysical Healing Properties:
- This stone will help you accept some hard realities regarding yourself, it will help liberate you from your bad habits for you to fully heal and transform.
- Show you how your personal power can be harnessed by converting your weaknesses into strengths and concentrating on your strengths.
- Eliminates fear, anxiety, anxiety, and body tension.
- As easy as having this stone near your personal auric field, you will get that boost of energy, it will replenish your energy supply, inspiration, or motivation.
- Also beneficial to your intuition and psychological perceptions. Great for past life, remember and guide you to the information you seek.

Physical Healing Properties:
- Strengthens the cells and tissues of the body, can also help to treat blood disorders and deal with blood flow problems.
- Abdominal distension, gastritis, ulcer, gout or rheumatism may be treated.
- Neutralizes over acidity and can benefit muscles and kidneys very much.
- Helps in any treatment related to the Skelton and the nervous system.

Chakra: Heart Chakra, Solar Plexus Chakra.

Silicon
The Stone of Element
- Found usually as part of something else.
- Can be found anywhere in the world, and there are wide and varied uses and benefits.

- A pure energy element.

Metaphysical Healing Properties:
- Improves your communication and clearly and positively transmits your thoughts, improves your focus and your mental agility.
- Sharpens your focus and increases your mental activity.
- Silicon energies will help you to decipher the truth from lies.
- Can assist you in identifying facts from a barrage of conflicting information.
- Promotes and enhances positive energies in all situations.

Physical Healing Properties:
- A master healing stone that can help heal headaches. It can also relieve the eye strain caused by overuse of your computer.
- A great booster of vitality to recharge and revitalize the body. Its healing energies can also consolidate teeth and bones.
- Can assist in the correct calcium assimilation for bone and joint maintenance and growth. Ensures good skeletal health for dislocation and fracture prevention.

Chakra: Crown Chakra, Root Chakra.

Merlinite
The Stone of Duality
- Speaks about light properties and dark ones.
- Their vibrations foster spiritual growth.
- Named after the Merlin wizard for the ability of stones to attract mystical and magical experiences to anyone wearing them.
- Only found in New Mexico, USA.

Metaphysical Healing Properties:

- Encourages the harmonization of heavenly and earthly energies.
- This stone will allow you to connect with the world of spirits and allow spirits into your life.
- Will help you become more open and accessible, it will also help you to embrace things that are out of the ordinary or different from your normal ways in your life.
- Working with this stone's energies will boost your creativity and enhance your overall organizational skills.
- Merlinite will enhance your magical and psychic abilities if you access higher levels of consciousness.
- Will also help you balance your masculine and feminine energies to better understand your inner god and goddess.

Physical Healing Properties:
- A powerful aid in the treatment of heart and intestine-related diseases and conditions.
- A known stabilization of the nervous system. It also helps with the circulatory and respiratory systems.
- Used to treat disorders affecting the veins, arteries, and skeletal structures.
- Can promote physical development and better circulation of blood. It is also a powerful cleaning stone, which can improve the lymph flow and excretion of the body.

Chakra: Solar Plexus Chakra, Third-eye Chakra.

Wonderstone
The Stone of Curiosity
- A type of Jasper.
- Wonderful stone for meditation.

Metaphysical Healing Properties:

- Will integrate your past with the present and heal unhealthy past life energies that affect your present, resulting in your total acceptance.
- Wonderstone will help you stay determined, especially when you experience a dry spell on your earnings and jobs.
- Can strengthen your psychic powers and enhance and maintain your channeling connections.
- Used often in psychological contact with your loved ones who have moved to the other side.
- has an incredible ability to channel tote animals and also to access internal wisdom.

Physical Healing Properties:

- Can combat most types of infection, especially from bites of animals and insects. It can also help calm general irritations of the skin.
- Can support the natural resistance of the body, provide physical vitality and muscle tone. It is known to be effective in relieving abdominal pain and back pain.
- The balancing properties of the nervous system and harmonious production can also be regulated with this stone.
- Can clean and clean the liver and enhance the immune system. It can also help people with multiple sclerosis, Parkinson's disease, and sciatica.

Chakra: Solar Plexus Chakra, Root Chakra, Heart Chakra.

Mariposite
Stone of the Night
- This stone comes from California's Mariposa County, and hence its name.
- The Spanish word "Mariposa," meaning butterfly, also derives this name.

Metaphysical Healing Properties:
- Will affect the physical, emotional, mental and spiritual aspects of your life in a positive way. Will also encourage you to be more flexible in your perspective and personality so that you can adapt to new environments and situations more easily and confidently.
- Mariposite may bring you dreams, revelations, and visions prophetic and phenomenal.
- Will help you to align yourselves with higher realms and your life.
- Can help to stimulate self-expression in your creative pursuits, which is why it should be regarded as a power stone for creative and artistic types
- This stone will help you to communicate better with everything in your environment and surroundings.

Physical Healing Properties:
- Can help to alleviate insomnia and sleeping problems.
- Will enhance the reproductive system functions of women.
- It can cure skin diseases and protect the sweat glands and the ovules.

Chakra: Heart Chakra.

Galaxite
The Galaxy Stone
- A micro-labradorite that holds powerful energy.
- The stone has an appearance of a galaxy of stars.
- Discovered in the small town of Galax, Virginia, USA.
- If you find yourself overly drawn to the beauty and energy of Galaxite, it might mean that you are looking for your next great adventure.
- Believed to be sent to earth by the angels

Metaphysical Healing Properties:

- This stone will enhance both your conscious and subconscious mind.
- Assists in contacting the higher realm, your spirit guides, your guardian angels, and even beings from other planes and dimensions.
- Eases stress and anxiety, as well as eliminates worries.
- Particularly helpful in astral projection and astral travel.

Physical Healing Properties:
- Aids with anxiety disorders, and is well known to be helpful with certain brain disorders as well.
- Known to be particularly effective against sinus infections, head colds, and regular colds.
- Can help with problems in digestion and metabolic illnesses.
- Can be used to ease the pains or discomfort that come with menstruation, such as PMS, menstrual cramps, bloating, headaches, or lethargy.

Chakra: Crown Chakra.

Okenite
Stone of the New Age
- Part of the Zeolites family.
- It looks like small white snowballs in some formations
- It is named after a German naturalist and can be found mainly in India.

Metaphysical Healing Properties:
- Supports the manifestation in this world of your higher self-energies.
- A stone that will help clear your way obstacles. If the road is clear and smooth, the possibilities are unlimited.
- Encourage you and others to forgive themselves and experience complete emotional healing.

- Gives you the strength to complete your objectives and tasks. The supporting energies of the stones will encourage you to break bad habits and to develop good habits that bring you closer to your objectives.
- This stone will help you to channel your chakras and purify them.

Physical Healing Properties:
- Helps to promote good milk flow for nursing mothers.
- stimulates and improves the circulation of the upper body.
- Can assist with blood and stomach disease treatment.
- This stone helps to balance emotions and hormone changes.

Chakra: Crown Chakra, Solar Plexus Chakra.

Wavellite
The Stone of Perspective
- Named after an English doctor who discovered the stone first.
- Found throughout the world.
- Crystal trade desirability is high for wavellite.

Metaphysical Healing Properties:
- This stone helps you to recognize that everyone is the same and that everyone comes from the same source.
- It will help remind you that it is only gained wisdom by determined observations, which help you conquer new struggles and challenges.
- Will aid you in managing problematic circumstances so that you can understand why these struggles and challenges lie before you.
- Can help you look at a larger picture before taking a decision or taking action.

- It has a very simple vibration and each new moon it grows more powerful. It develops your psychological skills and strengthens your intuition.

Physical Healing Properties:
- Used to treat dermatitis, blood flow increases, and stabilizes the blood count.
- Known also to clear any "cellular memory" that might otherwise have disease states induced.
- Wavellite is considered a great "energy flow balancer" that acts as a regulator for peak physical health.
- used in flow treatment (energy, blood)

Chakra: Heart Chakra, Third-eye Chakra.

Dravite
The Stone of Hard Work
- The least known stone in the Tourmaline family
- Derived from Southeast Austria.
- High temperature and high-pressure mineral.

Metaphysical Healing Properties:
- It has a reassuring, relaxing and soothing effect on your body, your mind, and your heart.
- This stone will help you to descend from the higher planes and strongly connect with the earth.
- A cleansing stone that removes the negative energies and gives you more endurance when difficult situations arise.
- Helps teach you how to accept yourself.
- Will balance your mind and stimulate your imagination and creativity. It will enhance your experiences so that you have a fuller and more enlightening life.
- Will show you how you can accept yourself more deeply, especially the parts you have not accepted.

Physical Healing Properties:
- Known to assist the absorption of food nutrients. It can also correct bowel problems, especially the disease of Crohn's and irritable bowel syndrome.
- Can enhance the immune system and help the lymph system. It can heal the blood, reduce skin spots and treat other skin disorders.
- Dravite energies can help with sexual dysfunction.
- Very beneficial for loss of brain function, paralysis of the brain and autism. It is also known that it helps with ADD and ADHD.

Chakra: Solar Plexus Chakra, Sacral Chakra.

Serpentine
Stone of Elements
- Often mistaken for jade, similar in color and texture.
- Found in Russia, Switzerland, USA, and Canada.
- Stimulates the arousal od the kundalini energies.

Metaphysical Healing Properties:
- Works for clearing blocked or stagnant energy in any chakra.
- Perfect stone to help heal your heart from changes in relationships, be it a friend, a lover, or someone with whom you have a relationship.
- Relaxation of the emotional body, letting you surrender your fear of hardship and change so you can look ahead to the future with excitement and expectation.
- Will help you to be more willing to contribute to the greater good time and energy and less self-centered.
- Help you to not be too sensitive to other people's opinions, comments, or thoughts.

Physical Healing Properties:

- Supports efforts and rebalancing with digestion.
- Good for cleansing detoxifies the blood and the body.
- Treats hypoglycemia and diabetes.
- Isolates the aura, protecting delicate DNA and cell energy structures.
- Relieves Alzheimer's and senile dementia symptoms, relieves pain from bites, and stings. It corrects low blood sugar, diabetes, and weakness of your muscles.
- Inflammation of the skin, eczema, varicose veins, warts, skin, and parasites of the hair.

Chakra: Root Chakra, Crown Chakra.

Angelite
Stone of Peace
- Is said to be able to aid you in connecting with the angels and spirit world.
- Has soothing energy that is overall calming and helps you feel more peaceful.
- This stone was discovered most recently among all of the other stones.
- Originally discovered and mined in Peru.

Metaphysical Healing Properties:
- Useful for people who find it difficult to cope with incarnation, death, and sorrow.
- Stabilizes your feelings. and emotional and physical bodies.
- Calms and enhances creativity and psychic ability.
- Helps you to become more compassionate and accepting.
- Transmutes pain and disorder into wholeness and healing and opens the way to inspiration.
- creates a deep sense of tranquility and peace.

Physical Healing Properties:

- Treats throat disorders, especially those caused by difficulty expressing yourself.
- Removes the spinal fluid that has been retained and accumulated as well as disperses swelling.
- Balances the Thyroid and parathyroid systems.
- Used in weight control and relates to lungs and arms, in particular.
- Reparation of the tissue and blood vessels, balancing the fluids in the body.

Chakra: Crown Chakra, Heart Chakra.

Selenite
The Master
- One of the only healing crystals that do not have to be recharged at all, but can be used to clean and recharge any other crystals.
- Translucent and colorless.
- There are such large quantities of Quartz crystal, which are found in evaporated ancient seas and lakes. It is considered the most abundant of them all. Often found in Mexico and Brazil)
- Named after the Greek goddess of the moon, Selene.

Metaphysical Healing Properties:
- The utmost level of consciousness and everything that is infinite— intuition, the universe, and spirit guides.
- Excellent for meditation work, because it brings profound peace so that meditation or visualization can be more easily achieved.
- Related to spiritual activation and reaching higher planes.
- Through radiating light energy, it promotes purity and honesty.
- Brings clarity of the mind and opens the crown chakra.

Physical Healing Properties:

- Selenite can be used for almost anything. Taking the stone with you and meditating can contribute to inner peace and great healing.
- Aligns the spinal column and encourages flexibility, which helps to prevent epileptic seizures.

Chakra: Crown Chakra.

Pearlite
The Stone of Wonder
- Forms in other rock types.
- Petalite energizes and activates all of the body's energy centers when carried on the body.
- Has a high content of lithium.
- Emits energy and dissipates electromagnetic energy when placed in a room.

Metaphysical Healing Properties:
- Excellent for healing all types of emotional trauma, but especially valuable for overcoming the patterns of abuse and abuse victims.
- Provides calmness, self-acceptance, and self-love frequency.
- Can be used to soothe and balance traumatized emotions and energies
- Helps balance emotions by keeping mood swings at bay, let this stone remind you to invite and invoke angel's help to feel safe and safe.

Physical Healing Properties:
- Can be used for ADD, ADHD, excessive stress or worry.
- Helpful to regulate blood pressure and counter attacks on anxiety.
- Aids in endocrine system healing. It is useful for AIDS and cancer treatment. Cells, eyes, lungs, muscle spasms and intestines benefit.

- Supports you when the chemicals are out of whack in your brain and you are going through a manic period.

Chakra: Throat Chakra, Crown Chakra.

Heulandite
Stone of Emotion
- A type of Zeolite mineral.
- A wide range of colors.
- Considered a high vibration stone, and powerful for meditation.
- Is of a karmic nature.

Metaphysical Healing Properties:
- Excellent emotional healer for loss and grief.
- Controls sarcasm and criticism when needed.
- For connecting experiences of a past life that are relevant to you today.
- Helps to bring practical, focused and balanced change to your life to make you feel more wholesome. Powerful to help you make significant changes in your life.
- Creates beautiful vibration that opens mind, heart, and soul together and creates extraordinary spiritual activation.
- Enhances your psychic abilities, your spiritual vision, and your dreaming skills.

Physical Healing Properties:
- Can assist in weight loss, digestion processes, and the respiratory system.
- Improves mobility by improving movement and reducing pain in the joints.
- Repairs damage to the nervous system and liver.
- Encourages the efficient processing of nutrients and assists in overcoming food intolerances
- Eases breathing difficulties

- Unpacks complex illnesses into their component parts so that lingering viral or bacterial infection can be efficiently and effectively treated.

Chakra: Third-eye Chakra, Solar Plexus Chakra.

Amethyst

The Materialization Stone
- Along with Crystal Quartz and Selenite, Amethyst is one of the New Age's most famous stones.
- Amethyst can be found almost worldwide.
- Known for many things, this amazing purple crystal is more acknowledged for is the manifestation.

Metaphysical Healing Properties:
- Wonderful stone in a time of confusion or chaos.
- Amethyst allows you to connect your yearnings and purposes of life with your heart, and then you can materialize them into your life!
- Supports neural signal transmission through the brain.
- This powerful stone is linked to the upper chakras, which helps us bring the ethereal realm to the physical level. This includes the realization of our earthly dreams. Low, calming frequencies resonate.

Physical Healing Properties:
- Amethyst can relieve headaches, help boost the nervous system, balance hormones, treat insomnia, and alleviate neck tension. Place the crystal under the pillow in front of the bed to sleep soundly and wake refreshed, ready to manifest.
- Aids to the pituitary and pineal glands and can relieve hawthorns.
- Relieves physical, psychological and emotional pain or stress, and blocks geopathic stress.

- Encourages water reabsorption and insomnia treatment, bringing a restful sleep.

Chakra: Third eye Chakra, Crown Chakra.

Staurolite
Stone of Growth
- Quite unique, they naturally form a cross within the stone.
- Useful to help stop smoking
- Comes from the Greek word "Stauros" meaning 'cross'

Metaphysical Healing Properties:
- Stone of consolation for someone suffering from an illness or loss
- Reduces stress in the human body and helps you to gain respect by keeping to your views
- Give strength and patience to all those who carry the burdens of others
- Helps you feel safe, protected and secure
- Beneficial to emotions and can help counter hysteria, excessive fear, and paralysis of the emotions. Staurolite is useful for stress relief.

Physical Healing Properties:
- Strengthen muscles and help them grow.
- Staurolite brings alignment of body, mind, and spirit in order to achieve total health.
- Assists in building muscle and blood. This stone maintains your general physical health.
- Excellent to be used to counteract normal aging effects.
- Regenerates the body aftercare, care or recovery from bad habits and abuse of oneself.
- Treats cellular disorders and growth that increases carbohydrate assimilation and has traditionally been used for fever.

Chakra: Base Chakra, Third Eye Chakra, Crown Chakra.

Scapolite
Stone of Smarts
- Scapolite has been mined in Sri Lanka and Myanmar.
- Helpful stone for those of you who work at computers, this stone absorbs and disperses electromagnetic emissions from electrical equipment
- Stimulates psychic abilities

Metaphysical Healing Properties:
- Will help you understand how you may be using your power to manipulate other people's emotions or actions.
- Enables you to break self-destructive patterns, it is a stone for natal depression and PMS.
- Soothes the body in times of stress by releasing tension in the back, shoulders, and back.
- An extremely calming stone that will cut through confusion, distress, anger, and fear of going deep within your emotional center.
- Removes emotional garbage that is preventing you from moving forward
- Releases blocked energy from the body, especially in the legs and veins.

Physical Healing Properties:
- Said to unblock varicose veins, cataracts, and glaucoma also assists with bone disorders and the shoulders.
- Can be used to balance hyperactivity and inattentiveness.
- Enhances the healing of infection in the glands and glandular fever.
- Assists arthritis and bone problems and may help relieve the effects of Alzheimer's disease and dementia.

Chakra: Throat Chakra, Third-eye Chakra.

Moonstone
The Stabilizer
- Moonstone is closely connected to the feminine energy of the moon.
- Perfect for the graceful creation of harmony within one's intuition and for the strengthening of it.
- In ancient India, it was considered the stone of goddesses and gods and perfectly fit for the king.

Metaphysical Healing Properties:
- Increases patience and helps to remain objective when empathic information is received from others.
- Moonstones can open you to other worlds as well as to the universe.
- Can also be used to fight materialism and manage the ego by using the powerful tool of self-observation for self-improvement and spiritual growth.
- Improves emotional stability and control so that users can learn not to react to inappropriate situations that can lead to strong emotions.

Physical Healing Properties:
- Easily helps with eyes, hair, skin, and fleshy organs like the pancreas and the liver degenerative conditions.
- It can be used to aid with obesity, hormonal and menstrual problems, pituitary gland, retention of water, digestive system.
- helps insomnia
- Balances hormonal cycles and relieves period pain, cramps, pregnancy-related tensions, and a variety of other women's conditions.

Chakra: Third-eye Chakra, Solar Plexus Chakra.

Diopside
The Stone of Worry
- Called cats eye for its various stones in the shades of green
- A 4 rayed star
- Because of its crystal shape, named after a Greek word that translates into "double appearance."

Metaphysical Healing Properties:
- Will help you to reconcile with anyone or anything that has hurt you in the past by pushing you gently to take the first step.
- Promotes and enhances your ability to feel and honor your real feelings, feelings, and thoughts. Love, dedication, and inner heart.
- Beneficial to those who can not show sorrow because it shows that there is nothing wrong with your feelings and letting go.
- Increases the sense of compassion by opening your heart to other people's suffering.

Physical Healing Properties:
- Increases surgery recovery, trauma or serious disease.
- Stone supports the balance of cellular memory, physical weakness, acid and alkaline as well as hormones.
- Beneficial for heart and kidney inflammation, muscle aches, spasms, stress.
- Increases the circulatory system's heating and helps to eliminate toxins from the body.
- Can reduce fevers, aches, and pain in your body.

Chakra: Heart Chakra.

Kyanite
The Stone of Affliction
- Kyanite aids one's mind to make energy passageways where there used to be none, specifically with regard to meditation and emotional development.
- It doesn't collect energy so that the stone doesn't have to be cleaned and can be used to clean other stones and spaces.
- Chakras and subtle bodies that clear paths and meridians are instantly aligned.
- The soothing blue-green tone is reminiscent of the sky, making it particularly supportive and soothing for the nerves.

Metaphysical Healing Properties:
- It can also aid the ones who are transitioning through loss or death, mentally.
- As it takes meditation to a more significant depth, while opening channels to the spiritual realm, Kyanite may intensify psychic abilities.
- Lightens the burdens of emotion.
- Encourage you by cutting through fears and blockages to speak your truth.
- Opens the throat chakra and promotes communication and self-expression.
- Can help arbitration, in diplomatic missions, negotiations, and other forms of disharmonious communication.
- Helps spiritual energy manifest into thought processes, so that they can then manifest into reality.

Physical Healing Properties:
- It can be used to relieve headaches, tension around or on the brow, and pain in the eyes if you look too long at the computer.
- It can improve the ability to communicate and is great to help cure any throat pain.
- Resolves respiratory health issues.
- Natural reliever of pain reduces blood pressure and cures infections.

- Can help bridge the energy gaps because of surgery and other intrusive trauma that aids tissues and nerves restore tracts throughout the trauma site, just like bone breakage.

Chakra: Throat Chakra, Brow Chakra, Heart Chakra.

Cinnabar
The Stone of Alignment
- Known as dragon's blood.
- Is toxic due to its mercury content, but is safe to wear.

Metaphysical Healing Properties:
- Connects with the acceptance that everything is in place at this moment and as it should be.
- Releases energy blocks and aligns energy centers
- Promotes longevity, physical warming, elevated mood, anti-suicide, and anti-senility.
- Focuses your life in the physical world rather than the spiritual world.
- Will make you more aware of the passing of time and your life moving along.

Physical Healing Properties:
- Excellent for treating deep-seated or systematic wounds, whether viral or bacterial
- Helps stimulate the immune system and purify the blood. It can be helpful in treating HIV, herpes, staph and strep infections.
- Useful in warts, lesions, and boils healing.
- Can be used to balance issues of sexual energy and fertility. Increases sales and cash flow in a business environment or work environment.

Chakra: Sacral Chakra, Root Chakra.

Aventurine
The Stone of Opportunity
- Well known for enhancing good luck, prosperity and wealth.
- A variety of quartz that attracts luck and helps new opportunities to be successfully exploited.

Metaphysical Healing Properties:
- In association with the heart chakra, Aventurine also generates a sense of emotional calm and general well-being, which also helps anxiety.
- Aventurine harmonizes emotional, physical and mental bodies and restores balance. Promotes wellness, compassion, and empathy and embraces perseverance.
- Encourages emotional recovery and enables your own heart to wish to live.

Physical Healing Properties:
- This stone supports the circulation of the heart, blood, and energy.
- Benefits the thymus gland, the tissue, and the nervous system.
- gives the body an anti-inflammatory effect.
- Works to heal the adrenals, lungs, sinuses, heart and muscle system.
- Can also help to accelerate recovery from injury, disease or surgery.

Chakra: Third eye Chakra, Throat Chakra, Solar Plexus Chakra, Sacral Chakra, and Heart Chakra.

Bronzite
Stone of Harmony
- Provides a dynamic state of nonaction and nondoing.

- Promotes positivity and is called Bronzite because of its resemblance to the element Bronze.
- Used mainly for protection purposes.

Metaphysical Healing Properties:
- Bronzite is effective against curses, a magical protector and turns negative thoughts and bad desires right back.
- Helps us with certainty and with our actions.
- Supports self-affirmation, restores composure and keeps the head cool.
- Helpful for stress overcoming and voluntary revision.

Physical Healing Properties:
- Support and balance the psyche's body with yin and yang energy.
- Aided for chronic exhaustion, iron assimilation, cramps, and nerves.
- Used in crystal healing for solar plexus chakra-related ailments.
- Assists in the reduction of muscle tension and the dissipation of agitation caused by emotional and psycho-physical disorders.

Chakra: Solar Plexus Chakra, Root Chakra.

Biotite
The Gold Stone
- Sometimes called "black mica"
- Can only be found in Canada, Sicily, and Russia.
- Named after the fresh physicist, who studied and investigated the optical properties of the stone.
- Often mistaken for gold

Metaphysical Healing Properties:

- Provides us with reflective qualities so that we can recognize our civilization's shortcomings while keeping our heart centered so that we can love what we see here.
- Helps us to get rid of anger, tantrums and nervous energy.
- Balances your ambitions with all your sense of compassion and fosters more kindness and understanding of the people with whom you interact with every day.
- Supports information maintenance and order within the mind.
- Promotes clarity and balances too much psychological perception and reduces your overwhelming psychological impressions.
- Helps release energy blocks and align chakras inside the body.

Physical Healing Properties:
- Used to diagnose diseases and disorders associated with disorganized cellular patterns.
- Used to treat eye problems, throat and voice conditions as well.
- Can help increase the energy flow at specific body locations.
- It helps to improve and maintain tissue, cell, and bone marrow health.
- A good stone to boost brain function and improve the functions of the neurological system as a whole.

Chakra: Heart Chakra, Crown Chakra.

Obsidian
The Mirror Stone
- This stone is the result from volcanic lava coming in contact with water, this process is what gives the black rock a gloss-like texture that looks like glass.

- It's a highly reflective surface and consistent coloring enables you to look deep inside to divulge your soul and the necessary healing to increase your vibration.
- This jet black stone is known as the mirror stone for its sight-enhancing power, the way you see the world and the circumstances of it.

Metaphysical Healing Properties:
- Obsidian dates back to the Stone Age, it is known to allow views of realms accessible from earth, of the soul itself, and of other worlds.
- Used to gain knowledge and wisdom.
- Use this to unravel your own flaws, weaknesses, and shadow so that you can understand yourself furthermore.
- Helps you identify outdated behavioral patterns and helps clean them.

- Shock and fear dissolve with it.
- Use obsidian to alleviate wiped out memory, ignored, or even long buried emotional distress.
- It can be utilized to relieve emotional trauma anxiety and stress.
- Helps you cope with sorrow, loss and separation pain.

Physical Healing Properties:
- Aids in digestion and detoxification, blockage and tension dissolving, including hardened arteries.
- If you have been shocked by injury, it will be dissolved on a cellular level and therefore helps staunch bleeding and accelerates wound healing.
- Reduces arthritis pain, joint pain, cramps, and injuries.
- Helps improve blood flow circulation.

Chakra: Base Chakra.

Seraphinite
The Stone of Serendipity
- This crystal can be found only in Sabena Lake Baikal, Russia.
- The name derives from its perceived link with seraphim, the highest order of angels due to the inclusion of feather-like mica in the stone.

Metaphysical Healing Properties:
- Every emotion is said to be removed.
- Helps to release emotional energies that don't serve. It brings the emotional body enlightenment and joyful energy and stimulates the flow and elasticity of your energy, ensuring you can react emotionally in a balanced and harmonious way.
- Cleanse feelings that do not serve you anymore by bringing clarity to the source of emotional imbalances.

Physical Healing Properties:
- Helps to release the belief systems or patterns that lead to the manifestation of the same physical diseases or diseases that you or your family members suffer.
- You can choose a different outcome with this stone and focus on breaking the pattern.
- Assists in regulating the growth and reproduction of all cancer cell types.
- Blood strengthener and can assist in cellular respiration and the delivery of nutrients to the cells.

Chakra: Heart Chakra, Crown Chakra.

Crystal Quartz
The Spirit Stone
- Crystal quartz in the metaphysical world is regarded as the most famous light window.

- A wide range of rock varieties can be found and is extremely abundant. • Supports your overall wellness essentially.
- This stone's clarity and understanding often alleviate disturbing feelings.

Metaphysical Healing Properties:
- This particular crystal contains the whole color spectrum and can be used from the spirit world to the physical world to amplify desires, prayers, and manifestations.
- Meditate the crystal with your intentions with this stone, and "program." This particular crystal contains the whole color range and can be used to increase desires, prayers, and manifestations from the spirit world to the physical world.
- Helps you stay focused on the objective at hand. The stone is useful for recalling memory, so use it for examinations or testing.
- Increase your ability to succeed in all life-related activities, including fertility, financial security, family, creativity, a happy home, a healthy body, blessings and more.

Physical Healing Properties:
- A master healing stone designed to stimulate the immune and circulatory systems, and also to increase the chi energy flow in the body.
- Stimulates the nervous system and fingernail and hair growth
- Can help remove bonding tissue adhesions.

Chakra: Crown Chakra.

Blue Topaz
The Stone of Creativity
- The bright blue color of this stone reflects the mind to learn more quickly and retain information that almost the rest of your life can draw on.

- It also helps to fire creativity and to open the mind to fresh ideas.

Metaphysical Healing Properties:
- Topaz is a mental stone, great to connect with one's spirit guides, loved ones who have passed on, and angels.
- Use topaz to open your soul, align with the realm of spirit, and expand your mind.
- Calms strong emotions and helps clear the mind with a sense of peace and tranquility.
- Inspires leadership and supports clear communication and natural authority.
- Helps you let go of anger and resentment, makes it easier for you and others to surrender to forgiveness.
- Help you control anger feelings by bringing hidden emotions calmly to the surface so that they can be treated in a positive way.

Physical Healing Properties:
- Ideal for treating liver and digestive system problems.
- It has always been known to help with eye disease, mental illness, dimness in sight, and to restore taste loss.
- Improve throat healing, eyes, ears, and nasal passage disease.
- The metabolism increases and the thyroid energizes.
- Reduces menopause side effects.
- Regenerates and revitalizes the physical body. It delays the aging process, disperses negative energy that attempts to weaken your resistance to disease.

Chakra: Sacral Chakra, Solar Plexus Chakra.

Hematite
The Grounding Stone
- This iron-rich stone is deeply grounded and earth-related.

- In ancient Greece, it was referred to as the "bloodstone" because of the red hue of the iron content found in nature.

Metaphysical Healing Properties:
- Hematite is linked to the root chakra and has a deeply grounded energy that reminds us of our human existence.
- Perfect stone to keep you out of " drama. "
- Excellent to organize your thoughts. Balances self-esteem and self-vision by the negative.
- Can be used to relieve anxiety about stress and to calm the nervous system.
- Supports financial stability flow.

Physical Healing Properties:
- Iron found in hematite can help us clean the blood, improve circulation, manage irregular menstrual flow and promote healthy heart conditions.
- Due to its grounding properties, it can relieve symptoms exacerbated by stress or anxiety.
- Positive heart and circulatory system effects.

Chakra: Root Chakra.

Citrine
The Money Stone
- Type of quartz with a golden yellow hue, the yellow colors of money, gold and wealth are associated.
- Powerful cleanser and regenerator that carry the sun's power are warming, energizing, and highly creative.
- Never require cleaning.
- Can guide you significantly in meditation when you make the most of your unique talents, you can easily enter a peaceful, calm meditative state using this stone.

Metaphysical Healing Properties:

- Take this stone to the bank, to financial business meetings, or place it on your desk while you are working.
- helps to understand information, analyze and guide situations in a positive direction. Makes you less critical, helps you develop a positive attitude and flow rather than in the past.
- Encourages inner calm to enable wisdom to emerge. Citrine can help you gain wealth, financial wealth and stability.
- Increases self-esteem in order to reduce self-injurious behaviors.

Physical Healing Properties:
- Citrine stimulates metabolism, helps to digest other conditions affecting the gastrointestinal system and nausea.
- Can also be used to boost nerve impulses, helping the brain to fire quickly and sharply.
- Facilitates the cure of ache, bedwetting, depression, diabetes, birth, sadness and problems of growth.
- Supports your mental and energy efforts.
- Purifies chakras.

Chakra: Crown Chakra, Solar Plexus Chakra, and Sacral Chakra.

Pearl
Gemstone of the Sea
- In contrast to other earth gemstones, pearls are formed in fresh and saltwater mollusks.
- If used, will make you wiser.

Metaphysical Healing Properties:
- A stone that will cultivate your inner wisdom, it will also show you how in your life to strengthen and nurture love.

Physical Healing Properties:

- Provides crystal healing by helping to treat disorders of the digestive tract and muscular system.
- It also helps maintain or restore your body's balance and natural rhythm. It can also regulate your hormone level.
- Beneficial for lung patients, such as chronic bronchitis, asthma, and tuberculosis;
- Helps with healing the heart and liver, urinary system, kidneys.

Chakra: Sacral Chakra.

Jade
The Dream Stone
- Another dynamic stone to be found throughout the world in a multitude of colors.
- Region ordinarily dictates stone color.
- Jade in ancient times was one of the most commonly used stones.

Metaphysical Healing Properties:
- The stone represents the ranking nobility and ideals.
- Promote autonomy and independence in an engaged relationship. If you are deeply attracted to this attraction of a stone, you may have an existential crisis and seek some reassurance.
- Jade promotes happiness and harmony in family life and in romantic relationships with you.
- This stone is connected to the heart and helps us to accept the truth, to express love (to oneself and to others) and to reach shamanic realms in the dream state.

Physical Healing Properties:
- Jade is good for filtering toxins and cleaning the body as a whole through the bloodstream in combination with the heart.

- A stone that can heal and soothe both the nervous system and the kidneys, gallbladder and the liver. It can help the renal system to remove kidney stones. Promotes cell recovery.
- Can reduce pain related to cramps, joints, and aches of the bone.
- Can also be used after surgery to relieve joint pain and accelerate the healing process.

***Chakra*:** Third-eye Chakra, Sacral Chakra.

Opal
The Eye Stone
- When moved into the light, this brilliant and colorful stone appears to be on fire with a rainbow spectrum of electric colors.
- It is related to the eye, as it is so pleasant to look, and to the Third Eye Chakra.
- A popular belief in France was that Opal could make his or her wearer invisible so that he or she could steal without being caught.
- There are more than 10 different opal types, all from different parts of the world with slightly different characteristics.

Metaphysical Healing Properties:
- Opal acts as a prism of the whole aura and brings the spiritual and energy body into the whole spectrum of light.
- Vibrant energy that is not commonly seen from other stones can be amplified in the soul.
- stimulates originality and dynamic creativity, helps you to access your true self and express it. Reinforces desire, eroticism, and sexuality. It makes us emotional, seductive, and unconventional and makes you love your life.
- Opal inspires optimism, happiness, appreciation, and welfare.

- Use Opal to awaken psychological and mystical qualities and connect ancient spiritual realms as a vehicle.

Physical Healing Properties:
- The Opal, referred to as the eye stone, can be used to promote eye health and improve vision.
- Treat the disease, infection, and fever of Parkinson.
- Memory can also be stimulated and neurotransmitter disturbances stabilized.
- Reinforces the will to live.
- Opal is beneficial to eye, kidney and skin health.
- Helpful if you are in need of dehydration or retention of water.

Chakra: All because of the variety of colors.

Fuchsite
Stone of Collecting
- Translucent to transparent crystals.
- Can be found almost anywhere.
- Fuchsite is really good for the function of blood cells and the body.
- Comes in colors of all types

Metaphysical Healing Properties:
- Collects unwanted emotions to cleanse and release the heart chakra, calms the process.
- Fosters light-heartedness, friendliness, compassion, and recovery from exercises that are spiritually damaging.
- Helps you understand your interactions with others and links to life's fundamental concerns.
- Releases you through sacrificial service to others from creating or maintaining your identity and self-value.

Physical Healing Properties:

- Helps to reduce swelling and pain caused by carpel tunnel syndrome.
- Aid for spinal alignment, muscles, immune system, throat, inflammation and sleep disorders.
- Helps relieve nausea
- More coordinated domestic schedules, such as childcare, school runs, visits to elderly or sick relationships and work commitments, can be provided when placed in your home.

Chakra: Heart Chakra.

Peacock Ore
Stone of Happiness
- Mainly used for decorative or cosmetic purposes.
- When exposed to some air, the colors change, making it look like a peacock with all the colors.
- is known for the effect of happiness it gives.

Metaphysical Healing Properties:
- This stone promotes awareness of inner wealth and awareness that wealth only comes from within.
- Helps us to cope with stress and obstacles blocking our path to a specific objective.
- helps to identify new ways and opportunities that can help us achieve our dreams and objectives.
- Helpful stone to protect against negative energy, it can also help you to recognize negative energy more clearly.
- Can stimulate your inner spirit to reach further heights, thus enhancing your ability to enjoy the momentary happiness.
- Useful to re-birth and to bring your emotions together with your intellect.

Physical Healing Properties:
- Synchronizes the cellular structure and metabolism of our body.

- Supports fever reduction and swelling.
- It helps to regulate adrenaline flow in our bodies.
- Blood circulation is also known to increase if you place it under the waist.
- Maintains the body's electrolyte balance.

Chakra: has the ability to align all of the Chakras.

Agate
Stone of Inner Stability
- You can find this varied stone in almost all colors with seemingly endless striation types.
- Often found as layers lining Geodes' internality.
- Strong chakras relationships.
- Agate incarnates the inner world and all its states.

Metaphysical Healing Properties:
- Agate raises self-consciousness, stabilizes the aura (in all its colors), transforms negative energy and is a powerful spiritual conduit.
- Agate gives you protection, security, and security by dissolving internal tensions, enabling you to withstand eternal influences better.
- Has the power to harmonize your yin and yang with the positive and negative forces in place in the universe. Gently facilitates self-acceptance, builds self-confidence.
- Use the stone to cure anger, emotional instability and feelings of self-worthlessness.

Physical Healing Properties:
- Known to enhance mental function by improving thought clarity.
- Good for centering assistance and physical energy establishment.
- Heals the eyes, stomach, uterus and cleanses the pancreas and lymphatic system.

- Agate is a wonderful stone to use when writing or gathering thoughts for a meaningful conversation with someone you care about and want to communicate clearly with before an important test.
- Useful for reprogramming cellular memory in a previous or present life after mortification of the flesh, emotions or spirit.
- Aids in hidden circumstances self-analysis and perception, bringing to your attention any disease that interferes with your well-being.

Chakra: Crown Chakra.

Moldavite
Rock of Glass
- Most often found in deserts.
- A transparent green type of glass that is thought to be formed by an impact on the surface of the earth by a meteor or other extraterrestrial object that causes the soil to cool and recrystallize into a tektite.
- It has been used as a talisman since the stone age.

Metaphysical Healing Properties:
- Moldovite brings you into contact with the higher self and improves other crystals.
- It takes you into the highest spiritual dimension and facilitates the process of ascension. Before using the stone, you must be grounded or you can feel spacious and rootless.
- Eliminates the blockages and aligns the chakras.
- The divine integrates and speeds up spiritual growth.
- Opens the chakra of the crown to receive the highest spiritual direction.
- Assists in developing worldly separation, worries about money and the future. It emphasizes qualities like empathy and compassion.

Physical Healing Properties:
- A great diagnostic tool that highlights the disease source and also supports the healing process due to its high vibrational energy.
- Prevents mental degeneration, retention of memory, balance maintenance and more.
- Infections of the respiratory tract, allergies, gout, and anemia also help.

Chakra: Crown Chakra.

Jet
Stone of Age
- A fossilized wood coalition that comes from a family of tall evergreen cone-bearing trees in South America and Australia.
- Been long used as a talisman.
- Usually black or brown.
- Could be significantly amplified if paired with other stones.

Metaphysical Healing Properties:
- Jet can be used to open yourself to psychic experiences and help you on your path to spiritual illumination.
- Balances mood swings, relieves depression and brings balance and stability.
- Works with you to restore your lost balance and harmony.
- Can attract knowledge and wisdom to deepen the meaning of your life.
- Will add excitation and fulfillment so that you can always look forward to something.

Physical Healing Properties:
- A migraine, epilepsy, bowel problems, mouth problems, grinding of teeth, gum disease and colds.

- Can decrease glandular and lymph swelling and cure pain in the stomach.
- Can cure aches of the stomach and menstrual cramps.
- Addresses health issues related to stress or sadness.
- Can also be used with people suffering from epilepsy.

Chakra: Root chakra.

Amazonite
The Stone of Courage
- Amazonite claims the spirit and soothes the greenish color of the soul.
- This stone enables you, without being overly emotional, to seek and express your inner truth with courage and conviction.
- Electromagnetic pollution protection.

Metaphysical Healing Properties:
- Used for balancing and cleaning all chakras.
- Helps you gain insight into a problem on both sides and helps to dispel aggravating and negative energy.
- Amazonite can relieve emotional trauma stored in the body and help prevent this trauma from manifesting into a physical disease.
- It is also useful to harmonize the relationship between intellect and intuition for a sound and well-founded balance.

Physical Healing Properties:
- Amazonite is typically used for well-being and is beneficial to the whole body.
- Calms the brain and nervous system and aligns the physical body with ethereal health.
- When used properly, negative energy dissipates and helps the nervous system.

- Use it, in particular, to soothe rashes, clear acne and prevent wound infection.
- Supports the absorption of calcium via parathyroid and thyroid.

Chakra: Heart Chakra, Throat Chakra.

Onyx
Stone of Sadness
- Onyx crystal name is derived from the Latin and Greek languages. It means " claw" or " fingernail."
- It consists of fine silica mineral growths.

Metaphysical Healing Properties:
- Heals grief that has lasted too long and helps to repair the heart.
- Assist in providing mental focus, grounding, and the ability to remain on the job.
- Gives support in mental or physical stressful times and in confusing or difficult situations.
- Stimulates the basic chakra and helps you to ground and connect to the Earth's electromagnetic energy.
- Onyx helps you learn lessons by giving you self-confidence and helping you feel comfortable in your environment.
- Can enhance spiritual vision and dream experiences related to that.

Physical Healing Properties:
- Enhances your financial strength and your ability to remain focused and achieve financial objectives.
- Can help to decrease the symptoms of headaches and to strengthen the eyes and optical nerves;
- Benefits for teeth, bone marrow, disorders of blood and feet.
- Increases general stamina and self-control.

Chakra: Root Chakra.

Tourmaline

The Grounding Stone

- Preferred protective talisman, tourmaline is used as a psychic shield to base your energy on the entry into your energy field of negative entities.
- Long used by magicians, shamans, witches, and wizards.
- Tourmaline can be found on all continents.

Metaphysical Healing Properties:
- As a black stone that acts as a sponge for harmful or dark energies, it absorbs light. It encourages you to stay shining in dark times.
- It is utilized to elevate your vibration and bring you into the light, keep away negative energies, even if it is black as night.
- Balances the right and left brain hemispheres and turns negative energies into positive ones.
- Removes obsessive or compulsive behaviors and releases chronic anxiety and anxiety.
- Attracts inspiration, compassion, tolerance, and prosperity.

Physical Healing Properties:
- Use tourmaline to relieve joint pain and help re-align the spine.
- It can also be used to strengthen the immune system, heart and adrenal glands—stress relief and tension release. Benefits the brain and the pulmonary. It corrects fluid disequilibrium by treating the kidneys, bladder, thymus, and thyroid.
- Insomnia, night sweats, sinusitis, and bacterial infections are helpful. Eases neck disease, pituitary disease, adrenal disease, and all major glands.

Chakra: Base Chakra, Throat, and Heart Chakra.

Phenacite

The Rare Stone
- Crystallizes often in short, hexagonal prisms.
- Advanced crystal workers are recommended.
- Comes from the Greek word meaning ' deceiver. ' This is because other crystals are easily mistaken for how varied they are in formations.
- Stone searched for due to its high energy, frequency, and vibration.

Metaphysical Healing Properties:
- Can relieve feelings of desperation and fear of change and make you more aware of the benefits of becoming a group or a community's energies.
- Phenacite helps increase your resolve so that your life can be changed to reflect more of your emotional and spiritual purpose.
- Allows you to access higher levels of consciousness and guidance quickly. It activates the third eye, the crown and the etheric chakras above the head, fostering mental perception, vision, and dreams of power.
- Can deepen meditation and help to bring into reality the high self-consciousness.
- Stimulates the light body by clear and pure light.

Physical Healing Properties:
- Excellent for nerve damage, brain imbalances, brain damage and genetic disorders that limit the function of the brain.
- Ease nausea and pain caused by migraine and headaches.
- Helps diseases in which conventional medicine does not work or in which chemotherapy, radiotherapy, genetic disorder or AIDS / HIV have weakened the body.

- Assists in stimulating and enhancing different aspects of brain function and brain activity.

Chakras: Third-Eye chakra.

Quantum Quattro
Stone of Transformations.
- Found in Namibia.
- Works at higher vibrational energy than other stones.

Metaphysical Healing Properties:
- Will inspire you through kindness and gentleness to express your own personal power.
- Supports tough love, but also shows where intervention would have a positive outcome and teaches you to walk away from everything that will not help your growth.
- Dissolves negative emotions such as solar plexus chakra guilt and grief, reverses destructive emotional programming and cures injury, betrayal, sorrow, and abandonment.
- Inspires creativity and environmental concert.
- This stone will help you to correct the imbalance whenever you feel something is off or out of alignment.
- Promotes a healthy, natural flow of energy and spiritual activation.
- The clearing of attachments, blockages, cords and karmic contracts can help.

Physical Healing Properties:
- Increases immune system healing, blood oxygenation, lungs, pancreas, addiction, thyroid, metabolism, and thymus.
- Increases the detoxification of all organs and systems, particularly intestines, liver, lungs, and kidney.
- Digestive, circulatory, reproductive and endocrine system healing.

- Can relieve arthritis pain, help with heart disease and control blood pressure.
- Can be useful for people who suffer from diabetes and calcium deficiencies.

Chakra: Solar Plexus Chakra, Throat Chakra, the Heart chakra.

Garnet
The Stone of Health and Creativity
- This highly vibrating and grounded stone is found in a variety of colors and compositions almost everywhere in the world.
- Most known for his ability to promote health and creativity and bring spirit to earth.

Metaphysical Healing Properties:
- Garnet helps eliminate taboos and inhibitions.
- Revitalizes, purifies, and balances energy with the necessary serenity of passion at the time.
- Inspires devotion and love.
- Allows the mind to think as freely and creatively as possible.
- Invites the spirit to participate in the physical realm and opens the channels of communication and creativity to external expression with the inner self.
- Has a connection to the hypnosis and can raise spiritual awareness of oneself.
- Boosts sexual expression and neutralizes the emotional aspect.

Physical Healing Properties:
- Garnet is a wonderful stone, known to stimulate the metabolism of the body, to make things flow in the body and, additionally, to help coagulate blood and stop bleeding.
- Works to restore the circulatory system through toxin cleaning and blood purification.

- Encourages blood formation and boosts the liver functions.
- It's also used to improve sexual libido and the heart's desires.

Chakra: Base Chakra, Heart Chakra.

Peridot
Stone of Evolution
- Assists in all kinds of transitions, especially that help you to rise above addiction.
- Egypt is where the best quality of this stone is found.

Metaphysical Healing Properties:
- This stone can help you to have the courage to fulfill your heart's wishes, to be generous to others, even as you pursue your own destiny.
- Protection against destructive jealousy caused by betrayal in past relationships and personal fears that you are unlovable, rather than in relation to the present relationship.
- Helps eliminate blockages to receive good energy, many spiritual people are adapted to give love, energy and time, but they may not be as good at receiving it.
- Makes you aware of the things that you have neglected to do and encourages you to compensate for the damage in healthy ways.
- Help you to think outside the box by opening your mind to the world's unlimited possibilities.

Physical Healing Properties:
- Strong detoxification effects and improves the overall functioning of the liver.
- Increases hepatic and gallbladder function stimulates metabolism and helps with skin problems, including warts.
- Will help to stimulate overdue work on the body, and to alleviate swelling and any unwanted growths.

- Can be used to mitigate heart heaviness and all kinds of heart-related imbalances.
- Helps to strengthen the blood circulation and to combat anemia and poor oxygenation in the lungs.

Chakra: Solar Plexus Chakra, Heart Chakra.

Rose Quartz
The Love Stone
- Pink shades of Quarts are associated with the heart and expressing unconditional love to self, others, and the planet.

Metaphysical Healing Properties:
- A magnificent stone to invite love, to help give love and even to attract your soul mate. Rose Quartz is heavily associated with the heart and heart chakra.
- It's a good stone for sorrow, loss of love, loss of friendship and better connection with children and babies.
- Impacts empathy, sensitivity and, at times, sensitivity on self-love, a strong stone for the heart, romance and allowing the ability to love wholeheartedly.
- To open yourself to finding love, carry or wear rose quartz. If you are in a relationship, it can help to deepen and nurture your love to each other.

Physical Healing Properties:
- Repairs and reinforces circulatory systems, releases body impurities, and helps with problems of the chest and lungs.
- When centered around the heart chakra, it is known to improve circulation and reduce blood pressure and can be used for deep emotional release and healing.
- Can also be used for reducing Virgo, easing palpitations or skipped beats and releasing tension.
- Cleans the body of toxins and excess fluids and makes it an ideal treatment crystal for water retention and edema conditions.

Chakra: Heart Chakra.

Ruby
Stone of Age
- Ancient legends in Myanmar say that you would become invincible by inserting a ruby into your flesh.
- Believed to communicate very good overall health to everybody that comes in contact with it.
- Lends you lifestyle and vigor.

Metaphysical Healing Properties:
- If you've lacked enthusiasm and feel generally bored, the ruby's energy will help to flow your blood.
- Intensifies your life passions and the emotions that are related to them.
- A talisman can be used to bring fortune, joy, sexual vigor, love, and power.
- Provides healthy tension and dynamism, enthusiastically motivates you and lifts you out of lethargy and exhaustion. It also has an impact on hyperactivity.

Physical Healing Properties:
- Can warm and energize even the most sluggish of auras, and as such is excellent for people who are convalesced or infirm.
- Can help cure infections, lower cholesterol, reduce blood clots, detoxify the blood and eliminate sobering difficulties.
- Stimulates circulation, menses and the pituitary gland, it is an excellent stone to keep your person cured of blood-related disorders or problems with blood pressure.
- It can often be used to treat sexual dysfunction and infertility to control your weight.
- Stimulates spleen, adrenal glands, and circulation as a whole.

- It helps to overcome infectious diseases like intestine diseases or flesh-eating bacteria's.

Chakras: Sacral Chakra, Third-eye Chakra, Heart Chakra.

Turquoise
The Stone of Safety
- Believed to be one of man's oldest known stones.
- Chiefs, shamans, kings, wizards and the like have long cherished Turquoise.
- In almost all ancient cultures, awarded as a symbol of wisdom, turquoise has been prevalent and has always been known as a protective stone.

Metaphysical Healing Properties:
- Shields emotion and heals irregular heartbeats and heartbreak.
- Turquoise strengthens the body's meridians and promotes intuition and better meditation.
- Connects physical and spiritual awareness, development and relaxation of inner strength.
- Helps you develop a sense of empathy for other people.
- Balances extreme mood fluctuation and dissolves an apathetic attitude of self-martyrdom. The brain is also refreshed if you are tired.
- It is also linked to the throat chakra, which supports clear communication with oneself and people around you, because of its blue hue.
- Turquoise is a talisman of protection and it channels the ancient wisdom it emits.

Physical Healing Properties:
- Assists with the brain, neck, ears, and throat issues.
- Assists with healing problems of the liver, anemia, health of the blood, nerve endings, physical strength, mobility, ear infections, and inner ear problems.

- Turquoise is strongly associated with the psychic realm, making it useful for clearing blockages and supporting the healthy flow of energy within the body, a truly great stone.
- Can help to improve vision, throat problems, bladder, weakness, the acidity of the stomach and issues in the stomach.

Chakra: Third Eye Chakra, Throat Chakra, Heart Chakra.

Diamond
The Stone of Colors
- Derived from the Greek word "Adamas" which means "invincible." This is precisely the theme that passes through the whole diamond mythology.
- Big symbol of courage and strength.
- For thousands of years, it was seen as a sign of wealth, and it still is today.
- The most popular gemstone in the world and most sought after.
- Was used to explore the spectrum of colors.
- Has been used as a purity symbol since ancient times.

Metaphysical Healing Properties:
- Their power productivity can be increased when used with other crystals.
- Clears mental and emotional pain, brings new beginnings to life, and reduces fear.
- Highly creative stone that stimulates your imagination and creative flow.
- Increase your personality, ethics, and fidelity to your own ideas and place in the world.
- helps you to overcome fear, depression and a sense of meaninglessness in life.

- Helps to promote harmony and balance in a partnership, marriage, or relationship.

Physical Healing Properties:
- Assists in the physical cure of concentration problems, artery sclerosis, bad memory, sight weakening, eye disease, gout, strokes, and cataracts.
- Strengthens blood vessels and glands that help blood flow.
- Heals organ diseases that directly affect mental functions in the brain.
- Ideal for people who have recently had a stroke, can initially reduce symptoms and helped you continue your life with little to no problems.

Chakra: Third-eye Chakra, Solar Plexus Chakra.

Fluorite
The Stone of Positivity
- One of the most undervalued but also among one of the most powerful stones.
- Known to suck negative energy and low vibrations from a space or your body quite literally and create space for light to shine in.
- Fluorite is actually a magic crystal found in multiple color variations.

Metaphysical healing properties:
- Used to raise your vibration, alchemize negative energy and calm a chaotic mind, used for auric protection among most people.
- Makes you more aware of emotions that you have suppressed. It does not emphasize its expression, however, but helps you gradually bring it to the surface.
- Fosters impartiality and diseases relating to the eyes, mouth, and ears.

- Rainbow Fluorite is best known to stabilize your mind, amplify your psychic connection and enhance your intuitive abilities.
- Neutralizes excess emotional energy by encouraging a better flow of energy throughout the chakras.

Physical Healing Properties:
- This dynamic stone can be used to clear your mind and sharpen your focus when studying.
- Can help with osteoporosis by reinforcing your spine and promoting a more upright posture, helps with stiffness and joint problems.
- Can also be used to relieve body inflammation, to dissipate cold symptoms and to cure the mucous membrane. Impacts the body, strengthening it and making it more resistant to illness and injury.
- Assists with dizziness, vertigo or disruptive off balance issues.

Chakra: Third eye Chakra, Throat Chakra, Heart Chakra.

Amber
The Stone of Self
- Amber dates back to around 2000 B.C. Or before that.
- Actually composed of tree resin and sticky semi-liquid, which has been hardened over the years.
- Technically, Amber should be considered a fossil and not a crystal, but is very often used in pieces of jewelry that incorporate high-class gemstones.
- Sometimes they have insects and pieces of nature formed within them.
- Found in the ancient tombs of Egypt as well as incorporated onto the tops of the tombs.

Metaphysical Healing Properties:

- This golden resin is highly protective against negative events. Especially useful if the negative is from psychological sources.
- Warm and bright energies of Ambers are transferred to a sunny, spontaneous arrangement which respects tradition from which Amber was made famous.
- Could help to counter suicidal and thoughts of depression. Links the spiritual self to the physical every day reminding you why you are here.
- Balances and encourages patience when decision-making.
- Strong stone to contribute to generating creativity for any occasion.

Physical Healing Properties:
- Relieves heart problems, arthritis, and pain absorbing.
- Encourages the balance and healing of your digestive system, adrenals, stomach, liver, and gallbladder.
- Allows the body to work on healing itself and restoring overall balance.
- Amber is a powerful cleanser and healer that helps to cure body diseases and revitalizes tissue that has been affected in any way.
- Assists in nutrient assimilation throughout the body, especially nutrient deficiencies.

Chakra: Solar Plexus Chakra Root Chakra, Throat Chakra.

Carnelian
The Stone of Action
- Used to guide and protect the dead, often used in burials thousands of years ago.
- The color depends on the crystals iron level and how old it is.
- Can help to clear bad energy when placed with other stones.

- Keeps an improved flow of life energy running through the blood.

Metaphysical Healing Properties:
- Accelerates your motivation and helps you clarify your objectives so that you can find the best direction in your life and exactly what you want.
- Grounds you and actually anchors you when you are feeling sad emotions.
- Excellent for motivation and vitality restoration in the older.
- Carnelian can encourage initiative, boldness, assertiveness, dramatic abilities, and affability when used correctly.

Physical Healing Properties:
- Heals uterus, fallopian tubes, ovaries, cervixes, tubes, and pelvis reproductive systems.
- Influences the reproductive organs of both men and women by increasing fertility, overcoming impotence and frigidity.
- Helps with bad inflammatory arthritis, mostly in the hands.
- Increases your metabolism and contributes to back issues that may be bothering you.
- It can help to stop severe bleeding if carnelian is placed directly on the bleeding wound.

Chakra: Heart chakra Throat Chakra.

Sodalite
Stone of Balance
- Found in the United States, Canada, Italy, India, and Brazil.
- Most commonly known as an Ornamental gemstone.
- Named for connection to Sodium.

Metaphysical Healing Properties:
- Balances rampant emotions, very helpful for your anger and frustration, to calm and release.

- Helps you to recognize and accept that your emotional problems are usually based on fluctuating hormone, estrogen, progesterone and testosterone levels.
- Helps you deal with releasing negative emotions and expressing them in a less aggressive, harmful way.
- Can reduce stress and anxiety by enabling you to see your reality from a higher and calmer perspective.
- Dissolves feelings of guilt and enables you to stand up for yourself and live your own feelings whatever they may be.

Physical Healing Properties:
- Reduces the body's calming energy inflammation and also relieves inflammatory conditions such as headaches and muscle strain.
- Can be used to help control blood pressure and to facilitate retention of water. Has a cooling effect and stimulates bodily fluid absorption.
- Balances metabolism, helps calcium deficiencies and purifies the lymph system and related organs.
- Helps boost the immune system.
- Helps with insomnia, throat issues, vocal cords, larynx, and digestive disorders.

Chakras: Throat Chakra, Root Chakra.

Kunzite
Stone of Benefits
- Kunzite helps with any soul work you need/want to do.
- Named after a specialist in gemstones who had spent a lot of time cataloging and describing the properties of this special crystal.
- Fosters alignment and healing of chakras in relation to karmatic aspects of life.

Metaphysical Healing Properties:

- Kunzite helps calm your nerves when you are getting ready for an examination or an interview.
- Will help you find out how to look after yourself without the help of anyone else.
- Provides loving energy for the health of your heart, so that you can reflect it back to others.
- Good for your physical health as well as the general health.
- Helps you to keep focusing on your heart chakra and unconditional love.
- Helps alleviate stress and dissolves heart tension that leads to helping solve joint problems.

Physical Healing Properties:
- Relieves heartbreaks and heartache from recent traumas.
- Helps attract healthy romance and loving friendships into your life.
- Helps you work on your compassion, kindness, and tolerance.
- Could reduce menopause effects and solve gynecological problems that you have yet to get checked out.
- Can reduce schizophrenia's side effects.
- Assists in removing resistance, helps you open up and learn how to commit to bigger things.

Chakra: Heart Chakra.

Tiger eye
Stone of Relativity
- Was made from the psychic miner protector asbestos, wonderful for business.
- First discovered in South Africa.
- In the Greek language, it means "false form."

Metaphysical Healing Properties:
- Helps you find your emotional balance in life.

- Can help harmonize people with different points of view, religious beliefs or approaches to life. It is an excellent contribution to bringing the family together and the relationship's harmony.
- Help you to keep your distance from external influences that can negatively influence or affect you. Mitigates the influence of stressful moods and situations.

Physical Healing Properties:
- Strengthens your blood to support your general vitality.
- Strengthens the endocrine system and helps balance your hormones and biochemistry.
- Can aid in heavy pain relief.
- Slows the energy flow in the body and dampens the excitement of the nerves and the stimulation of the adrenal glands.
- Helps to improve general eyesight and can over time heal eyesight completely.

Chakra: Solar Plexus Chakra, Sacral Chakra, Base Chakra.

Lapis Lazuli
Stone of Relief
- Can help to bring out one's internal truth and is also very protective from negative entities that could live among you.
- helps you recognize the vibration of truth and works to resonate enlightenment within yourself.
- The powerful blue stones are designed to open the third eye and stimulate the pineal gland.
- The Persian word " Lazar" means " blue stone."

Metaphysical Healing Properties:
- Helps to alleviate anger and negative thoughts, as well as to intensify growth of your intuition.

- Creates depth and better clarity in your thinking and communication with yourself and other people
- Will clarify your mind and set your imagination free. Encourage better self-care in your life.
- Helps move your consciousness beyond the worldly and allows you to identify habits, patterns, and lessons that may be difficult to perceive consciously and that may block you from spiritual advancement.

Physical Healing Properties:
- May help to cure problems associated with hearing loss and vertigo.
- Will help your immune, breathing, and nervous system immensely.
- Especially known to help ease migraines.
- Very common in nerve calming and anxiety.
- Helps identify karmic disease roots, otherwise known as karmatic issues in the ancestry of one's family.
- Can help to detect habitual patterns and emotions that sabotage the healing process.
- Aids the endocrine system, migraines, lymph glands, ears, and reduces pain and inflammation in the nasal passages, also are thought to be good for autism and Asperger's syndrome.

Chakra: Third eye Chakra, Throat Chakra.

Vitalite
Stone of Compromise
- Stone affected by various mineral traces such as Quartz, Muscovite and Plemontite.
- Recognized as the stone with the strongest energy release.
- Provides a cleansing influence.

Metaphysical Healing Properties:

- Fosters love and courage, two of the most important virtues of the heart.
- Stimulates a general sense of well-being and helps to reduce anxiety, stress, depression and/or irritability.
- Can dislodge repressed emotions, but it has such a positive influence it rarely takes the form of anger even though it helps absorb repressed negative emotions.
- Currents from this stone may help clear the way to a healthier flow of energy throughout the body.
- Known as the generosity stone.

Physical Healing Properties:
- This stone has such a strong chi, that it affects the whole body at the cell level and promotes a healthy flow of life in every cell, organ, and system.
- Vitalizes the flow of energies to the heart, bringing new vitality not only to the heart but also to the circulatory system, lungs, liver, and digestive system.
- Speaks to the consciousness of the cell, pushes the cells to live, and exist in a joyful, flowing energy.

Chakra: Throat Chakra, Heart Chakra.

Smoky Quartz
Stone of Psychic Protection
- Grounding and anchoring stones, these stones are highly protective and at all times and they are excellent for us all to keep in our aura.

Metaphysical Healing Properties:
- Highly beneficial for you to use and transmute energy when you need protection against any kind of negativity.
- Wonderful for bringing prosperity, abundance, and attraction of good health into your life.

- Can boost your spiritual growth and help clarify your thinking, initially helping you to make any process in your life easier to proceed.

Physical Healing Properties:
- Relaxes pain anywhere in the body.
- Helps soothe cramps and soothe on edge nerves.
- It also helps to relieve headaches, benefits the heart, absorbs electromagnetic, electronic radiation, and facilitates spasms.

Chakra: Root Chakra.

Lazurite
The Stone of Self Awareness
- This composition forms Lapis lazuli mineral when combined with pyrite and calcite.
- Mined in Afghanistan for more than 6,000 years.
- it was used as a pigment in painting and tissue dyeing since at least the sixth or seventh centuries.

Metaphysical Healing Properties:
- Encourages self-consciousness, dynamism, honesty, and straightforwardness.
- Helps you to face the truth and be able to accept it while expressing your own opinion at the same time.
- brings a disturbed mind balance, calmness, and strength to become undisturbed.
- Grants you wisdom and helps to reveal your own inner truth to yourself. Can help balance your physical and spiritual aspects of life so that they can work in harmony together.

Physical Healing Properties:
- Heals neck, larynx, and vocal chord problems.

- Lowers blood pressure and helps to properly regulate thyroid gland function.
- known to prolong the menstrual cycle if needed.
- Restores harmony between the brains hemispheres.
- Helps to cure you of dyslexia and schizophrenia disorders.

Chakra: Heart Chakra, Solar Plexus Chakra.

Calcite
Stone of Achievement
- A hexagonal structure means that calcite is a mineral that helps you to achieve your desires, so it is excellent for manifestation work.
- Brings a huge increase in good vibes to your life.

Metaphysical Healing Properties:
- Clears blockages and helps to remove lingering negative body energy.
- Enhance your memory.
- Amplifies and projects positive energy.
- Bring your life some hope and daily motivation.
- Helps to combat laziness so that you can be more energetic on all levels.

Physical Healing Properties:
- Cleans the removal organs such as the bladder, intestines, and kidneys.
- Helps in calcium absorption throughout the body, especially if you have calcium deficiencies.
- Strengthens the immune system and promotes the growth of under-dimensional children.
- Strengthens the joints and the skeleton.

Chakra: Root Chakra, Throat Chakra.

Labradorite
Stone of Magic
- Known as a stone of magic, and for awakening within your mystical and magical abilities and psychic powers.
- Can be used to bring amazing changes to multiple aspects of your life.

Metaphysical Healing Properties:
- Seals and helps prevent leaks of energy.
- This crystal will help you to recharge mentally, physically, and spiritually.
- Brings synchronicity and serendipity to you.
- Can help to uncover unconscious and subconscious patterns of belief that create unpleasant emotions within you.
- Guides you to understand your own relationship with yourself or with others.

Physical Healing Properties:
- Can help reveal the nature of 'mystery diseases.' The patterns that have created the disease can be revealed over time with this stone.
- Beneficial to the general eye, nerve, brain, bone and spinal cord health.
- Relieves recent stress and controls metabolism.
- This stone helps in rebalancing the sharing of chemicals in your brain, particularly those with cerebral paralysis, sclerosis, optic neuritis, Parkinson's disease, psychotic episodes, and retinal problems.
- Known for treating the common cold, gout, rheumatism, balancing hormones and menstrual tension relief.

Chakra: Throat Chakra, Third eye, Crown Chakra.

Emerald
Letting Go Stone
- These crystals create only positive actions and outcomes; they help to give you the strength to overcome any problems in your everyday life.
- Highly sought after and one of the most valued stones today.

Metaphysical Healing Properties:
- Calms your emotions when upset and generates positive vibrations throughout your body.
- Relieves stress and improves your memory to give you clarity and comprehension.
- Encourages prosperity, wealth, growth, peace, patience, love, harmony, faithfulness, and honesty into your life.
- Ensures an emotional, physical, and mental balance.

Physical Healing Properties:
- Helps you to recover from diseases and infections you may have recently had.
- Heals sinus, congestion, problems with the lungs, clears the eyes and aids in repairing your vision.
- Reinforces your spine and back muscles.
- Detoxifies the heart, liver, and spleen.
- Helps respiratory problems and heart problems. If you have swollen lymph nodes, Emeralds are recommended for you. Even can help spikes in diabetes and hypoglycemia in blood sugar.

Chakra: Solar Plexus, Heart Chakra, Root Chakra.

Crystals for Zodiacs
If you are a follower of astrology and universe signs, you know that each sign has a particular gem, flower, and animal associated with it.

Here are the Gems:

Aquarius: Amethyst, Hematite, Amber.

Pisces: Opal, Amethyst, Bloodstone, Aquamarine, Fire Opal, Coral.

Aries: Aquamarine, Fire Agate, Citrine, Bloodstone, Diamond, Jade, Emerald.

Taurus: Diamond, Carnelian, Chrysocolla, Blue Tourmaline, Rose Quartz.

Gemini: Aquamarine, Rusticated Quartz, Blue Sapphire, Jade, Emerald, Pearl.

Cancer: Ruby, Moonstone, Opal, Fire Opal, Carnelian.

Leo: Amber, Citrine, Jasper, Garnet, Diamond, Carnelian.

Virgo: Watermelon Tourmaline, Smoky Quartz, Moss Agate, Amethyst, Geodes.

Libra: Tourmaline, Rose Quartz, Bloodstone, Jade, Citrine, Opal, Moonstone.

Scorpio: Moldavite, Turquoise, Moonstone, Malachite, Peridot, Opal, Ruby.

Sagittarius: Obsidian, Lapis lazuli, Azurite, Topaz, Smoky Quartz, Turquoise, Chalcedony.

Capricorn: Jade, Tigers Eye, Green Tourmaline, Black Tourmaline, Smoky Quartz, Garnet.

CHAPTER 8
Crystal Mining And Collecting For Yourself

Sometimes you go crystal hunting for hours on end and you can't seem to find anything, a lot of work has been put into this hunt. Other times you barely dig into the earth and you find something that really catches your eye or is of value.

How to go about crystal hunting:
This largely depends on where you live. In some countries, access to mines is strictly forbidden, that is not recommended at all. But in some countries, there are privately owned mines that you can visit by paying a small entrance fee.

If you decide to go crystal hunting, make sure you are dressed appropriately and prepared for the occasion. Crystal mining season usually depends on the weather, but most prospectors prefer spring or autumn when the earth is still moist. Make sure you bring water, a light meal, sturdy shoes, and a charged headlamp no matter the occasion.

Birthstones

Garnet – January

Amethyst – February

Aquamarine – March

Diamond – April

Emerald – May

Pearl – June

Ruby – July

Peridot – August

Sapphire – September

Pink Opal – October

Citrine – November

Turquoise – December

Chakra Balancing Stones

Root Chakra – Alexandrite, fire opal, garnet, red carnelian, red jasper, red tiger's eye, red tourmaline, rhodochrosite, rhodonite, ruby.

Sacral Chakra – Amber, orange calcite, citrine, orange carnelian, sunstone, tiger's eye, topaz.

Solar Plexus Chakra – Amber, citrine, golden calcite, honey, calcite, pyrite, sunstone, tigers eye, topaz, yellow jasper.

Heart Chakra – alexandrite, aventurine, bloodstone, green calcite, emerald, green fluorite, green obsidian, green tourmaline, jade, malachite, moldavite, moss agate, peridot.

Throat Chakra – Angelite, Azurite, Blue Goldstone, Blue Lace Agate, Blue Obsidian, Kyanite, Labradorite, Lapis lazuli, Sapphire.

Third eye Chakra – Apatite, Lapis lazuli, Sugilite, Tranzanite.

Crown Chakra – Amethyst, Ametrine, Charoite, Purple Fluorite, Purple Agate, Sugilite.

Stones to Attract or Enhance

Calm – Rose Quartz
Confidence and Courage – Agate, Bloodstone, Dacite, Carnelian, Charoite, Diamond, Hematite, Tigers Eye
Communication – Blue and green stones: Amazonite, Aquamarine, Blue Lace Agate, Turquoise
Creativity – Yellow for intellect: Calcite, Citrine, Opal, Topaz, Green for growth: Amazonite
Energy – fiery red and orange stones: Carnelian, Garnet Red Jasper
Family harmony – Clusters
General health – Emerald, Aventurine, Green Calcite, Green Tourmaline, Malachite
Happiness – Orange Calcite, Sunstone, Blue Kyanite
Love – Amber, Amethyst, Diamond, Emerald, Jade, Lapis Lazuli,

Malachite, Moonstone, Opal, Pearl, Rose Quartz, Sapphire, Topaz, Tourmaline, turquoise
Money – Aventurine, Emerald, Green Tourmaline, Jade, Malachite, Citrine, Golden Calcite. Pyrite, and Tigers Eye
Psychic ability – Amethyst, Clear Quartz
Sex – Ruby and Garnet

Stones to Repel or Eliminate
Addiction – Amethyst
Anger – Amethyst, Carnelian, Emerald, Green Calcite, Green Tourmaline, Topaz
Anxiety – Rose Quartz, Rhodochrosite, Rhodonite, Peridot, Aventurine
Depression – Blue Agate, Kunzite, Amber, Topaz
Fear – Onyx, Smoky Quartz
Heartbreak – Rose Quartz
Jealousy – Peridot, Chrysoprase
Nightmares – Amethyst
Stress – Black Tourmaline, Hematite, Obsidian, Smoky Quartz, Rhodochrosite, Rhodonite

CHAPTER 9
Benefits Of Crystal And Energy Healing

Energy Healing Benefits

One of the greatest benefits of healing energy is stress reduction and relaxation, which triggers the natural healing skills of the body and improves and maintains health. Energy healing is a natural therapy that smoothly balances the life force of the body and gives the recipient health and wellness.

Energy healing is excellent for the healing of all physical, mental, emotional or spiritual problems. Some health benefits include:
- Aids better sleep
- Blood pressure reduction
- Can help with acute injuries and chronic problems (asthma, eczema, headaches, etc.) and medication breakage aids.
- Relieves pain
- Removes energy blockages
- Assists the body in the cleansing of toxins
- Supports the immune system
- Increases vitality
- Increases the frequency of vibration

When we are relaxed and stress-free, we are able to restore our natural ability to heal. To keep the positive energy flowing and the body healing itself, we can turn to crystal healing which is affordable, beneficial, and fascinating to learn about.

Crystal Healing Benefits

Crystals have been used to release physical, mental, and spiritual blockages. Crystals come from the earth, and so when placed on the body, they can help you connect to the healing energies of the planet. The belief is that there is a resonance between crystals and humans. Each crystal has its own healing properties. If a body part or the emotions are affected by stress or illness, the whole body gets affected. The unique healing vibrations need to be introduced to your body to bring it back into balance.

Holistic healing techniques, which include crystal healing, encourage us to rely on our intuition, to listen to the things our soul is trying to tell us, to feel our emotions and nurture our spirit.

How can crystals strengthen our spirit? They can do so by bringing you into alignment with your true self through aura and chakra balancing, through helping you develop your intuition, and through cleaning up and protecting your living space. All of this will help raise your vibrations and contribute to a general sense of well-being.

Crystals and Their Healing

Stones like rose quartz, jade, and amethyst carries a belief in crystal therapy that it can all connect individually with the energy flow of the human body and can help realign the energy channels that interrupt the positive flow of energy that should help the body heal itself.

Red Crystals: Red crystals activate, energize and stimulate. They are related to your ability to use practical skills on a daily basis. They strongly symbolize life, love, and physical vitality. Red stones can help speed up cell growth, release stiffness, and motivate you to improve your love life physically.

Pink Crystals: Pink crystals exude a soft and gentle energy, making them have a calm way of pushing things towards a resolution. Pink brings emotions and sensitivity to our daily actions, it shows the universal color of love and it is excellent for a better and happier life filled with love, affection, and happiness.

Orange Crystals: Orange crystals combine energizing and focusing qualities to give birth to creative and artistic abilities. Used to encourage you to use your personal power, which makes them very beneficial to people who can use a little more self-confidence and self-esteem.

Yellow Crystals: Yellow is the color of the sun, life force, and vitality. Yellow crystals have to do with the function of the body's nervous, digestive and immune systems. Stress, fear, satisfaction, and positivity are all associated with this color. They will bring in more energy and make you feel more uplifting about life.

Green Crystals: Green symbolizes the beauty of life and embraces the abundance and the energies of nature. These crystals are directly associated with the heart. They balance emotions and relationships, promote personal space and growth and create a sense of tranquility. It looked like a restful color.

Light Blue Crystals: Blue is the color of sincerity, inspiration, and spirituality. Light blue crystals and thus all forms of communication are associated with the throat. Taste, sight, smell, feel, hear, feel. Your internal communication is the most important because it is the way you deal with yourself and talk to each other, your thoughts and your ability to express yourself are all influenced by the vibration of light.

Indigo Crystals: Dark blue strengthen your self-esteem and promotes your well-being. Indigo crystals are connected to the third chakra of your eye. Indigo is attributed to perception, understanding, and intuition as well as a profound sense of peace.

Violet Crystals: Violet identifies with mystical and purifying qualities. Violet crystals inspire, fancy, empathy and a sense of service to others. Violet and purple stores help to balance extremes in the body's systems so that they can be useful if you are not sure about the nature of the problem. These crystals are often used for meditation to increase your psychic awareness and strengthen your connection to your higher self.

White Crystals: Clean or white stones are controlled by the moon and represent the potential to reflect all the energy around them. White has to do with the concepts of clarity, protection, and purification. They are linked to sleep and psychological energy and attract fortune and protect.

Black Crystals: While white rocks reflect light and clarity, black rocks absorb light. White reflects the visible, black shows you the hidden potential. Black manifests and solidifies. It holds all energies in itself quietly and therefore requires patience to fully explore. Black stones usually ground, acting as energy anchors to help you get back to normal working conditions. Many things will also reveal hidden aspects so that they can be handled, black stones play a purifying role in this respect and are the most misunderstood of all crystals.

CONCLUSION

Thank for making it through to the end of *Crystals for Beginners*, let's hope it was informative and able to provide you with all of the tools you need to achieve your goals whatever they may be. I hope that you learned a thing or two about the intricacies of crystal healing and how it can benefit you, your life, your relationships, and your reality. Remember to use this book to submit yourself to the positivity of the universe with each healing session. This way, you can harness the powers of the stars and all of the nature around you, bringing you to newer heights in all aspects of your life, and revealing new truths and strengths that can help you meet the height of your spiritual, physical, emotional, and cognitive potential.

The next step is to stop reading and get started doing what you need to do in order to ensure that you are staring/expanding your journey to a more enlightened life through crystal use. You will have better end results the more you practice and the more knowledge you take in on the subject. This book is simply for beginners; how deep you dive into crystals is all up to you!

Studies show that working with crystal can provide you with hundreds of positive benefits for the physical, mental, and emotional bodies when used correctly. You have to put minimal dedication into crystal healing but you do have to put in effort when really trying to access higher consciousness and health benefits associated with doing so. Once you have read this book, reevaluated your life, and thought about ways to begin the process... Give it a try! It could be the best thing you've ever done for yourself.

Finally, if you found this book useful in any way, a review on Amazon is always appreciated!

DESCRIPTION

If you want to start working with crystals and types of beneficial healing but don't know where or how to begin, then *Crystals for beginners* is the book that you have been looking for!

This book discusses every aspect of mind, body, and soul. If you are interested in crystals, it is really important that you know how to choose them, use them and integrate them into your consciousness. Stones can be more powerful sometimes than we can believe. Chakras, energy healing and crystal healing are subjects that many people don't get into, most people don't even know that they exist to such a positive extent.

Crystals and gaining a perspective on your higher consciousness is always a good way to become more in tune with yourself and the earth. There are so many ways you can go about incorporating crystals into your daily / weekly routine. Rebalancing the mind, body, and soul is important to the human condition. Keep your crystals cleansed, keep them safe, and keep them close. Once you're done reading this book go tell your friends about what you've learned, it is always good to help give the people you spend time with a perspective on the matter as well.

CRYSTAL HEALING BIBLE

The Ultimate Guide to Gain Enlightenment and Awaken Your Energetic Potential with the Healing Powers of Crystals

Crystal Lee

© Copyright 2018 by Crystal Lee - All rights reserved.

No part of this book may be reproduced or transmitted in any form or by any means, electronic or mechanical, including photocopying, recording or by any information storage and retrieval system without written permission of the publisher, except for the inclusion of brief quotations in a review.

INTRODUCTION

Hello, and welcome to my book, Crystal Healing Bible. In the chapters to follow, you will be learning the ultimate guide that will help you gain enlightenment and awaken your energetic potential with the healing powers of crystals. Whether you are new to healing crystals or have some practice, there is always something new to learn! I have filled this book with everything you need to know to get started with healing crystals. I hope that by the end, you feel at peace and secure with utilizing healing crystals to benefit your life.

In the first chapter, we will be going over the very basics of crystal healing. You will learn the basic concepts of crystal healing and how to get started. Along with this information, we will also be going over the power that crystals can hold and the vast history that has given us the power of the crystals. Once you understand this, we will delve into starting a collection of your very own!

Of course, you will know which crystals you will want to collect once you learn the incredible benefits of healing crystals. You will find how to heal different problems from addiction to increasing compassion, to finding happiness, patience, and even more. As you will learn, there are numerous benefits you can collect from healing crystals. You will learn a number of aspects from the configuration of the crystals, to the type of stone you can use whether it is the focus stone, intention stone, or perimeter stone.

In the third chapter, we will be going over your chakra connections and how crystals can help you heal and balance your chakras. If you have never studied chakras before, we will go over the basics, so you can begin to practice on your own. Chakras are the energy centers of your body. In Sanskrit, Chakra means "disk" or "wheel." You can think of these as spinning wheels of energy within your body. Our Chakras are in charge of keeping us functioning at optimal levels. You can use crystals to help heal these spots if you feel your energy is out of whack.

The fourth chapter will bring all of the information on some of the more popular crystals out there in the universe. You will be provided with information such as origin, shape, energy, color, placement, and use of each crystal. Knowing your crystals is going to be important, especially as you start your own collection. If you ever have any questions, feel free to refer back to this chapter so you can assure you are using the correct crystal in proper form.

Once you have learned some of the crystals and some of the amazing benefits, the fifth chapter will bring you even more uses for your crystals. You may be surprised to learn that you can use them for more than just health benefits! There are crystals for energizing your body, crystals that can be helpful for meditation, love stones if you lack in that department, and crystals to decorate and protect your home. As you will find out, crystals are incredibly versatile!

Finally, you will learn how to care for your crystals once you have started your own collection. This information will be vital when it comes to not only cleaning your collection but also recharging them. Much like our bodies, crystals can only do so much until they need a recharge. When your crystals are fully charged, you will be able to re-energize your own body and clear your mind of any negative energy. When you are ready to start your crystal journey, we can begin.

CHAPTER ONE
What Is Crystal Healing?

In the modern world, we seem to have an affinity with crystals and stones. They are found in our jewelry and our homes as sparkling decoration. What you may not realize is that the use of crystals dates back to the beginnings of our history. Crystals can be dated back to 60,000 years ago and are found in reference to both history and religion. Before we dive into the incredible benefits of the crystals, we will learn about its rich history, first.

Amulets

One of the first known usages of crystals were found in amulets. It is believed that some of the oldest amulets dated back to 30,000 years ago. The oldest amulets, the Baltic amber followed by amber beads, believed to be 10,000 years old. Other popular stones and crystals were jet beads discovered in Paleolithic gravesites in both Belgium and Switzerland.

It was in 335 AD that certain amulets were banned by Christian churches. Despite the ban, gem and crystals tend to have a role in all different types of religions. In the bible comes the first mention of birthstones. In the book of Exodus, there is a mention of the breastplate of Aaron, also known as the High Priest's Breastplate. On top of this, there is also the mention of stones and crystals in the Koran. One of the more popular examples comes from the Kalpa Tree. This tree is the representation of an offering to the Hindu Gods. It was thought to be made out of precious stones. In another example of a Buddhist text, there was thought to be a diamond throne near the Tree of Knowledge. As you can see, crystals are part of our religion's history, but they can also be found in other spots of our history, such as the Renaissance!

Renaissance

In school, you may have learned all about the Renaissance and all of the incredible advancements that came from that time period, but what you may not have learned about was the extensive use of crystals! In Europe, there were a number of medical treatises using precious and semi-precious stones used to treat certain ailments. Typically, the stones were used hand-in-hand with herbal remedies.

On top of the healing ailments, stones were also thought to have qualities of protection and strength. One example of this comes from a chief justiciar in 1232 known as Hubert de Burgh. He was accused of stealing gems from King Henry III. It was believed that whoever wore these stolen stones would be invincible. He ended up giving these stones to King Henry's enemy, Llewellyn, who was the King of Whales.

These stones were thought to be corrupted by the sins of Adam, meaning the stones were inhabited by demons. With this state of mind, gems and crystals were always sanctified and consecrated before anyone was able to wear the crystals. This is why we cleanse and program our crystals in the modern world before performing any crystal healing. You will learn in our final chapter how you can perform a cleanse yourself, so you can avoid any problems.

The Beginning of Crystal Healing

The start of crystal healing can be dated back to 1609. The first person to suggest the virtue of gemstones comes from Anselmus de Boot who was a court physician in Germany. He suggested that the gemstones have a virtue due to the good and bad angels. Boot believed that good angels were able to grace certain gems, but on the other hand, bad angels were able to tempt humans to believe the stone itself as opposed to God's gift that was bestowed upon it. It wasn't until later in history that a man named Thomas Nichols introduced the concept of "Faithful Lapidary," meaning that inanimate objects could not possess effects from the past. During the Age of Enlightenment, precious stones were used more than ever to help with protection and healing.

What are Crystals?

You know that crystals can help with ailments, but what are crystals exactly? Crystals are natural elements that are created right here on earth. A true crystal has a lattice pattern known as a crystal system. As of now, six different lattice patterns have been found in healing crystals.

1. **Hexagonal**
   Hexagonal crystals look much like a 3D hexagon. Typically, these crystals are used to help with manifestation.

2. **Isometric**
   Isometric crystals have a cubic structure on their interior. These crystals are used to amplify energies and can help improve certain situations.

3. **Monoclinic**
   Monoclinic crystals have a 3D parallelogram shape. For the most part, these crystals are used for protection.

4. **Orthorhombic**
   Orthorhombic crystals are shaped like diamonds. These Orthorhombic crystals are used to help remove blockages, clean, and also clear any negative energy.

5. **Tetragonal**
   Tetragonal crystals have an interior structure that is rectangular. These tetragonal crystals are used to make things more attractive and can help attract certain things to the wearer.

6. **Triclinic**
   Finally, we have the Triclinic crystals. These crystals have three inclined axes. Typically, the triclinic crystals are helpful to ward off energies that are unwanted and are able to retain positive energies.

Another way we determine crystals are their different colors! As you may already realize, the color of the crystal can change how attracted you are to certain crystals. What you may not realize is that the color of crystals has a major role in the healing impact of crystals and their energy. You will learn later in the book how the color changes the healing powers of the crystals and which will be the best for your use.

Three different aspects create the color of the crystal. First, the color will change depending on how the crystal is able to absorb light. The color is also affected depending on the certain chemicals and minerals that are within the crystal. Another factor that can change the color of the crystal is any impurities it may have. The minerals and impurities impact the wavelengths of light that the crystal absorbs. One example of this would be a crystal that is able to absorb the entire light wavelength. Can you guess what color it will be? Black! The opposite is true for a crystal that is unable to absorb any light wavelength. If this happens, the crystal appears to be clear!

With the growing popularity of crystals and gemstones, there has been an increase in laboratory-created gemstones. For the most part, these crystals and gemstones are used in cheap jewelry. You can tell when a gem is made in the laboratory because it will be much less expensive compared to crystals that have been naturally formed.

Crystals that are formed within the earth can take millions of years to be created. This is why these crystals are thought to have strong, energetic power. While lab-made crystals still carry power and have the ability to retain energy, they are less pure. You will learn later how to sense energy from various crystals and how to feel the energy you need at any given moment.

Using Crystal Terms

If you research crystals, there seem to be several different terms such as rock, mineral, gems, and crystals. Most of the time, people use these terms interchangeably. It is important to realize that certain substances aren't crystals. To avoid confusion, here is a quick overview on which each term is:

1. **Crystal**
   As you already learned, crystals are a mineral that has a crystalline interior structure.

2. **Gem**
   A gem, on the other hand, is a crystal, mineral, or rock that has been cut and polished. An example of this could be a cut diamond. This cut diamond is a mineral, crystal, and rock. These minerals can be referred to as gems or gemstones. Other substances that are considered gemstones are amber and pearls, but they are not crystals, rocks, or minerals. You can probably see where the confusion comes from.

3. **Mineral**
   A mineral is a naturally-occurring substance. These minerals have a specific chemical composition and an ordered structure that isn't always crystalline. An example of this would be Opal. Opal is a gemstone and a rock but does not have a crystalline structure.

4. **Rock**
   A rock is a combination of minerals. One example of this is Marble. Marble is made up of several minerals and is a metamorphic rock. Metamorphic rocks are rocks that are subjected to pressure and heat over a certain amount of time.

Crystal Energy

Everything in our vast world has energy. Crystals have energy, and so does your body. You may not even understand your own energy at the moment, but over time, you will learn more. Imagine you are out with a group of friends and you get a bad feeling from a certain person, you just don't vibe with them and you don't quite understand why. When we experience this dislike for certain people, you are sensing their energy, and it simply isn't compatible with your energy.

This energy is the same for those negative and positive people in your lives. Have you ever been around a negative person and felt your mood take a dive? Your energy is being drained due to their negative energy. The same can be said for the energy of a positive person. Typically, the positive energy of this individual can help re-energize your energy and enhance your mood.

Crystal and Electric Effect

Another neat aspect of crystals is their electrical effects. One of these effects is known as the piezoelectric effect. This effect occurs when nonconducting crystals are able to generate an electric charge when placed under mechanical stress. One of the more popular crystals that demonstrate this effect would be Quartz. This is why this crystal is used in watches, radios, and other digital circuits.

In fact, Quartz crystals have been used in our technology as far back as the late 1800s. These crystals were used in several pieces of equipment such as radio, watches, and sonar. The use of Quartz can be found in military radios used in World War II. The military used oscillators made of quartz to help control the frequency of their radio transmissions. While these oscillators were precise, they were unfortunately hard to mass-produce. These quartz oscillators were also popular in watches. The crystals were excellent in timekeeping and only required a tiny piece of quartz.

On top of this, crystals also have their own vibration. As you learn to work with crystals, you will begin to notice how they are able to change your mind, spirit, and body energies. With this change in vibration to the body, it is thought that the vibration within the crystal can change as well. Typically, crystals have higher vibrations compared to our body, which is why they are helpful with advancing the body in a more positive direction.

Feeling Crystal Energy

There are metaphysicians, energy healers, mystics, and psychic mediums who have dedicated hours of their lives to communicate with spirits, meditate, and feel the energy that surrounds them. As a beginner, you may not have the experience or the ability to sense energy just yet. There are several ways you can learn how to feel crystal energy but remember that you will need time and practice.

First, it is important that you are open to the experience. There are plenty of people out there that are skeptical that crystals can carry power. If you lack belief in the crystal healing power, you are blocking the energy from coming in your direction. With this, you will also need to set aside any preconceived notions about crystals you may already have. You can't walk into this with high expectations of healing yourself instantly. You will learn to understand that the universe has a plan for you. If you allow yourself to be in the moment with your crystal, you will understand what it is trying to do for you.

Everyone has a unique experience with crystals. As a beginner, you will want to start with a crystal that attracts you. Your very first crystal should be exciting, one that truly calls for you. This crystal will be used for healing work because it is most likely calling to you for a reason. Later, you will learn the many different crystals and their healing powers but always listen to your own energy.

You may be wondering how you will feel when you first hold a crystal. This sensation from the crystal will change depending on your energy and the energy of the crystal. When you first start, all you will need to do is observe how you feel. You will want to pay special attention to any thoughts that arise, emotions you feel, and physical sensations you feel. It will be vital that you allow these to occur without any blocking or judgment. As you start, keep an open mind and experience the shifting of vibration. For some people, this may be subtle, for others, it will be much more noticeable.

It is important to realize that not everyone will react the same way to the crystals. For some, they are able to feel certain crystals lift their energy to high levels. For others, they may not feel anything. This doesn't mean that the crystal isn't working. It just means that the energy levels are different! How you end up experiencing crystals will change depending on your needs, beliefs, and own perspectives.

Crystal Myths

As mentioned earlier, an important aspect of harnessing the healing power of crystals is to keep an open mind. Unfortunately, many myths around crystals can cause disbelief in the powers of the crystals. One strong example of this is believing that the healing power is all in your head. When you work with crystals, you are meant to get out of your head. You will want to focus on the sensation alone. Thanks to the power of the crystal, there is no need to explain or rationalize what is happening. If you do feel concerned about using crystals, those thoughts are only in your mind. Instead of being focused on why it won't work, allow yourself to experience the sensations that come from the crystals and rationalize about those feelings later.

Another popular myth that circulates around crystals is the thought that if they are able to help people, they can also harm them. You will learn later that your crystals vibrate the energy that entrains with your energy. One of the major factors of using healing crystals will be your mindset and intention. If you go into the situation expecting the crystal to harm you, this, of course, is possible. Your belief in the crystal will change your experience and outcome. In general, you will want to approach the healing crystal with the intention of shifting your vibration to more positive energy.

The third myth about crystals is the mindset that you need to be spiritual in order to use crystals. While this is helpful, it isn't necessary. Just about anyone can use crystals. All you will need is to have an open mindset and the desire to change your energy. Even those who aren't spiritual or new-age have the ability to experience the healing power of the crystal.

A final myth I will mention here is the thought that more expensive crystals are the most powerful. One of the most powerful crystals is Quartz. Typically, quartz is fairly common and can be inexpensive. When you are starting your crystal collection, the amount of money you spend will make no difference on how effective the crystals are — the only factor that truly matters for the crystals is your energy and mindset. Sometimes, the least expensive crystals will be the ones that give you what you need.

As a beginner, you may feel the need to know everything at once. You could spend months immersing yourself in information, but you will need hands-on experience. Of course, you will need to educate yourself to help guide your crystal healing journey but remember to pick up the crystal along the way. With that in mind, we will now dive into starting your own crystal collection. Remember to find the crystal that attracts you. When you do, you will want to wear it, hold it, or even place it in your pocket. The more you experience crystals, the easier it will become to sense their energy.

Starting a Collection

Now that you have learned some of the crystal basics, it is time to get started on the fun part; starting a crystal collection of your own! Some people have crystals everywhere in their house while others just carry a few crystals in their pocket. You don't necessarily need a plethora of crystals to have a collection. All you will need is one or two. The major goal of a crystal collection will be to select your crystals mindfully. As you go through this book, you will be guided to the crystals as long as you follow your intuition.

I believe that crystals choose you just as much as you choose the crystal. You will learn that some crystals will serve a temporary need, and others, you will give to benefit other people who need them more. As you collect, you will buy some crystals for their beauty and others for their healing benefits. Later in the book, we will be going over different crystals in detail to help you select the best one for your life.

Places to Shop for Crystals

The first suggested place to shop for crystals would be a crystal/metaphysical shops. When you are selecting crystals, you will want to hold them and feel their energy. Many cities and towns have crystal outlets. Most times, these stores are listed as New Age shops, crystal stores, or even metaphysical bookshops.

Another location to purchase crystals would be a crystal, mineral, and gem show. These are traveling shows for crystals and are great for buying crystals at good prices. It should be noted that you will most likely have to travel to these shows and pay an entry fee. If you see a show coming to your town, you will definitely want to plan a trip. At these shows, the dealers typically have a vast knowledge of crystals and will allow you to handle them before any purchase.

Finally, you can always find an online retailer for your crystals. There are different craft sites such as Amazon, Etsy, or eBay. This can be tricky as you cannot hold the crystal to feel their power. Instead, try checking out the seller feedback before buying any crystals and checking their overall rating. This way, you get a good vibe from the seller, and hopefully, good vibes from the crystals as well.

Understanding Crystal Shapes

When you first start purchasing crystals, you will find two basic categories for the crystal shape. It is natural and polished. In general, the natural stones, also known as raw or rough, will have more powerful energy. It should be noted that more power isn't always better. In the case for beginners, it is better to start with polished stones as they have subtler energy.

Rough Stones

One of the main factors of rough stones you will notice is that they look very much like they were just removed from the earth. Some of the raw stones you find may appear as though they have broken off into smaller stones. In general, rough stones maintain their natural form and have never had any human intervention. There are a few different rough stones as followed:

1. Blades
   Blades are rough stones that are exactly as they sound. These stones are typically long and flat. A blade stone has jagged areas and is best known as a worry stone. This stone is great to rub your thumb along the smooth area to help soothe any stress you may have.

2. Cluster
   A cluster rough stone contains a group of crystals. One of the more popular cluster stone would be a cluster of quartz. These stones are best for direct energy if it is needed in a specific area.

3. Geodes
   Geodes are rough stones that have open cavities in which are lined with crystals. Typically, this type of rough stone is used for decorating the house.

4. Point
   Point stones have one pointed end known as single-terminated or two pointed ends known as double-terminated. The stone will also have one flat end. A popular point stone is a smoky quartz. This rough stone is typically used to point direct energy toward something.

5. Rough Crystals
   Rough crystals often just look like rocks. These types of rough stones have no certain shape and can change size. Depending on the size of the stone, these crystals can help with a number of healing factors.

6. Wand
   As you could have guessed, a wand natural stone is long and narrow. The difference is, the stone isn't shaped deliberately. It appears naturally in the earth. A wand rough stone is also an excellent choice for a worry stone.

Cut and Polished Stones

While rough stones look the way they sound, cut and polished stones are glossy and smooth. While some still have their natural shape, other crystals can be cut into a specific shape. As you will learn, different shapes hold different properties. When you work with this type of crystal, the shape of the crystal is able to impart properties of both the sacred shape as well as the power of the crystal itself. Below, I will explain some of the more popular shapes to help you decide which would benefit you most.

1. Dodecahedron
   The Dodecahedron looks much like a circle with edges. This shape is mostly associated with an element known as Ethers. It is thought that this shape helps connect individuals to their intuition and higher realms.

2. Hexahedron
   A hexahedron is also known as a cube. This shape is known to represent the element of earth. For most people, this shape helps with grounding and stability.

3. Icosahedron
   An Icosahedron is mostly known for its link to the element of water. This shape helps people connect to the way they change and flow in any given situation.

4. Octahedron
   An Octahedron looks like two triangles placed together. This shape is best known to represent the element of air. For the holder, it promotes feelings of love, forgiveness, kindness, and compassion.

5. Sphere
   A sphere crystal looks much like a marble. It is thought that this shape holds energy that helps people feel whole, complete, and one with the world.

6. Tetrahedron
   A tetrahedron is the shape of a triangle or pyramid. This crystal shape is best represented with the element of fire. This crystal helps the holder promote stability, balance, and introduces the ability to create change.

7. Merkaba
   A Merkaba is the shape of a 3D star. This shape contains all of the elements of those above and combines them so that the holder can experience the effects of each element. Mostly, this crystal shape is associated with eternal wisdom and sacred truth.

Choosing your Crystals

If you are a true beginner with crystals, you may have absolutely no idea where to start. While of course in the third chapter, we will be going over many different crystals, there are ten crystals that make for an excellent starter kit. These crystals are known as crystal workhorses and are crystals that absolutely everyone should have. Of course, these crystals are just a suggestion, but you can always add on and use these as a jumping off point.

1. Clear Quartz
   Any crystal collector should have clear quartz in their collection. Clear quartz is a great crystal to have as the crystal is able to work with every type of energy.

2. Citrine
   Citrine is an excellent crystal to have for any beginner as it is able to help promote both prosperity as well as self-esteem.

3. Smoky Quartz
   You will learn later in this book that smoky quartz is a manifestation stone. This stone is able to convert any negative energy into more positive energy.

4. Turquoise
   While also beautiful, turquoise stones have the ability to promote personal power, prosperity, as well as luck.

5. Rose Quartz
   If you are seeking love in your life, rose quartz will be vital for your collection. This stone is able to support all different types of love such as romantic love or even unconditional love.

6. Hematite
   Hematite is a stone that is used to attract energies into your life. It is also associated with centering and grounding and is a protective stone.

7. Amethyst

If you are looking to tune guidance and intuition into your life, amethyst will be good to add to your first collection. This stone also has the power to help with your dreams.

8. Carnelian
   Are you looking to become a more creative individual? Carnelian will be essential for your crystal collection. This stone is able to help with integrity and also allows individuals to set appropriate boundaries for themselves.

9. Black Tourmaline
   As a crystal collector, you will need a protector. Black tourmaline is great for this and can also help keep negative energies at bay if that is something you typically experience.

10. Rainbow Fluorite
    Finally, we have rainbow fluorite. This crystal is best known to promote love, facilitate clear communication, and also has the ability to deepen intuition.

As I said, these are mere suggestions. In the third chapter, you will have a better understanding of crystals for your own needs and collection. You will want to choose crystals based on their system. Later in this book, we will explain the different crystal systems and how they each have certain properties. Some of these crystal systems include:

1. Triclinic Crystals
   These ward off energies

2. Tetragonal Crystals
   These attract energies

3. Orthorhombic Crystals
   These clear, unblock, and release energies

4. Monoclinic Crystals
   These crystals help protect you

5. Isometric Crystals

These crystals can help amplify energy and improve situations

6. Hexagonal Crystals
   These have the ability to manifest

Another way people choose their crystals is by their color. As you will learn, each crystal's color will have vibrational energy that is connected to their healing property. Later in this book, we will be going over the different colors and their specific property. By having this knowledge, you will be able to select your crystals for certain conditions.

Finally, you will want to choose your crystal based on how they make you feel. Crystal selection relies heavily on intuition. This is why I suggest you hold the crystals in your hand and let them tell you how they make you feel. In hand, you will instantly be able to tell if a crystal makes you feel comfortable or not. You will want to feel a pleasing sensation before you buy, if not, it isn't the right crystal! You will always want to pay attention to the attraction you feel toward any crystal as they are most likely calling to you for a reason.

Tips and Tricks for Crystal Shopping

1. Ground Yourself
   As a crystal beginner, you may feel a bit disoriented when you enter a crystal shop. The energy of the store itself can seem overwhelming, which is why you will want to ground yourself before entering the shop. You can do this by closing your eyes and visualizing your roots growing from your feet and into the earth. If you still feel lightheaded in the shop, try picking up a black stone to help ground you.

2. Follow your Intuition
   This is vital when shopping in a crystal store. You will more than likely be drawn to a certain location. It is the crystal calling to you. Remember, always to follow your intuition as it is happening for a reason.

3. Ask Away
   If you walk into a shop or gem store, you will most likely find an expert in the crystal department. If you have any questions on finding the right crystal, never be afraid to ask. Asking questions is also a wonderful way to educate yourself. On top of asking questions, feel free to reference this book!

4. Don't Jump
   If you are just starting your collection, it is easy to get overwhelmed, especially by shiny objects. You should never just grab the first pretty stone you see. Instead, shop around and see which stones are calling to you. Once you have selected your stone, you will want to compare prices and find the best price for the crystal you want.

5. Reputation of Seller
   Before you stop into a store, you will want to check out the reputation of the seller. Unfortunately, there are scammers out there who are just looking to make a buck. Take to the internet to search for reviews before you hand over your hard-earned cash to just any person selling crystals.

6. Touch
   Any true crystal seller will allow you to hold the crystals before you purchase them. It is important that you handle the crystal to see how they make you feel. You will instantly sense the energy coming from the crystal to see if it is calling out to you or not. If the owner of the shop says no touching, walk out. Most likely, this person doesn't really understand how healing crystals work.

Power of Crystals

While collecting crystals is one part of the journey, the other part is to understand the healing powers of each crystal. One of the major reasons that healing crystals work is due to the energy you feel when you hold them in your hand. They are concrete examples that help individuals move to other modalities when they become more comfortable with crystals. Eventually, you will be able to move to chakra work, sound practice, meditation, mantras, and even more. At the end of the day, you will practice healing practices that resonate most with you. One major way you can further your practice with crystal is learning how to use crystals in conjunction with other crystals. This is known as a crystal grid. A crystal grid is when you combine crystals based on their sacred geometry. By doing this, you will be able to grow the energy of the crystals to be more focused and much more powerful. A grid can be simple or complex depending on how comfortable you are with crystals. In order to use a grid, you can place them anywhere whether it is on your bed or even on your disk. Below, I will go over some grid shape examples to help you get started.

1. Spirals
   A spiral grid is used to represent a path to consciousness.

2. Circles
   If you use a circle grid, this is perfect to represent unity and oneness.

3. Vesica Piscis
   This grid is two circles that combine. This is helpful if you are trying to represent creation.

4. Squares
   A square grid represents the earth's elements.

5. Triangles
   If you create a triangle grid with your crystals, this helps create a connection between the mind, body, and the spirit.

On top of the placement, the grid arrangement will also be important. Your grid will need to follow certain elements for it to work. To start, you will want to place your focus stone in the center of the grid. You can think of this as the stone that holds the primary energy you would like to achieve. Once in place, you will place the appropriate surrounding stones to help amplify the energy. By doing this, you allow the energy to flow outward from the focus point.

If you desire, you can also place outer stones around the surrounding stones, though this isn't required. Outer stones are often placed to be a source of intention for the primary energy you are trying to achieve. These stones can also be a perimeter stone if you wish to keep the intentional energy within your grid.

One example of a grid arrangement would be a grid for creativity. The configuration you will want to use is the Vesica Piscis. As you will recall, this looks like two circles that are intertwined. To achieve the most creativity, you will want to place the citrine as your focus stones, surrounded by amethyst for your perimeter stone.

Another example of a grid arrangement will be if you are seeking forgiveness, whether it is for yourself or from another person. The configuration you would use would be a spiral. Start by placing your focus stone, selenite, in the center. Going out from this stone, you would want to use clear quartz points to amplify the energy through the perimeter stones. As you learn more about crystals, you will be able to put your own grids together eventually.

Now that you understand the basics of crystals, it is time to understand the health benefits that come from the crystals. As you go through the different benefits such as help for addiction, increased happiness, or creating patience, take mental notes on what you wish to improve in your life. By thoroughly understanding the healing powers of crystals, you will have a thorough understanding of which crystals you will need to introduce into your life.

CHAPTER TWO
Health Benefits Of Crystal Healing

As you work more with crystals, you will learn different strategies that work for you. The following information in this chapter is mere suggestions. The more you work with crystals, the more you will be able to choose crystals that work best for you. What you will need to remember is that healing will take some time. In order to make any changes, you must have an open heart and an open mind.

Being a beginner, you will need to learn how to set aside any doubts or fears you may have about crystals. Instead, enter your practice with a receptive and positive mindset to help with your healing. You can only heal if you are willing to receive the powers of the healing crystals. Due to this, I will grace you with a mantra to start each session with. In the chapter to follow, you will find a mantra for the problem, followed by two healing stones that can be used, and a grid that may be helpful with your practice. You can start with these suggestions, and then come up with some solutions of your own as you learn more about crystals.

Addiction

Many people struggle with addiction. While some people have an addiction to alcohol or drugs, other people have an addiction to unhealthy relationships and unhealthy diets. No matter what you are addicted to, you can often feel helpless in any given situation. Luckily, there are some remedies you can try to help you release from any unhealthy attachments you have and gain the strength to free yourself from any given addiction.

> **Mantra:**
>
> I have an addiction. I choose to release this unhealthy attachment. I will move forward and release myself from this addiction
>
> **Healing Stone:**
>
> 1. **Hematite**

In the chapter to follow, you will be learning more about your chakras. It is thought that most addictions stem from our root chakra. In this case, you will want to use a crystal that can help bring balance to this chakra. Hematite is a crystal that is able to absorb energy to help take away any power an addiction may hold over you.

One way to use the hematite is to place it beneath a place you sit through the day. Some examples of this could be on your bed or your chair at work. You can also carry the crystal with you, so it is with you through the day. For those moments when you feel the addiction urges wash over you, simply hold the hematite in your dominant hand and repeat the mantra until the addiction urge passes. Remember to cleanse the hematite after using it all day. We will be going over the cleansing process in the final chapter.

2. Amethyst

This crystal is often referred to as the sobriety stone. It is thought to help protect individuals from becoming drunk. If you are an individual who is addicted to any substance that alters your mind such as alcohol, caffeine, or even nicotine, amethyst will be beneficial for you. To use this crystal, you will just need to carry it in your pocket. When your addiction urges strike, place the crystal in your dominant hand and repeat the mantra until you feel better.

Healing Grid

As mentioned, addiction can be related to your root chakra. The healing grid you will want to create with your healing crystals is going to be a basic layout of chakra stones. You will want to create this grid in a location where you typically spend most of your time. We suggest placing it on your bed or on your desk. Each one of the crystals will absorb your chakras from any excess energy that may be causing your addiction.

Configuration: Vertical Line

Stones Needed:

- Howlite (Crown)
- Lapis Lazuli (Third-Eye)
- Sodalite (Throat)
- Malachite (Heart)
- Yellow Tigers Eye (Solar Plexus)
- Carnelian (Sacral)
- Black Tourmaline (Root)

Anger

Anger. It is an emotion that we all experience from time to time. We get angry when we are stuck in traffic and are late to work. We get angry when our loved one doesn't listen to what we say. We even get angry when our food gets burned! It is so easy to get angry about things that are out of our control. This emotion can become debilitating when you suffer from long-term anger. Sometimes, these emotions can come out as resentment, frustration, or even rage. When you start working with healing crystals, the powers can help you release some of this anger, so you can move forward with your life.

Mantra:

At this moment, I am feeling anger. I have the power to control my anger. I will choose to be calm and positive.

Healing Stones:

1. **Malachite**
   It is believed that anger is linked to our heart chakra. Anger is an emotion of excess energy and over-expression. This emotion can be absorbed by an opaque crystal. This crystal is able to absorb the energy as you release it. The malachite crystal is a deep green color and holds the ability to absorb any excess energy you are releasing. If anger and rage are emotions you experience daily, try wearing the malachite on a long cord so that it

lies over your heart. In the case that wearing the crystal doesn't work, place the crystal in your hand and repeat the mantra until the feelings pass you by.

2. **Black and Red Jasper**
For some people, anger happens when they are afraid. Anger is a defense mechanism that can protect you from feeling afraid. If this resonates with you, you could benefit from a red or black opaque stone such as Jasper. This stone can help you by just simply carrying it in your pocket. In the chance that you are feeling afraid and angry, simply place the stone into your hand and plant your feet to the floor. Close your eyes and visualize a cloud draining through your feet and repeat the mantra until you feel more secure.

Healing Grid:

When it comes to anger release, a circular grid will be most helpful. As you already learned, a circle grid stands for unity and oneness. As you place your stones, they will amplify compassion as well as absorb any anger you are feeling. You will want to place this grid under your bed or anywhere you spend a lot of time.

Configuration: Circle

Stones Needed:

- Malachite (Focus Stone)
- Rose Quartz (Intention Stones)

Balance

It should come as no surprise that balance is vital in our lives. When we feel out of control, we feel unbalanced and unhappy. Unfortunately, a lack of balance in certain areas can lead to a lack of balance in other parts of your life like work, love, and friendship. The very first step you will need to take is to recognize that you are out of balance in the first place. Once you have come to terms, you can use some crystals to help you find your balance again.

Mantra:

I have the power to balance myself. I am balanced and at peace.

Healing Stones:

1. **Rainbow Fluorite**
   You will be learning in the next chapter that rainbow fluorite has a wide array of colors. Thanks to the colors, this crystal is able to help balance energies. The crystal is also so beautiful. It is perfect to wear as jewelry to bring you to balance through the day. If at any point, you begin to feel imbalanced, all you will need to do is place it in your non-dominant hand a repeat your mantra.

2. **Turquoise**
   This stone is often known as the stone of harmony. By wearing turquoise in your jewelry, it can help balance your energy so that you can bring peace back to your life.

Healing Grid:

The healing grid to find your balance is a bit different. You will need black tourmaline and clear quartz for this healing grid. What you will need to do is find a comfortable place in your home and lie down. I suggest your bed or even the sofa. Once in place, you will place the black tourmaline on your root chakra and the quartz near your crown chakra. If you have no idea where these are, we go further into your chakras in the next chapter. After, you will close your eyes and imagine your energy flowing from each chakra. As you do this, repeat your mantra until you feel balanced.

Compassion

Compassion is an important quality for just about anyone, but it is something that people often forget. We forget to have compassion for not only others but also for ourselves. Compassion can be difficult and frustrating, but it is necessary if you wish to experience yourself in a Divine manner. Several crystals can help you develop more compassion.

Mantra:

I have the ability to see everyone and everything with eyes of compassion. I am a compassionate and loving person.

Healing Stones:

1. **Rose Quartz**

   As you probably already know, compassion is an emotion that comes not only from our hearts but also from our spirits. In order to experience an emotion such as compassion, you will want to choose a stone that amplifies the desire to nurture and grow compassion. Rose quartz is the perfect stone for this as it has one of the highest vibrations to cultivate compassion.

   You can use rose quartz in a few different ways. If you are searching for self-compassion, you will want to hold the stone in your non-dominant hand, hold it at your heart, and repeat your mantra. If it is compassion for others you are searching for, place the stone in your dominant hand, hold at your heart, and repeat the mantra as many times as you need to.

2. **Aquamarine**

   When it comes to compassion, it can be hard to experience unless you release any judgments you may be having about certain individuals. Aquamarine holds power to help you let go of these emotions. If you experience yourself being judgmental, all you will need to do is hold the stone in your dominant hand, close your eyes, and picture yourself releasing this emotion. You will want to repeat a mantra such as, "I will allow compassion for this person. I am choosing to release my judgment."

Healing Grid:

For this practice, you will need Peridot. Peridot, known as a heart stone, is best known for its quality of compassion. For this practice, you will need first to find a comfortable location. We suggest your bed or a nice, soft sofa. When you find this place, lie down on your back and place the peridot on your heart chakra. When you feel safe, close your eyes and notice the beating of your heart. As you focus on your breath, visualize a person who you have compassion for. Notice your emotions and sensations for this person and feel it through your whole body. Practice for as long as you need to help bring more compassion into your life.

Confidence

While there seems to be a bad reputation behind confidence, it is essential for life. It is important to realize that there is a very fine line between confidence and arrogance. If someone comes across too confident, people are turned off by this quality. When you are confident in yourself, it brings balance to your life to be successful and joyful. If you feel you are lacking in the self-confidence department, there are a few crystals that can help you out.

Mantra:

I love myself. I accept myself unconditionally. Being confident is okay.

Healing Stones:

1. **Yellow Tigers Eye**
   If you lack self-confidence, you may benefit from meditation with a yellow tiger's eye in hand. This stone helps absorb any negative energy you feel for yourself and can absorb excess confidence that makes people come across arrogant. While you meditate, hold the stone in your dominant hand and repeat your mantra to remind yourself that you will accept yourself for who you truly are.

2. **Citrine**

Citrine is a stone that has the ability to amplify self-confidence. This is only useful if you recognize the confidence within yourself already. Of course, this will be something that you will need to practice. You can build your confidence and strengthen it by holding the stone in your non-dominant hand and meditate quietly. You will want to visualize a golden light around you, flowing through the stone and into your body.

3. Amber

Finally, you can use amber to help build your confidence. Most of our confidence comes from our solar plexus chakra. Many people wear amber in their jewelry to help build their self-confidence when they need it most out in public. You can wear a necklace or bracelet as a visual reminder that it is okay to be confident.

Courage

When the lion was on his way to see the Wizard of Oz, he was going to ask for courage. What he found was that it was within him all along. Finding courage isn't always due to being afraid of something, it can be finding the courage to do what is best for you. If you ever find you need more courage in a trying situation, there are a few crystals that could help you on that path.

Mantra:

I have the courage within my mind and soul to do what is best for me.

Healing Stones:

1. Citrine

Citrine has a golden yellow color that is able to amplify the energy to your solar plexus. It is thought that courage arises from this chakra, so in times that you are looking for courage, this stone is excellent to create a power source. For it to work, you will hold the stone in your non-dominant hand and repeat the mantra from above.

2. **Aquamarine**

   Another stone that represents courage is aquamarine. This stone is beautiful and looks great in jewelry. If you feel you need courage through your day, for any situation, you can wear this on a daily basis. For the moments you need an extra boost of courage, call to the stone and repeat your mantra for the courage.

Healing Grid:

The healing grid for courage is called a courage grid. You will want to place this grid in a location you spend a lot of time in. You will need the following stones to help amplify the energy.

Configuration: Square

Stones Needed:

- Amazonite (Focus Stone)
- Aquamarine (Intention Stone)
- Citrine (Intention Stone)
- Clear Quartz Points (Perimeter Stone)

Forgiveness

There is a lot of misunderstanding about what forgiveness can mean. For some, it is about letting go of anger or resentment to another person, but that isn't necessarily always true. Forgiveness truly happens when you let go of the pain that is caused by another's actions. You will also want to learn how to forgive yourself. Often, we are our own demise. It is important that you learn how to love yourself just as you love others. Crystals can help with all different types of forgiveness whether you need it for yourself, or a person you have had a struggling relationship with.

Mantra:

I am choosing to let go of the pain I have felt in the past. I will move forward with love, compassion, and forgiveness in my heart.

Healing Stones:

1. **Apache Tears**

   Apache Tears are the perfect stones if you are looking to overcome any painful or difficult feelings you are experiencing. These stones grant the ability to let go of negative feelings so that you will be able to forgive and move forward with your life. For this stone to work, you will hold it in your dominant hand and close your eyes. As you find your breath, imagine there is a dark shadow floating from your heart, down your arm, and into the crystal. Once you feel clear from this negative energy, imagine telling the person or yourself, I forgive you.

2. **Rhodochrosite**
   Rhodochrosite is a stone that is also able to help with forgiveness. This stone is a pink color that some people find themselves instantly attracted to. For this stone to work, all you will need to do is hold the stone over your heart using both hands. Once in place, close your eyes and repeat your mantra of forgiveness until you feel the pain leaving your body.

Healing Grid:

Earlier in the book, we described the forgiveness grid. Please feel free to go back to check out this grid before moving forward. When your grid is in place, you will just need to visualize the person you are seeking to forgive. Imagine that you are fixing the energy ties between the two of you and repeat your Mantra. Once you forgive the person, imagine a lovely and positive white energy that surrounds them.

Grief

Unfortunately, grief is a natural part of life. We experience this emotion when we lose something we love. Of course, it is vital that you allow yourself to experience this emotion fully in order to move past this moment. It does become an issue when you get stuck in this emotion. When we are stuck grieving, we often miss out on life's moment that is meant to be joyful. Luckily, working with crystals can help the grief pass in a healthy manner. With the use of crystals, you will be able to remove any blockages so that you can move forward with your life.

Mantra:

I will let go of this grief. I am filled with love and love will heal my pain.

Healing Stones:

1. **Apache Tears**
   Much like with forgiveness, this stone also works for grief. While the stone itself can't make the emotion go away, it will help you healthily process the emotion. If you are in the middle of grieving, try carrying the crystal with you to help process the emotion. It is helpful to place it next to your bed, so its energy is near you while you are sleeping.

2. **Ruby**
   When we are grieving, our hearts are wounded. Ruby is an excellent stone to help heal your heart. To use this stone, lie down with the ruby held gently to your heart chakra. You will want to repeat your mantra for grief and visualize a healing light enter your heart chakra, washing away any grief you are experiencing.

Healing Grid:

You will want to create a grief grid to help heal yourself. This is also known as a stages-of-grief grid. Much like with other grids, you will want to create it where you spend a lot of time. Each stone will represent a different stage of grief. You will notice that there is no true focus or perimeter stone. Instead, focus on each stone to help go through each stage of grief.

Configuration: Spiral

Stones Needed:

- Apache Tear (First Stone, Grief)
- Hematite (Anger)
- Rainbow Fluorite (Denial)
- Blue Kyanite (Bargaining)
- Smoky Quartz (Depression)
- Amethyst (Acceptance)

Happiness

While I think we all wish we could be happy all of the time, it is something we can easily lose sight of. We often become overwhelmed with our day-to-day lives and can get stressed out. Often, we can forget to experience happiness or joy. With the help of crystals, you will have a reminder to choose to be happy. It is okay to get stressed out; it is going to happen. It is important to let go and be happy!

Mantra:

At this moment, I choose to have happiness and joy.

Healing Stones:

1. **Amber**
   Amber is often associated with happiness. First, it has a gorgeous golden color that radiates natural warmth. Many people wear amber to help cultivate the energy of happiness. You can wear it as a visual reminder to be happy. It is something you can choose, no matter what the situation is. If you ever fall under the spell of stress, hold the amber in your non-dominant hand and repeat your mantra until you feel the happiness return to your soul.

2. **Smoky Quartz**
   Smoky quartz is a stone that is able to turn negative energy into positive energy. If you feel more stressed out than usual, you can take a moment to meditate with this stone in each hand. As you sit or lie down to meditate,

close your eyes and visualize the negative energy flowing through you. Once you have it in your mind, imagine the energy flowing into each stone in your hands. The negative energy leaves your body and is replaced with warm, happy energy.

3. Citrine

Citrine is a stone that has the ability to spread joy and happiness. If you are going to a social situation but aren't in a good mood, try holding citrine before you leave. You will want to place it in your dominant hand and tell yourself; I will spread only happiness. Repeat this mantra until you believe it in your soul, and then pop the stone into your pocket. It will be your reminder to spread happiness to those who surround you.

Love

You are loved, even if you don't realize it. It is important to remember that not all love is a romantic love. However, when we lack this type of love, people often feel lonely. One of the most popular reasons people get into crystal healing is to help with love. With the help of crystals, you will be able to help with all different types of love in your life.

Mantra:

I choose to give love to others, and I receive this love in my heart and soul.

Healing Stones:

1. Rose Quartz

Rose Quartz is the most widely used crystal for those seeking unconditional love in their life. Most people find this stone in a heart-shape. However, it isn't necessary for your use. If it is romantic love you are looking for, you will want to meditate with this stone held against your heart chakra. As you settle into your meditation, imagine a love energy coming from your heart, flowing to your crystal, and exploding into the universe. You can think of this stone as a magnet to attract love in your direction. As you meditate, remember to repeat your own mantra about love.

2. **Peridot**
Difficulty in relationships can be taxing and frustrating. Whether this love is romantic or platonic, the peridot stone is an excellent source to help release any hurt feeling or anger you may be experiencing at the moment. The peridot brings healing energy to you and your relationship when used during meditation. As you settle in, you will want to hold this stone against your heart chakra. Once in place, you will want to visualize the person you are having difficulty with. As you picture them, imagine a green light extending from your heart, through the stone, and to the heart of this individual. This light will heal your emotions and relationship as you repeat your mantra.

3. **Pink Tourmaline**

A final crystal that is known to help with the emotions with love is pink tourmaline. If you find yourself in a relationship where you lack trust, this is a major block for love. By using pink tourmaline, the crystal healing powers may help you build this trust toward another person. For this crystal to work, you will want to hold the stone in your dominant hand and visualize the energy surrounding you. You will feel the warmth and trust building up inside you. Repeat your mantra until you believe it in your heart and soul.

Motivation

Sometimes, motivation is hard to find. When we want to accomplish our dreams, it takes a lot of self-motivation. It is thought that motivation comes from our solar plexus. The solar plexus is in charge of our personal will which can experience imbalances of energy. When this happens, we can lack motivation. With the help of crystals, you can help restore and rebalance these energies to get you moving in a positive direction.

Mantra:

I choose to be motivated. I can do it, and I will be it.

Healing Stones:

1. **Yellow Tigers Eye**
   Yellow Tigers Eye is a stone that can help you with your personal will. For this stone to work, you will want to begin meditation and place the stone against your solar plexus chakra. Once you do this, you will repeat your mantra until you believe it in your heart and soul. If you don't have time to meditate, place the stone in your hand, close your eyes, and state a mantra for the activity you are trying to gain motivation for. An example of this would be if you are trying to find the motivation to eat healthily. Try saying, I choose to consume foods that support my health. You will want to repeat this until you believe it.

2. **Rainbow Fluorite**
   Rainbow Fluorite is a stone that is commonly known to help with both motivated and keeping individuals focused. If you are a person who lacks motivation constantly, try wearing this stone on a necklace so that it is with you at all times. On the days you need more motivation, place the stone in your dominant hand and repeat your mantra.

3. **Citrine**
   A final way to use crystals for motivation is to combine citrine with essential oils. When these are combined, it can help you improve your motivation and your focus. While each person is different, you can try a lemon or orange oil to get you started. You will want to diffuse the oil as you meditate. Once in place, hold the citrine near your solar plexus and repeat your mantra until you feel motivated.

Negativity

Negativity can come into our lives in a number of forms. Sometimes, this energy comes from other people while other times, it comes from events that happen to us. One thing for sure is that these negative energies can drain us, making it almost impossible to focus on the things in life that really matter. On top of that, you probably don't feel well if you are living in a negative space. There are crystals that can help transform your negative energy into positive energy.

Mantra:

I choose to be a positive person. Everything I say and do, I will do in a positive manner.

Healing Stones:

1. **Smoky Quartz**
   Smoky quartz is one of the most popular stones to use for negative energy. It is a stone you can have all around your house to help create a positive space to work in. I suggest placing it under your bed or even under your desk at work!

2. **Hematite**
   Hematite stones have the ability to absorb negative energy. It can work on your own negative energy, negative energy from your environment, or even another individual. There are special hematite rings you can purchase if you tend to be in a negative space more than you would like — all you need to do is place the ring on your finger and state your mantra.

3. **Himalayan Salt**
   Another way to rid of negative energy in a space is to purchase a Himalayan salt lamp. You will want to place this lamp in the rooms that you spend the most time in. When the lightbulb heats up the Himalayan salt, it sends a positive energy field through the room, helping cleanse any negative energy and creates a positive space.

Patience

We have all lost our patience at some point in our lives. Whether it was with a co-worker, a child, or a loved one, it happens! Under certain circumstances, anyone can lack patience. If you find your patience is being tried, some crystals can help when you need a little extra support.

Mantra:

Everything is temporary. This feeling will pass.

Healing Stones:

1. **Howlite**
   Howlite is a stone that has the ability to teach anyone patience. If you have a lifestyle that is filled with impatience, this is the perfect stone for you. Whether you are dealing with crazy parking lots, yelling children, or a stressful situation at work, howlite can give you the support you need. All you will need to do is keep a smooth piece of howlite on your person. As the impatience starts to build, treat the stone as a worry stone and rub your thumb over it. When you rub the stone, repeat your mantra and become mindful of the patience you need for any given situation.

2. **Amazonite**
   Some people lack patience, in general. If you find that you are typically an impatient person, amazonite may be the crystal to benefit you most. This stone has the ability to sooth the highest of nerves. The energy of this stone helps with patience and grants the ability to help you chill out. You can keep the stone in your pocket or sleep with it under your bed to experience the most benefit.

3. **Labradorite**
   There will be times in your life when you need to be kind and patience with yourself. Labradorite can be helpful with this and can act as a reminder to be patient. Many people wear labradorite as jewelry so that they always

have it on their person. If you find that you need patience with yourself, try holding the stone in your non-dominant hand and tell yourself, I am at peace. I am going to be patient.

Regret

In life, we have emotions that simply don't help us at all. Regret is one of these emotions. Unfortunately, this emotion stems from unresolved shame or guilt that sticks with us. When we fail to focus on life and instead, dwell of something we have already done, it can keep you from living your best life. When you regret, you are keeping yourself rooted in the past as opposed to the here and now, where you should be. Self-forgiveness is very important, and some crystals can help with this problem.

Mantra:

I choose to forgive myself. I will live in the here and now. I will let go of my past.

Healing Stones:

1. **Rose Quartz**
   One major aspect of letting go of regret is having self-compassion. When you have self-compassion, you will be able to release regret sooner. As you already learned, rose quartz is a popular stone that will help you forgive yourself and release any regret you are holding onto. For this to work, you must place the rose quartz on your heart, close your eyes, and repeat your mantra.

2. **Smoky Quartz**
   Another benefit of smoky quartz is the stone's ability to help you release any old beliefs you may be holding onto. For many, regret is an old belief that is no longer serving you in the here and the now. If you feel regret over something that happened in your past, try carrying a piece of smoky quartz in your pocket for quick access. If you ever feel regret slipping into your mind, hold the

stone in your dominant hand and repeat your mantra until this emotion fades.

Healing Grid:

If you still feel regret and feel you need something a bit stronger to help you overcome these emotions, a releasing regret grid may do the trick for you. I suggest creating this grid under your bed or on a flat surface you spend a lot of time near.

Configuration: Triangle, to connect your spirit, mind, and body.

Stones Needed:

- Smoky Quartz (Focus Stone)
- Aquamarine (Intention Stone)
- Black Tourmaline (Perimeter Stones)

Rejection

When we get rejected, it can hurt a lot. Sometimes, we are rejected in relationships. Other times, we are rejected by things like a job. It can be very hard to put yourself out there when you risk rejection. It is important to realize that rejection is just a part of life. More than likely, you are rejected because you are meant for something different, something better! Nonetheless, rejection is still painful. If you fear rejection, it can hold you back from trying new things. Below, we will go over some crystals that can help you overcome your fear of rejection, so you can get out there and experience life to the fullest.

Mantra:

I am not afraid of rejection. I can take risks that benefit me. I am brave.

Healing Stones:

1. **Rose Quartz**

When we are rejected by someone or something, we typically take that emotion to heart. Unfortunately, we have no control over whether people like us or not, but that doesn't mean that we don't get hurt when this happens. Rose quartz is the perfect stone to use to help heal the pain you feel. After rejection, it will be important to return to an emotion of self-love. If you feel the sting of rejection, try to wear rose quartz as jewelry. As the emotion creeps in, hold onto the stone and remind yourself that you are loved, and this rejection is not a reflection of yourself.

2. **Hematite**
We have all experienced rejection at some point in our lives. Some develop a deep fear of rejection and avoid any risky situations to avoid this feeling. Fear is rooted deep in our root chakra and is associated with our need for safety and security. The hematite stone is able to provide us with both. To use this stone, place it in your non-dominant hand and repeat your mantra. As you do this, you will want to visualize this fear of rejection like a cloud over your head. Imagine that this cloud flows from above you and into the stone, releasing all of your fear. Once you release your fear of rejection, you can do more exciting things in life.

3. **Yellow Tigers Eye**
Along with the heart, rejection can also affect our self-worth and self-imagine. These emotions are typically located in our solar plexus. You can use a yellow tiger's eye stone to help strengthen this chakra. By doing this, you can overcome past rejections and the pain that it has caused you. The more you practice getting over the fear of rejection, the less likely this fear will cripple you in the future. You can practice by placing the crystal over your solar plexus chakra. As you lay down, imagine the energy from the stone flowing into your body and strengthening your self-worth. When you do this, you will want to tell yourself that there is no amount of rejection that can keep you down.

Stress

In general, life can be pretty stressful at times. If you think about it, we stress about a lot of small things throughout the day. We stress about getting to work on time, we stress about getting the kids ready for school, we even stress about what we are going to eat! When life seems to be spiraling out of control and you feel yourself falling apart, there is a crystal that can help you in this situation. When you manage stress properly, you can increase your health.

Mantra:

I choose to let this stress go. I will be healthy and happy.

Healing Stones:

1. **Yellow Tiger's Eye**
   When you are stressed, this has a major effect on your adrenal gland. The part of your chakra that is associated with your adrenal glands is your solar plexus. The stone of yellow tiger's eye has the ability to absorb any excess energy you may be taking in. When there is too much energy, it causes stress from an imbalance of energy. The stone is able to absorb this energy and helps you rebalance in the process. For this stone to work, simply lay down where you are most comfortable and place the stone over your solar plexus chakra. As you relax, take a deep breath and repeat your mantra to yourself until you begin to feel balanced.

2. **Smoky Quartz**
   As you have already learned up to this point, smoky quartz has many amazing qualities. Another benefit of this stone is that it has the ability to stabilize energy. When the world feels like it is spinning around you, the stone can help you regain your balance. For some people, they enter the fight-or-flight mode when they are stressed out. The stone will help prevent this from happening in the first place when used properly. Many people choose to wear this stone to feel balanced

throughout the day. If you ever find yourself in a situation you can't handle, take the stone in your hand, close your eyes, and state your mantra. You can do this for as long as you need until you feel a sense of calm wash over you.

3. **Hematite**
   Another response to stress is fear. Luckily, the stone Hematite has the ability to absorb this fear if it is something you ever experience. For this to work, simply place the stone in your non-dominant hand and squeeze it. When you close your eyes, imagine that there is a black cloud over you. Once you see the cloud, imagine the cloud flowing through you and into your stone. You will want to meditate until this emotion vanishes, and you are feeling peaceful and stress-free again.

Trust

Trust is a hard concept for a lot of people. Unfortunately, there are some events we can go through that create a lack of trust in our future. Some traumas affect us emotionally, mentally, and sometimes, physically. When this happens, it can be hard to trust other people or even feel safe around them. Some crystals can help you build your trust in people. By working on the issue, you may find yourself feeling safe and secure in more situations.

Mantra:

I am safe. I am loved. I place my trust in the universe.

Healing Stones:

1. **Garnet**
   It is believed that our sense of security and safety comes from our root chakra. When we lack trust, it may mean that our root chakra is out of whack. In order to restore trust in humanity, you will need to restore the energy in your root chakra to feel safe. Garnet is the perfect stone to accomplish this task. For this crystal to work, you will want to begin your meditation on your back and place

the stone near your root chakra. When you feel safe and secure in your location, you can close your eyes and state your mantra. You will want to repeat this mantra until you feel better.

2. **Carnelian**
While sometimes our trust issues are with other people, these trust issues can also stem from our selves. Sometimes, we break promises we keep for ourselves, and often lack trust in our own integrity. This lack of trust with yourself comes from your sacral chakra. Carnelian is one stone that may be able to help with this lack of trust in yourself. For this stone to work, you can use it while you are meditating. All you will need to do is lie down on your back, place the stone near your sacral chakra, and repeat your mantra. You can change the above mantra to become more fitting for your own being. You can try something like, I trust myself because I will always keep my word.

3. **Amethyst**
If none of these situations match you, perhaps, you just lack the universe in general. If you are fearful to leave your house or trust anyone in your life, Amethyst is a stone that can help you connect to the universe. The universe is always there for you, even when it feels as though it is acting against you. For this stone to work, try placing it against your third eye chakra and take a few moments to meditate. Repeat your mantra until you feel a sense of trust flow through you. Even if you can't trust others, always place your trust in the universe.

You have noticed through this chapter that a lot of our issues seem to stem from a lack of balance in our chakra. If you have no idea what your chakras are or what they do, you are not alone! In the next chapter, I will be teaching you everything you need to know. We will go over each chakra, what they do for you, and how to balance them out. Once you learn about your chakras, you will get a sense of the crystals you need, and then we can get started on learning the crystals and their incredible benefits as well!

CHAPTER THREE
Chakra Connections And Crystals

In the prior chapter, you may have been shaking your head, wondering what all this talk about our chakras was. Believe it or not, chakras actually have a huge impact on your daily life. When energy is blocked in any of your chakras, this can have major effects on you spiritually, mentally, emotionally, and even physically. In order to balance your chakras, you will need to have a further understanding of them and how they work.

The first lesson you will need to learn is that we are more than just our physical body.

Our chakras, much like everything else in the universe, are created through energy. Everything from our atoms to our organs, to our muscles, is all made up of energy. Your whole entire body is an energy field that can expand past your physical body. While the physical is made in intricate layers such as the skeletal system, the nervous system, and musculature, the energy within your body is a whole other complicated layer. Together, all of these layers of energy are called your aura. While this aura does interact with your physical body, it is also a part of your chakras.

In Sanskrit, the word chakra means wheel. These energy centers within your body are known as energy vortexes. The vortexes have the ability to transport energy from your body and aura into the universe. If it helps, picture your chakra system like a bloodstream of your spirit. The system helps you balance and regulate your body.

While all living things have a chakra system, we will be focusing on yours today. Within your body, you have seven major chakras. There are also other minor ones, but we won't throw too much at you for now. Each major chakra in your system is connected to certain glands and organs. This holds true for the physical dysfunctions of these systems whether they are spiritual, mental, or even emotional.

As you learn more about your chakras, you will be able to tell where your imbalances may be stemming from. By using crystals, you will be mindful of your healing through not only your mind but your spirit too. While physical activities can help some of your issues, cleaning your spirit via crystals may work wonders for you too. For now, we will start with the basics of the chakras.

Feeling the Energy

Before we rocket off into learning all about the chakras, it is time to learn your own energy. As you first start, try to get in touch with the energy within your body. You can do this by holding your hands together and have your palms face one another. As you do this, you may notice slight warmth exchanging between your hands. If you don't, don't worry! It will take some time and practice. Once you do feel the heat between your hands, separate your hands a little more and stretch the energy between your palms. When you feel comfortable with this motion, you can then try to condense the energy by bringing your palms closer together. Feel free to repeat this a few times until you feel comfortable with your energy.

Before Getting Started

As a beginner, you may feel nervous about engaging with your chakras. There are a few factors to remember as you get started. The first detail to remember is that you must be patient with yourself. There are many people who try to learn too much at once! It will be important to understand that you should never judge yourself when it seems as though you are "failing." You are on your own timeline. Everything is happening exactly as it should; this includes your healing with crystals.

No matter how hard you try, healing simply isn't something that you can speed up. Instead, try to focus on the healing journey. As you practice and take more steps toward healing, you may learn more about yourself than you ever thought was possible. Your transformation is going to take both compassion and patience, remember to always be kind to yourself.

With that being said, it will also be vital that you never push yourself out of your comfort zone. There are repercussions to forcing your energy, and you will most likely burn yourself out. Of course, you are probably very eager to connect to your chakras, but you will want to take your time. Much like learning the energy between your hands, you will be learning how to connect to each chakra. If you push too hard, you could potentially give yourself a headache. If you find practicing is too stressful and you feel resistance to the energy, try taking a break and then come back to the practice.

Finally, it is important to point out that at some points, you may need a professional. While there is a lot you can accomplish on your own, guidance is always helpful. This is especially true if you ever hit a point where you feel like you are hitting a wall. If you do choose to go down this path, you will want to be sure that the practitioner is certified or licensed. Luckily with the internet, you can check out their reviews before you make an appointment. Once you meet them, remember that certain people will be a better fit for you than others. You should always take your time and choose what is best for you, not what other people say is best for you. With those bits of advice, it is time to learn how to take matters into your own hands!

Activating Kundalini Energy

As stated earlier, the foundation of your chakra system is made up of seven different chakras. Each one of these chakras serves a purpose, but they are also all interconnected as you will be learning later in this chapter. Before we get into each chakra, you will need to learn how to activate your kundalini energy.

What is kundalini energy, you may be asking? It is the energy that has the ability to awaken your chakras. While all of us have this energy within us, it is often dormant and coiled at the base of our spine. As you work with your chakras, you will begin to awaken this energy.

It should be noted that this energy doesn't just suddenly awaken one day. This process will take a period of time and will require constant practice through your life. You can do this by performing energy work on yourself or going to a yoga class every week.

For other people, kundalini energy can be awakened randomly. If you are not prepared for this to happen, it could block your chakras or become stuck in a certain area. When this happens, it can cause some painful symptoms caused by the surge of energy. It can also cause mental and physical instability. This is why it is vital to start slow and work overtime with your practice. Once you begin, you will learn how to send this energy in beneficial ways. For now, we will get started with one of your basic chakras; the root chakra.

Root Chakra

The root chakra is one of the first physical chakras you have. This chakra is in charge of your sense of safety and security. When this chakra is out of harmony, you may feel that you cannot trust the universe around you. At points, you may feel ungrounded and have issues in creating relationships with people around you. It also creates a false sense of understanding your basic needs like shelter, love, and food. You will begin to function out of fear as opposed to love.

When this chakra is balanced, you will start to feel grounded again. You will be able to move with the ebb and flow of life and trust the people around you again. A balanced root chakra also helps you connect with family and loved ones when you feel safe again.

1. **Location**
   Your root chakra is located at the base of your spine.

2. **Color**
   Red

3. **Element**
   Earth

4. **Other Names**
   You may notice through research that the root chakra has several names it can be referred to as. Some other names include the first chakra, base chakra, and Muladhara, which is the Sanskrit name for root chakra.

5. **Physical Body Parts**

Your root chakra is in charge of several body parts including the base of the spine, rectum, feet, bones, legs, your immune system, the large intestine, and your teeth.

6. **Physical Dysfunction**
Unfortunately, an imbalance of the root chakra can show in several different physical dysfunctions. These include weight problems, depression, immune disorders, knee issues, arthritis, constipation, rectal tumors, varicose veins, back pain, and more.

7. **Emotional and Mental Dysfunctions**
On top of the physical dysfunctions that come from an imbalance in your root chakra, it can also block the ability for you to stand up for yourself, to provide life's necessities, or experience safety and security. These may stem from an energy block from fear or guilt.

8. **Crystals**
Some of the following crystals can help bring balance back into your life if you feel your root chakra is blocked or out of whack.
Fire Agate, Smoky Quartz, Lodestone, Red Jasper, Onyx, Obsidian, Hematite, Bloodstone, Black Tourmaline, Garnet, Ruby.

Sacral Plexus Chakra

Your solar plexus chakra is located just above the root chakra. This chakra is in charge of your reproductive and sexual activities. The chakra can also play a major role in your creativity and your emotions. You may feel your sacral plexus chakra is out of balance if you feel the inability to express your feelings. At some points in your life, you may feel you are holding onto anger and are out of touch of the things that have brought you pleasure in life. If you feel stifled in your creativity or are experiencing relationship issues, this could be the root of the problem.

Once you have balanced this chakra, you will have the ability to get in touch with the pleasurable things in life again. When you return to a balanced state, you will be able to grow healthy relationships and connect to others socially and sexually. It will also help you develop a healthy relationship with life and money.

1. **Location**
   Your sacral plexus chakra is located about two inches under your navel.

2. **Color**
   Orange

3. **Element**
   Water

4. **Other Names**
   The sacral plexus chakra has been known to be referred to by several other names. These names include naval chakra, pelvic chakra, sacral chakra, second chakra, or Svadisthana.

5. **Physical Body Parts**
   Kidneys, hips, bladder, appendix, pelvis, lower vertebra, womb, and genitals.

6. **Physical Dysfunction**
   An imbalance of the sacral plexus chakra can lead to a few physical dysfunctions. These can include kidney issues, bladder issues, impotence, pelvic pain, gynecological issues, and even lower back pain.

7. **Emotional and Mental Dysfunction**
   On top of the physical ailments, you may find that an imbalance of this chakra can have effects on your emotional and mental states as well. Some of these issues include ethics, relationship honor, creativity, lack of power and control, issues with sex, money problems, guilt emotions, and even blame of other people. It is thought that these blocks of energy can stem from issues like rape, trauma, sexual abuse, or gender issues.

8. **Crystals**

Luckily, several crystals can help you if you feel that this chakra is out of balance. Some of these crystals include Sunstone, orange tourmaline, coral, moonstone, amber, and carnelian.

Solar Plexus Chakra

The next chakra we will be going over is the solar plexus chakra. This chakra is in charge of your sense of worth, self-esteem, and your personality. When this chakra is out of harmony, an individual may feel the need to have constant control and will dominate any situation. If you feel the need to keep up with your appearance and be better than others, your chakra may be out of balance! A block of this chakra often creates an overwhelming feeling of being inadequate, and with this emotion, you may not respect yourself. The opposite can be true for others, as an imbalance of the solar plexus chakra could cause you to give your powers to others if you feel no sense of self.

Once your solar plexus chakra is back in harmony, you may feel a sense of wholeness again. You will learn how to cultivate your power in a healthy way and gain a sense of self-worth. When this chakra is balanced, there is a healthy balance between the material world and the spiritual world. At this point, you will feel true calmness and inner peace within your soul.

1. **Location**
   Your solar plexus chakra is located two inches above your navel.

2. **Color**
   Yellow

3. **Element**
   Fire

4. **Other Names**
   The solar plexus chakra can be referred to as the power chakra, the third chakra, or its Sanskrit name, Manipura.

5. **Physical Body Part**
   Middle spine, spleen, gallbladder, liver, upper intestines, stomach, and the abdomen.

6. **Physical Dysfunction**
   If your solar plexus chakra is out of balance, you may be experiencing some of the several health issues: diabetes, hepatitis, fatigue, adrenal dysfunction, liver dysfunction, bulimia, anorexia, indigestion, intestinal problems, colon issues, gastric ulcers, or arthritis.

7. **Emotional and Mental Dysfunction**
   On top of the ailments mentioned above, you could also be experiencing some of the emotional dysfunctions listed such as lack of personal honor, sensitivity to criticism, a lack of responsibility to make decisions, lack of self-care, lack of self-respect, no self-confidence, lowered self-esteem, a sense of intimidation from others and a lack of trust and/or fear. It is believed that these issues can occur due to issues of control, repressed anger, or issues of control related to power.

8. **Crystals**
   If you experience any of the above physical, mental, or emotional dysfunctions, some crystals can help you out. These crystals include Rutilated Quartz, Yellow Agate, Yellow Tiger's Eye, Yellow Topaz, Amber, and Yellow Citrine.

The Heart Chakra

Next, we will be going over the heart chakra. You may already be aware, but this chakra is in charge of the physical and spiritual aspects of our beings. The heart chakra is a pivotal location as it connects both your spiritual and physical chakra. If you are looking to get in touch with your Higher Self, the heart chakra is where you will want to look.

When the heart chakra is out of harmony with the rest of the chakras, you may be feeling like you are disconnected from yourself. An imbalance of this chakra may make you feel like you are not deserving of love and cannot love yourself properly. Many people who experience this, become depressed and lose touch of who they truly are.

Once your heart chakra is back in harmony, you will be able to cultivate joy in your life. With the balance, you will be able to love and accept yourself for who you really are. It is only at this point that you will be able to not only give but also receive the love that you deserve. Once you are in balance, you will understand what it means to have compassion for yourself and others in the universe.

1. **Location**
   It is located in the center of your chest.

2. **Color**
   Green

3. **Element**
   Air

4. **Other Names**
   It can be referred to by its Sanskrit name, Anahata or the fourth chakra.

5. **Physical Body Parts**
   The Heart chakra is in charge of your diaphragm, breasts, ribs, shoulders, arms, lungs, the circulatory system, and of course, the heart.

6. **Physical Dysfunction**
   If your heart chakra is out of balance, it is possible that you could be having the following physical dysfunctions. These include high blood pressure, breast cancer, lung disease, pneumonia, lung cancer, asthma, allergies, heart disease, heart attack, or heart failure.

7. **Emotional or Mental Dysfunction**

Some of the emotional or mental dysfunctions you can experience due to the heart chakra being out of harmony could include lack of trust, no hope, zero compassion toward others, a sense of loneliness, being self-centered, grief, resentment, and hatred for everyone. It is thought that the potential cause of energy block in this location could be due to heartache or even grief.

8. **Crystals**
   If you suffer from any of the ailments above, some crystals can help you in this situation. The crystals include Peridot, Green Kyanite, Green Calcite, Jade, Green Tourmaline, Emerald, or Rose Quartz.

The Throat Chakra

Now, it is time to move into learning the first spiritual chakra. The throat chakra is in charge of our authentic voice, our faith, and our understanding of others. When this chakra is out of harmony, it may become difficult to speak the truth and to express yourself. If you have recently been feeling that you are out of touch with your will to live, this chakra may be imbalanced.

Once you balance the chakra, you will be able to speak your truth and follow your dreams. When your values are in place, you have the strength to say what you mean and express yourself to others in an authentic manner. You must learn the delicate balance between speech and silence and when it is appropriate for each action.

1. **Location**
   The throat chakra is located in the hollow of your collarbone and at the front of the base of your neck.

2. **Color**
   Light Blue

3. **Element**
   Sound

4. **Other Names**

The throat chakra is referred to as Vishuddha in Sanskrit and also the fifth chakra.

5. **Physical Body Part**
   The throat chakra is in charge of the hands, arms, shoulders, esophagus, hypothalamus, teeth, gums, mouth, neck vertebrae, the trachea, and the throat.

6. **Physical Dysfunction**
   If your throat chakra is out of balance, you may experience thyroid problems or swollen glands. It is also possible you could develop a stiff neck, TMJ, scoliosis, gym difficulties, mouth ulcers, a sore throat, or a raspy voice.

7. **Emotional and Mental Dysfunction**
   If you don't have any of the physical dysfunctions from above, there are also some dysfunctions that can happen mentally or emotionally. These issues include lack of faith, criticism, judgment, addiction, inability to make a decision, problems with following your dreams or losing your will. It is thought that these blocks can come from suppressing your creative talent, swallowing your words, or never expressing yourself.

8. **Crystals**
   If you suffer from any of the dysfunctions from above, there are several crystals that may be able to help you out. Some of the crystals include Lapis Lazuli, Sodalite, Iolite, Celestite, Aquamarine, Blue Kyanite, and even Turquoise.

The Third Eye Chakra

As we move up your chakras, the next one is the third eye chakra. Often times, this chakra is associated with your sixth sense which is in charge of your intuition, spiritual insight, as well as your wisdom. You may notice that this chakra is unbalanced if you find yourself lacking faith in your own intuition. Often times, people who have energy blocked to their sixth chakra only have the ability to see their physical reality. When this happens, it is possible you may fear your own inner wisdom.

With the help of crystals, you may be able to return your awareness and intuition. It is vital that you trust your inner vision and allow your intuition to guide you through life. As we mentioned before, there is so much more than what we can just physically see.

1. **Location**
   The third eye chakra is located between your eyebrows.

2. **Color**
   Indigo

3. **Element**
   Light

4. **Other Names**
   The third chakra is often referred to as the sixth chakra, forehead chakra, or brow chakra. It can also be called by the Sanskrit name, Ajna.

5. **Physical Body Parts**
   This chakra is in charge of your nose, ears, eyes, brain, and the whole nervous system.

6. **Physical Dysfunction**
   If your third eye chakra is blocked or imbalanced, you could be experiencing some of the following physical dysfunctions. These include blurred vision, headaches, seizures, learning disabilities, spinal difficulties, deafness, blindness, neurological issues, stroke, or even brain tumors.

7. **Emotional and Mental Dysfunction**
   An imbalanced third eye chakra could also lead to some mental and emotional disturbances. It's possible you lack the ability to learn from new experiences, have the inability to open to others, have some feelings of inadequacy, doubt your intellectual abilities, lack the ability to evaluate yourself or feel you can never tell the truth. It is believed that these issues are caused by a lack of intuition.

8. **Crystals**
   Kyanite, Star Sapphire, Clear Quartz, Tanzanite, Sugilite, Lepidolite, Fluorite, Amethyst, Lapis Lazuli

The Crown Chakra

As mentioned earlier, there are several other chakras, but the crown chakra is the last of the major chakras. This chakra is the source which connects to your higher self and the Divine. When this chakra is out of harmony, you may feel the sense that you are disconnected from your self as well as the universe. Perhaps, lately, you have been feeling angry at God. You feel lost and feel life has become difficult. If you feel depressed and alone, your crown chakra may be creating all of these feelings.

Once you balance your crown chakra, you will begin to connect to the universe again. It is important to understand that you are an individual and you will need to trust the path you are on. Our identity is so much more than just our physical form. When you are able to love and accept yourself for who you are, it will be easier to elevate your consciousness.

1. **Location**
   This chakra is located at the top of your head, in the center.

2. **Color**
   Gold, white, and purple.

3. **Element**
   Thought

4. **Other Names**
   Seventh Chakra or Sahasrara

5. **Physical Body Parts**
   The crown chakra is in charge of your central nervous system, the cerebral cortex, skeletal system, and the muscular system.

6. **Physical Dysfunction**

If your crown chakra is out of balance, you may experience several physical dysfunctions. These issues range from the sense of alienation, apathy, confusion, sensitivity to your environment, physical disorder, chronic exhaustion, depression, and other energetic disorders.

7. **Emotional and Mental Dysfunctions**
With these physical dysfunctions, it is also possible you may be experiencing emotional dysfunctions from a blocked chakra. You could lack devotion, spirituality, faith, or seeing the bigger picture. You may also have the inability to trust your ethics or values, lack courage, and act selfishly. These issues seem to stem from a lack of trust in the Divine or an unresolved anger.

8. **Crystals**
White Topaz, Apophyllite, Kunzite, Phenacite, Selenite, Moonstone, Labradorite, Herkimer Diamond, Clear Quartz, Amethyst.

Using Crystals to Heal Chakras

As you can tell, there is a certain magic when you combine crystals with your internal energy. This is because crystals have the ability to draw out energy and can also redirect it when needed. When this happens, you will be able to develop the strength with the associated stone. On top of these wonderful benefits, the crystals can also help you heal these issues and rebalance your energy.

The whole reason for working with crystals is to help you engage with the Earth, and its natural energy. When you practice this, you will be able to nourish any of your natural gifts and strengths. As you practice more, remember that it will be important to release emotions that no longer serve you. Once your energy is restored and rebalanced, you will be able to tap into your gifts and elevate your consciousness.

Luckily, there are a few different ways to work with crystals, as mentioned slightly in the previous chapter. You may have noted that one of the most popular ways to use a crystal is to keep it on your person. When shopping, you will notice all the different types of jewelry like bracelets, earrings, or pendants. If you aren't a jewelry person, you can always carry the crystal in your pocket.

Another major way to use crystals to heal your chakras is through meditation. When you combine crystals with meditation, the crystal will amplify the energy you are working on, whether you are looking to gain energy or release it. Remember that practice will help you out in the long run. You won't be a master after a couple of sessions and that is okay!

The pros of using crystals to heal your chakras are that they are incredibly versatile to work with. On top of that, they are also aesthetically pleasing. Many people enjoy crystals to heal themselves because they are easy to use, and the healing power can be easily felt. As you begin, you may also feel the pulsing in your hand that holds the crystals.

The downfall of using crystals is that it will take some time to become familiar with crystals. Remember that as you start your collection, it will take some time before you find the right crystals that work for you. The crystals you buy will vary depending on the individual. I suggest you do your research before you dive into any big purchases. This is exactly why in the next chapter, we will be going over a number of crystals. With all of the information within these pages, you will be able to buy the crystals that work best for you!

CHAPTER FOUR
Crystals To Know

In this chapter, we will be listing off different crystals in alphabetical order. As you will see, each crystal will have their own color, physical cures, mental cures, and affirmations. In the chapter above, we went over several of the different ailments crystals can be used for. It will be up to you to take this information and apply it to your life. I hope that within this chapter, you will be able to find at least one crystal to help you.

Actinolite

This crystal is best known for its shielding properties. Actinolite has the ability to fill gaps of energy that may be in your chakras, resulting in unwanted negativity, illness, and stress. The crystal can help you balance your spirit, body, and mind. It also can boost self-esteem by releasing negative energy you may be holding onto.

1. **Chakra**
   Heart Chakra

2. **Color**
   Black and Green

3. **Rarity**
   Common

4. **Physical Uses**
   Actinolite is excellent for several physical ailments. Some of the more common usages are to strengthen the immune system. It can also help if you have kidney problems, liver problems, or cancer.

5. **Emotional Uses**
   This crystal has been known to help refuse stress and tension. It is also great to help individuals cope with change and find harmony in their life. On top of these wonderful benefits, actinolite is also excellent if you lack self-confidence or self-worth.

6. **Spiritual Uses**
   Actinolite is wonderful to help with the following spiritual issues you may be experiencing. These ailments include lack of visualization, shielding, growth, balance, or awareness. The crystal can also help remove any energy blocks you may be experiencing.

Agate

Agate is a crystal that is most commonly known for its quiet energy. If you are looking to achieve balance and stability in your life, agate will be the perfect crystal for you. Many individuals use this stone as it works on the cause of an issue as opposed to the symptom of the problem. This crystal can work on mental functions and improve clarity. It should be noted that while the energy of this crystal works slowly due to the gentle nature, it works very deliberately and will have a lasting impact when used correctly.

1. **Chakra**
   Agate comes in several colors and will work with different chakras depending on the color.

2. **Color**
   Yellow, White, Light Brown, Red, Pink, Orange, Green, Brown, Blue, Black

3. **Rarity**
   Common

4. **Physical Uses**
   This crystal is excellent for a number of physical ailments. These issues include problems with the uterus, constipation, diarrhea, stomach issues, skin infections, rheumatism, pancreas problems, gastritis, eye infections, digestion health, blood vessels, and aids.

5. **Emotional Uses**
   With these physical fixes, agate can also help with some emotional ailments. It can help you tell the truth, helps work through trauma, has the ability to soothe stressed out

individuals, can increase self-confident, enhance perception, increase courage, helps with bitterness, and grants the ability to release any anger you may be holding onto.

6. **Emotional Uses**
   Agate can help bring balance and clarity back into your life. It also helps ground individuals and helps them grow to become their true selves.

Amazonite

This crystal is best used if you struggle with non-verbal expression. Often times, amazonite is used to connect to Nature Spirits and is known as the stone of success and abundance. It has the ability to attract good luck and focus, leading to a peaceful transition, especially if your time on earth is coming to an end. This crystal can assist in balancing your yin and yang energies and restore any separation you may have from the Divine.

1. **Chakra**
   Heart Chakra and Throat Chakra

2. **Color**
   Turquoise and Green

3. **Rarity**
   Common

4. **Physical Uses**
   Amazonite can help with a wide range of physical ailments. On top of helping with the yin and yang energy, it can also help to balance the thyroid health, reflexology, osteoporosis, nutrient absorption, nervous system regeneration, muscle pains, mental clarity, liver disorders, heart issues, gout, dental problems, breast health, balance issues, and even can assist with chemotherapy.

5. **Emotional Uses**
   If you are looking to use amazonite with emotional uses, it is also incredibly versatile here. Amazonite can help with

worrying, trauma, helps soothe stress, can boost self-confidence, increase joy, decrease fear, helps cope with grief, can help guild compassion, build communication, creates clarity, and can help you release anger you may be holding onto.

6. **Spiritual Uses**
   With these wonderful benefits, amazonite can also help with balance, clarity, universal love, manifestation, and grants an enhanced intuition.

Amber

Amber is one of the more popular healing crystals. It is an excellent crystal to add to your collection if you are a beginner, as it has gentle energy and can help heal and cleanse. Amber is also versatile as it has the ability to aid in physical healing as well as emotional healing and environmental clearing. On top of these wonderful benefits, amber is also very protective and can help promote fertility.

1. **Chakra**
   Solar Plexus Chakra

2. **Color**
   Orange and Yellow

3. **Rarity**
   Common

4. **Physical Uses**
   Amber can help with a number of physical ailments. As mentioned earlier, this crystal is very versatile. It can help with viruses, urinary tract health, trauma, toxins, tonsillitis, throat issues, stomach issues, spleen problems, skin infections, pregnancy, pneumonia, pancreas health, pain relief, ovarian disorders, nervous system problems, lungs, laryngitis, intestinal disorders, infections, immune system strengthening, headaches, migraines, gallbladder issues, ear infections, dental pains, colds, breathing problems,

brain disorders, bone disorders, birthing issues, asthma, arthritis, and even wounds.

5. **Emotional Uses**
   Amber is an excellent crystal to use if you are looking to reduce tension or stress in your life. It can also help individuals with their patience and can help ease depression. If you need to increase patience or help with grounding, amber is a great crystal to add to your collection.

6. **Spiritual Uses**
   This crystal is used often for people to help balance their aura. It is also thought to help with ancient wisdom and knowledge if that is something you're seeking. Amber is also used to help recall past life events, which helps some people heal in their own ways.

Amethyst

Amethyst is the first crystal many metaphysicians choose to use due to its protective and powerful nature. Often times, amethyst was used in ancient times to help people with addictions and is now known as the stone of sobriety. This crystal has strong healing energy that can help transform any negative energy in your spirit into love energy. If you feel that your third eye chakra is out of balance, amethyst has the ability to provide the peaceful energy you will need for meditation. It can also be used to activate the crown chakra to connect to the Divine and enhance your spiritual awareness.

1. **Chakra**
   Third Eye Chakra and Crown Chakra

2. **Color**
   Purple and Lavender

3. **Rarity**
   Common

4. **Physical Uses**

Amethyst is excellent for a number of physical uses. It can help with some of the following issues such as wrinkle, overall well-being, weakness, viruses, tumors, swelling, smoking addiction, sleep issues, skin infections, respiratory health, post-surgery healing, pituitary gland problems, pain relief, issues with overindulgence, night terrors, mental health, itching, insomnia, injuries, supports the immune system, hormone production, hearing issues, headaches, endocrine system problems, eczema, digestion, the dying process, cancer, burns, bruising, brain disorders, alcoholism, addiction, and acne!

5. **Emotional Uses**

   With these physical benefits, amethyst is also a powerful crystal to help with emotional ailments you may be experiencing. Some of the more popular issues that amethyst benefits include increasing inner serenity, reducing stress, defusing rage, increases peace, helps with focus, increases love, motivation, and decreases night terrors. It can also be used to help release negativity, creates emotional balance, helps cope with loss, copes with grief, and increases your ability to cope with change or anxiety you may be experiencing.

6. **Spiritual Uses**

   Amethyst is a popular stone to help with spiritual ailments. It can help increase wisdom, telekinesis, increases spiritual protection, and is used very often in meditation. This crystal also helps enhance psychic abilities, increases intuition, and can bring individuals cosmic awareness if that is something they are searching for. Amethyst also helps people open up to their own awareness and can help you connect to your inner child. It is also used for astral projection and can help individuals interpret and recall their dreams.

Aquamarine

When you find aquamarine crystals, you may notice that they resonate with the ocean. The energy of this crystal connects to the spirit of the sea. Historically, seamen carried this crystal to help travel safe in the water and were meant to protect them from drowning. This crystal is known as the stone of courage and protection. Most times, it helps promote self-expression and can enhance communication blocks you may be experiencing. It is also a very popular crystal to help enhance and align your chakras.

1. **Chakras**
   Throat Chakra and Heart Chakra

2. **Color**
   Turquoise and Blue

3. **Rarity**
   Common

4. **Physical Uses**
   Aquamarine is used for a number of physical ailments. Some of these issues it can benefit include water retention, traveling, thyroid issues, skin infections, sinus problems, issues with the pituitary gland, neck issues, nausea, liver disorders, jaw problems, foot problems, eye disorders, edema, eczema, dental problems, brain disorders, issues with the bladder, allergies, acne, and other autoimmune disorders.

5. **Emotional Uses**
   While aquamarine does help with a number of physical problems, it is also great for emotional problems you may be experiencing. This crystal grants serenity, peace, inspiration, harmony, and can help individuals cope with changes. It is also excellent if you are looking to release anger you are holding onto or can help with any anxiety you may have.

6. **Spiritual Uses**
   Aquamarine is a popular crystal people use to help communicate with angels. It can also help communicate with your higher-self, your inner child, or even just to use during meditation. As mentioned earlier, aquamarine is a great protector and helps give people the strength to tell the truth.

Black Tourmaline

You may have noticed that black tourmaline has been mentioned several times in this book already. This stone is an excellent source of protection and can help block any negative energy that comes your way. It also has the ability to remove this negative energy if it already exists in your person and assists to purify your energy into a lighter vibration. On top of these benefits, it is also used to help balance and harmonize your chakras.

1. **Chakra**
   Root Chakra

2. **Color**
   Black

3. **Rarity**
   Common

4. **Physical Uses**
   Black Tourmaline is mostly used for physical protection. It has also been known to help with physical ailments such as dyslexia, chemotherapy, arthritis, addiction, and radiation complications.

5. **Emotional Uses**
   As for emotional benefits, black tourmaline can help reduce any stress or tension you may be feeling. We also mentioned that this stone can help with anxiety, criticism, and can help balance your sense of serenity.

6. **Spiritual Uses**
   Black Tourmaline is mostly used for spiritual and psychic protection. It also has been known to help balance your aura and protect you from electromagnetic frequencies and pollution. There is also a belief that black tourmaline can protect you from aliens and other extraterrestrial communication!

Bloodstone

Bloodstone is an interesting crystal as it is composed of Chalcedony but also has small dots of Red Jasper. This stone has been used for thousands of years and is a powerful healing stone. Often times, it can be used if you are looking to detoxify and purify your body of any negative energy. It also has the ability to enhance clarity, brain function, and increases energy by removing any energy blocks you may have. As a beginner, this may be a good choice to start your crystal collection with.

1. **Chakra**
   Heart Chakra, Solar Plexus Chakra, and the Sacral Chakra

2. **Color**
   Red and Green

3. **Rarity**
   Common

4. **Physical Uses**
   Bloodstone has the ability to work on a wide variety of physical ailments. Some of the benefits include help with tumor growth, stroke, pancreas health, nose bleeds, muscle pain, lung issues, liver disorders, kidney disorders, immune strengthening, high blood pressure, heart issues, eye issues, colon issues, circulatory problems, cancer, bronchitis, body detox, blood disorders, blood clotting, blood cleansing, blood circulation, bleeding, and anemia.

5. **Emotional and Spiritual Uses**
   With these wonderful physical benefits, bloodstone also comes with a few emotional benefits. Bloodstone can help increase compassion and courage. It also can help individuals become gentler by releasing any retained anger.

Bowenite

You may have heard of Bowenite before, as it is Rhode Island's state mineral. Often times, it can be confused with Jade, and while it is close in comparison, it is a variety of Antigorite. This crystal is a semi-precious stone and is usually made of a higher-grade material. Historically, this crystal was worn as an amulet as it has the ability to protect individuals from destructive forces. It also makes well for a dream stone and helps release emotions that may be suppressed.

1. **Chakra**
   Heart Chakra

2. **Color**
   Green

3. **Rarity**
   Pretty Common

4. **Physical Uses**
   Bowenite is the perfect crystal to use if you are looking to balance your masculinity or feminine attributes as it can help with your hormonal balance. It is also great to help regulate blood sugar and diabetes.

5. **Emotional Uses**
   This crystal is wonderful if you are searching for protection from external forces. It can also help with relationships when it comes to love and friendships. Bowenite also has the ability to help with anxiety if that is something you have.

6. **Spiritual Uses**
   One of the more common uses for bowenite is for spiritual protection. The crystal is also excellent for dream interpretation, as it has the ability to help enhance and recall dreams. It has also been known to help with shielding against negative forces.

Calcite

Calcite is most commonly known as an energy amplifier and cleanser. When this stone is used properly, it can help restore any negative energy whether it is in your house or your body. You can use this stone to remove any old patterns you may have to help increase personal drive and motivation. It is most commonly known as the Stone of the Mind. It can help increase your memory as well as learning abilities. If you are a student, this could be a useful stone to have in your collection.

1. **Chakra**
   Varies depending on the color.

2. **Color**
   Yellow, Sky Blue, Pink, Red, Peach, Orange, Green, Clear, Blue

3. **Rarity**
   Common

4. **Physical Uses**
   Calcite can help with several physical ailments. These include issues with the skeletal system, nutrient absorption, helps with mental clarity, joint pain, dental issues, and bone disorders.

5. **Emotional and Spiritual Uses**
   This stone can help increase your motivation and ability to learn. It can also benefit you if you are looking to relax. Spiritual wise, Calcite is often used to help with long distance healing as its vibrations are fairly powerful.

Carnelian

Carnelian was a stone used back in ancient times to help the dead protect themselves as they traveled into the afterlife. It is believed that this stone has the ability to calm fears of death and rebirth. The powers of this stone grant the ability to accept the cycle of life and bring a sense of serenity about everything. Carnelian can also increase your physical energy as well as give you courage while boosting your creativity. Many people choose to wear this stone to enhance their vitality.

1. **Chakra**
   Sacral Chakra

2. **Color**
   Orange

3. **Rarity**
   Common

4. **Physical Uses**
   Many people choose to have carnelian in their crystal collection because it has so many incredible benefits. This stone can help with a number of physical ailments including weakness, urinary tract issues, tissue health, scoliosis, reproductive issues, pancreas health, ovarian disorders, memory problems, low blood pressure, liver disorders, kidney disorders, intestinal disorders, problems with infertility, infections, edema, colon disorders, colds, body balance, blood circulation, back problems, appetite control, and even allergies.

5. **Emotional Uses**
   Emotional wise, carnelian helps a lot with understanding death, as I mentioned before. It also helps many people gain their confidence back and helps increase their courage. This stone can also be used to diffuse anger and helps if you have gone through emotional abuse.

6. **Spiritual Uses**
   Carnelian is known as a protector and can help bring balance to your chakras. It has also been known to benefit people to enhance their appreciation for life. On top of those benefits, carnelian can also help bring serenity and may be able to help recall past life events.

Chalcedony

If you are looking for a crystal that helps promote peace and joy, Chalcedony is the right stone for you. This is made out of a group of cryptocrystalline quartz minerals that form masses. There is a variety of this stone that comes in a wide array of colors. This crystal has the ability to relieve negative emotions and promotes overall happiness. Chalcedony is often referred to as the stone of brotherhood as it can promote group stability.

1. **Chakra**
   Varies depending on the color

2. **Color**
   White, Gray, Blue

3. **Rarity**
   Common

4. **Physical Uses**
   The most common use for this stone is to help balance and restore energy. It has also been known to help with nightmares, night terrors, and Alzheimer's disease.

5. **Emotional Uses**
   Chalcedony is an excellent stone if you are looking to enhance your happiness in life. It has the ability to increase self-worth, self-confidence, and your emotional balance. This stone is also beneficial if you are looking to cope with grief or release negativity from your life. You may find that it brings you a sense of peace and has a calming effect.

Citrine

Citrine is another fairly popular stone as it has a very joyful vibration that has the ability to transmit its energies to those who surround it. This is very popular if you have suppressed anger or suffer from depression. Citrine is known to help increase optimism and will bring a more positive conscious mind over time. It is thought that this crystal is powered by the sun, which is why it has the ability to energize and cleanse the soul. If you are looking to cleanse your chakras, this crystal will benefit you most.

1. **Chakra**
   Sacral Chakra

2. **Color**
   Yellow

3. **Rarity**
   Common

4. **Physical Uses**
   Citrine has many wonderful benefits when it comes to physical ailments. It can help with verbal communication, tissue health, thyroid balance, spleen disorders, seasonal

disorders, pancreas health, kidney disorders, headaches, food poisoning, eye disorders, digestive health, diabetes, and circulatory problems.

5. **Emotional Uses**
If you have been having suicidal thoughts, citrine will be a must have for your collection. It can also help boost self-confidence, self-worth, and give you the hope you've been searching for in your life. The stone has also been known to increase courage, enjoyment, honestly, and even hope. If you are looking to boost your creative expression, this may work for you as well.

6. **Spiritual Uses**
Citrine is great if you are looking to reduce the negative energy in your life. It also has the ability to help activate will and increase some individual's psychic abilities. Citrine can also be used to maximize your energy flow and can help ease phobias.

Clear Quartz

You have seen clear quartz mentioned several times throughout this book. It is one of the most popular and most versatile healing stones out there. This is due to its powerful healing nature and ability to work with just about any condition. Clear Quartz is a power stone and has the ability to boost energy and intention. It can also help individuals attune to their higher self, reduce negativity, and can relieve pain.

1. **Chakra**
Clear Quartz can work on all chakras.

2. **Color**
Clear

3. **Rarity**
Common

4. **Physical Uses**

As I mentioned earlier, clear quartz is very versatile. It can be beneficial for physical ailments such as vitality, vertigo, thyroid issues, sleep issues, post-surgery healing, pain relief, memory health, kidney disorders, immune system problems, heartburn, dental pain, burns, and problems associated with AIDS and HIV.

5. **Emotional Uses**
Clear Quartz is commonly used to help reduce tension and stress. It is also excellent for emotional balancing, healing, and stabilizing. This stone has also been known to help create joy, harmony, and acceptance in people's lives.

6. **Spiritual Uses**
Clear Quartz is great for spiritual uses. It can help with a number of issues including unity, telepathy, spiritual guidance and awakening, increases consciousness, creates connection to your Divine, connection with your inner child, communicating with spirit guides, communicating with angels, and can help with affirmation.

Danburite

As of today, danburite is one of the highest vibration minerals found. This crystal has the ability to connect the heart of your mind with the mind of your heart. This stone is highly sought after due to having high spiritual properties and is very powerful with the heart chakra. Danburite has the ability to work with your heart chakra to relieve emotional pain and increase the self. It is most commonly known to help an individual's true light shine through. It is very popular due to having gentle energy that is still fairly powerful. If you are going through a time of extreme change, danburite will be an excellent crystal to have with you to help ease the transition.

1. **Chakra**
Heart Chakra and Crown Chakra

2. **Color**
Clear

3. **Rarity**
   Common

4. **Physical Uses**
   Danburite is used to help several physical ailments. It can be used for tumors, tissue health, muscular issues, liver disorders, infertility, gallbladder problems, body weight management, body detox, and allergies.

5. **Emotional Uses**
   This stone helps individuals open and revitalize their auras. It can also reduce stress, tension, and increase your sense of belonging with friends and family. As I mentioned earlier, it is also excellent to help cope with extreme changes in your life.

6. **Spiritual Uses**
   Danburite is an extremely spiritual stone. It can help with a number of spiritual journeys such as truth-seeking, reiki, psychic work, spiritual work, protection, and can help some people communicate with angels. It is also popular with enhancing an individual's intuition and can protect you as well.

Dioptase

If you are searching for a stone that can help you relax and relieve mental stress, dioptase will be a great addition to your crystal collection. This stone has the ability to stimulate and clear all of your chakras so that you will be able to enter a higher level of awareness and bring refreshing energy to your body and soul. Dioptase is also beneficial if you are looking to further your spiritual attunement as it has the ability to stimulate your past life memories and promotes prosperity.

1. **Chakra**
   Heart Chakra

2. **Color**
   Turquoise or Green

3. **Rarity**
   Uncommon

4. **Physical Uses**
   Dioptase can help with several physical ailments. The powers of this stone can help with tumors, removing toxins, PMS symptoms, pain relief, muscle pain, lung problems, liver disorders, heartburn, heart problems, headaches, chronic pain, cancer, blood pressure issues, and abrasions.

5. **Emotional and Spiritual Uses**
   Dioptase is often used to help ease depression and balance your emotions. It is also beneficial if you are looking to reduce stress and create a sense of tranquility in your life. On top of these benefits, it can also help you clear and cleanse your aura.

Emerald

Emerald is mostly associated with the Heart Chakra. This crystal is mostly used to enhance wisdom, unity, loyalty, and love for peoples' lives. When you use emerald on a group of people, it has been known to encourage bonding and increase both understanding and communication. On top of these amazing benefits, emerald is also useful if you are looking for mental clarity and enhance memory. If you are looking to connect to Divine Love, you can use the crystal in meditation to help you open your heart and accept all things.

1. **Chakra**
   Heart Chakra

2. **Color**
   Green

3. **Rarity**
   Common

4. **Physical Uses**
   Emerald is an excellent stone to use for a number of physical ailments. These can include overall weakness, vomiting,

ulcers, nausea, memory health, liver disorders, immune system problems, heart issues, fever, infections, eye problems, colds, cancer, blood pressure, and arthritis.

5. **Emotional and Spiritual Uses**
   This stone is mostly used to help individuals calm down and creates a sense of tranquility in your life. It also has the ability to inspire some people and creates a sense of serenity and compassion. Emerald has also been known to help people cope with grief and gives them a sense of clarity.

Epidote

Epidote has the ability to enhance the energy of whatever this stone touches, this includes other stones which is why it is so popular. If you have other energies you are looking to enhance, you will need to add epidote to your crystal collection. This stone is excellent for releasing negative energy and increasing the perception of spiritual beings. It can also restore one's sense of optimism and can clear energy blockages.

1. **Chakra**
   Heart Chakra

2. **Color**
   Green

3. **Rarity**
   Common

4. **Physical Uses**
   Epidote can help with several physical ailments. Some of the more popular issues this stone can help include physical strength and recovery, vitamin absorption, kidney issues, weak immune systems, dehydration, and brain disorders.

5. **Emotional and Spiritual Uses**
   This stone is beneficial in several ways. For one, it has the ability to increase an individual's self-worth and self-confidence. It is also helpful if you are looking to ease depression. On the spiritual side, epidote is helpful if you

are looking to raise vibrations and create a balance in your chakras.

Fluorite

Fluorite is another crystal that is fairly popular in the crystal healing world. This stone is very protective and is useful if you are looking to ground yourself. Mostly, this crystal works with your upper chakras and can help connect your mind to the universal consciousness. It also has the ability to clear your aura of energies that may be dragging you down.

Fluorite comes in several different colors. One example of this would be green fluorite. This version has the ability to access intuition. It can ground you and absorb any excess energy you may have. Use green fluorite if you wish to renew and cleanse your chakras.

Another popular version of fluorite is blue fluorite. The blue color helps clear communication between your physical and spiritual planes. This crystal is used to create a sense of serenity and calmness to help bring you inner peace.

1. **Chakra**
   Varies depending on the color

2. **Color**
   Purple, Green, Clear, and Blue

3. **Rarity**
   Common

4. **Physical Uses**
   Depending on the color of the fluorite you buy, it will have different physical benefits. This crystal can help with issues such as viruses, ulcers, spleen issues, sinus problems, pneumonia, physical coordination, pain relief, nutrition problems, vitamin absorption, muscle toning, memory health, lung problems, kidney issues, herpes, health, gallbladder problems, eating disorders, dental problems,

broken bones, bone strengthening, bone disorders, arthritis, and issues with ADD and ADHD.

5. **Emotional and Spiritual Uses**
   Fluorite is a great stone to have if you are looking to balance your emotions. The power of the stone grants the ability to release any negativity or denial you may be holding onto. It can also help with healing and enhancing your intuition.

Fuchsite

This is the mineral of renewal and rejuvenation. Fuchsite is a stone that helps bring out your inner child and often sparks joy. It is a wonderful reminder that no matter how old we get, your heart and soul have an attitude of its own. Fuchsite can assist in clearing your consciousness and creates a balance in your mental and emotional states. This stone also has the ability to increase energy when combined with other crystals. If you are a healer, this will be a wonderful addition to your collection.

1. **Chakra**
   Heart Chakra and Throat Chakra

2. **Color**
   Green

3. **Rarity**
   Common

4. **Physical Uses**
   Fuchsite is an excellent stone to help with several physical ailments. It can help with issues of the throat, spine, snoring, larynx issues, inflammation, immune system problems, eczema, cellular disorders, and carpal tunnel problems.

5. **Emotional and Spiritual Uses**
   As mentioned, fuchsite is excellent to strengthen your emotional balances while bringing you both fun and joy. It also grants the ability to connect with angels and connect with the nature around you.

Garnet

Garnet is a popular crystal to have as it can help inspire a sense of brightness and light in your life. This is especially helpful if you are looking to help with depression or simply bring more joy back into your life. The crystal is also beneficial to help release the anger that you may be holding onto, especially if that anger is targeted at yourself. The fire of Garnet is known to bring courage and willpower to those who hold it in their hands. It can even "light a fire" under you to help you bring feelings to the surface. If the Garnet is powerful, it is also known to clean chakras of negative energies so that you can re-energize them.

1. **Chakra**
   Root Chakra, Heart Chakra, and Sacral Chakra.

2. **Color**
   Red

3. **Rarity**
   Common

4. **Physical Uses**
   Garnet is a crystal that can help with a number of physical ailments. Some of these issues include vitality, thyroid health, stomach problems diarrhea, constipation, pancreas health, pituitary gland issues, menopause, low blood pressure, libido, leg problems, kidney disorders, intestinal disorders, hyperactivity, heart issues, fatigue, exhaustion, colic, blood disorders, blood detoxing, blood circulation, arthritis, anemia, and abdominal pain.

5. **Emotional Uses**
   This crystal can also bring several benefits to your life on an emotional level. Garnet can help increase self-confidence, willpower, and self-worth. It has also been known to help with emotional issues that are involved with relationships, love, and loyalty to others. On top of these benefits, the stone may be able to increase your compassion as well.

6. **Spiritual Uses**
   Garnet is known to help people prosper and transform into the person they are meant to be. It can also be used to help create unity in your life as well as manifestation. Garnet can also come in a green color that helps people express themselves in situations where they are fearful to do so.

Halite

You may have heard of halite before as it is more commonly known as rock salt. This salt is mined in the Khewra Salt mines, which is one of the biggest salt mines in the world. While many of us typically use table salt, halite can be beneficial in your diet. This stone has the ability to cleanse your aura and can help deflect any negative energy in your life. Halite also has purification properties and is often kept in a bowl to rid of negative energies in a room. There are also halite salt lamps to help clear indoor pollutants.

1. **Chakra**
   Heart Chakra and Sacral Chakra

2. **Color**
   White, Pink, and Peach

3. **Rarity**
   Very Common

4. **Physical Uses**
   Halite has wonderful benefits for a number of popular ailments. One of the major reasons to introduce this stone into your home is to help with Seasonal Affective Disorder. It can also help with your nervous system, lung problems, infections, headache relief, migraine relief, chemical imbalance, fevers, asthma, and allergies.

5. **Emotional and Spiritual Uses**
   If you find yourself lacking self-confidence or self-worth, halite may be beneficial for you. It can also help with judgment and worrying. On top of these wonderful benefits, halite also can help you remove energy blocks and balance your aura.

Hematite

If you are looking for a crystal that has the ability to absorb negative energy and bring stress relief into your life, hematite will be an excellent option for you. This stone is protective and can help individuals stay grounded in a number of different situations. It is also beneficial if you want to work with your root chakra to help change your negative energy into positive vibrations. You can carry this stone with you if you need equilibrium or balance in your life. It is also beneficial if you need help focusing.

Please take note that when hematite is in its natural state, it has a slight magnetic charge. If you have a pacemaker, you will want to consult with your doctor before working with this stone. If a stone is marked Magnetic Hematite, it should be avoided if you have a pacemaker.

1. **Chakra**
   Root Chakra

2. **Color**
   Silver and Metallic Gray

3. **Rarity**
   Common

4. **Physical Uses**
   Hematite is a wonderful stone to add to your collection as it can be used on a wide variety of physical ailments. Some of these include issues with yin and yang energy, weakness, tissue healing, smoking addiction, physical strength, pain relief, nutrient absorption, nose bleeds, nervous disorders, multiple-sclerosis, cramps, menstruation, leg cramps, kidney disorders, inflammation, insomnia, high blood pressure, focus, detoxifying, circulatory issues, broken bones, blood clotting problems, blood detoxing, back issues, anemia, and other addiction problems.

5. **Emotional Uses**
   If you are looking to diffuse anger or release it from yourself, hematite can help you with this. It can also help balance

your emotions as well as increase your self-worth and your self-confidence. This stone also has the ability to dispel any negativity in your life as well.

6. **Spiritual Uses**
   As you start your crystal collection, you will want to have a spiritual protector. Hematite has the ability to protect you while also creating a sense of balance and harmony in your life. This stone will help bring awareness to the world around you and will also help to ground you through your life.

Howlite

Howlite is a popular crystal as it is an attunement stone. This means that it has the ability to connect you to higher spiritual consciousness. The stone will help prepare and open your mind to receive the wisdom of the attunements and the energy it provides. Howlite can also help if you experience stress, tension, and anxiety on a daily basis. By eliminating these stressors, it can help encourage the emotional expression of any individuals and help soothe them.

1. **Chakra**
   All Chakras but primarily the crown chakra

2. **Color**
   White

3. **Rarity**
   Common

4. **Physical Uses**
   Howlite is beneficial for several physical ailments. It can help with skeletal system problems, osteoporosis, lactating, dental issues, and bone disorders.

5. **Emotional Uses**
   This stone is used more for its emotional benefits. It can help diffuse any rage you may have and helps release anger you are holding onto. Howlite can also be beneficial to calm

yourself and creates a higher sense of creative expression in some individuals. It has also been known to help people become unselfish as well.

6. **Spiritual Uses**
   Howlite has several spiritual benefits aside from helping people clear and cleanse their aura. It can also help maximize your energy flow and connects you to spirit guides. Some people also use howlite to help recall past life events.

Jadeite

Jadeite is the second member of the jade family. This stone is known as the stone of harmony and can help bring people together in a group setting. This is an excellent crystal to have if you are looking to strengthen the relationships between friends, family, or even business colleagues. This stone also works if you are looking to fix a relationship that was torn apart due to a loss or separation. Jadeite is also extremely helpful for children who are dealing with changing hormones or feel alone.

1. **Chakra**
   Heart Chakra and Root Chakra

2. **Color**
   Yellow, White, Red, Pink, Orange, Lavender, Green, Blue, and Black

3. **Rarity**
   Fairly Common

4. **Physical Uses**
   Jadeite is beneficial for several physical issues. These can include skin infections, issues with reproductive organs, cramps, cellular disorders, bone disorders, and blood pressure regulation.

5. **Emotional and Spiritual Uses**
   If you are looking to enhance and recall lucid dreaming, jadeite will be a must-have for your crystal collection. It can

also help with love and all different kinds of relationships. Jadeite has the ability to create harmony in people's lives and can help with abundance and prosperity for some.

Kyanite

Specifically, we will be discussing black kyanite. This stone helps with clairvoyance and the manifestation of vision. This stone is a favorite among healers as it is full of healing energy and is helpful in healing any of the chakras. Kyanite helps send energy to any holes or tears that exist in your chakras and can help sweep away any negative energy you may be experiencing.

Black Kyanite is also beneficial if you are looking to open communication between people. With this, it is also used to ground individuals while their chakras are being aligned. It is popular to use while healing because it has the ability to heal and energize at the same time and makes for a wonderful meditation tool.

Overall, this stone has the ability to amplify energy, making it a wonderful tool for attunements as well. Kyanite may help bring tranquility to your life and can calm you for meditation.

1. **Chakra**
   Root Chakra

2. **Color**
   Black, Blue, Green, Orange

3. **Rarity**
   Common

4. **Emotional Uses**
   Kyanite is a popular stone to use when looking to enhance communication and expression. It is also beneficial if you are looking to get in touch with your creative expression. With these benefits, the crystal carries a calming effect that people are often searching for when they are trying to heal themselves.

5. **Spiritual Uses**
   Kyanite is mostly used for spiritual benefits. It can help with several spiritual issues such as spiritual protection, vision quests, recalling past life events, dream recalling and interpretation, clairvoyance, balancing the chakras, and also helps with attunements.

Labradorite

Labradorite is thought to be highly mystical. It is a crystalline form of Feldspar but is widely known for its flash when it catches the light. This stone is wonderful to heighten your intuition and also has the ability to enhance psychic abilities. Many people use labradorite to work with their third eye chakra because it is able to balance both intellect and intuition. On top of these wonderful benefits, the stone can also protect individuals from negative energies while balancing their strength and aura from any energy leaks at the same time.

1. **Chakra**
   Third Eye Chakra and Crown Chakra

2. **Color**
   Iridescent

3. **Rarity**
   Common

4. **Physical Uses**
   Labradorite has the ability to help people with a number of different physical ailments. Some of these problems could be stomach issues, diarrhea, constipation, addiction to smoking, certain skin infections, seizures, can boost metabolism, helps with eye disorders, emphysema, brain disorders, and other addictions.

5. **Emotional Uses**
   If you are looking to increase your self-confidence or your self-worth, labradorite may be beneficial for you. This stone also has the ability to enhance codependence if that is something you need to work on.

6. **Spiritual Uses**
   Labradorite is a very spiritual stone and can be beneficial for a number of spiritual ailments. As mentioned earlier, this stone is mostly used to help balance the third chakra. On top of this benefit, it can also help with telepathy, psychic attacks, personal empowerment, mediumship, meditation, stimulating and enhancing creams, cosmic awareness, consciousness, communication with spirits, communication with the higher self, clairvoyance, helps to protect the aura, cleans the aura, and can help with the ascension process.

Lapis Lazuli

This stone is made of a combination of several different minerals. These minerals include Lazurite, Pyrite, and Calcite. It is believed that Lapis Lazuli has existed since the birth of time and was used by ancient Hebrews. This is why the stone is best known for the power of spoken words. If you are looking to open and balance your throat chakras, Lapis Lazuli can help you with verbal expression.

Lapis Lazuli also has the ability to open the third eye chakra. It is thought that this stone can connect to the celestial and physical kingdoms. This stone is very peaceful and can connect with physical guardians. It is also known to help shield individuals from negative energy and can protect against psychic attacks.

1. **Chakra**
   Throat Chakra and Third Eye Chakra

2. **Color**
   Indigo

3. **Rarity**
   Common

4. **Physical Uses**
   Lapis Lazuli is used for many different physical ailments. Some of the more popular problems it can help with include vomiting, vertigo, throat issues, sleep apnea, shingles, pregnancy problems, panic attacks, pain, menstrual cramps, menopause, laryngitis, insomnia, immune system support, herpes, hearing issues, migraine and headache relief, fainting, eye disorders, epilepsy, ear infections, dizziness, dental issues, cramps, coma, chronic pain, brain disorders, problems with bone marrow, bone disorders, body detox, birthing problems, birthing pains, asthma, and other aches and pains.

5. **Emotional Uses**
   As for emotional uses, this stone also carries many benefits for a number of ailments. Some of these problems can include issues with self-worth and self-confidence, suicidal thoughts, reduces stress, helps with panics attacks and perseverance, helps with obsessive-compulsive disorder, melancholy, hope, emotional healing, emotional abuse, helps with criticism, grief, calming, and overall anxiety.

6. **Spiritual Uses**
   As mentioned, Lapis Lazuli is mostly used to help balance the third eye chakra. It can also help with spiritual protection, spiritually uplifting, psychic protection, psychic attacks, reincarnation, meditation, and karma. It is also known to help enhance intuition, psychic abilities, and the

ability to spirits. Lapis Lazuli may also help with balancing your aura.

Malachite

This stone is one of the more popular healing crystals as it has the ability to absorb energy and helps draw certain emotions to the surface. Malachite is known as the stone of intention, manifestation, abundance, and balance. It can help you clear your chakra and stimulate them. This stone is mostly used to clean energy and bring positive transformation to those who use it. Due to Malachite's ability to amplify all types of energies, it is recommended you use this stone in small doses.

1. **Chakra**
   Heart Chakra

2. **Color**
   Green

3. **Rarity**
   Common

4. **Physical Uses**
   Malachite is known to help with several physical ailments. Some of these issues include tumor growths, vertigo, toxins, skin infections, scoliosis, radiation, post-surgery healing, pancreas health, pain relief, muscular issues, muscle pain, liver disorders, joint pain, inflammation, infertility, immune system issues, healing, headaches, migraines, dizziness, dental pain, congestion, colic, chemotherapy, cancer, bone disorders, body detox, birthing issues, viral infections, back problems, asthma, and arthritis.

5. **Emotional Uses**
   With physical benefits, malachite can also help with several emotional ailments. If you feel your emotions are out of whack, this stone can help you remove any blockages you may have so you can restore your emotional energy. This stone can also help increase self-confidence, self-worth, and hope in your life. It has also been known to help shy individuals be able to express themselves.

6. **Spiritual Uses**
   As mentioned, this stone is mostly used to help with the heart chakra. It can also help absorb energy and protect your spirit.

Moonstone

As you can probably already tell, moonstone is associated with the moon and can help people connect to the Goddess within them. This stone is best known for its ability to balance the emotional body and helps individuals connect to their intuition. Moonstone is best for those who typically have an aggressive personality as it helps relieve stress and can also offer protective energies.

1. **Chakra**
   Sacral Chakra, Crown Chakra, Third Eye Chakra

2. **Color**
   White, Tan, and Cream

3. **Rarity**
   Common

4. **Physical Uses**
   Moonstone has some wonderful physical benefits. Some of the more common issues that it can help with includes water retention, vomiting, stomach issues, pregnancy, PMS, pituitary gland problems, muscular and skeletal issues, multiple sclerosis, menstrual cramps, menstruation, insomnia, insect bites, infertility, health, headache relief, edema, circulatory problems, breast health, birthing issues, and arthritis.

5. **Emotional Uses**
   Moonstone offers some emotional benefits alongside the physical benefits as well. It has the ability to help with postpartum depression, enhances positive energy, can help with letting go, mood swings, fear of the dark, emotional healing, emotional balancing, happiness, centering, composure, and also helps release anger.

6. **Spiritual Uses**
   Sometimes, we suffer from spiritual ailments. Moonstone can help with spiritual protection, visual quests, stimulating and enhancing dreams, enhancing intuition, and can help individuals connect to a higher realm. It is also known to increase ancient wisdom and bring awareness back into your life. If you are looking to revitalize and balance your aura, moonstone can help with this too.

Obsidian

While there are a few different versions of obsidian, we are going to focus on black obsidian. Oftentimes, it is referred to as the wizard stone as it is thought to have magical problems. In the modern world, many people choose to wear this stone to help protect them against hostile environments, stress, and negative energy. It can also be used as décor in your home to help protect you against electromagnetic fields.

1. **Chakra**
   Root Chakra

2. **Color**
   Black

3. **Rarity**
   Common

4. **Physical Uses**
   Mostly, obsidian is helpful for physical protection and pain relief. It may also be able to help with physical ailments such as knee pain, joint pain, circulatory problems, blockages, and arthritis.

5. **Emotional and Spiritual Uses**
   Obsidian is a beneficial crystal to have if you are looking to release any stress or emotional blockages you may be suffering from. It is also great if you need positive energy in

your life or helps to ground yourself. This crystal also has the ability to protect you against psychic attacks.

Onyx

Onyx is a powerful protection stone that has the ability to absorb and transform any negative energy in your life. This is important as negative energy often drains our personal energy. By getting rid of the negativity, you may find that your physical and emotional strength will increase as you become less stressed.

This stone also encourages good fortune and happiness, helping people heal from past life issues they may be holding onto. On top of this benefit, many people use black onyx while they are dreaming or meditating to help ground themselves.

1. **Chakra**
   Root Chakra

2. **Color**
   Black

3. **Rarity**
   Common

4. **Physical Uses**
   Onyx is beneficial for several physical issues. Some of these ailments include ovarian disorders, obesity, birthing problems, allergies, alcoholism, and other addictions.

5. **Emotional and Spiritual Uses**
   This stone is excellent if you are looking to reduce or release any negative energy in your life. It also has the ability to soothe the soul and can help people who have anxiety. On top of these benefits, onyx is also known to help ground individuals when they need it most.

Peridot

Peridot is a crystal that helps bring positive energy to those going through traumatic situations and is highly vibrational with your heart chakra. This stone also has the power to bring out unconditional love for those who seek it and can help with several relationship roles. For this reason, peridot is often worn during social interactions.

1. **Chakra**
   Heart Chakra and Solar Plexus Chakra

2. **Color**
   Green

3. **Rarity**
   Common

4. **Physical Uses**
   Peridot has the ability to work with a wide range of physical ailments. Some of the more common treatments can be for trauma, tissue healing, thyroid balance, spleen issues, smoking addiction, muscle toning, lungs, liver disorders, intestinal issues, indigestion, heartburn, eye infections, breast health, blood sugar regulation, and birthing problems.

5. **Emotional Uses**
   This crystal is most commonly used for emotional benefits. Peridot can help with resentment, reduces stress and tension, diffuses rage, lessens jealousy, decreases irritability, can ease depression, help cope with grief, and is found to be a very comforting healing stone. This stone can also be used to help with emotional abuse and emotional healing.

6. **Spiritual Uses**
   Peridot has been known to have several spiritual benefits as well. It can be used to stimulate spiritual insight, enhances creative expression, can cleanse the aura, and may even help in vision quests.

Rose Quartz

As you may have already guessed, rose quartz is one of the most popular healing crystals. This stone is the stone of unconditional love and works with the heart chakra to help open your heart to all different kinds of love. Whether you are seeking the love of family, romantic love, or even the love of friends, the high energy of this stone can help you.

Rose Quartz also has soothing energy. It helps many people foster emotions of forgiveness, reconciliation, and empathy toward others. While lowering your stress levels, this stone can help clear any resentment, jealousy, or anger you are harnessing toward others. Instead, you will attract love through the romance stone and help yourself express feelings you may be keeping bottled up inside.

1. **Chakra**
   Heart Chakra

2. **Color**
   Pink

3. **Rarity**
   Common

4. **Physical Uses**
   Rose Quartz may be able to help you with a number of physical problems. Some issues include skin infections, shingles, PTSD, pain relief, neck problems, menstrual cramps, lung issues, kidney disorders, infertility, headache relief, fatigue, eating disorders, dying process, dementia, coughing, burns, bruising, and Alzheimer's disease.

5. **Emotional Uses**
   This stone is excellent if you are looking for a healing stone to help with your emotions. Rose Quartz can help with all types of relationships, reduce stress, enhance love, decrease jealousy and guilt, decrease fear while increasing emotional strength, and helps some people cope with grief. If you are looking to diffuse anger and create a sense of calm for yourself, rose quartz can help with this too.

6. **Spiritual Uses**
   Rose Quartz is most commonly used to bring users unconditional love. It also can help with spiritual love, increases positive energy, and helps some people connect with the Christ consciousness. On top of this, the stone is also known to help connect with the divine love through the heart chakra.

Ruby

Are you looking to open your heart chakra? Ruby is a very powerful heart stone that can help protect against lost heart energy and can dissolve any emotional congestion you may have. This stone has the ability to balance and heal emotions involved with connecting to others. Ruby grants the ability to express love and facilitate new relationships.

1. **Chakra**
   Heart Chakra and Root Chakra

2. **Color**
   Red

3. **Rarity**
   Common

4. **Physical Uses**
   Ruby is a stone that is used often with a number of physical ailments. This stone can help with urinary tract issues, ulcers, stomach problems, skin infections, sexual abuse, pregnancy, reproductive organ issues, physical strength, night terrors, menstrual cramps, menopause, leg issues, kidney problems, intestinal disorders, infertility, heart problems, fever, brain disorders, bone disorders, blood pressure regulation, blood circulation problems, bleeding, anemia, and abrasions.

5. **Emotional Uses**
   Ruby is an excellent stone if you are looking to build your self-confidence and self-worth. It is also beneficial to gain courage, happiness, inspiration, and passion. If you are

looking to balance and stabilize your emotion, this will be an excellent addition to your crystal collection.

6. **Spiritual Uses**
   Ruby is also beneficial for spiritual uses. This stone is known to help reduce negative energy and has the ability to create long distance healing. If you are looking to work with your heart chakra or strengthen your aura, ruby may be able to work for you as well.

Sapphire

Sapphire is most popularly known as a stone of tranquility, peace, and spiritual truth. If you are looking to channel healing energies from a higher source, this is an excellent stone to add to your collection, especially if you practice Reiki. Sapphire has the ability to guide users on the spiritual path and can help boost both spiritual and psychic powers.

I mentioned earlier that there are Biblical references of Sapphire being placed in the breastplate of High Priests. It is believed that this stone has protective powers and seems to have been used through history. There are many different colors of sapphire depending on the trace metals they have.

1. **Chakra**
   Throat Chakra, Crown Chakra, and Third Eye Chakra

2. **Color**
   Purple, Pink, and Blue

3. **Rarity**
   Common

4. **Physical Uses**
   Sapphire can help with several physical ailments. Some believe it helps with tumors, nausea, motion sickness, hearing problems, eye disorders, eczema, brain disorders, and altitude sickness.

5. **Emotional and Spiritual Uses**
   Sapphire is beneficial for a number of emotional and spiritual issues. It helps many bring happiness, hope, and wisdom back into their lives. It also has a calming effect that

helps many individuals release negative energy they are holding onto. Sapphire is also thought to help some people communicate with spirits and can be beneficial to use during meditation.

Smoky Quartz

Throughout this book, you have seen smoky quartz mentioned several times. This is a very powerful stone and emits high levels of energy. Mostly, smoky quartz is used to ground people and is used to work with both the solar plexus chakra and the root chakra. This stone can be highly beneficial because it has the ability to transmute and absorb negative energy. It also provides relief and can help after a strong energy session. The best part of this stone is the fact that the energy is slow and steady but still powerful. It has the ability to help you transform your dreams into reality.

1. **Chakra**
   Root Chakra

2. **Color**
   Brown

3. **Rarity**
   Common

4. **Physical Uses**
   Smoky Quartz is popular for a number of physical ailments. It can help with understanding death, tumor growth, skin infections, toxin removal, radiation, pancreas issues, pain relief, night terrors, nightmares, kidney issues, infertility, headaches, migraines, foot problems, chemotherapy, cancer, balancing issues, and abdominal problems.

5. **Emotional Uses**
   This stone can also benefit users if they are having emotional problems. It can help ease any stress or tension in your life. Smoky quartz is also beneficial to ground individuals and helps ease depression. If you are holding onto resentment toward another individual, it can also help with that.

6. **Spiritual Use**
   Smoky Quartz is a powerful spiritual healing stone. It can help with the root chakra and has the ability to help individuals release and dispel any negativity they are holding onto. It is also thought to have psychic protection and can help individuals cleanse and clear their aura. Smoky Quartz is beneficial in the home as well as it can protect people from pollutions, smog, and electromagnetic frequencies.

Tiger Eye

While there are several different versions of Tiger's Eye, we will be focusing on golden or brown tiger eye. This stone has the ability to draw spiritual energy to the earth. Golden Tiger Eye specifically has the power to bring optimism and brightness into your life, while shining light on any issues you may be having. It is also widely known to protect travelers and can bring individuals good luck.

If you add this stone to your collection, it is great to carry around with you when you need help dealing with any issues that include concentration, control, will, or power. It is also beneficial for those looking to boost their creative energy. Overall, it works closely with your solar plexus chakra to help increase your power.

1. **Chakra**
   Solar Plexus Chakra, Sacral Chakra, and Third Eye Chakra

2. **Color**
   Yellow and Gold

3. **Rarity**
   Common

4. **Physical Uses**
   Tiger Eye can be beneficial for a number of physical ailments. It has been known to help with the throat, reproductive organs, mental diseases, hepatitis, gallbladder problems, fatigue, eye disorders, bone disorders, and balance problems.

5. **Emotional Uses**
   This stone is excellent to work with your emotions thanks to its ability to ground users. It can help with self-criticism, self-confidence, pride, personality disorders, goals, depression, creative expression, coping with change, commitment problems, and balancing problems.

6. **Spiritual Uses**
   It is believed that Tiger Eye can help enhance psychic ability. It is also known to increase spiritual protection and creates a sense of balance. Some also believe that Tiger's Eye can help some communicate with animals!

Tourmaline

Tourmaline is a popular crystal used in metaphysical circles. It is believed that this stone has the ability to balance the brain, clear energy blockages, and can transmute any negative energy you may have. It is also beneficial as a healer and a protector stone by boosting sympathy, empathy, and compassion.

1. **Chakra**
   Dependent on Color

2. **Color**
   Pink, Green, Clear, Brown, Blue, and Black

3. **Rarity**
   Common

4. **Physical Uses**
   This stone can help with some physical uses. Some ailments tourmaline can benefit include tonsillitis, the sense of taste and smell, muscular problems, muscle pain, lymphatic system issues, low blood pressure, indigestion, immune support, hearing issues, epilepsy, cancer, anemia, and abrasions.

5. **Emotional and Spiritual Uses**

Tourmaline is known to help with several emotional and spiritual ailments. This stone can help bring peace, happiness, and harmony back into your life. It is also popularly used to cleanse auras and balance masculine energy. On top of these wonderful benefits, tourmaline also has the ability to help people cope with grief and bring courage back into their life. This is especially true for those looking to stabilize their emotions after going through specific types of abuse.

Turquoise

Turquoise is believed to be the bridge between heaven and earth. Several cultures believe this stone has the ability to connect our minds to the universe. This may be why it is so popular in jewelry all around the world. Turquoise has wonderful benefits including releasing and removing any old behaviors you may have such as self-sabotage.

This stone works closely with the throat chakra, granting people the ability to speak honestly and clearly, especially in public. With turquoise, you may find you have the ability to express yourself freely while the stone provides you with both strength and purification of your heart and soul.

1. **Chakra**
   Throat Chakra

2. **Color**
   Green-Blue, Sky Blue, Green, and Blue

3. **Rarity**
   Common

4. **Physical Uses**
   Turquoise can be used for several different ailments. These include rheumatism, pain relief, nutrient absorption, night terrors, nightmares, muscle pain, lung problems, infection, healing, migraine relief, eye disorders, breathing issues, and blood oxygenation.

5. **Emotional and Spiritual Uses**
   Mostly, turquoise is used to bring peace and kindness into people's lives. It can also help promote empathy and friendship for other people. Turquoise has wonderful benefits with mental clarity and public speaking if that is something you have trouble with.

Zircon

Finally, we end with zircon as crystals you should consider for your collection. For a very long time, zircon has been known as a protective stone. Depending on the color of the stone, it has the ability to renew your sense of joy and enthusiasm for life. It also helps some people to bring peace into their life after they have gone through a traumatic event.

It should be noted that if you have epilepsy or wear a pacemaker, you should not wear Zircon. Some people have noted that this stone can cause dizziness if you have either of these ailments.

1. **Chakra**
   Root Chakra

2. **Color**
   Yellow, Grey, Green, Copper, Clear, Brown, Black

3. **Rarity**
   Fairly Common

4. **Physical Uses**
   Zircon can benefit some specific physical ailments. Most commonly, it is used for viruses, vertigo, ulcers, sexually transmitted diseases, poison, muscle pain, insomnia, brain disorders, bone disorders, and allergies.

5. **Emotional and Spiritual Uses**
   If you are looking to clear and cleanse your aura, zircon may be beneficial for your collection. It is also known to bring an individual's vitality, protection, and joy!

CHAPTER FIVE
Other Uses For Crystals

With all of these incredible healing benefits crystals can bring into your life, it may be hard to believe that people use crystals for anything else! Indeed, crystals can have several roles in your life. Some other uses for crystals include energizing, grounding, meditating, decorating, and more! In the chapter to follow, we will be going over just some of the other ways you can use your crystal collection.

Energizing

As we go through our day, sometimes, we need a little boost of energy. There are energizing stones that can help you get through tough times when you are feeling weak or fatigued. It should be noted that these types of crystals have higher vibrations and should be used sparingly. If you are looking to temper the healing crystal, try wrapping them in gold. You can also keep the crystals on your bedside if you are looking for a good night's rest. Two of the most popular energizing crystals include topaz and opal.

Grounding

You may not realize it just yet, but the ground beneath you is more important than you realize. Everyone needs to have solid ground beneath them to be the best version of themselves. A grounding stone will keep you from floating away or forgetting who you are. A powerful healing stone can help root you and bring awareness back into your life. Some popular grounding stones include smoky quartz, petrified wood, hematite, coral, and bloodstone.

Manifesting

Some people choose to have healing stones and crystals to help manifest certain powers. These stones can help you focus on the things in life you really want. They can also help you maintain a positive mindset when you need it most. Some of the more popular stones used for this purpose include onyx, sapphire, green quartz, bloodstone, and citrine.

You can also use manifesting stones to help during the meditation process. Stones such as alabaster, amethyst, and geode can help connect to your power source. If you need help focusing during meditation, try holding lapis, iolite, or lepidolite.

Record Keeping

In the crystal healing community, people believe that stones are both wise and ancient. Certain stones have the ability to absorb and retain memories. In general, it seems as thought red-colored stones are the best at holding onto information. If you are a student, stones such as ruby, garnet, or carnelian may be beneficial to carry with you to class. The stone can help you focus and stay grounded during lecture. It may also be beneficial to bring this memory-keeper with you to exam days for some extra help!

Protection and Shielding

As you have already learned throughout this book, healing crystals have certain energy shields that can help protect you. If you wear certain crystals, they can shield and absorb energies around you. Stones such as pyrite, yellow jasper, diamond, and fluorite can absorb bad vibrations around you, so you can remain happy and positive.

Love

If you are looking for love in your life, there are love stones you can add to your collection. These stones typically have warm and soft energies that can bring love into your life. Typically, the love stones attract love and help people learn how to love themselves. If you are looking to bring more compassion in your life, try kunzite, moonstone, morganite, rose quartz, or even apatite.

Enlightenment

These stones are known as seeker stones. Stones such as celestite, moldavite, topaz, and Tiger's Eye can help elevate energetic vibrations. If you are looking to gain knowledge from the astral plane or connect to your higher self, an enlightenment stone will be beneficial to add to your collection. Some other seeker stones include selenite, sodalite, and Sunstone.

Goddess Energy

Are you looking to increase your feminine energy? There are healing stones for that! You don't need to be female to seek feminine energy. Each and every person is a blend of both feminine and masculine aspects. If you are looking to soften yourself in a difficult situation, you can try any of the goddess energy stones like peridot, moonstone, or chrysocolla.

Decorating

Your home can mean a number of different things to you. Your home is your sacred space, your sanctuary, your safe haven, your personal space, and where your heart is. Oftentimes, we decorate our homes with different pieces of arts, plants, and items that are important to us. Some people choose to add crystals to their décor because not only do they look beautiful, they can also have healing effects too.

One of the more popular crystals to decorate with is black obsidian. This crystal is a glossy black color and is a very strong protection stone. Black obsidian has the ability to cleanse your house of negative energy, anger, fear, greed, or resentment. I suggest using this crystal in your study or TV room to help absorb any electromagnetic emissions from appliances in your home. You can also place it near your front door to help stop any negative energy from entering your home in the first place.

Another stone you can place at the front door to greet friends and family is rose quartz! This stone helps increase happiness and joy in a gentle and loving manner. If you are looking to increase love and friendship in your home, rose quartz will be an excellent addition.

Next, we have rock salt! This crystal is most beneficial in your kitchen. It can be used for cooking but also can be a symbol of hospitality and prosperity. Rock Salts have energy that helps clear away any negative energy you may have in your environment. It also helps promote family harmony and can be used to cleanse your energy.

Another room you may want to decorate in your house is the bathroom. With healing crystals, you can help make this space serene and relaxing. I suggest using amethyst or rose quartz to help cleanse your physical body of any negative emotions and create a serene and stress-free environment. You can even place these stones in the bath water with you when you aren't displaying them!

Finally, it is time to take a look at your bedroom. Many of us spend a lot of time in the bedroom and crystals can help depending on what your goal is. Before you decorate, you must first ask yourself what you want from the crystals. Are you looking to sleep better? Perhaps you are looking to increase your love and intimacy in the bedroom. Once you have your goal set, you can do some research to find the perfect crystal for your space.

One of the more classic crystal placements for this room is right under the mattress. Many people place three quartz crystals to help bring a protective and relaxing energy to your bed. This is perfect if you are looking to sleep better. You will want to be careful when selecting your crystals as some people are sensitive to the energy from crystals.

If you are looking to boost love in the bedroom, you will want to consider rose quartz. As you will recall, this is the stone for universal love. This stone can emit calming energy to help anyone in the room open their heart and remove negative energy. On top of having healing energy, rose quartz is also very pretty to look at. I suggest placing this stone in every corner of the room to benefit the most from the energy.

Of course, you are welcome to get as creative as you wish with crystals! These are just some suggestions if you are looking for other ways to use your collection. Now that you know all of the wonderful benefits that come with healing crystals, it is time to learn how to take care of them. In the chapter to follow, we will be going over how to cleanse and recharge your crystal, so you can continue to benefit from them!

CHAPTER SIX
How To Care For Crystals

As you begin to collect crystals, it will be important that you cleanse them on a regular basis. I highly suggest cleansing a crystal when you first receive it. You already know that crystals naturally absorb energy. When you cleanse the crystal, it can remove any energy it picked up before it landed in your hands. This will be especially important if you are planning on working energetically with crystals through meditation or healing work. If you do not cleanse your crystal when you first receive it, it could pass the energy from the last person onto you.

When Should I Clean My Crystal?

As you work more with crystals, you will have a better idea of when your crystals need to be cleansed. One crystal you can tell that needs cleaning is quartz crystals. This stone becomes cloudy and loses its luster when it needs to be cleansed. Other crystals will typically become heavier as they carry an extra load of energy.

If you have crystals you use around the house or wear on your person often, I suggest cleansing these on a more regular basis. You will know a crystal needs cleansing if you feel a lack of energy from them. Crystals such as quartz also need to be cleansed if you are planning on reprogramming the energy to benefit something new.

Methods of Cleansing Crystals

There are several different methods you can use to cleanse your crystals. As you work with healing crystals more, you will be able to find which works best for you. At the end of the day, you will want your crystals to be clear of all energy, so you can continue to use them.

The first method we will discuss is cleansing the crystals with your own energy. You will do this through intention and a focused mind. To cleanse the crystal with your energy, try holding the crystal in your hand and imagine immersing the crystal with a white light. This white light have the ability to clear any unwanted energy. It can also help re-energize the crystal as you hold it and ask the crystal to transform all of the energy into divine love and light.

Another method of cleaning crystal is through running water. It is believed that most crystals enjoy running water, so you can hold it under the tap and allow cold water to wash over it. As you do this, focus your mind on the crystals and visualize any negative energy within the crystal washing away and dissolving. This focus will help transform the energy into positive healing energy.

It should be noted that when you use water to cleanse your crystals, you will want it to be cold. You should never use hot or warm water to cleanse the stones. Please also understand that water is not recommended for all crystals. Some stones you will not want to use water include calcite, opals, turquoise, malachite, hanksite, celestite, or pearls. These stones have a composition that can be damaged by water. You will also want to use natural water as chlorine and other chemicals can also damage the crystals.

People have also been known to bathe their crystals in rainwater or water that comes from a natural source such as the river, ocean, or spring. If you soak in natural water, you will want to dry them in natural sunlight, too. Morning sunlight and moonlight allow light to filter through the crystal to help cleanse them. The best time to cleanse your crystal through moonlight is when you have a full moon.

Smoke is another popular method of cleaning crystal. You will want to use sacred herbs like lavender, cedar, or sage to cleanse the energetic matrix of your crystals. You can smudge with white sage if you are looking to remove negative energy. To smudge the crystals, you will light the herb, burn them, and when the flame dies, you can run the crystal through the smoke to help purify it.

The last two methods of cleansing crystals take a bit more time. One of these methods is to place the crystals on a rock salt bed for a day or two. This has been known to help max a crystal's energetic matrix. Another method is to bury the crystal in the earth for two to seven days. The longer you leave the crystals in, the deeper the cleanse will be. You will want to make sure you choose a safe location so that the crystals won't be lost or stolen. This method is a very slow but gentle way to cleanse your healing stones.

Methods of Recharging Crystals

Once you have cleansed your crystal, you will want to recharge them and renew their energy. There are a few different methods you can try. As you work with your crystal collection, you will be able to find a method that works best for them!

The first method of recharging crystal is through sunlight. You will want to place your crystals in the sunlight for an hour or two. You can place them on a windowsill or on the earth. Crystals can be charged under the stars, moon, or sun. The moon is typically a gentler method of recharging your crystals. A full moon is best for penetrating your crystals to recharge.

Another way of recharging your crystals is to place them in dynamic weather conditions. If you get a chance, try recharging your crystals in a thunderstorm. The energy from the storm can provide electromagnetic charge to your crystals, and you may feel the energy when you use them soon after the storm.

Crystal Storage

Crystals are very fragile and need to be treated carefully. Typically, crystals enjoy being out in the open so that they can work to their full potential, but if you need to store them, there are certain methods you can use to keep them safe and sound.

First, you will want to select a location that is dry and clean. If you choose an area that has a lot of moisture or dust, this can destroy or damage your crystal. One location for fragile crystals is a box. This can help keep your crystals protected from the environment.

If you have crystals that are smaller or more fragile, you will want to keep them in divided containers. While some people use egg cartons, others choose to invest in special crystal boxes. It is important to keep some crystals separate, so they don't damage softer materials. You can do this by lining your box with cotton balls or pads.

If you have polished crystals, you can keep them in a few different places. They typically do well in pockets, under pillows, or even in a bowl. How you store your crystals is ultimately up to you. Remember that each crystal is unique, and the energy of that crystal can never be replaced. These crystals are true gifts from the universe and should be taken care of as such.

CONCLUSION

I wish to thank you for reading through my book on healing crystals. I hope that you were able to find all of the information you were seeking and that I was able to provide you with the tools you need for your crystal healing journey. Now that you have been granted with all of this wonderful information, the next step is to try some of the techniques in your life and figure out which method works best for you. Remember that there truly are numerous benefits healing crystals can bring to you. It will take time and effort to build your own crystal collection, but you will find it will be worth it.

If you enjoyed this book, I would appreciate if you took the time to rate it on Amazon. Your honest review will be appreciated. I thank you for taking the time to learn from crystals and wish you the best of luck on your crystal healing journey. May you benefit from the healing powers and live your life to the fullest. Thank you!

DESCRIPTION

Are you looking to balance your body, mind, and soul? If so, there may be a healing crystal for you. Holistic healing methods can help bring positive energy into your life to help you become the best version of you! In this book, *Crystal Healing Bible: The Ultimate Guide to Gain Enlightenment and Awaken Your Energetic Potential with the Healing Powers of Crystals*, author Crystal Lee will walk you through everything you need to know to get you started on your healing journey.

This book will provide you with:

- Basics of Crystal Healing
- How to Start Your Own Crystal Collection
- Incredible Benefits of Crystal Healing
- Basics of Chakra Connections and Crystals
- Over 40 Crystals You Need to Know
- How to Harness the Power of Crystals
- And More!

If you suffer from issues such as trust, stress, self-confidence, rejection, regret, negativity, motivation, or love, there is a crystal for you. Start today and discover the incredible natural cures crystals can perform for you.

CRYSTAL HEALING FOR BEGINNERS

Introduction to Crystal Healing: Learn How to Achieve Higher Consciousness and Enhance Your Spiritual Balance with the Power of Crystals and Healing Stones

**By
Crystal Lee**

© Copyright 2018 by Crystal Lee All rights reserved.

The following eBook is reproduced below with the goal of providing information that is as accurate and reliable as possible. Regardless, purchasing this eBook can be seen as consent to the fact that both the publisher and the author of this book are in no way experts on the topics discussed within and that any recommendations or suggestions that are made herein are for entertainment purposes only. Professionals should be consulted as needed prior to undertaking any of the action endorsed herein.

This declaration is deemed fair and valid by both the American Bar Association and the Committee of Publishers Association and is legally binding throughout the United States.

Furthermore, the transmission, duplication or reproduction of any of the following work including specific information will be considered an illegal act irrespective of if it is done electronically or in print. This extends to creating a secondary or tertiary copy of the work or a recorded copy and is only allowed with an express written consent from the Publisher. All additional rights reserved.

The information in the following pages is broadly considered to be a truthful and accurate account of facts and as such any inattention, use, or misuse of the information in question by the reader will render any resulting actions solely under their purview. There are no scenarios in which the publisher or the original author of this work can be in any fashion deemed liable for any hardship or damages that may befall them after undertaking information described herein.

Additionally, the information in the following pages is intended only for informational purposes and should thus be thought of as universal. As befitting its nature, it is presented without assurance regarding its prolonged validity or interim quality. Trademarks that are mentioned are done without written consent and can in no way be considered an endorsement from the trademark holder.

INTRODUCTION

Welcome to *Crystal Healing for Beginners*. By downloading this book, you should consider yourself both lucky and blessed, for the contents that follow will surely change your world. Congratulations for the download and for beginning (or continuing) your adventure with healing crystals through this text in particular.

In the following pages, you'll be introduced to many aspects of crystal healing, but you'll start with the basics. In the first chapter, we explore the history of crystal healing and what it is exactly as well as its importance and the importance of *you* learning it. Finally, we'll examine the effects of crystal healing on the mind, body, emotions, and more.

In the second chapter, we get right into it with a set of guidelines and instructions to begin crystal healing in your own life. We'll practice how to feel the energy of our crystals and connect with them, how to cleanse them, how to create grids with them, and *then* how to explicitly heal with the assistance of crystals.

The third chapter is essentially an index of over one hundred stones, minerals, and crystals as well as a guide to which *types* – which *forms* – of crystals do what. For example, sometimes you'll be working with raw and rough crystals that perhaps you found yourself while most of the time, you'll likely be healing with imported and polished (or "tumbled") low-grade "gems," stones, and crystals instead. What *type* of crystal you have to use makes a relative difference in its energy, and the more you know, the more efficient your crystal healing abilities will become.

The fourth chapter provides the details of the chakras, kundalini, and how crystal healing relates to both. If you're coming to crystal healing hoping for assistance with awakening as well as general healing, this chapter will be right up your alley, for it will help you diagnose "disease" that lies in your chakras and that goes deeper than surface hurts. By connecting to your inner subtle energy vortexes in this way, you'll find yourself changed for the better in no time.

In the fifth chapter, we dive deeper into a discussion on what subtle energy is, how crystals affect it, what other modalities of divination and healing exist, and how to tie crystals into any of those modalities without issue. Finally, chapter six provides even more details on how crystal healing works as well as an introduction on how to pair or group crystals into healing pouches specifically designed for any one person, theme, or level of disease.

By the end of this book, you will have been flooded with important knowledge regarding crystal healing, and you will feel ready and excited to begin experimenting with it in your own life. You'll be surprised how soon it'll be *you* whose pockets jingle with the daily assortment of nature bits, small faceted crystals, and tumbled stones. Thank you for the download, and welcome!

CHAPTER 1
Explaining Crystal Healing

As we start off on our journey with crystal healing, we'll touch base on its origins and what it will mean for your life. While these tiny and tough nature bits look like they're just glorified paperweights, you might be surprised what potential they actually contain and how long that potential has been tapped into by our own humanoid ancestors.

The History of Crystal Healing

Humans have been using pieces of the earth as talismans and jewelry for as far back as we can study, essentially. Early beads were traded economically and were carved from bones, coral, and teeth of the animals our ancestors caught and ate to survive. From as long ago as 60,000 years, Russians made beads from mammoth tusks and buried them with their dead. As long as 30,000 years ago, amulets made from amber in the Baltic region were traded and made for fashion.

Early humans from as late as 10,000 years ago began to become increasingly skilled in their stone and gem trades. Around this time, Brits began trading amulets ever increasingly, using stones of amber, jet, rhyolite, and more. When the ancient Egyptians and Greeks came to the historical foreground, both cultures relied heavily on crystal accents for nobility and for high priests/priestesses. In fact, the word "crystal" itself comes from the ancient Greek word for "ice."

In addition, ancient Chinese peoples were fashioning incredible things, from beads to armor and masks out of jade, and the Scandinavian Vikings used translucent calcite to navigate across their narrow sea, enabling their Western raids on England, France, Italy, Africa, and more. In many religions, crystals were becoming considered holy and coveted possessions. In fact, Christianity around 350 AD had to ban the use of amulets in its followers, for crystal healing became increasingly associated with paganism and "unholy" earth worship around that time. For them, only the elite of the church was worthy and incorruptible by these nature bits' incredible powers.

In the Renaissance period, crystals were used a bit more and more frequently as cures for ailments, but only for upper nobility, and the rising and falling religions of the time made it hard to tell which rulers supported crystal healing and which didn't. The last thing you wanted was to recommend a gem cure to a staunchly pious ruler. During the Renaissance period, too, the "modern-day" study of crystal healing was officially established by a physician at the German court. In a time of increasing religious skepticism, this physician talked of good (or bad) angels working within the stones for (or against) healing, and the crowd (and the King) ate it right up. Since then, the onset of the Age of Enlightenment and Reason caused the crystals another fall from grace, but as the centuries and decades pass to now, crystals seem to be accepted *almost* more than ever for their healing capacities.

While it is true that gem and crystal healing has existed across time in varying degrees (starting with those earthen amulets and talismans of the past, leading up to the "sophisticated" attempts at gridding and crystal healing today), a new age dawns in terms of its appreciation. Starting in the '70s loosely and burgeoning widely in the 1980s, crystal healing has become something that straddles the line between a bonafide healing method and a hippie's placebo effect.

Regardless what you *think* of crystal healing, however, the physical and historical reality of the practice remains clear, and the resurgence today only proves that we're entering an age of increased energetic and vibrational sensitivity. We're entering a return to the feminine vibration, to the potential of subtle energy healing, and to the effects that crystals can have on us, and in this flooding-in feminine age, any tools the earth has to give us are both valid and life-altering. It comes down to us as to whether they're used and how much credit we give to our earth.

What Is Crystal Healing Exactly?

Crystal healing is a modality of subtle energy healing that relies on crystals, gems, minerals, and stones to make its point, and the point is fundamentally this; every carbon-based life-form has a vibrational expression, too, and that vibrational expression provides healing aid to others lacking in that vibration. For crystal healing, it's these rough and tough little nature bits pack quite the energetic punch when they're used and treated in the right ways.

Crystals can be used to give energy boosts and to calm people down, to attract what people want in life and to protect them from their worst fears, to enhance certain personality traits and to tone down unproductive ones, to heal physical ailments and alleviate pressure and pains, and so much more. Crystals, whether raw, polished, large, or small, are an underappreciated and influential healing modality.

To many inhabitants of today's world, the sound of a phrase like "crystals can make you feel better," in any capacity, will be received not as truth but as madness. For these people in this contemporary, highly scientific and technological world, it seems utterly impossible that a small chunk of earth can do anything but hold down paper. However, the millennia of crystal work before our time speaks to another type of truth; the truth of crystal healing. In fact, crystals are used today to store, transmute, and focus energy to make watches, ultrasound machines, lasers, certain surgeries, computers, and other numerous electronics, which goes to show that their value is hardly nil, even to the scientifically-minded.

Crystal healing works based on vibrations, frequencies, and resonances, but that doesn't mean it's all a bunch of hooey. Crystals and minerals can harness light and sound into beams of energy that a crystal practitioner can then direct for healing purposes. Sometimes, it is the metal within a stone that helps, creates, or amplifies its healing vibration, such as with malachite and its copper contents. Sometimes, it is the location the crystal or mineral was mined or harvested from. Sometimes, it is the stone's positive or negative electric charge. Sometimes, it's the dye the crystal's powder creates and those connotations, and sometimes, it's even the crystal's power that aids with (physical & emotional) troubles within.

When it comes to crystal healing with complexes of disease and chronic illness, those vibrations and qualities of remedy that naturally exist within each mineral can be used to both treat symptoms of the disease and, at times, mitigate its presence altogether. Ancient Chinese people found that jade worked to mitigate kidney ailments millennia ago, and shamans of many cultures seem to have realized the crystals' harnessing power and then used it to their tribes' advantages. Crystal healers today are just tapping into this ancient tradition with renewed vigor, and each individual's practice makes the collective smarter and stronger, without us ever physically communicating.

The Importance of Learning & Practicing Crystal Healing

It makes a lot of sense that so many people would be drawn to crystal healing at this time in earth's present history. The earth is experiencing a period of great turmoil. Regardless of what you call it and why you think it happened, the earth's temperatures are increasing, and our planet is heating up. Our winters are becoming colder and fiercer too. The magnetic poles are shifting, and those temperature extremes are amplifying, just like watching a young child being pushed on a swing by a powerful adult. The tips of the pendulum arc become higher and higher, more and more extreme by the minute.

Not only is our earth going through menopause, basically, but our cultures are going through great strife, with an increased desire to separate rather than join forces together. War is as prevalent as ever, and it exists for as exploitative reasons as ever. Hunger and famine and poverty reign in certain parts of the world. Humans are in almost constant conflict, it seems, with one another, animals, and the earth itself. Even the very crystals we use for our healing have been taken harshly from the earth, but now that they're extracted, it's up to us to send back love, solidarity, respect, and healing straight to that earthen source.

So many people are coming to crystal healing now because we and our planet so desperately need it. We need to return to the power of collective healing, even if it happens first on an individual level. We need to remember the power of the earth, and what better way to do that than to work with her gorgeous nature bits and amplify love right back to their source. Being alive on this planet at this time grants us a huge responsibility. Either we live freely and unconsciously exploit the earth and plunder resources to the detriment of humanity's future, or we choose to live consciously and righteously in partnership with the earth, promising to give love where love has always been due in exchange for this powerful healing potential.

You are being called to crystal healing for a reason. Whether it's to heal yourself, someone close to you, or a group of people in the future, you're fascinated by these incredible earthen materials so that you'll remember your origin and feel connected to a divine purpose. No matter what healing work you're here for, you're sure to be blown away by the potential of your relationship with these crystals in no time.

The Effects of Crystal Healing

Crystal healing's effects on the human body, mind, and soul, are too numerous to just list outright, so it will be helpful in this case to divide our approach to discuss the multiple benefits of crystal healing in terms of *where* the effect will be housed. We'll start with the effects on the mind and mental faculties before moving onto the physical body and human physiology generally. Then, we'll discuss how crystals can affect emotions and emotional health before ending with their abilities to build and focus one's personal power toward a variety of ends.

...On the Mind

As far as the effects of this healing modality on the mind go, they are both numerous and highly beneficial. Having certain crystals and minerals around, in whatever form, can increase the individual or group's focus, creativity, organization, productivity, clear communication, psychic abilities, multitasking capacity, abilities to attract love and a romantic partner, abilities to attract wealth, abilities to protect one's home, and abilities to protect from pollution (environmentally and technologically). It can also help the individual clear unproductive thought cycles, it can give a boost to one's intellect, and it can help one work through destructive personality traits to the other side where things are decidedly a bit less harsh.

...On the Body

As far as the effects of this healing modality on the body go, they can do so much it's almost innumerable. Crystals can help with any of the ailments that follow: degenerative brain disorders, cancer, addiction or drug dependency, respiratory problems, blood pressure issues, blood sugar issues, diabetes, circulatory problems, heart defects, joint pain or insecurity, general pain and back pain, headaches and migraines, broken bones, strained muscles, tired or diseased eyes and vision, sore throat, asthma constrictions, infections (whether bacterial or fungal, in any part of the body), autoimmune disorders, depressive neurotransmitter imbalances, infertility, menstruation and menopause, nutritional absorption issues, digestive issues, and general inflammation.

...On Emotions

As far as the effects of this healing modality on one's emotions go, they're so positive and numerous that it's comforting to even consider. For people struggling with breaking a habit, loss and grief, depression, manic-depressive tendencies or bipolar disorder, broken heart, anxiety or stress-related chronic illnesses, panic attacks, feelings of being unlovable, feelings of listlessness and purposelessness, and even feelings of unworthiness, crystals can be an incredible aid through both their potential to comfort generally, as a weight in one's hand, and to mitigate the physiological responses that feed into some emotional complexes. For people seeking peace, calm, solace, mental balance, emotional clarity, anger management, and help with defensiveness, crystals can also be an incredible boon through just their presence, if not, then with their presence *applied* to healing.

...On Your Personal Power

As far as the effects of this healing modality on your personal power will go, I almost don't want to tell you so that you can be pleasantly surprised. I'll let you know a good bit of what's in store for you, at least. As you reconnect with your personal power through crystal healing, you'll come to realize that is it your *relationship* of working with the stones that make things happen in your life, and you'll come to reconnect with yourself. You might find that you become connected to yourself through past life visions too, for a handful of minerals and crystals even listed in this book have the abilities to connect you in that way. You might also find that you have the potential to make a connection with your spirit guides or surrounding angels and that potential is almost inexplicably enormous.

You might finally find that you grow in strength and capacity through your application of crystal healing in a way that brings you confidence. You may find a connection with your personal power through your voice, your assertiveness, and your abilities to live out your life the way that best suits *you*. Essentially, crystal healing has several effects on the body, mind, and soul, but perhaps none are so moving and influential as its ability to connect you with the best version of yourself in real time. Just wait and see what you can make happen.

CHAPTER 2
Guidelines For Engaging In Crystal Healing

Before just jump right into crystal healing, step back and take it all in. It might seem like a lot, but you still have a long way to go. You'll have to learn the essentials – the intricate inner workings of crystal healing – to see what you're in for before you decide if it's right for you*.

* Spoiler Alert: If you've made it this far, it's probably right for you!
*
How to Feel the Energy of Crystals

As someone who may be just getting started with crystal healing, you likely need an introduction on where to even begin. That's absolutely understandable, and you needn't worry. I'll walk you through exactly what to do to begin your incredible and healing relationship with these wondrous little nature bits. We'll start with just feeling the energy of the crystals and getting in touch with them in that way before going all the way into the use of them for healing. After feeling things out, we'll learn about cleansing, programming one's intentions, gridding, and *then*, finally, healing.

If you've ever been given a crystal before, or if you've had one or two random ones since you were young for no reason, go find those stones! If you definitely have never been gifted one, and you're certain you have none, go out to a metaphysical or mineral store and pick out just one or two to start. Once you have your starter minerals and crystals gathered, it's time to try closing your eyes and getting better attuned with the stones' inner vibrations.

The following exercise can be used on any mineral or crystal to help you feel connected to its energy and get a sense of its nature. This exercise can also be used to connect with the vibrational essences of plants, trees, herbs, flowers, and more, so don't be afraid to use this technique for any form of healing and knowledge gathering. It can take you farther than you know. The exercise is essentially this; holding the stones, you'll close your eyes and quiet your mind of excess thought, waiting to feel the vibration of the stone in your hand. If you're extra patient, you may even be able to intuit its healing capacity, too.

Meditating is a crucial part of how one can better feel the energy of crystals. The ability to close one's eyes and close out the world, to a certain degree, is immensely helpful when attuning to the vibration of a stone so small it fits, perhaps, on your thumbnail. By quieting the noise of the world and the chatter of the mind, the individual can learn to sense those quiet things that normally go so unnoticed. Like the glistening path of a snail on the sidewalk or the chirp of a cardinal, the vibrational essence of a crystal is small, but to some, it can be loud. To those who have trained themselves to silence out the unnecessary, even these small gestures can mean healing.

With your eyes closed, then, and the stone or stones in your hand, try to feel out the essence. You might feel it in terms of an amplified heartbeat under the crystal or a muscle spasm. You might feel it in terms of relaxation in your one arm or overall peace and satisfaction. Simply be calm and quiet; breathe and be still, and just wait to see what surfaces. Breathe evenly and deeply and take in this moment with this crystal. If any distracting thoughts or emotions or urges enter your mind, simply breathe them in or blow them away like smoke or fog or clouds.

As you meditate with the stone in your hand and begin to feel its vibration, make note of how it makes you feel. Make note of its effects, too; you could even keep a crystal journal if you like doing that sort of thing, and you can keep more detailed notes about your experiences and occurrences with each stone. After a little while, you will likely feel encouraged to carry certain crystals with you throughout the day, whether placed in your car, your pocket, your purse, or otherwise. And then, you can note the differences of how the crystal affects your *day*, rather than just how its vibration feels in your hand. With a crystal in your pocket, you're well on your way to learning and actualizing the full and potential intricacies of crystal healing in your life.

How to Cleanse Your Crystals

Crystals can take on a lot of energetic weight as you begin to work with them more and more. Even with one just sitting in your hand or being carried through the day in your pocket, it can pick up certain things from you and hold onto them until you help it find its release. Some crystals can cleanse themselves and won't need you. For example, selenite, quartz, and carnelian are excellent self-cleansers, and they're so strong they can clear the energies of any others they're near.

However, other stones are not so low-maintenance, and for those crystals and minerals, the following guide will become imminently helpful. As far as when to cleanse your crystals goes, you'll want to do it if or when any of the following 10 things happen: (1) you've just used the crystal, (2) you're just about to use it after a long time of it sitting, (3) someone else handled your crystal, especially if you don't trust or like that person, (4) someone else used the crystal to heal him or herself, (5) you think the crystal was mistreated or misused in some way, (6) you or someone else brought intense negative energy around the crystal, (7) it actually looks dirty or feels sticky, (8) you're preparing for a special ritual, (9) something major has changed for you/in your life, or (10) you're using a crystal you normally use for yourself on someone else.

If your crystals are polished, the easiest and most stress-free method is to put them under running water. You can choose to use sink water, poured spring or filtered water, naturally-running spring or creek water, still lake water, or even puddle water for this task, but the most ideal would be to find a natural source of running water and take your crystals there for a cleansing ritual. Be careful when using even polished versions of calcites and malachite for this type of cleansing, however, for the copper in malachite will become dull and the exterior of the calcite will begin to dissolve. Use these types of stones for the following method instead.

If your crystals are raw or in crystalline form, you'll want to try something different. You could always lay these crystals out on a selenite sheet or slab, or you could lay them onto the points of a quartz cluster. You could also put them onto a plate (or inside an opaque bag) with a piece or two of carnelian. However, the best method for crystals of this nature will always be to bathe them in the moonlight. Crystals that are raw and flaky are called friable, and these often dissolve in water and drastically fade (color-wise) in daylight. In order to protect crystals of this nature and other sensitive raw ones, choose moonlight as your cleanser and charger. Full moonlight is always best, but any night when the moon is out can work for a moment of cleansing. Just lay your crystals out in view of the moon, and the rest is up to nature.

If you'd like to try something different, there are a variety of other options at your disposal as well. Generally, you can apply the conditions you already listed. You can set any stone in running water (based on its physical qualities) or even a bowl of water for cleansing. You can set any stone in a pouch with another cleansing crystal, or you can set the stone on a cluster of cleansing crystals instead. You can use moonlight, as with friable, raw, and sensitive stones and minerals, and then the fun begins.

You can also use techniques for cleansing your crystals that involve other minerals, such as salt or soil. You can bury any stone, mineral, or crystal into a bowl of salt or soil to cleanse it from any energetic intensity. Furthermore, you can use indirect techniques of bathing your crystals in sunlight (be careful with amethysts though, they might fade!) or in an energetic shield of visualization on your behalf. Through meditation, you can visualize any amount and degree of cleansing any crystal may desire. Finally, you can use the "more direct" indirect means of cleansing, as through sound and incense smoke. The sonorous sound of a struck singing bowl, gong, bell, or chime can cleanse and refocus the energy of a crystal, and the smoke of an incense stick, as well as the smudge smoke from both sage and palo santo, can do the same.

How to Connect with Your Crystals

When it comes to connecting with your crystals after they're cleansed and ready to go, your relationship will be entirely changed. You won't be protecting, cleaning, and almost coddling the stone back to its healthiest, purest state of being; it will be time to put things into focus. It will be time to program your crystals with your specific healing intention, and while that may sound like a daunting task, I promise, it's easier than it sounds, and it will become second nature in no time.

As you learned when you sat and felt the vibration of the crystals a few sections ago, some crystals have a specific healing goal in mind, and with the right application of intuition, you can tell what the crystal *wants* to do. When you sit with your cleansed crystal now, how does its vibration feel? Was it affected by the cleansing, or does it largely feel the same? Is there anything worthy of note in your crystal journal? Most importantly, does it feel like the crystal wants to do any sort of work in particular? When you sit and meditatively feel that vibration, do you receive answers of this nature? If so, follow up with that direction. If not, provide your own.

If it comes down to providing your own direction and healing intention, the best way to "program" your crystal with that information is as follows. First, cleanse the space you're sharing with the crystal. You want to make sure that the environment you're inhabiting doesn't imprint any distracting energies onto the crystal while you're attempting this work, and you also want to make sure that any lingering energies of anyone else who's entered the space don't get attached to the crystal instead of or before your own. Smudge the room with sage or palo santo smoke to accomplish this feat.

Second, set all electronic devices out of the room completely. Get any distracting electromagnetic radiation and pollution out of the space so the crystal doesn't get too focused on something that's not you right off the bat. Third, hold the crystal in your hand and begin to meditate. Imagine what you want the crystal to do. Visualize that potential if you can. Really imagine it with detail. See the outcome, the circumstances that would lead up to it, and its resolution. See the togetherness and the community. See the success and achievement. Whatever you're hoping for, visualize it with this crystal held gently but with purpose.

Fourth and finally, breathe in all that intention, open your eyes, and exhale, blowing out your intentions and goals onto the crystal itself. Imagine that your goals are getting physically stuck to the crystal and that the crystal will want to work to solve or actualize those dreams in order to clear itself and get back to its most natural state. Visualize that the crystal is grateful for the task, and make sure to express your own sense of gratitude for the crystal's work, too. The more respected the subtle energy of the crystal is, the better its work will turn out. It might sound crazy, but it's true: the purer and kinder the approach, the better this technique will work overall.

How to Grid with Crystals

When it comes to crystal healing, one of the most effective and impactful methods is to set up a grid and then place your intention and energizing abilities onto that specific crystal set up. As you continue learning about minerals and what crystals work well together (and then when you read through the final chapter of this book and start thinking explicitly about crystal pairings and groupings), it will become obvious to you how one's healing intentions can be strengthened when several minerals are used that can work together for the same purpose.

Until you get to this point, it will suffice to know that grids are setups of crystals that usually involve two or more types of crystals (for example, the two types could be amethyst and rose quartz) which are then attuned to work together (whether naturally, intentionally, or both) to achieve a specific healing goal. Once it's agreed on what type of healing will be done and what crystals will be used, the individual can then plan what the grid itself will look like and what format is best for the style of healing in question.

Sometimes, the healing project deals with individual struggles, physiological alterations, or personality adjustments. In these cases, it's appropriate to formulate the grid *around the individual in question* so that the crystals' energies work together directly in relation to that person. Sometimes, the grid can even be established around the individual's workspace, bedroom, bed, or office so that the maximum effect can be achieved through a long-standing setup.

Sometimes, the healing project deals with altering the energies of environments or physical spaces. For these healing goals, it would be best to set the grid up around the edges of the space in question. If it's a natural space like a park, set up a few stones all the way around the park's perimeter if you can. If it's a room, grid the border, and if it's a home, you can even make a grid outside the residence with stones.

Sometimes still, the project involves healing a group of people. In this case, the grid would be a little more complicated and you have two main options. First, you can set up a stationary grid in your home that represents everyone involved, with a crystal or two focused on healing each person. Second, you can give each person a few stones from the grid to carry on them always, and as the individuals move about the world, the shape of the grid will change, giving everyone a transformative and interactive healing experience.

A few, more specific, guides to crystal gridding can be found in chapter 5. If you're really fascinated by this concept, flip forward, for basic grids to benefit those experiencing heartbreak, recent home invasion or feelings of insecurity and household unsafety, excessive stress, chakra imbalance, and (auto-)immune problems are included when other modalities of crystal healing are discussed in this later chapter.

How to Heal with Crystals

After you've set your intention with the crystal's approval and meditatively connected your energies in that way, you'll have to move forward. However, you might be at the point where you haven't even chosen the crystal for the task yet, and clearly, that's the place to start. If this situation describes yours, you can try several different techniques to choose the right crystal for you.

First, you could just go to a mineral store (whether online or in person) and intuitively choose a crystal without doing any research and then begin your work with it when it arrives at your home. Second, you could do research based on what ailments you want to heal, choose the right stones respectively, and then put them to action. Third and finally, you could do research based on a stone you're drawn to and then use it regardless of its healing capacities because you know it will benefit you somehow.

Regardless of what method you use, choose your stone or stones and prepare them for healing. Cleanse them, connect with them, and set your intention after doing your choosing and research. Then comes the good stuff. At this point, you'll have to energize your crystal so that it has all the power it needs to do that good work you asked it to do (and technically, you can do this energizing step before you complete the intentional programming, depending on how things play out; it doesn't matter *too* much the order here).

A few different ways you can energize your crystal, stone, or mineral include using water, moonlight, sunlight, or physical contact with the hands (or inflicted body part) of the person in need of healing. Energizing with water would involve sitting your stone in running water if able, or in a bowl of water if it's too sensitive. If it's too sensitive for water contact whatsoever, you can put the stone next to a glass of water in the sunlight or in an enclosed jar that's immersed in water.

Energizing with moonlight or sunlight involves using those natural light energies to give a boost to the potential of the stone in question. Use indirect sunlight for light-colored stones, as they may fade in direct light. Finally, energizing with physical contact reflects on an ancient Native American tradition, whereby nothing was used to amplify the potential of a stone other than the hands of the person it would be used to heal. Connecting one's energy with the stone in this way can be exactly what the crystal's essence needs to link with you for the future work of healing.

Finally, you'll want to consider where you'll put the stone or crystal when it comes down to that healing work. Certain placements work better than others, especially depending on the theme of the healing. Are you working for protection? Make a grid in your home or set stones right inside the doorway. Are you working to heal one of your organs? Find a way to hold that stone with you daily and keep it as near to that organ as possible. Are you working to clear the energy of a room or set of rooms? Make a gem essence (see chapter 5) and spritz it into the room out of a spray bottle whenever help is needed. Overall, placements to consider are nearby or on the person in question, in the room, in a spray bottle for the room, in the home (as inside main doorways), on a prayer altar, or worm in pockets or as jewelry.

CHAPTER 3
Crystal Index

This chapter will become your best friend as you continue building your relationship with these little, powerful nature bits. Eventually, you may use this chapter as a go-to for finding out what healing crystals and stones do what. The following pages delineate over 100 crystals and their abilities for aiding and manifesting metaphysical learning, spiritual development, personal transformation, financial abundance, and more.

After the general index of crystal details, you'll find another section that addresses the formations of these special stones. This section will become as important to you as the extensive beginning section of this chapter, for the form of crystals or stones affects and *enhances* their abilities even to an exponential degree at times. In time, you'll realize what the difference is between an Amethyst geode and a piece of polished Red Jasper.

What Crystals Do What

A

Agate

Any form of this stone is notable for its peculiar repeated pattern. Usually, there are banded layers of internal forms within the stone that help you tell which form of agate is which. For instance, blue lace agate produces a pattern within that looks like white lace on a pale blue background, while moss agate varies in color but looks like it contains moss on the inside when polished. Generally, agates are good for protection and attracting luck and wealth. They're essential for earth healing and training with strength or endurance.

Blue Lace Agate works with the throat chakra and third eye chakra. It encourages kind and compassionate communication of one's truth as well as peace and wisdom, generally.

Fire Agate grounds and inspires its holder or wearer while protecting them fiercely. It ignites passion as well as personal awareness of one's soul mission, life purpose, or ultimate adventure.

Moss Agate stabilizes and reinvigorates one's energy, based on what one needs. It is especially attuned to earthwork and earth-related healing. It's also a great stone for self-esteem, as it boosts self-compassion and capacity for self-love even when times are tough.

Tree Agate provides a deep sense of inner calm and rejuvenates one's connection to the natural world. It also fights stagnation if you're having trouble with laziness or procrastination.

Amazonite

This crystal helps one feel at peace and works in support of the throat and heart chakras. It helps your self-expression be as genuine and heartfelt as possible, especially during times of great stress. It encourages an overall return to health and mental well-being.

Amethyst

This stone works for so many different things. It's a pain reliever, a psychic awakener, a sleep aid, a health booster, an energizer, and more. It's also incredibly helpful for meditation and finding one's truth despite hard times or trauma.

Chevron Amethyst helps to attune one's intuition and generally opens the third eye when applied in meditation. It also works to cleanse and heal subtle energy injuries and aura wounds.

Vera Cruz Amethyst, in particular, brings about good mood and reminds of the importance of play.

Apatite

Apatite helps reduce feelings of hunger while encouraging mental and emotional creativity. It boosts intellect, clairvoyance, confidence, and clarity.

Apophyllite

This crystal helps people who struggle with allergies as well as those who want a stronger connection to the spiritual side of things. In addition, apophyllite helps one perceive and act on their truth. For those skilled with meditation, apophyllite has the ability to open portals through space and time.

B

Beryl

This stone lets one release emotional baggage that may have been accumulating. It also helps one reach his or her greatest potential while encouraging their solar plexus and crown chakras to open. Beryl is also a powerful stress reliever that works for the circulatory system generally. It even fights infections in the body and issues with digestion.

Bloodstone

This green and red stone help with any issues related to blood, the heart, and circulation. It also connects its wearer or holder to their root and heart chakras for healing purposes. It grounds and centers as well as encourages devoted friendships and lasting loves.

Boji Stone

Boji stones are some of the best grounding stones, for they even help to root their holder in the present moment despite over-stimulation or stress. They help strengthen one's connection to earth generally, and they help one get over hurtful situations or lingering emotional wounds. Healing-wise, boji stones work well for pain relief and even tissue regeneration. They work best in pairs.

C

Calcite

Found in a wide variety of colors, calcite works with chakras of almost any color, too. Furthermore, it allows the release of stress and fear while invoking happiness and laughter to fill their places. Calcites are also generally good energy amplifiers.

Blue Calcite helps reduce blood pressure and relieve pain. It also dissolves energy blockages for the best possible recuperation and recovery.

Green Calcite allows one to release old habits without detriment to the mind or soul. It helps one "cut out the fat," so to speak, of his or her life and personality.

Orange Calcite promotes happiness and joy while providing healing power to the reproductive and digestive systems.

Yellow (or Gold) Calcite banishes negative energies surrounding the individual and heightens the experience of meditation.

Carnelian

This stone provides healing and balance for the sacral and solar plexus chakras while restoring one's overall energy and cleansing any stones or crystals near to it. Carnelian protects and draws abundance when placed inside the front door of one's home, too. It boosts energy, encourages interest and love of life, and helps with kidney disorders.

Chrysocolla

This stone heals the heart and throat chakras while relieving deep physical and psychological pains related to past trauma. It helps build one's strength and vitality to be able to grow past those hurts.

Citrine

Crystals of citrine are powerful attractors of abundance. They also enhance one's communication abilities while making him or her more decisive and confident. Citrine also helps boost creativity while clearing any negativity in the space or individual. Use these crystals for sacral or solar plexus healing.

D

Danburite

This crystal helps for those who need a self-acceptance boost. It works well for people who need help accepting others, too. It creates the sensation of lasting peace for the holder or wearer, despite any lingering emotional pain (no matter how deeply it's hiding). It is intimately connected to the heart chakra.

Diamond

As the hardest gemstones on Earth, diamonds encourage resilience, endurance, trust, and constancy along with everlasting love. Even rough diamonds can strengthen your energy field.

Dolomite

Dolomite harmonizes energies within any shared field, and it helps to release great sorrow. Athletes can use the stone for increased strength and stamina, while writers and artists can use it for boosted creativity and frequency of insightful thoughts.

Dumortierite

This crystal is the best stone for work on patience. It helps increase intuition and insight as it activates the third eye chakra, and for the physical body, it heals pains, diarrhea, and various intestinal problems. If you're having trouble choosing something or deciding what to do in life, this stone will be of great help to you, too.

E

Emerald

Emerald is a stone of the goddess that aligns with the heart chakra. Furthermore, it works to attract peace and harmony in one's life. For the physical body, emerald helps to heal eyesight, the heart, and the immune system.

Epidote

This crystal helps increase contact with entities outside this dimension and planet. It's a vibrational and energetic amplifier in that sense. Epidote also relieves feelings of depression and hopefulness by raising one's vibration to new potential (that was always the true potential in the first place).

Eudialyte

Eudialyte is particularly gifted when it comes to healing a broken heart, as it clears up negative energy build-up from something like a break-up or loss. It generally replaces negative feelings towards others with more positive, beneficial ones. Finally, this crystal clears out old, stagnant, unhelpful energy from the root, sacral, and heart chakras (even energy as old as would linger from a childhood trauma).

F

Fairy Stone

Fairy stones are naturally occurring calcium deposits, but they're also undeniably, energetically strong because of it. They help establish strong bones or strengthen weak ones, they make the skin stronger and more resilient, they help individuals cut bad habits completely, they relieve tensions or pain from radiation or chemotherapy, and they boost happiness and connectivity to nature.

Feldspar

Feldspar is almost unmatched in its abilities to trigger and enhance creativity, but it also helps you achieve standard goals through a simple boost of productively creative thinking. Feldspar helps you become more self-aware, too, while increasing self-acceptance and feelings of self-worth. It will essentially allow you to feel grounded and loving to all through your own experience of self-love.

Fluorite

This semi-transparent crystal comes in a variety of colors, but it always packs the same punch: it enhances focus, mental clarity, memory capacity, and organizational productivity. Furthermore, fluorite helps broaden one's mind and acceptance of others while protecting against viral infection.

Fulgurite

Through prayer, manifestation goals become immediate and material with the aid of fulgurite. They're stones of purification that help clear out what's unproductive in order to make way for larger, more impactful experience, not excluding one's own psychic/soul awakening.

Fuchsite

Fuchsite helps clear blockages on all levels while recreating balance and tranquility within once that clearing work is complete. It's an energetic amplifier of other crystals, and it also triggers a deep and lasting sense of compassion and understanding for others.

Fuchsite with Ruby works specifically to heal one's own heart and dissolve blockages of energy there. It opens the individual up, psychically, once that heart chakra work is finished.

G

Galena

This harmony stone helps reduce inflammation while stimulating the circulatory system. It works well to increase or maintain hair growth and helps the body absorb its necessary nutrients. It encourages safe intellectual exploration, too.

Galaxite

This stone is wonderful for dissolving stress and for healing conditions or illnesses related to the experiences or stress or chronic anxiety. For those with brain disorders, galaxite helps limit degeneration and backward progress. Finally, this stone works to aid digestion and boost metabolism while creating a lasting sense of peace and calm with one's life.

Garnet

This root chakra crystal is one of the most powerful energy boosters. When you're having a low day, grab a garnet! It also promotes overall health and attracts spice for your love life (or a love life in the first place, if that's where you find yourself starting from). Finally, garnet helps one access higher states of consciousness as well as the pain relief and blood healing one desires.

Gaspeite

This crystal is a powerful and impacting healer that maintains a healing vibration no matter how much negativity it happens to pick up. All the while, it imparts that healing vibration onto its holder or wearer, as well as that person's surroundings. It grounds you while opening your eyes, providing a spiritual perspective of any situation you encounter.

Gold

Gold works metaphysically to heal feelings of impurity, unworthiness, and general negativity. It encourages belief in one's inner strength and all the while attracts abundance.

Goldstone

This human-made stone glimmers with potential and it imparts that energy onto you too. Goldstone helps boost your life force energy, which you can call chi, prana, etc. Because it contains copper, it helps heal the circulatory system while easing inflammation of many types. It's also great for detoxification and strength building.

Green Aventurine

This stone is great for comfort and general healing assistance, but particularly for the heart, green aventurine provides incredible healing potential. It harmonizes the heart chakra while protecting the physical heart from a relapse into disease once healed. This stone can also settle feelings of nausea, disorder, and distress.

H

Heliodor

A great crystal for leaders and leadership, heliodor ignites charisma and inspired work. It will draw towards you such wonderful traits as confidence, self-awareness, group-awareness, assertiveness, decisiveness, and wisdom. If others come to you often with intention of manipulation, heliodor can help you see through their falseness while boosting your strength to shut them down.

Hematite

This metallic stone activates the root chakra while enhancing feelings of groundedness. It helps one find a balance between their masculine and feminine aspects as well. For those with blood issues, hematite will be a necessary companion.

Herkimer Diamond

These "diamonds" are actually a variety of quartz that aligns with the crown and third eye chakras. They increase dream activity and dream recall while grounding people who are often too "fiery." They clear all chakras, too, when used for chakra healing and meditations, helping the individual reach their highest possible potential (through clairvoyance, clairaudience, dream insights, and more).

Howlite

Howlite is a calming stone that strengthens manifestation abilities, reduces experiences of insomnia, connects one with wisdom and true insight, redirects anger sent your way, and helps dissolve triggers of any kind. Furthermore, this stone will work to balance calcium levels in the body for the benefit of one's overall health.

Blue Howlite, in particular, works well with sleep and dreaming. It increases abilities to fall asleep easily and stay asleep deeper, but it also aids in dream recall while enhancing your ability to process and interpret those dreams.

I

Infinite

This crystal works wonders for pain relief, both physical and emotional, but it also helps one process where those pains came from and what they mean for the past, present, and future. It also gradually increases one's capacities of dealing with others, other energies, and external stresses (especially for those people who are highly sensitive or empathic).

Iolite

Like hematite, iolite helps one find balance between his or her masculine and feminine features, aspects, traits, etc. In this way, iolite helps one find self-acceptance on a whole new level. Additionally, this crystal increases one's abilities of intuition and imagination while dissolving any emotional baggage that keeps the individual from feeling like he or she can handle the responsibility of any sort. Iolite can also promote psychic visions and crown, third eye, and throat chakra cleansing and alignment.

J

Jade

Jade works to promote many things. First of all, it aligns with the heart chakra to trigger feelings of love, wisdom, courage, and even mercy. Second, it works for overall good health and will help you live a good life. Third, it boosts strength, fertility, immunity, and more. Fourth and finally, jade can encourage the integration of healthy coping mechanisms in replacement of those that have failed or become unhealthy.

Jasper

Jasper generally works well for protection, earth connectivity, grounding, and overall health.

Basanite is technically a black jasper that can take you far away into altered states of consciousness along the lines of dreamwork and prophecy.

Blue Jasper also connects the individual to spiritual realms. It provides lasting energy during trying times, too, and it fights degenerative disease.

Brown Jasper heals examples of environmental stress, both on the individual and on the environment. It connects the individual to past lives in order to help heal as a whole being alongside the Earth. Finally, brown jasper has the potential to regenerate organ and immune health.

Green Jasper connects with the energy of the goddess while bringing your attention back to those things that have brought you joy in the past. It works well to heal skin disorders, to reduce inflammation generally, and to detoxify specifically and generally.

Mookaite, or Australian Jasper, is a great stone for couples, for it helps one see all sides of a situation before acting. Furthermore, it stabilizes and grounds the individual while purifying the blood, fighting infection, and healing a variety of wounds.

Orbicular Jasper demonstrates a circular pattern in its coloring, and it works to help those who work in the service of others maintain patience, respect, and individuality. Furthermore, it heals respiration, circulation, and systems of detoxification.

Picture Jasper conveys messages from the Earth to its children, all of animal-kind (including humanity). It helps us learn from past and present mistakes to heal the future, and it can kickstart a weakened immune system.

Purple Jasper works well with the crown chakra by reducing hypocrisy and unintentional (or intentional!) self-contradiction.

Red Jasper is the so-called "worry stone" that anxious, stressed-out, or worrisome people should carry with them always. It grounds, provides energy, increases insight, and stabilizes the body. Furthermore, it works to the benefit of one's liver, blood, and bile ducts.

Yellow Jasper works as a protector during travel of many sorts, and it can help one travel to spiritual realms, too. It aligns with the solar plexus chakra, so its effects heal digestion, the stomach, and the toxins that float around inside.

Jet

This stark black stone helps heal and reverse disease or illness that is related to sorrow or anxiety. Furthermore, the jet is a protector and energetic purifier that can keep unproductive, pessimistic, or generally negative energies (and entities) at bay.

K

Kunzite

This crystal allows the heart chakra to accept healing that it thinks it doesn't deserve, and the healing it enacts tends to reverberate out onto one's community without too much effort on the individual's part. It calms the over-excitable nervous system, too.

Kyanite

This "bladed" crystal has the potential to align all the chakras. It boosts energy by removing blockages and strengthening intuition. Through its use, one's speech and thoughts will become more and more aligned with one's deeper sense of truth.

Black Kyanite, the stone of revitalization, clears blockages, stimulates energetic awakening, and helps one ground during the process.

Blue Kyanite helps its holder or wearer receive psychic messages and unlock psychic gifts.

L

Labradorite

As one of the most impressively beautiful crystals in existence (in my opinion), labradorite is also packed with healing potential. It connects one with his or her soul mission, helps the individual see the light in dark times, encourages patience and acceptance of flaws, and inspires with its gorgeous flashes of color. It can even help release feelings of exhaustion caused by over-working and distraction.

Lapis Lazuli

This stunning stone links with the throat and third eye chakras, so it allows one to overcome psychic roadblocks as well as ones dealing with communication or self-expression. It essentially encourages the individual to speak up for what he or she believes in. Furthermore, this stone is incredibly effective in healing the nervous system, the throat, and in reversing any issues relating to metabolism.

Larimar

Larimar is an incredibly useful stone that helps those seeking inspiration or understanding. It also links with the throat, third eye, and crown chakras, encouraging awakening and enlightenment on several levels. It's a great stone for diagnosing places in your body that hold disease (even if you're not consciously aware of it yet).

Lepidolite

This purple crystal helps those in need of immediate transition. Whether you're moving, changing jobs, switching gears in life, or otherwise, lepidolite will be your best aid in those highly changeable (and often frustrating) moments. Furthermore, lepidolite reduces stress and opens one up to senses of universal awareness far greater than he or she is alone. It also can locate places that hold disease in the body, just like larimar.

Lodestone

Naturally, magnetic lodestone provides a visual aid for what it does. Just like it can draw iron shavings its way, it pulls in abundance from all corners of the world just for its holder and that person's community. Associated with luck, endurance, growth, and relief from pain, confusion, or burden, lodestone has a lot to provide. It can even help one establish balance and help heal the blood or broken bones.

M

Magnesite

Magnesite is a great meditation aid. It also boosts unconditional love of others, and it provides a general sense of calm for its wearer or holder. It brings about an overall feeling of harmony for anyone around it. Physically, magnesite is also high in magnesium, which allows it to heal muscle pains and aches, encourage muscle growth, and reduce the frequency of cramps. This stone also brings down fever effectively, eliminating one's sickness, and its related irritabilities.

Magnetite

Like lodestone, magnetite is naturally magnetic, but it works less through drawing in abundance than lodestone does. Instead, magnetite pulls together and eliminates toxicity, physically, energetically, and aurally. It can provide the opposite energy level that you're currently experiencing through its magnetic capacities, too. If you're an asthmatic or someone who has frequent nosebleeds, magnetite will also be incredibly helpful to ease your physical symptoms.

Malachite

This powerful energetic amplifier works well against arthritis and other joint pains/issues. For friendships, it enhances feelings of love and trust. For healing, it eliminates stress and helps the heart. For well-being, it clears the heart chakra and paves the way for productive transformation.

Moldavite

Moldavite is a fragment of meteorite, so its abilities are fairly unique. This dark green stone aids spiritual development, increases receptivity to visions and sparks important life changes. It also relates to the circulation system through its connection to the heart chakra (as well as to the optical system through the third eye chakra and the nervous system through the crown chakra).

Moonstone

Moonstone is highly connected with feminine universal energy, women, and the literal moon of Earth. It can help one become more accepting of their cycles and fluctuations, however, even if they're not female or overly feminine. Essentially, this stone boosts your psychic powers and protects your energy.

Black Moonstone is a little more complex than standard moonstone, for it relates to the energy of the Black Madonna, Lilith, Kali, Hekate, and more. Instead of focusing on the bright, illuminating powers of the moon, this stone looks at the power of remaining hidden and what shadow really is (spoiler alert: it's not evil, it's just an energetic compliment to light).

Morganite

This stone helps one process trauma by cleansing the heart chakra of its lingering wounds, and it also helps encourage emotional growth toward wisdom. It reminds its holder or wearer that we are all vessels of and channels for divine love. For those with anxiety or stress disorders, morganite will be a godsend. For those goals of astral travel and healing, morganite will be your closest ally.

Muscovite

Muscovite is a form of naturally-occurring mica. It helps one connect to his or her higher self to receive guidance or healing, and it encourages transformation on all levels. For those with kidney, sleep, or allergy problems, muscovite might do just the trick! For those with anxiety and stress issues, too, this crystal is a keeper.

N

Natrolite

This crystal is a highly energetic form of zeolite, and it works well to heal vision or brain disorders because it also connects with the third eye and crown chakras. If you seek guidance in your healing from ascended masters, your higher self, your ancestors, or higher dimensional beings, natrolite can help you make and maintain contact to suit that goal.

Nebula Stone

Nebula stone enacts its best healing potential on the cellular level. If you want to kickstart autophagy or fight a degenerative disorder, this stone will be a go-to for you. Similarly, if you're healing from any major injury, a nebula stone by your side *could* work miracles.

Nuummite

This black stone works well to maintain a healthy balance of blood sugar, as it naturally purifies the blood of its holder or wearer. If you have troubles with pain or sleep, nuummite is good to have handy, for it neutralizes pain and helps to induce periods of insightful and deep rest. It can also help one feel empowered to face his or her fears and grow beyond them.

O

Obsidian

Generally, obsidian protects its holder and absorbs negative energy, whether emotionally, electromagnetically, or otherwise.

Obsidian is a good stone for people who struggle with depression, too, because it allows one to see the bright side of things and relax enough to enjoy what's happening. Furthermore, all obsidians are skilled at revitalization and resolution. Finally, if you're still trying to figure out what exactly to heal within you, obsidian can help pinpoint the source of your disease.

Apache Tear can help resolve ancestral and past live traumas or wounds. It is also attuned to heal in times of incredible distress in the present. In general, it's a good detoxifying stone, too.

Rainbow Obsidian has somewhat of a gentler energy than harsher, completely black obsidian. For those in need of help with grounding or with healing one's connection to the earth, this type of obsidian will be perfect.

Snowflake Obsidian has a great tie to ancestral healing, and it resonates with the sacral chakra. Its effect is soothing and centering. For help with circulation and skeletal strength, this stone is a go-to.

Onyx

Onyx is a very supportive stone. Whatever you're going through, onyx can make the situation seem easier or more approachable or manageable. It builds confidence and focuses one's attention. Like other black stones, it can help resolve feelings of grief or sadness, too. For physical healing, onyx has an affinity for the bones, teeth, and feet.

Opal

This brilliant mostly white stone has the ability to awaken your true potential, whether magically, intellectually, athletically, or otherwise. It helps its holder or wearer stay calm but focused on his or her current mission. It connects with the dream world and healthy sleep, and it can reduce or eliminate infections, fevers, and all-consuming anger.

Black-Brown-Gray Opal, in particular, heals one's reproductive system and can help the individual separate sexual compulsions from their emotional origins, allowing him or her to heal the emotional problem first before lashing out sexually.

Blue Opal builds and boosts confidence through demeanor and speech. It has a calming energy, too, that helps the holder or wearer stay connected to his or her higher self despite struggles or stress.

Cherry Opal can help dissolve headaches, muscle pains, and menopausal struggles. It's great for blood and tissue healing as well.

Chrysopal is blue-green in color, and it has an effect on its holder or wearer that he or she is looking through rose-colored glasses at the world. It's a liver detoxifier, too, and it works wonders for chest congestion.

Fire Opal gives warning signs against danger as it protects its holder or wearer. It rejuvenates one's passion and fire for life, and it helps those who work against injustice. For the physical body, fire opal has an affinity for the kidneys, adrenals, reproductive organs, and intestines.

Green Opal helps one recover from toxic or painful relationships by adjusting the mind to handle what happened, learn from it, and grow. It boosts the immune system, too, and works like a champ against any flu or cold symptoms.

Hyalite is a water opal that connects with spiritual worlds, both alongside and far removed from our own. Use during meditation or astral traveling for grounding and connectivity with the divine.

P

Peridot

Peridot helps lonely people make friends, and then it can also help people who have troubles with jealousy or anger be more rational to keep the friends they have. It links to the heart chakra but heals wounds on mind, body, and soul levels.

Petalite

This crystal is said to connect its holder to the angels or highest dimensional realms and consciousnesses. For those who aren't quite there yet, it can awaken shamanic capacities, help one find their path, allow one to trigger their soul mission, and activate huge growth patterns. Physically, petalite can help those suffering from AIDS and cancer through its cellular, intestinal, respiratory, and muscular benefits.

Prehnite

This green stone connects with the heart chakra and allows its holder or wearer to experience and reflect outwards unconditional love. It's protective and motivating. In terms of helping others find peace, it can work particularly well for hoarders, hyperactive individuals and kids, bipolar individuals, and those out of touch with nature.

Pyrite

Iron pyrite, or fool's gold, is a powerful stone for people with hormonal imbalances. In addition, people who are teased for being feminine or masculine when they "shouldn't" be will find comfort through this stone, and it is a great companion for anyone transitioning physically in terms of sex or socially in terms of gender identity. It also protects its wearer or holder from environmental and electromagnetic pollutants. Finally, it aids in boosting willpower, immunity, and cardiovascular health.

Pyrolusite

This shiny, fanlike mineral helps transform disease into future strength, manipulation into communication, and expectations into acceptance. Generally, it's a motivator of transformation on all levels, but only when the transformation suits one's overall health, growth, soul mission, and overall potential. For the physical body, pyrolusite aids with metabolism regulation, bronchitis & eyesight treatments, and circulation strengthening.

Q

Quartz

While there are tens if not hundreds of different types of quartz, they all work incredibly well with the healing of many natures. Regardless of what part of the body you're working on or what aspect of personality, quartz can help you discern what needs fixing and what to do about it. Then, quartz can store and amplify energies in order to go about the healing you desire. It's great for any chakra and any ailment or situation.

R

Rhodochrosite

This pink and white stone has an affinity for love and the heart chakra. It helps one connect to and love the earth as well, especially if the individual has already conquered the self-love bit. For those experiencing personality deficit or mid-life crisis, rhodochrosite can help you remember and reconnect to who you truly are. Physically, rhodochrosite heals the lungs and eases breathing-related problems.

Rhodonite

Rhodonite helps even the lowliest hermit connect to the sense of brotherly love that inspires all of humanity. It's great for anti-social individuals in that sense. In addition, it helps people healing PTSD through its affinity for those in the fight, flight, or freeze modes. Whether you're feeling shock, paralysis, panic, or fear, rhodonite can help you move past that and remember how to be yourself again or how to become the *new you*. Physically, it heals insect bites, reduces the presence of scars, fights inflammation on a number of levels (including ulcers!), and eases autoimmune diseases.

Rhyolite

This more-rare stone inspires deep and moving creativity without forcing its flow. It connects to deep meditation states and heals past life wounds with ease. Rhyolite has an emotional balancing effect that encourages strength and self-esteem even against the most challenging emotional ordeals. Physically, rhyolite can be used to mitigate infections and assimilate vitamin B. It's good for body-builders or those working on strength training, too, due to its ability to increase both strength and muscle tone.

Rose Quartz

Rose quartz is a crystal intimately tied up in ideas of love. It attracts love, but only the love we think we deserve, for it teaches the holder or wearer that one cannot "deserve" a love that one cannot afford oneself. It works for circulatory system healing and relieves symptoms of emotional or physical traumas. Use this crystal for any healing work dealing with self-esteem, personality, love, forgiveness, or the literal and physical heart.

Ruby

Ruby, whether in gemstone form or simply polished or uncut, is a powerful motivator, connector to bliss, and locator of passions. It's an incredibly dynamic stone that gives energy to whatever area of your life needs it. Whether you need help with becoming a better leader, healing the blood, fighting infection, stimulating overall health, expressing emotionally, or what have you, ruby will help you concentrate and achieve your goals.

S

Sapphire

This stone comes in a variety of colors and forms, but it always helps enact genuine and creative self-expression. Sapphire also builds a sense of deep inner peace and attracts romantic love when desired. It works specifically well to heal the eyes, the glands, and the veins. It's commonly called the wisdom stone, too, with its intrinsic links to the third eye and throat chakras.

Sardonyx

Sardonyx is good for regulating, strength-building, endurance-boosting, and protecting. It encourages happiness and good luck as well as self-control and stamina. In terms of the physical body, sardonyx helps one absorb all the nutrients of one's food, and it encourages the waste elimination process to work well. Furthermore, works incredibly well for skeletal and respiratory healing.

Selenite

Selenite crystals are powerful cleansers and chargers. When you're looking for a way to cleanse your crystals, look to selenite first! Get a selenite slab or block to make things easy on yourself. This crystal absorbs and transmutes all negative energy into that which your higher self can work with. It connects with past life healing, too. Physically, selenite strengthens the spine, removes toxic metals from the blood, encourages healthy breastfeeding, and protects against epileptic seizures.

Serpentine

Serpentine clears all the chakras and helps the crown chakra open to receive information and teachings from the higher self. It helps one feel more in control of his or her life, and it eliminates parasites of all natures. Figuratively, serpentine removes psychic vampires and energetic parasites from your path. Literally, serpentine cleanse your gut and body of parasites that harm your abilities to absorb nutrients and build strong bones. This stone also works well for diabetics.

Smoky Quartz

This crystal is a version of clear brown quartz that has the special capacity to remove negative energies from your path. Whether they arrive in the form of electromagnetic radiation or pollutants, negative emotions from others, or bad habits of your own, these negative energies will have no choice but to be eradicated in the presence of smoky quartz. If you struggle with removing these shadows from your life even with smoky quartz, try boosting your willpower and strengthening the solar plexus chakra, too. Use a piece of gold or yellow quartz along with your smoky quartz and see what happens.

Sodalite

Sodalite is a great stone for group work, as it encourages feelings of friendship, trust, companionship, and solidarity for the task at hand. It also helps you stay true to yourself despite any adversaries, and for those who struggle with defensiveness or defensive personality traits, sodalite can help melt your harsh exterior and pave the way for growth.

Stichtite

This purple stone has a powerful connection to the third eye and the heart chakras. If you're feeling emotional distress of any nature, stichtite will be there to comfort you. If you're having issues with digestion, stichtite may help you realize how your problems have an emotional root (as well as what steps to take to fix the situation). If you feel alone and lost without anyone to help you, stichtite's rescuing nature will be activated too, calling to you people who will be able to help. It's a powerful healing stone for many emotional imbalances.

Sugilite

Sugilite is a stone oriented to boost love. It helps you love yourself and understand why you chose this life for this current incarnation. It also helps you love others and practice forgiveness in any format. It helps one understand the connection between mind and body, too, and that understanding is pivotal in the healing of overall disease. For help with headaches, restless limbs, and general discomfort, sugilite is a great choice. Hold next to the body part that hurts to receive the greatest relief.

Sunstone

Sunstone helps fight depression by turning sorrow into lasting happiness and bliss for life. It helps you remember how to nurture yourself in times of need, and it can also attract nurturing help if you're unable to get there yourself. If you're feeling drained or exhausted, sunstone can pick you up and give you the energy you need. If you're feeling low and pessimistic, sunstone can get you back to seeing the glass as half full. For the physical body, sunstone removes ulcers, relieves sore throats, kickstarts the immune system, and reminds you of your abilities to heal yourself from the start.

T

Tanzanite

This crystal works amazingly well for skin and vision issues. Figuratively, too, it helps you achieve the foresight you need to attain your goals, and it allows you the ability to receive psychic visions through meditation. It connects to the crown, third eye, and throat chakras, too, bringing voice to the body itself.

Tektite

This extraterrestrial stone helps one communicate with other worlds. It balances energy flow in the body and clears the chakras, sometimes fully opening them on contact (as with the third eye chakra). Physically, tektite is a good companion for anyone seeking a fertility boost, and it can reduce the intensity of any fever. After surgery, tektite is beneficial to have around to stimulate easy, quick healing.

Tiger's Eye

Tiger's eye has a lucky, abundant vibe that wants to attract wealth and success into your life. It connects with the solar plexus chakra to bring feelings of confidence, willpower, positivity, and true joy. If you're dealing with feelings of unworthiness, tiger's eye is a must-have. Physically, tiger's eye links with the eyes and helps repair broken bones.

Blue Tiger's Eye calms down one's energy. If you're overactive in terms of sex, metabolism, anger, or fears, this stone will help you reground and re-center yourself in relation to those intense stresses and their true emotional causes.

Hawk's Eye is a particular pattern within the tiger's eye banding that looks like the eye of a hawk, and it helps with literal vision healing as well as figurative third-eye healing through divination capabilities, insight and intuition, and psychic abilities like clairvoyance and clairaudience.

Red Tiger's Eye boosts one's energy. If you're feeling lazy, unproductive, stagnant, lost, or lethargic, this stone can help you find your drive and motivation once more.

Topaz

Topaz of any color encourages openness, trust, and friendship through increased understanding and patience. It encourages one to feel generous and fortunate in all situations. That self-realization is key to one's ability to attract future abundance with this stone as well. Physically, this crystal links with regenerative tissue capacities.

Imperial Topaz reminds one of the highest possible good and helps one align his or her work with this potential. Furthermore, it strengthens manifestation abilities and enforces transformative success.

Tourmaline

Tourmaline fights stagnation of any kind. It encourages action and fights fatigue. If fatigue is triggered by anemia, tourmaline goes straight to the source and works to heal the imbalance. It also connects with overall energies of attracting success and love into its holder's (or wearer's) life.

Black Tourmaline works for grounding and balancing the individual. It also redirects negativity send your way, and it can remind you of the benefits of reasonable control and discipline.

Pink Tourmaline is also known as rubellite, and it heals the heart both physically and figuratively. Its soothing and insightful energy is particularly helpful for break-ups or loss.

Watermelon Tourmaline works well for people who are easily overwhelmed or highly sensitive. It can help you maintain perspective in any situation, no matter how difficult. It also activates the heart chakra and works to purify the blood.

Turquoise

Turquoise is a good meditation aid for any situation, as it relaxes and purifies the mind. It also helps one channel kindness constantly by detoxifying the aura when interacting with other people. Furthermore, it detoxifies the body and works to fight inflammation in a variety of ways. It also builds tissue, helps nutrient absorption, and defeats infection with ease.

U

Ulexite

Ulexite is a crystal also known as TV stone, and it's called that for its incredible clarity and ability to magnify what's seen through it. It helps to cleanse problem routines and activate healthier ones, and it allows you to see your hopes manifested in the physical world. Physically, it heals the eyes and can fight aging in the skin.

Unakite

This green and pink stone have great reproductive healing potential as well as the potential for psychic awakening. When you combine those two purposes of the stone, it becomes clear how the stone could encourage the *rebirthing* of yourself into higher levels of your potential! Physically, unakite boosts recovery in any situation and maintains hair and tissue growth. Furthermore, it does several things to make sure you have the most healthy pregnancy possible, such as maintain proper body weight, cleanse the reproductive system, and align mama's system with baby's as best as possible.

V

Vanadinite

This crystal works well to heal bladder and prostate problems in men that cause excessive urination. For people of all genders, vanadinite assists comfort on earth and abilities to travel to other dimensions. Furthermore, it gives a boost in meditation through its abilities to cut off excess mental chatter when you attempt to concentrate on the moment and your breath.

Variscite

Variscite reminds of the importance of hope. For people with terminal or chronic conditions – or people who are home-bound / house-bound or differently-abled – this crystal keeps the spirits up and the goals focused. It relaxes the troubled mind and makes sure one's dreams for healing are realistic but not fatalistic. Physically, it encourages elasticity of skin and plasticity of the brain. It even neutralizes problematic acidic conditions in the body that can lead to cancer.

Vesuvianite

This crystal is also sometimes called idocrase, and it generally aids with self-awareness and self-restraint, especially for those triggered by thoughts (or memories) of literal imprisonment or restraint. Furthermore, this stone encourages desires for freedom and connects the individual with outlets for his or her creativity. For those struggling with fear, it will release you. For those hungry to learn, it will direct you.

W

Wavellite

This mineral is known to balance one's energy flow, whether it's the flow of blood, breath, emotions, or life energy (also called *prana* or *chi*). It brings awareness to the individual of this energy flow, too, reminding them of the law of One and the importance of peace and love in the universe. For skin conditions and abusive living situations, wavellite helps the individual finally find some relief.

Wulfenite

This crystal helps one accept and transmute negativity in certain situations to positivity if the individual starts to get depressed about things. Furthermore, if you've had trouble sugarcoating things and looking too much on the bright side unrealistically, wulfenite can remind of the importance of hardship and strife. It's a grounding stone that connects knowledge and pain directly to wisdom and growth. Physically, it builds or conserves your energy, when needed.

Z

Zebra Stone

Zebra stone stimulates energy and ends stagnant cycles. It also affirms strength, endurance, and stamina. In that sense, this stone is a great companion for athletes and competitive runners. Furthermore, it is wonderful for anyone who struggles with procrastination for any type of work. Physically, zebra stone has an affinity for skeletal healing with particular focuses on the spine and on the bones of older individuals. For people dealing with heart murmurs, heart spasms, or muscle tremors, zebra stone is equally helpful.

Zeolite

This type of crystal is actually a generic name for any group of crystals growing in a cluster on a matrix of standard rock or standard quartz. The combination of the crystal points in the cluster magnifies the energy of the piece and focuses it on tasks like detoxifying, aligning energies, igniting awareness, building strength, encouraging fertility, or anything else you decide as your goal. Physically, zeolite clusters work well to treat goiters and eliminate addictions (and their underlying emotional causes).

Zincite

Zincite is able to stimulate, align, and cleanse all the chakras while providing an energy boost to the rest of your system, too. It's especially powerful when it comes to rebuilding one's passion and fire for life, and it links well with courageous goals. In terms of the physical body, zincite heals both the hair and the skin, and for men, its effects on the prostate are unmatched, while for women, its assistance during menopause is a blessing.

Zircon

Sometimes we judge ourselves far harsher than anyone else would dare. Even if we don't realize we're falling into that pattern of action, zircon can snap anyone out of it. It awakens self-awareness and shuts down bad habits and routines. As it cuts out the "should" and "have to" energy of your self-judgment, zircon enables you to meet and validate your *true* and most authentic self. In that sense, it encourages transformative growth.

Zoisite

Zoisite protects against electromagnetic radiations that are problematic for the human body, so keep a piece on your laptop or next to your phone when it's charging! It also encourages feelings of appreciation, vitality, and divine love (even in the face of despair and rejection). It can also help you become aware of your defense mechanisms and restructure them to be healthier and more productive. Physically, zoisite is a detoxifier that stimulates health of the reproductive, cellular, circulatory, endocrine, and immune systems.

What Forms of Crystals Do What?

Particularly when it comes to grid work with crystals, simply knowing which one is which and sensing where to put it may not be enough. The added layer to complete your work will be learning what *forms* of crystals do what. It could be that a pointed crystal completes your grid in a way that a polished version of the same specimen cannot.

It could also be that your grids are equally powerful regardless of what form of the crystal you use. It partially depends on your mindset and partially depends on your abilities, financially, spiritually, and otherwise. Regardless of your current means, however, the knowledge is always helpful, I say! When you *are* able to, the following details will become applicable, but for now, take in what you can and intuit the rest as you're able.

Polished

All polished or "tumbled" stones are considered basically **egg-shaped crystals**, and they carry with them an intrinsically balancing, comforting energy, especially when they're larger polished stones.

These egg-shaped crystals can be large enough to fit in your palm, and then they're called **palm stones**, and they're usually flat on one side and rounded otherwise. These varieties are more grounding than simply balancing, and they'll also work well as reflexology or massage tools.

Sometimes, you'll find these tumbled stones in the true **sphere, or ball format**. The beauty of these balls is that it looks smooth and perfect on the outside, but if the crystal is even semi-translucent, you can see the imperfections, flaws, and separate planes inside that space which makes the ball a more complex healing medium. It can amplify energies in ways a flattened side cannot, and it's said that these ball shapes can even be used as so-called "windows" into time, space, or other worlds.

Generally, polished stones hold a more harnessed and compact energy and vibration than, say, a raw mineral or a pointed crystal would. These "tumbled" stones have likely spent hours in a rock tumbler to become that way, which both shocks the stone and *affirms* its vibration, again and again, honing and perfecting its own energetic intention. Therefore, if you only have tumbled stones to work with, fear not! You've got a powerful set of minerals and crystals at your disposal, to be sure, and their form affirms that completely.

Raw & Geodes

Tumbled and polished stones and gems, of course, have to start somewhere! There is a gorgeous raw format of each mineral and crystal, whether it's a small and perfect ruby gemstone in a matrix of clear quartz or a giant slab of selenite. When it comes to the details of those raw versions, there are a few things to keep in mind.

First, consider the **cluster of crystals**. The cluster naturally has several pointed ends coming from the same surface or base. Those points may all go out in various directions or they all may point the same way, but the general effect in healing and gridding is the same. Because there are so many of the same type growing out of the same base, clusters, therefore, expel their energy and healing vibration out exponentially more efficiently than a single point would. The energy of a cluster can fill a room or even a home without much effort on its holder's part.

Second, consider the **geode**! Geodes are essentially a world of crystals contained within what looks like a rock. When you crack the rock open, you see that it's been completely lined on the inside with the crystal you desire. In this format, therefore, the crystals' vibrations exude a gentler and less direct force on their surroundings. Think about it, the crystals are homed in this cave-like vessel, and their points will all face one another; that inward-faced energy sends out slow and steady vibrational assistance to the geode's surroundings, depending on how big the geode cluster is (in both size and number). Geodes have a guardian-like presence in healing, too, and work particularly well to break bad habits and reprogram addictions.

Third, consider the **naturally-occurring square** (also called "cube") or **triangle** (also called "pyramid") crystalline structures. Some minerals that naturally grow into square shapes are fluorite and iron pyrite, while the most common triangular ones are often apophyllite. Essentially, squares are excellent for grounding and intentional work, for they keep their energy locked inside their forms. They offer a more concentrated, focused healing effort than, say, a cluster or a geode. They're good to keep in your pocket throughout the day or to use in the center of a grid.

On the other hand, triangles are often human-made by cutting off a single-pointed crystal right at the base of the point, but even when they're human-made, the effect is generally the same. These pyramid formations magnify the energy of your intention and focus it through the top point, honing your intention and fully concentrating your healing efforts. Triangle formations are powerful aids in chakra healing as well because they can draw out negativity or blockages from your chakras, transmuting all that into positivity then releasing it all out and through their pyramids' tips. (Clearly, as mentioned before, the naturally-occurring triangle formation is more ideal than the human-altered one, but you should take what you can get!)

And fourth, consider the generally **amorphous raw mineral**. Without any inherent structure aside from being unpolished, these minerals and crystals have a fiercer, relatively less structured effect in their healing compared to the cube, pyramid, or even the geode. It happens that their vibrations are stalwartly expressed in the instant with direct effect toward your intention. Raw and formless minerals like this are great centerpieces for grids, as the surrounding assembly of crystals can help to focus and sustain the amorphous vibration for more intensive healing work.

Finally, your raw crystals can be pointed on one or both ends, causing them to have facets, and that's a whole other ballgame, which we'll venture into momentarily. For now, know that the four main raw forms of crystals and minerals affect their energies and expressions in terms of healing. However, if all you have happens to be an amorphous tiger's eye, don't go out and replace it with a polished one just because!

There's no reason to rush or overspend when working with crystal healing. Just remember to trust in the Goddess, your guides, the universe, God, truth, or whatever you call that energy that's bigger than us. Trust in that energy, and trust that all the tools you believe you need for healing will come to you in time.

Faceted

Faceted crystals are described in these terms to express the multi-sided nature of that raw crystal. Within the category of faceted crystals, there are several different forms to work with, four of which we'll walk through today. First, there's the generally **single-pointed crystal**. Maybe it grew out of a matrix of another stone or maybe it broke off of a cluster of its buddies. Regardless, this crystal has one side that's dull and one side that's naturally pointed.

This first type of crystal would have the ability to harness energy toward the direction of the mineral's tip. Essentially, that single point works incredibly well for healing, because it allows the healer to extract pure energy from him or herself and send it into the patient purified with the vibration of the crystal – or because it allows the individual to draw out what's impure from him or herself and direct it away by pointing the tip elsewhere and expelling it from the crystal afterward.

Second, the crystal could be naturally double-ended in points, and then it would be called "**double-terminated**." Crystals like Herkimer diamond are naturally double-terminated, so they (and others like them) are able to release or absorb energy equally well out of each side. These crystals and minerals would be able to move energy *through* them in one direction like pointed crystals, but their special form would enable them to move energy in *two* directions at once, making a (potentially) more balanced approach to energetic healing.

Third, the crystal could be **tabular**, which is when it's almost a flat sheet with single- or double-pointed ends. Instead of having anywhere from three to ten facets on the sides, therefore, it would really just have two well-defined, broadsides. These types of crystals and minerals likely have notches and raw exposures connecting those two well-defined sides, and there's extra potential in healing if you have these crystals to rub those side notches. This gesture will activate and focus the crystal's energy and any healing guidance it might contain for you.

Fourth and finally, the crystal could be a **long point** that just formed itself that way. This version is similar to a double-terminated crystal, but it's usually much longer and thinner. These thin wand-like growths of crystals have similar energy to what they resemble. If you're hoping to focus the crystal's energy, hold the formation like a wand and direct its vibration. These types of formations are applicable for ritual work and deep cleansing work of any healing inclination.

Harvested Yourself

Raw minerals and crystals can be found anywhere on Earth. Sometimes, they can even be found in your own backyard! You'd be surprised what minerals and crystals comprise the bedrock of your town and then end up scattered in its surrounding soils.

That being said, you can choose to sift through your soil and see what's there (often just a bit of mica and plenty of quartz, but it always depends!), or you can go crystal hunting! Based on where you are in the world, your range of options may be incredibly limited or bountiful. You may have to drive hours to days, or you may have to drive 5 minutes away.

Look into it! Do the research and see where your favorite minerals and crystals are found in real time. If you can go there, go there! Guaranteed, there are mines you can go to or places you can hike to that grant you the opportunity to extract minerals for yourself, and that experience compares to none other.

True, you might not have all the tools you need but you can surely pick up a few!

True, you might not be that skilled with the area when you arrive at the location, but you can always make friends with someone from the community and figure out the lay of the land!

True, you might not get those "perfect" specimens that get sold online for small fortunes. However, the experience of going out yourself and connecting to the earth and its blessings (these beautiful nature bits), your relationship with the mineral will be completely different, and its vibration will be all the more attuned to you, your goals, and your healing intentions.

Imported

The complete reverse of the minerals you harvest yourself is those that come imported from the opposite side of the planet. Surely, these stones are powerful and vibrationally energetic, just like you need them to be. There's nothing inherently *wrong* with these imported specimens, but there is one main thing to be conscious of when you *do* pick up crystals of this nature.

Consider *where* the stone came from. If you have the ability to know what country or continent it came from, do a little research. What is the quality of life like? How do most people make their living? Are peoples' lives in this area tied to a mineral economy in that location? Could it be that your purchase subtly influences a problematic regime?

The more conscious you are about your purchases, the more enlightened your healing will become. If it happens to be that you're using an imported crystal from a strife-torn area, cleanse it a little extra before you use it on yourself, and when you *do* use it, send a little love to the miner and country of origin!

If you have more than one of this type of stone, devote a little extra love to them. You could try cleansing them all together (see chapter 2 for some cleansing tips and instructions!) and sending some healing vibrations out into the world for the people who mined them from the earth. Respect toward this origin space, environmentally and culturally, in your healing work will help both *it* and *you* evolve.

CHAPTER 4
Explaining Chakra Healing

A lot of the crystal listings of the previous chapter kept mentioning a particular (and potentially unfamiliar) word again and again. I wonder if you noticed it? "Chakra." The listings read that this crystal opens that chakra. This mineral clears all the chakras, and more as the list goes on.

While some of you will already know what this word means, others may not. Even if you do know, there's always more to learn! And what's more, it can't help to be reminded of the incredible healing capacity you hold when you combine crystal healing with chakra healing.

What Are the Chakras? What Is the Kundalini?

"Chakra" is another word for the wheel in Sanskrit, a language that originated from ancient India almost 4,000 years ago. While chakra literally translates to the wheel, however, it more so means an energetic wheel that churns and spins, pushing life force energy through anything with life. As humans, we have 7 chakras housed in our physical bodies, and these energy wheels connect to 7 main glands in the lymphatic system across our bodies.

While the chakras connect to glands, they also correlate with specific things, experiences, and emotions as well as particular colors. The first chakra called the Root Chakra or "Muladhara" is located in the genitals, and it relates to the color red, affecting one's senses of safety, security, well-being, survival, and sexuality. The second chakra called the Sacral Chakra or "Svadhishthana" is located below the belly button, and it relates to the color orange, affecting one's capacities of pleasure, belongingness, community, creativity, and emotionality. The third chakra called the Solar Plexus Chakra or "Manipura" is located on the diaphragm, and it relates to the color yellow, affecting one's will-power, the force of desire, assertiveness, need for control, and confidence.

The fourth chakra called the Heart Chakra or "Anahata" is located at the heart, and it relates to the color green, affecting one's abilities to feel love, compassion, relatability, understanding, warmth, and joy. The fifth chakra called the Throat Chakra or "Vishuddha" is located in the throat and neck, and it relates to the color blue, affecting one's capacities of speech, self-expression, group communication, listening, and purpose-finding. The sixth chakra called the Third Eye Chakra or "Anja" is located between one's eyebrows, and it relates to the color indigo, affecting one's powers of foresight, intuition, self-awareness, psychism, and higher consciousness. Finally, the seventh chakra called the Crown Chakra or "Sahasrara" is located at the top point of the skull, and it relates to the color violet, affecting one's connection to the divine, spirituality, the Universe, the Earth, and more.

In chapter 5, we'll go on to discuss how particular colors have vibrations oriented to heal in different ways, but for now, it will suffice to say that these chakras and their respective colors made links with certain energetic expressions of the individual. If one's chakras are imbalanced in any way by being blocked, spinning backward, spinning too slow, or spinning too fast, chakra *healing* would come into the mix.

Chakra healing focuses on the flow of these energy wheels in the body, the health of their respective glands, and their effect on the overall person. Chakra healing aims to open, cleanse, and align all the chakras so that energy flows as freely and limitlessly as possible, allowing for the kundalini to rise.

"Kundalini" is another Indian Sanskrit term, and this one means small, coiled one. What it refers to is what the language calls a serpent lying coiled and dormant at the base of one's spine until awakened and invited to dance through the free-flowing chakra wheels, providing healing to the individual's entire body and spirit.

What Is a Kundalini Awakening?

When the kundalini becomes awakened, that small, coiled one becomes larger and vibrant with life. During this period, the chakras must have already been cleared, opened, and aligned or balanced to a certain degree so that at least all are open-ish and flowing in the right direction. With this relative free-flow of inner subtle energies, the serpent at the base of one's spine gets excited and begins its track of movement.

It may sound like this all happens very quickly, but it's exactly the opposite. It can take months to years to be able to heal, cleanse, and open a stubborn or traumatized chakra, and even then, it could be that your other chakras become blocked because of such long-standing focus on just one. That being said, simply balancing one's chakras can take a good bit of time, but once they're becoming open and balanced, that serpent can't help but become engaged.

The kundalini symbolizes one's connection to the divine. It is that divine energy (like "prana," "chi," or even "reiki") of the universe that inspires the kundalini's movement when the chakras work with a balanced flow. That divine energy is termed Shakti in this tradition of study and healing, but the gist is quite clear; once one's body is open enough for the spirit to move freely, his or her connection to the divine will be boosted, bringing the individual to an enlightened, awakened energetic state.

As you progress through your own kundalini awakening, meditation will be your best and most supportive friend. Through conscious and mindful meditation, you'll become able to guide the snake's movement through your chakras, feeling its flow bringing enlightenment and insight to your various energy centers. You'll be able to slow down your attention and focus, drowning out the stresses of the day in order to focus on the healing going on inside of you, for the movement of the kundalini reverberates its own type of a cure out from the inside out with each turn of its tail.

Once your kundalini becomes awakened through conscious attention, mindfulness, visualization, or otherwise, some things you might experience are as follows, and during the first stages of one's kundalini awakening, things will not be easy, for the energetic healing of the kundalini will make things uncomfortable at first. You might get literally stinky. You might get moody. You might have an emotional outburst. You might feel uncomfortable in your own skin but stick through it! Some things need to be cleansed out in order for growth to be made!

Once you get through that harsh first set of steps, you'll experience more positive effects, such as clearer sense of life direction, connection to soul purpose, confidence in one's self and purpose, awareness of one's true potential, heightened senses, increased joy and openness, budding or bursting creativity, and manifestation capabilities.

However, alongside all this positive, hopeful news, one thing must be kept in mind: the kundalini cannot (and will not) be awakened with self-serving thoughts. The trick to this process is to act and meditate selflessly, allowing the ego to become muted and one's connection to pure universal energy to flourish. Focusing on the end-goal will not work, for it's all about the process and what's taught (and learned) along the way.

How Is Crystal Healing Connected with the Chakras?

Crystal healing and chakra healing have an intimate and intrinsic connection. Chakra healing spends its remedial attention on the flow of our internal energies. These energies are physical, sure, relating to specific parts of the body, self-expression, organs, glands, lymphatic systems, and more, but they're also so much more than just physical.

Sometimes, studying the patterns of the physical itself can also teach us a lot about how energy works and flows, and these studies are based in what's called the *meta*physical. Metaphysically, energy, blood, vibrations, fluids, and more all want to *flow*, and blockages in that flow happen. However, they don't always happen due to these directly-physical causes. Instead, sometimes looking closer at things, at the metaphysical details, can be all the help one needs.

In the process of chakra healing, blockages and flow are central. They're studied to figure out what needs to be fixed and what's working, as well as what needs just a little boost or adjustment to flow correctly. When you meet a blockage head-on, however, the cause of the blockage will likely still be unclear, and then those metaphysical clues are one's greatest help. When you think about the blockage there, what comes to mind? With a heart blockage, for instance, what associations surface? What causes can you intuit, and what symptoms would you expect from this malady, based on the patterns of those physical behaviors?

Once you can intuit these metaphysical connections, you'll be in a good place to add crystals to the mix. On one hand, your metaphysical associations will enable you to intuitively choose crystals, stones, and minerals that you think will work well for your healing. On the other hand, all chakras already have a color and theme associated with them, making them all the more inclined to mesh well with the metaphysical healing capacities of stones of that same color.

Whether your mixture of crystal and chakra healing focuses on this color association or the more specific healing abilities of individual stones, in particular, the energetic vibrations of each realm of healing work well when combined together. Stones can help bring awareness to issues or successes with that internal and emotional free-flow, and they can also help point out charkas that you may not realize are spinning the exact opposite direction as they should be.

Essentially, crystal healing can work like a metaphysical magnifying glass for those interested in chakra healing, and that relationship is beautiful while being mutually-beneficial, for you'll certainly learn more about each healing modality by combining them both together to meet these specific aims.

On Clearing, Aligning, and Balancing Your Chakras with Crystals

As you read before in chapter 3's index, certain crystals, minerals, gems, and stones have different metaphysical and energetic capabilities when it comes to chakra healing. Sometimes, a stone clears just one chakra, while other times one stone clears them all. Sometimes, a stone can align every chakra with one another, while other times it just works on balancing two or three in a harmony together.

Generally, what it means when it says a crystal can clear or open a chakra, this phrasing means that the crystal can pinpoint chakra blockages and work directly against that closing, destructive effort. The crystal's presence will help you process what's been holding up that chakra's flow and what it means for you personally and your day-to-day experiences. The crystal may even encourage you to see action plans for working against that blockage, but it could be that the stone just teaches you and lets you decide on *process* and *action* for yourself.

When it comes to those crystals that can align the chakras, the index refers mainly to situations where the chakras' energies might be flowing the wrong way or in noncompatible speeds. In these cases, aligners come in and help readjust the flow to be going the most productive direction, and these aligners also help to get the speed of that flow established at a rhythm that's helpful for all chakras but not too harsh on anyone. Aligners get the energy flowing the right way, but they're not always the most helpful with opening and blasting away blockages. Try pairing an aligner with an opener and see what happens! The effect may be even more powerful and impacting than what a balancer can do!

When the index says that a crystal will balance chakras, it means that it may provide some opening, clearing boosting power to your chakra healing as-is in order to get each energy wheel open and ready for business. Then, this crystal will get the energy moving in an even amount through each chakra so that the flow is established once more. Some people who approach balancers for the chakras will find that they have to do a lot of work on just one or two chakras to get this process to come to fruition – and even then, maybe only two or three found balance. Others will find that they have to work a little bit on each one and then the energy starts flowing through all seven chakras.

On another level, some people will find that their chakras blow wide open with the help of balancers, while others will feel that there are still partial blockages in each chakra that the balancer couldn't help with. In this case, it depends partially on the individual, his or her strength, and his or her degree of disease in any particular chakra, and it also depends partially on the crystal itself, for some are far more effective and naturally powerful than others, depending on the type of crystal and form.

CHAPTER 5
Other Methods Of Crystal Healing

Combining chakra healing with crystals is *literally* just the beginning.

In fact, crystal healing in and of itself is just scratching the surface of your incredible potential as an energetic being in this all-too-human existence. As you learn to trust and harness your intuition for crystal healing, you may find that you become drawn to other expressions of subtle energy as well. And what is subtle energy? Well, I'm glad you asked.

On Subtle Energy

Subtle energy exists all around us. It is released in terms of electromagnetic fields, so-called "energetic vibrations," which every carbon-based lifeforce on this planet possesses. By attuning yourself to crystal energy, as you learned how to do in chapter 2, you have started to pay closer attention to that subtle energy as it is expressed through mineral and crystal nature bits.

Subtle energy is what the ancients tapped into when they used crystals for healing and energy storage in their time. They must have been so intuitive. They were at least sensitive enough to realize that even metals, minerals, and flowers released vibrations that aligned with specific healing goals.

Subtle energy is also technically related to how chakras affect us. These "wheels" of energy that spin within us can get kicked into spinning backward or not spinning at all. The subtle energy that affects that spin comes from real-world incidents but then reverberates through you, subtly, until you find closure and/or heal yourself.

Subtle energy is expressed and affirmed through divination attempts as well. Divination almost literally means seeking into the supernatural and subtle energetic realms. In addition, any gesture encouraged by your intuition works alongside this type of vibration, and of course, subtle energy is expressed by crystals and minerals, too. That's partially what you were sensing through those experiments in chapter 2, as mentioned above.

All this means to say that crystals' subtle energy and intention affirmation finds itself amplified and directed through divination attempts, and this chapter will dive directly into that reality. We'll start off with a few more-obvious ways to amplify the subtle energy of your work, getting into direct divination-crystal correlation towards the end of this first section.

Then, we'll address five major modes of healing that lie on a spectrum, from being directly physical to predominantly energetic. As this chapter comes to a close, we'll prepare you for the future that exists outside this specific learning experience. There's only so much that can be conveyed in one book, so the final section will prepare you with an important piece of information: how to apply these crystal techniques to any mode of healing that you may run into without me as your guide.

Modalities of Crystal Healing

Crystals have so much potential. They can move and store so much information, and our abilities to learn from them are only growing. The sky's the limit, but the following section will provide details on nine specific healing capacities of crystals beyond their mere presence, which is already a lot and a blessing!

Chakra Healing

As mentioned in the previous chapter, chakra healing clearly has a space for crystal boosters. With each chakra being a different color and with them being incredibly positively affected by pyramid shapes, triangular-shaped stones of any of the 7 chakra colors are innately attuned to chakra healing work. Even if you don't have 7 pyramid stones, one of each chakra color, just one quartz or apophyllite pyramid can do the trick when used on one chakra at a time. Even more, 7 stones that aren't pyramids can work for the chakras if they're each colored after their own chakra. But of course, if you only have tumbled quartz, you can use that for each chakra instead, working one after the other or just on the one you have trouble with.

Aura Cleansing

The electromagnetic field that surrounds you has a name that you may have heard thrown around casually in spiritual circles in the past. The name is "aura," and it isn't just something people have been talking about to feel enlightened. The aura is real, and whether or not it has colors, I don't know, I don't have the gift of seeing them unlocked yet, but I do know that its presence has been verified by scientific studies and that it can be measured and healed.

As you go about aura healing, even if you can't see auras, your intuition with crystal companions will be your best guide. Without your crystals and your intuition, you might not have any direct "tap" into your aural reality, but with these things in play, you certainly will and do.

Diagnosing Sites of Disease

There are multiple crystals and minerals listed in chapter 3's Index that have specific attunements toward a diagnosis. For example, obsidian, quartz, lepidolite, and larimar are able to point out where the illness lies, and they're just four of perhaps fifty or more options. Using crystal healing to pinpoint sites of disease relies on two basic techniques.

First, you essentially use chakra healing to open, cleanse, or awaken your third eye. In this process, you'll find that your so-called "sixth sense" is ignited, and even with your eyes closed, you'll be able to intuit knowledge and receive guidance for your personal journey and healing. With this ability awakened, adding crystals that point out disease makes it a much more focused endeavor.

The second technique is meditation. Once you have your crystals and your third eye at least cleansed, come to a place of meditation where you simply focus on your breath with the intention of quieting your mind of all thoughts and emotions.

Then let your hands and the crystals do the talking. Move them over your body slowly with your energy focused into your third eye until each stone settles somewhere. It could be they all go to the same place, but it might not. This process works incredibly well for highly intuitive people.

Mitigating Illness

Through various crystal healing techniques, it is said that one can mitigate the symptoms of illness and help encourage overall wellness. Several other techniques are included in this section already, so in this segment, it should suffice to focus on remedies in the form of crystal essences.

Some stones and crystals are not suited for this type of work because you're essentially putting a stone directly in water and capturing the subtle energy of it in the liquid. Raw minerals and crystals are liable to disintegrate or lose their intricacies in water, but tumbled stones don't pose that same risk.

Therefore, to lessen the effects of certain illnesses or diseases, look up a particular crystal to find its abilities. When you have one or two that match your aims, try to make sure they're tumbled but if they're not, we have another option! Then set each one in a bowl of purified or spring water. Let the stone sit in water that's exposed to sunlight for 12 hours, if possible. If it has to be 12 hours over two or more days, that's absolutely fine.

Afterward, pour that water into a large bottle to save it and preserve it with a tablespoon or two of 50% vodka or brandy added to the mix. Generally, you can then take ¼ teaspoon up to three times a day until you see improvement of your condition. Your ¼ teaspoon can be applied to the skin over where the disease rests, or it can be taken internally, like cough syrup. You can also add the ¼ teaspoon to any cool drink you're already imbibing or to any chilled food you may be eating.

Two tips for this method are as follows: (1) if you're using stones that are raw, simply put that stone into a small jar first and then set the jar into your bowl of water. This indirect method of extracting the gem essence works just as well and poses no damage to the structural integrity of your stone. (2) If you're using an elixir or essence focused on the eyes, do not add the vodka or brandy preservative. Keep this crystal essence in the refrigerator if you need to preserve it for longer than a week.

Grid Work

While the basics of how to grid with crystals are explained in chapter 2, this section explains how to harness the energies of certain crystals in order to enact particular healing in the body, mind, community, or world as a whole. In this section, we'll walk through five types of grids that can offer solace for some more common ailments and concerns, such as heartbreak, home protection and defense, stress relief, and more.

A **Heartbreak Grid** would be composed of stones such as eudialyte, rose quartz, watermelon tourmaline, dioptase, and unakite. You would make yourself the center of this grid and lay the chosen stones around you, alternating as possible between the unakite, rose quartz, and eudialyte on the exterior of your body and holding the tourmaline and/or dioptase directly over your heart. When the minerals are assembled and, in their formation, you'd close your eyes and meditate or simply lay in their presence for anywhere from twenty minutes to an hour. You'll surely feel alleviated of your pains and ready for future prospects in a matter of days with this practice of meditation and gridding.

A **Home Protection & Defense Grid** would be composed of several stones placed inside the doors of your home or just outside them. You could use stones and minerals such as black tourmaline, obsidian, onyx, selenite, sardonyx, and carnelian to provide your protective shield. This grid would be a little different from the ones more focused on the physical body in that the crystals would ideally stay in their place for as long as you inhabit the home. Once you have the crystals and minerals you'll work with, go around your home, placing them inside each window and exterior doorway. If you only have one or two, place the stone above the door jamb of the main door you use, as possible. Meditatively place these crystals and imagine your home being protected for as long as you're there. Feel secure in your actions and know that you're doing good work.

Next, a **Stress Relief Grid** would be incredibly simple to build. You could even just use a few pieces of amethyst to complete your task. Lie down or sit in a meditative position and surround yourself with these amethyst pieces or points. If you know where you tend to hold in stress, whether it's your throat, your eyes, your hands, your heart, or otherwise, you could also place an amethyst directly over that space in your body to help. Now that everything's situated, you'd close your eyes and meditate or lay in the arrangement for about fifteen minutes, but if you really needed to detox from stress and anxiety, you could stay as long as you like. You could even arrange these amethyst points or pieces around your bed so that they're always boosting your rest with their calming potential.

A **Chakra Healing Grid** would utilize one stone of each chakra color, placed on your body near or over top the associated chakra. You could also place one brownstone for grounding at the base of your feet and one white, higher-vibration stone for ascension about five inches above the top of your head. Essentially, you would have this brownstone at your feet, a red one near your genitals, an orange one about three inches below your belly button, a yellow one on your solar plexus, a green or pink one over your heart, a blue one on your throat, an indigo stone on your third eye, and a purple one at the tip of your head followed by that bright white or clear one up top. You'd stay in this position and meditate or simply lay in the crystals' presence for anywhere from 5 minutes to an hour.

And finally, an **Immunity Booster Grid** for those with the flu or auto-immune issues would incorporate stones like emerald, brown jasper & picture jasper, green opal, rhodonite, sunstone, or zoisite from this book as well as others, such as green tourmaline, pink smithsonite, and energetic amplifiers such as quartz and malachite. You would surround yourself with the amplifiers and place the other crystals on your body. You could place the crystals intuitively where you feel they need to go, or you could focus their gathering over your throat and your heart. Once the minerals are in place, close your eyes and meditate or simply lay in their presence. After ten minutes, you could get up, or you can stay in this position for as long as an hour for a bigger boost.

Pendulum Work

If you're not sure where to start with crystal healing and you'd like more guidance than just the words I've afforded you, you might be the type for a pendulum. Across all the modalities of crystal healing, pendulum use is potentially the least-well understood, but we'll work to combat that here.

Pendulums are tricky devices. It's not so simple as taking your pendulum, swinging it between alternatives and letting it settle where it will to divine an answer. The pendulum doesn't connect with higher beings, necessarily, and it doesn't put you in contact with ghosts; not unless you ask it to!

What pendulums actually do is that they connect with your unconscious instincts. When you close your eyes and hold your pendulum completely still, you can ask it questions. Essentially, you ask *yourself* these questions, and the pendulum shows you what your unconscious self *really* wants, without those desires being cloaked by ego or anxiety or what have you.

First, you'd want to connect with your pendulum and ask it some verifiable true or false questions. Again, close your eyes and hold the pendulum completely still before you ask these questions, then ask them with confidence. After about 30 seconds, open your eyes to see how the pendulum is moving.

Sometimes, one receives "yes" from the pendulum in the form of a back and forth swing; sometimes, it's a circular motion or a complete stillness. Now try a question where the answer is "no." See how the pendulum moves after 30 seconds of your eyes being closed. Attempt this yes/no style of questioning until you're sure what your pendulum's yes and no look like.

Now for the connection with crystal healing: imagine that you'd be choosing between crystals for a healing purpose and you'd truly not know which one is best for your condition. Maybe you're unsure what your condition even is, so you're choosing between two stones you felt drawn to, but you want a more concrete answer of which is best than simply what you're physically drawn to.

In this case, you'd close your eyes and hold your pendulum still before asking, "Is the first stone (*call it by name, though*) the right one for this healing?" After 30 seconds or so, open your eyes to see the pendulum's response. Then, repeat the question for the other crystal or crystals you're choosing between. You might be surprised just how well this works for you and your process of healing.

Channeling

Some crystal healing deals with connecting to the intelligence, love, and wisdom of entities outside the earth plane. Sometimes, it means connecting to the spirits of the dead to resolve issues, conflict, or tension. Sometimes, still, it means reaching out to one's ancestors for guidance in times of great turmoil.

Crystal healing often deals with the energies of the souls that surround us. For example, we need help de-stressing from others' presences or we need encouragement to find a partner or we even need to detoxify interpersonal pollution from, say, our places of work. What's more than that, however, is that crystals can help us connect with souls that are not so obviously *material* or *physical* in order to receive overall guidance for this lifetime and beyond.

This point is where channeling comes in. For those who happen to know they're reincarnated souls from other stars or planets or galaxies, for those who happen to know that they're dealing with certain ancestors' spirits, for those who are unfortunately haunted by lingering earth souls with malice; crystal-guided channeling can be the ultimate blessing for the hope of resolution.

Through channeling stones like apophyllite, morganite, turquoise, labradorite, and more, one can meditate on these otherworldly (and occasionally supernatural) issues and receive guidance. Using apophyllite, in particular, can be groundbreaking for those connecting to entities in other dimensions or in other star systems. It's said that when you look from the base of an apophyllite crystal into its point, you open a channel for interstellar and interdimensional travel, with the right meditative focus.

Color Divination

Incredibly enough, even just a bag of crystals with one of each color of the rainbow can work wonders for those interested in divination. This type of healing connects the individual to his or her intuition, higher chakras, and higher self. Essentially, you'd choose a fabric bag that's entirely opaque and not see-through at all. Then, you'd gather up to 13 stones with any or all of the following colors: pink, red, orange, yellow, green, blue, indigo, violet, black, brown, grey, white, and clear.

Each color has a specific vibration and wavelength, due to the physics of light, which means that each color comes with a specific healing frequency and focus. For example, pink associates with love and friendship, red with passion and change, orange with creativity and growth, yellow with travel and communication, green with grounding and health, blue with sleeping and overall health, indigo with insight and guidance, and purple with spirituality and expansion.

Once you've got an assortment of stones of different colors and your non-see-through bag, put them inside and settle on a question you'd like an answer to. You can come up with a daily routine where you ask a question in the morning and see how accurate it is as the day goes along, or you could wait until the end of the day to ask guidance on how things went. Differently still, you could ask a general question whenever you like and then see what answers you receive.

Once you've asked your question, close your eyes and grab a stone or two at the behest of your intuition. With them in your hand, you can keep your eyes closed and try to sense their vibrations and then check with your vision, or you can just look to see what you've drawn. These stones and their color frequency should provide insight into your situation and somewhat of an answer to your question, and through that power of knowledge, you should find yourself one step closer to overall healing.

General Divination

With an opaque pouch filled with tens of different stones (including at least one carnelian to cleanse and recharge the rest simply and efficiently), you can try a similar divination technique to the section above with a less guided structure. Instead of asking questions for this one, you'd simply draw a stone or two to provide guidance and advice regarding life, love, work, and creation in general.

You can make yourself a list of the stones you have to work with and one or two words about each one and what it does for healing. Once you have this easy "cheat-sheet" list, you can put those stones into your non-see-through bag and pull one or two at random. Based on your "cheat-sheet," then, you will know what the stones have to say and their general advice for your situation.

You could still try asking a question and choosing stones as a means of receiving answers, but you don't *have to* use that much structure with this mode of divination. In fact, you can alter this mode of divination to suit any particular needs you might have.

For example, you could use the crystal pull of this technique to tell you something about a loved one, you could use it for help making decisions, you could use it for direction in your artistic work, and you could even use it to trigger clairvoyant visions. This style of divination is inherently flexible, and it aims to encourage your creativity, so trust your intuition and claim the sky as your limit!

Modalities of Subtle Energy Healing

Even without crystals, our abilities to heal ourselves and one another are practically endless. By laying our hands on one another through massage and surgery, we can make life-altering adjustments for people, but even without touching someone else, energy flows out in ripples that can't help but do good work.

For example, prayer is becoming more and more validated, scientifically, for its abilities to affect positive outcomes. Even without touching someone, prayer focused on any topic has positive effects at exponential rates, and the effects of prayer on the pray*er* (not the prayed-for) are healing in ways that can manifest as faith or religion but regardless, these remedies can last a lifetime.

Energy Centering, Healing, and Clearing

The more and more conscious you become of subtle energy, the easier it will be to tap into your mental, physical, and emotional health even if you have had trouble picking up on those themes in your life up until now. Subtle energy is loud for some, but for others, it's a whisper that gets bigger and louder by the day, with practice and focused attention. Regardless of where you are in your process of noticing and sensing subtle energy, there are several energetic techniques you can do to heal yours and go from there.

First, let's discuss the potential to center and ground yourself and your subtle energy. With the right application of meditative focus and healthy breathing, you can start to notice when your energy gets erratic or overly influenced by others. You can start to note when your energy gets pulled one way or the other by one person in particular, too, and when you become aware of these subtle energy hooks and interactions, you can learn how to cut loose and reground yourself in your own energetic center.

It starts with this energetic self-awareness, and then it all comes down to the powers of visualization. Once you know you need to find the center and reground yourself, it's as simple as regaining collected, calm breathing and visualizing that you have a cord that grows from the soles of your feet and connects to the earthen nature beneath. No matter how far above the soil you are, visualize that this cord can extend to be as long as needed in order to make that connection. Breathe and visualize this connection with the nature that surrounds you, and you'll be so much more able to tell what's (energetically and emotionally) yours despite any distractions or stressors.

Next, let's explore the general healing potential tied up in your subtle energetic expression. With this increased awareness of your own energetic patterns, you can become conscious of how your internal illnesses or states of disease actually ripple out, affecting your overall self-expression and energy level. While you may have always been aware of this connection between the presence of sickness and energy level, you will now be truly able to *see* the effects and their interrelation with the overall cause more clearly.

In fact, it could be that the cause of your *internal* disease was actually the *energetic* imbalance in the first place. It could be that you were internalizing, perhaps, something your parents keep fighting about or that you're taking someone's criticisms of you very personally. There are many reasons how this energetic exchange can happen, but it matters that once you know where that illness came from, you'll have the ability to change your situation for the better.

Finally, let's discuss clearing any bad or built-up energy as well as clearing cycles that could get your subtle energy stuck in a rut. Differently than *healing* your overall energy and subtle expressions, clearing something vibrationally means that you're working on just one aspect of something that's often less physical and more *meta*physical than what can be done with explicit energetic healing (like, for example, personality traits, vices, phobias, anxiety patterns, and more).

For those who notice these unproductive traits and want to do something about it, the responsibility comes in the next step. Noticing is one thing but *deciding you're ready to change* is another. Through attention to subtle energy and appreciation of how those ripples inwards and outwards work, one can accept that responsibility and approach one's own self as a canvas ready to be repainted. For those interested, you can try energetic cleansing and chakra healing to solve the vibrational issue. You can even try massage, reiki, or acupuncture to help out. Whatever you do, if you've made the decision to work out the energetic kink, be ready to shed some real-time emotional baggage, but trust that it will be for the best.

Overall, subtle energy has multiple modes of expression even just in one human body, and these techniques can help you to harness, notice, and heal that field of energy. Adding in crystals to the mix is easy to do and at some point, it will just *feel right*. For now, however, even practicing these techniques alone will be productive to your overall growth. Start with that and see where you can go.

Reiki Healing

An explicit mode of healing that's different from just subtle energetic awareness is what's called Reiki. Reiki is an ancient Japanese technique that relates back to what we discussed in the last major section about channeling, but in this case, the physical method of energetic transfer that allows one individual to *channel* energetic healing to another individual (by means of the chakras and more) to help that diseased person be able to connect with the energy of life better.

Originally, Reiki was not practiced as a massage technique whatsoever, although it has largely become that these days, with its increasingly Westernized rehearsal. It was originally just a means of using a human channel to vibrationally adjust someone else's bodily environment in order to induce that person's future healing. It still is largely this same practice overall, but the laying of hands-on skin to skin contact and the giving of massage have been added to amplify the diseased human's abilities of future healing.

Interestingly, just like the concepts of Hindu "kundalini" and "Shakti" (along with "chi," "prana," and more), Japanese "reiki" represents that life-force; giving, creative, and soulful energy of the universe. Reiki, however, is not associated with any particular religion, it simply is. Reiki work done on one another then represents this type of energy work to heal, correct, adjust, or make ready for healing anyone's vibrational essence.

Reiki healing easily aligns with chakra healing, for (as long as he or she knows about the chakras and chakra healing) the reiki healer will notice with ease and relative clarity when the individual's chakras are blocked or imbalanced. Being the energetic channel that he or she is, the reiki healer should then be able to open, adjust, clear, and rebalance the chakras by way of (massage-based or touchless) energy work. Even if this healer isn't as skilled yet in his or her work, the adjustments made on the diseased person's energy should pave the way for future progress and healing with or without the healer's additional support.

Spiritual Healing

Some veins of healing focus just on the connection one have (or strives to have) with divinity. In that sense, spiritual healing might be the right venue for people who have such interests. If you're working on blossoming your third eye and crown chakras most of all or if you're at the point where you're thinking beyond your own seven chakras out into the other 15 we have potential access to; you're doing healing work oriented with your connection to divinity. In addition, if you find yourself meditating frequently, if not daily, and if you're extra interested in aspects like reincarnation, past lives, karma, justice, or revolution, you're very likely doing spiritual self-healing work, possibly without even knowing it.

Sometimes, people are born into this lifetime thinking they'll never be good enough for God (or generally, for divinity). Some people are born with great connections to the divine that fade with time or through experiences like abuse or stifling. Some people, too, are born into this life with the potential to do great things with divinity, based on their past life careers (for example, being a shaman, clergyman, martyr, saint, etc.) but onlookers would never know otherwise.

We all are born into this lifetime with some connection to the divine, even if it's just through the fact that we're all literally *born*, coming into life through the omnipresent, creative force of the universe. Often, however, it is so much more than this simple fact of our births. We spend our whole life with proof of the divine calling out to us in multiple ways. Divinity was fractured and manifested through so many different religions and mythologies, and divinity also exists within us, for our abilities to procreate and manifest our will into existence other ways.

Divinity leaves nature as a gift for us, which we often take for granted. Divinity gives us the potential for a great feeling, which draws to us people who prove again and again that love and creativity are real and worth celebrating. Despite all that divinity does, however, some of us are more conscious, more cognizant than others, and for those who are not (or for those who experience blockages in appreciating divinity's gifts), spiritual healing is a must.

Whether one goes about spiritual healing through guided past-life meditations, attempts at channeling divinity, work devoted to relieving past-life karma, social justice work, or divinity-based educations and careers, the potential for healing is real, it is great, and it is out there. Like so many of these subtle energy healing modalities, however, it first takes one's awareness of his or her blockages and *the desire to change* before that end-goal is secured.

Ancestral Healing

Something else all of us could benefit from working on is ancestral healing. Differently, from work done on past lives, ancestral healing deals with those real-time actions our own ancestors took that put us in the places we inhabit today, in terms of one's literal home, one's socio-economic standing, one's diseases and illnesses, one's social mobility, and more. Our ancestors' actions determine so much more for us than we often imagine. They can even affect the countries we live in, the travel we have access to, and the literal meaning of our last names.

For instance, many last names deal with the trade one's ancestors worked, traced back through the male bloodline for the most part due to patriarchal naming traditions. Millers were literally that, while Browns were leatherworkers or farmers, Williamsons were descendants of a man named William, Tanners worked as leather tanners, and more. However, some last names reveal a little of what the family should be shamed for. Some last names translate back to the root of "thief" or "liar," while others like Black, Blackman, or Freeman have race-based connotations that may have been unkind.

Aside from just this naming, however, it is true that our ancestors' actions, strife, woes, successes, and advancements affect their progeny today. Sometimes, this connection we have to the past means that we live out something like a curse that our ancestors were doomed with for their faults, crimes, or flaws. Sometimes, this connection means that we live out success at the exploitation and sorrow of others. For those interested in these ancestral "hauntings" and remnants, subtle energy healing can once again come to your aid.

Through subtle & energetic dreamwork, one can attempt to reach out to one's ancestors on the plane of dreams and work out his or her connections to these long, lost dead in that way. In another way, one can use guided meditations about ancestral healing and resolution that reverberates out into peace through the generations. In another way, too, one can take on actions and responsibilities that directly *undo* the damage caused by his or her ancestors in the past.

Whether you're ancestrally aware or blind, in touch or out of touch, there may come a time when you're ready to attempt this type of subtle energetic work, and the vibrational effects in your life will be both long-standing and inspirational. However, it will take, as with this section's other techniques, a true commitment to changing oneself and a trust in one's awareness of the past; all of which crystals can greatly help with.

Trauma Healing

The more physical avenue of trauma healing also has ties to one's subtle energy field and its expression. As mentioned before with energetic healing and clearing, it can be the case that energetic wounds cause physical trauma just as easily as physical trauma causes energetic wounds. This cycle of hurt can actually bounce back and forth, creating a reverberating chamber of so-called "ripples" of hurt until lasting actions are taken.

For individuals working through trauma of any nature (physical, emotional, psychic, mental, or any combination thereof), subtle energy healing can often be of great help. Subtle energy healing comes in so many other forms than just meditation, self-awareness, and past life work. It is also imparted through herbs, essential oils, metals, and flowers that can help to boost your trauma recovery.

In the old world, herbs, oils, metals, and flowers would have been the essence and completion of any healing remedy, especially from situations of trauma. Today, we're so bent on using pharmaceutical cures that we forget how much help these old-world remedies can still be to us. While they will likely not entirely cure your situation, they will always be of help. Especially for those who are sensitive (or becoming sensitive) to subtle energies, healing done with herbs, oils, metals, and flowers can be the best body & attitude boost of all.

With the potential of herbal healing, there are a few options, of which essential oils are one. Herbs across the globe all have healing affinities. Whether they work for the blood, for digestion, for poison, or for enlightenment, herbs have always been incredibly gifted healers. Today, people suffering through trauma with PTSD and more can use herbs to make day-to-day life easier. Whether herbs are used to boost the individual's diet or to alleviate symptoms through with aromatherapies (as with incense, essential oils, and more), the herbal potential is vast and should not be taken for granted.

Metals can also be used for curative means. While metals are not ingestible like herbs or flowers, their mere presence can be strengthening and affirming. Copper is said to help with digestive, lymphatic, and immune issues, while iron supports the blood and heart. Silver works for the urinary system and fights bacterial infections. Gold strengthens in many ways, such as with memory, for cardiovascular health, with respiration, and against the effects of aging.

Finally, flowers can come into play. Certainly, the scents of flowers work an aromatherapy related to herbal healing, and essential oils exist of flowers, too. However, flowers can have their "essences" extracted in a similar way that crystals can, which provides a whole new layer of subtle energy healing. Sometimes, we're so stuck in certain ways of living that we can't imagine healing. Sometimes, we're content to wallow in disease. Sometimes, we think we're not worthy to heal, and in all these occasions, flower essences can be of great help.

These extracted and focused energies of flowers can be taken daily to boost your subtle energy in ways that make space for future healing mechanisms. Even if you're not ready to fully heal yet, for whatever reason, start taking flower essences (such as Star of Bethlehem to alleviate soul tension and frustrations, Wild Rose to increase multitasking and end procrastination, Saguaro to enhance psychic abilities and receptiveness, and more) and after a few weeks, you'll be surprised what you're ready for in terms of healing and how much your symptoms have already been changed for the better.

How to Incorporate Crystals into Any Modality

As you go out into the world without me (as it was before me, my book, and my words), you're sure to encounter incredible and life-changing healing techniques that are ripe for a crystalline boost. In order to make you feel as prepared as possible for those moments, the following section will provide a brief guide to how you can do exactly that. The guide divides any relation between healing and crystals into a process comprised of 5 steps.

First, **assess the situation**. Take in the healing needs of the individual in question and your healing *abilities* as the individual likely approaching things as a healer (even if you're healing yourself). Think about what that healing goal will look like when it's all said and done. Think about what the situation may have been caused by and its implications on the individual's body, mind, and soul. Consider as many angles of the situation as possible to be able to develop the most intuitive remedy.

Second, **match the situation to this new strategy**. As you think of what the end-goal will look like, you will be using a new remedy or curative technique (the new healing modality to incorporate crystals into) as a potentially successful "cure." Now recall what that new cure will look like. Remember what the tenants of this new healing technique are. Think through it all, even if it's far-fetched. Think about that cure's details and just let your intuition, your reason, and your judgment work their combined magic. There's a reason why this new healing strategy was brought to you, and it might just be because it perfectly brings in line what you know about crystals and what needs to be done.

Third, **determine the strategy's weak spots**. As you think of this new healing strategy, the new potential "cure"; there will be obvious weak spots. There will be more weak spots if the "cure" is especially "far-fetched," but that just means there are more holes to fill gaps in with crystals! These weak spots are essentially that; they're invitations to tie in crystal healing. Now that you've considered the healing situation on all angles and have pondered what you know of this new strategy, look again at the weak spots and let your intuition be your guide. Some ideas of crystals or minerals *will* certainly fill your mind, and the more ideas you have, the better.

Fourth, **meditate** with the dilemma and your chosen crystals. This can look different for everyone, based on what your relationship with meditation is like and based on what crystals you actually have at your disposal. It might just look like you are closing your eyes and thinking about the situation deeply. It might be completely different and look like literal research for you. Instead, if you're practiced with meditation and have a connection with your spirit guides or guardians, you can simply ask for their advice to make sure you make the right connections for the situation.

Fifth and lastly, **fortify the strategy with crystals** for the benefit of the overall healing situation. Any case for healing has space for crystal boosters; you just have to open yourself to the possibility and do a little meditation or research to affirm your instincts. Once you have those intuitions confirmed (or altered, and that's okay too!), acquire the crystals and begin to incorporate them into your new technique.

CHAPTER 6
Advanced Crystal Healing And Details Of The Craft

When it comes to the subtle energies of crystals involved in healing or divination or what have you, there's more to it than just what I say each crystal does. For example, your intuition may be a better guide to you (eventually or now!) regarding what stones do what for which disease, and you can actually learn to guide, to hone that intuition by simply learning the "gender," elemental, and solar system/planetary associations for each stone and working from there instead.

If it's easier for you to remember what stone does what in the first place, then this chapter will just sprinkle a little extra context on top of those associations. Eventually, you will learn what it means to consider stones, crystals, and minerals with gendered, elemental, and planetary associations. You will also be introduced to the concept of crystal pairing and grouping so that you can start to create crystal healing pouches for yourself and others in need.

As one final bombshell, the end of this chapter touches on the connections between Western astrology and crystal healing. For, if each crystal has a gendered, an elemental, and a planetary alignment, surely some crystals would connect better with, say, a Pisces than a Libra, etc. We will not get into debates over esoteric astrology, the 13th sign, or other complicated astrological matters. I'm simply going to introduce you to some concepts and associations and let you decide for yourself.

By the end of this chapter, you should find your internal warehouse of knowledge on crystal healing becoming fine-tuned, and there should certainly be a few crystals that come to mind for you to begin healing yourself (and others, as your intuition and reason guide you). Essentially, you should be ready for action.

Feminine or Masculine?

To think of each stone or crystal with a gendered association does not mean to engage with debates about gender identity in the world today. It is simply to say that the universe demonstrates the existence of two gendered extremes: masculinity and femininity, and those gendered extremes are imprinted onto all life *within* that universe. This statement corresponds to the Hermetic & Universal Law of Gender, which is one of twelve that work together to define the nature of our reality.

Within humans, gendered extremes can become meshed through hormonal imbalances, gender identity, gender expression, and otherwise, but stones and crystals are far simpler than we are in this sense. The vibrations of crystals can easily align with either masculine or feminine potential, with complete exclusion of the other, and when you come to learn which stones align which way (gender-wise), you'll find that their overall energy signatures and healing potentials become more and more clear.

This universal sense of **Femininity** corresponds to passive, receptive energy. It is observant, sometimes aloof, accepting, and more subtly energetic. It hides and obscures, as well as illuminates, reveals, and enlightens. It can be sneaky and passive-aggressive, but regardless, it is oriented towards receptive interpersonal alignments and understandings. Feminine crystals are also oriented towards styles of healing that are soothing, love-related, de-stressing, wisdom-related, compassion-related, sleep-related, empowering, growth-related, and community-related.

Some **feminine** stones, minerals, and crystals are as follows: (blue, green, & moss) agate(s), amethyst, aquamarine, azurite, beryl, (blue, green, & pink) calcite(s), chrysocolla, coal, coral, emerald, fossils, geodes, jade, (brown & green) jasper(s), jet, kunzite, lapis lazuli, malachite, marble, moonstone, opal, pearl, peridot, petrified wood, (regular, blue, green, rose, & smoky) quartz(s), salt, sapphire, selenite, sodalite, sugilite, (black, blue, green, & pink) tourmaline(s), and turquoise.

This universal sense of **Masculinity**, on the other end of the spectrum, corresponds to active, forceful energy. It is assertive, sometimes demanding, controlling, and openly energetic. It presents, projects, represents and actualizes. It can be protective and defensive, but regardless, it is oriented towards forceful interpersonal interactions. Masculine crystals are also oriented towards styles of healing that are protective, intellect-related, exorcism-related, luck-related, success-related, power-boosting, confidence-boosting, courage-boosting, and will power-related.

Some **masculine** stones, minerals, and crystals are as follows: (red, banded, black, & brown) agate(s), apache tear, aventurine, bloodstone, (orange) calcite, carnelian (agate), citrine, fluorite, garnet, hematite, (red) jasper, obsidian, onyx, (fire) opal, (rutilated & tourmalinated) quartz (s), rhodochrosite, rhodonite, ruby, sardonyx, serpentine, spinel, sunstone, tiger's eye, topaz, (red) tourmaline, and zircon.

Fire, Earth, Air, or Water?

Thinking of crystals and stones with elemental associations may sound redundant to some. These people may consider that rocks, stones, crystals, minerals, etc. are harvested from the earth and should, therefore, be linked to that element more clearly than to any other. However, I wonder what these people might say about a stone-like, say, Obsidian, which is a naturally-occurring form of *volcanic glass* or about a mineral like Ammolite, which is technically a fossilized, opalized *ancient sea critter*?

Crystal healing gets complex, but it is much easier for me to break it all down into groups. The basic elemental designations are fire, earth, air, and water, and becoming familiar with those energies will hopefully be helpful for your journey with crystal healing, too.

When it comes to **fire**, the energy is associated with universal masculinity. Some minerals, stones, and crystals associated with fire are as follows: (banded, black, red, or brown) agate(s), amber, apache tear, asbestos, carnelian, citrine, diamond, garnet, hematite, (red) jasper, lava, obsidian, onyx, rhodochrosite, ruby, sardonyx, serpentine, spinel, sunstone, (regular & red) tiger's eye(s), topaz, (red & watermelon) tourmaline(s), and zircon.

When it comes to **earth**, the energy is associated with universal femininity. Some minerals, stones, and crystals associated with earth are as follows: (green & moss) agate(s), alum, (orange) calcite, chrysoprase, coal, diamond, emerald, (brown & green) jasper(s), jet, kunzite, malachite, onyx, peridot, salt, stalagmites & stalactites, (black & green) tourmaline(s), and turquoise.

When it comes to **air**, the energy is associated with universal masculinity. Some minerals, stones, and crystals associated with air are as follows: aventurine, (white) fluorite, jasper, mica, opal, pumice, (regular & blue) tiger's eye(s), topaz, and certain types of turquoise.

When it comes to **water**, the energy is associated with universal femininity. Some minerals, stones, and crystals associated with water are as follows: (blue lace) agate, amethyst, aquamarine, azurite, beryl, (pink & blue) calcite(s), chrysocolla, coral, geodes, jade, lapis lazuli, lepidolite, moonstone, mother of pearl, pearl, quartz, sapphire, selenite, sodalite, sugilite, and (pink, blue, or green) tourmaline(s).

Solar System Associations?

Crystals having solar system associations might be the wildest set of associations of this chapter for most of my listeners (and readers) to accept, but there's an easier way to explain what I mean. Of course, with the exception of "crystals" formed by meteorite debris (such as desert glass, pieces of the meteorite itself, moldavite, space diamonds, and tektite), all of the nature bits included in this text originate from Earth. The planetary or solar systemic associations of each stone are different than that.

Energetically, each crystal correlates to the vibration of a planet in our solar system or a star beyond. For example, Jupiter's energy is (through mythological associations) said to be linked to travel, expansion, higher education, spiritual studies, and luck, so the lucky abundance stone, Lodestone, relates with that energy well and clearly associates to that planet's vibration. Once you learn what these associations look like, you can intuit information and potential about a healing stone in question to determine whether it will work best for your goals or not.

The **"planetary" energy of the Sun** is about the self and self-expression, and solar healing focuses on work dealing with legal matters, general healing, protection, success attraction, literal or metaphorical illumination, and energy boosting or morale. Stones and crystals linked with this Sun energy are as follows: amber, orange calcite, carnelian, diamond, quartz, sunstone, tiger's eye, topaz, and zircon.

The **"planetary" energy of the Moon** is about emotions and self-actualization, and lunar healing focuses on work dealing with sleep & dreaming, prophecy, gardening, love, general healing, water- or sea-related healing, birth & reproduction, fertility, the home, peace, compassion, and general spirituality. Stones and crystals linked with this Moon energy are as follows: aquamarine, beryl, moonstone, mother of pearl, pearl, quartz, sapphire, and selenite.

The **"planetary" energy of Mercury** is about communication and self-expression, and mercurial healing focuses on work dealing with strengthening, mental boosting, literal or mental eloquence, divination, general studying or specific studies, self-improvement, travel, and wisdom. Stones and crystals linked with this Mercury energy are as follows: (blue lace & fire) agates(s), aventurine, jasper, mica, and pumice.

The **"planetary" energy of Venus** is about beauty and self-confidence, and Venusian healing focuses on work dealing with love, self-promotion or group promotion, fidelity, reconciliation, forgiveness, interpersonal interaction or exchanges, beauty & youth, joy & happiness, pleasure, luck, friendship, meditation, and femininity in any aspect. Stones and crystals linked with this Venus energy are as follows: amazonite, azurite, (blue, green, or pink) calcite(s), chrysocolla, coral, emerald, jade, (green) jasper, lapis lazuli, malachite, peridot, rose quartz, sodalite (pink, blue, green, or watermelon) tourmaline(s), and turquoise.

The **"planetary" energy of Mars** is about aggression and self-assertion, and Mars-based healing focuses on growing courage, building and honing aggression, recovery, physical strength, political endeavors, sexual expression, exorcism, protective & defensive work, and masculinity in any aspect. Stones and crystals linked with this Mars energy are as follows: bloodstone, garnet, (red) jasper, lava, onyx, rhodochrosite, ruby, sardonyx, and (red & watermelon) tourmaline(s).

The **"planetary" energy of Jupiter** is about luck and self-fulfillment, and Jupiter-based healing focuses on linking with spirituality, meditation, growing psychic gifts, and religious ritual in any format for healing. Stones and crystals linked with this Jupiter energy are as follows: amethyst, azurite, lapis lazuli, lepidolite, lodestone, sugilite, and (white) topaz.

The **"planetary" energy of Saturn** is about authority and self-restriction, and Saturn-based healing focuses on grounding, centering, limiting, habit breaking, protecting, purifying, and drawing appropriate luck. Stones and crystals linked with this Saturn energy are as follows: apache tear, coal, hematite, (brown) jasper, jet, lodestone, obsidian, onyx, salt, serpentine, and (black) tourmaline.

The **"planetary" energy of Uranus** is about transformation, and self-immolation and Uranus-based healing focus on guidance (for the self, the group, or both) through rebellion or transformation. Stones and crystals linked with this Uranus energy are as follows: aventurine, azurite, chrysocolla, diamond, labradorite, all quartz (esp. rutilated & tourmalinated), and (blue) topaz.

The **"planetary" energy of Neptune** is about idealism and self-delusion, and Neptune-based healing focuses on dreamwork, sleep, habit breaking, delusion-bursting, awakening, and bring ideals and goals to life. Stones and crystals linked with this Neptune energy are as follows; amethyst, celestite, Herkimer diamond, (blue & regular) howlite, jade, lepidolite, mother of pearl, sapphire, and turquoise.

The **"planetary" energy of Pluto** is about revolution and ego-death, and Pluto-based healing focuses on larger group transformation, the cycle of life, coping with death, grief, religious ritual, and general moving on. Stones and crystals linked with this Pluto energy are as follows: kunzite, malachite, obsidian, (tourmalinated & smoky) quartz(s), ruby, spinel, and topaz.

What Goes Well with What?

Now that you have a working knowledge of the associations that stones, minerals, and crystals have with gender, elements, and bodies of our solar system, you can become able to take things in your journey with crystal healing past the point of just *knowing* toward a place of *synthesis*. With this knowledge, you're at the point where you can find yourself making connections between crystals. These groupings will become essential as you progress with crystal healing, for they will allow you to actually create healing grids, make your own chakra stone set, and generally take your healing work to a whole new level.

As you start drawing these connections, and these associations begin happening for you (if they haven't begun to do so already), you have two main options. Generally, you can *pair* crystals, or you can *group* them together. The connotation here is clear: either you work with just two crystals together and focus on their energetic combination and healing potential, or you look outside a duo and begin to pull together connections and potentials for three or more allied crystals at once.

If you haven't begun to note which crystals and stones seem to go well together, we can touch on a few basics to help you along in your process first. Overall, let's start small and just look at pairings in this section before moving onto groupings in the following.

While we're starting small, think back to what you learned in chapter 2 regarding the energetic *feeling* of each crystal and how you can establish your connection to it. For just a moment, try to forget what you learned in terms of the verbose listings of the past few sections and chapters, and just go back to that intuitive sensory knowledge.

Remember how it's done? With one stone in your hand, it is relatively simple to pick up its vibration. By breathing deeply and essentially meditating with that one crystal, you get to tune into its frequency, but when you add two to one hand or hold one crystal in each hand, things get a little more interesting. They get even *more* interesting when you *do try* two crystals together and their energies feel instantly harmonious or chaotic together.

You can practice the exercise from chapter 2 again now with two crystals together. First, try holding one in each hand. See if you can tell that there are two different stones in your hands if you close your eyes. Without focusing on how those items literally *feel*, can you sense their vibration in the palm of your hand? Can you feel *more* than just that frequency, perhaps? Do you have the ability to intuit what the stone might do for healing purposes?

Regardless of where you're at with your intuition, just try to see how these stones feel. Then, you might try holding them both in one hand and intuiting how their energies are affected and altered. Do this combination and the proximity change things? Can you sense that chaotic or harmonious balance? Practice this technique, and you'll become better at it in time. There are certainly other methods to use in the meantime.

Once you've mastered or have decided to move past this intuitive connection capacity, there are two more methods you can try to see "what goes well with what." First, you can use your intuition in an entirely different way. It can certainly be said that stones that have the same abilities work well together, but stones with different yet *supportive* abilities work just as well if not better!

Go back to the index and chapter 3, go back to the sections before this (the ones with all their listings), and just read through the details again. As you read, you may realize how well certain qualities will work together, and that's exactly what I'm going for. For example, if you're trying to heal defensiveness of personality, a stone for clarity (azurite, fluorite, charoite, etc.) and one for healing defensiveness itself (red jasper, sodalite, rose quartz, malachite, etc.) may stand out to you as supportive and productive, and that intuition would be entirely sound.

Second and finally, you can let go of the intuition feature and simply do the research. Practice choosing crystals that balance one another through opposition and ones that harmonize with each other through shared intention. Put together the pairings and see what happens. Practice pairing crystals by reading around for which ones are from similar geological locations. Maybe that origin location vibration would affect healing capacity even if the stones weren't necessarily allied before!

Let the sky be the limit here. Get creative with your goals of healing, and you will easily find new crystal pairings to test out on a daily basis. If you don't have the crystals to test out just yet, don't give up! Instead, keep a journal of your findings for the future! You never know when you'll be able to come into crystal "wealth" and get to test out what you had studiously connected in the past!

How to Create Healing Pouches

When you're working with groups of crystals, it becomes much easier to look at explicit traits rather than to intuitively sense out connections, for the sheer number of crystals in the group can easily become overwhelming to keep track of even for a more experienced crystal healer. Therefore, simply look at the facts.

Gather together multiple feminine-orientation crystals for help with menstruation or menopause. Gather together several water-oriented crystals to cool you down if you struggle through hot flashes. Pull together several Jupiter-related crystals to attract luck or future travel connections. Having trouble with authority? Try meditating with some Saturn- or Uranus-oriented crystals.

Just by looking at the associations of this chapter, you can determine what is similar and how certain energies align. However, you can always go back to chapter 3 and the general index of crystals and their healing traits. You can try to pull together several stones that, for example, all work against anxiety, or you could gather together several separately-oriented stones, one for each bodily space where you need help.

When you do come to the point where you can create "pouches" of healing stones all working toward a common cause, keep these four pointers in mind. First, take into account the work the stones will do. If they're going to suck out bad energy or neutralize bad energy in any way, they will need to be cleansed more often. Furthermore, if your work focuses on explicit bodily or energetic healing, your crystals will need to be cleansed at least weekly to deal with the effort you expect them to undergo. **Basically, consider the weight of the work, and cleanse your crystals appropriately.** Otherwise, you risk holding onto exactly what you want to release.

Second, **don't overly concern yourself with "balancing" the pouch** with masculine and feminine energies, one of each of the elements, and something from each planet. There are far too many other avenues of grouped crystal healing to go down for you to stay focused on balancing something that's not your explicit healing goal. *If you really want a pouch that's constantly self-cleansing, add in a piece of carnelian.* If your focus is a compulsive balance, however, try shifting your focus elsewhere and see how your crystal grouping potentials blossom.

Third, **listen to your intuition**! If you're being drawn to crystal healing, there's surely a reason for it, and your intuition (as mentioned before) may be your greatest and most trustworthy guide of all. Let your instincts play out but do a little research after the association comes to you to see more clearly what you were picking up on.

Fourth and finally, **if you have an idea for a pouch, don't limit yourself; go for it**! This book may not provide all the answers you seek, but that's okay! Chapters like this one, in particular, are designed to ignite your ability to ask those creative and complicated questions, so don't be afraid to do additional research and to look up more statistics, details, and facts on the internet or in encyclopedias and other books. Essentially, if you come up with an idea for a pouch and this book doesn't provide helpful information for it, don't give up! Ride that intuitive wave through other sources of information until you can actualize your dream. The effort will be more than worth it.

10 Healing Pouches

This section will give you some explicit ideas of ten healing pouches that can work for a variety of goals. It should help you conceptualize what to look for with allied stones, what types of pouches are possible, and what types of healing potential exists for crystals in general.

1. Attracting Love and Growing Self-Love

    Contains: Rose quartz, amethyst, rhodonite, and tree agate.
    Goals & Intentions: To use their commonalities to boost one's self-love and romantic love capacities.

2. Technology Shield

    Contains: Aventurine, amazonite, sodalite, fluorite, and lepidolite.

Goals & Intentions: To protect from the electromagnetic radiation that technology gives off with the combined vibrations of these crystals.

3. Fighting Depression

    Contains: Sunstone, lapis lazuli, lepidolite, rose quartz, and tree
    Agate.
    Goals & Intentions: To work against the imbalance of hormones that causes your depression and to reverse the effects of depression in your life.

4. Pain-Killer Stones

    Contains: Lapis lazuli, aventurine, fluorite, and amethyst.
    Goals & Intentions: To dull the sensation of, or relieve entirely one's pain.

5. Allergy Aid

    Contains: Apophyllite, lepidolite, and aventurine.
    Goals & Intentions: To assist in the relief of allergy symptoms.

6. Healing for Breast Cancer

    Contains: Moss agate, bloodstone, rose quartz, rhodonite, and
    Moonstone.
    Goals & Intentions: To relieve pain and kick-start healing.

7. To Break a Fever

    Contains: Sodalite, labradorite, kyanite, hematite, and moss agate.
    Goals & Intentions: To naturally cut down a fever.

8. Helper During Menstruation

Contains: Amethyst, citrine, regular moonstone, black moonstone, and labradorite.
Goals & Intentions: To make PMS and menstruation a bit easier.

9. Helper for the Upset Stomach

    Contains: Turquoise, sodalite, agate, amethyst, and carnelian.
    Goals & Intentions: To work against upset stomach and help restore
    internal order.

10. Increased Respiratory Health

    Contains: Lapis lazuli, aventurine, amethyst, and rose quartz.
    Goals & Intentions: To boost immunity, aid in respiratory repair,
    and help keep things flowing well with one's breath.

10 Additional Ideas

Now that you have a sense of what to look out for and what grouped stones can do together, here are ten additional ideas that you can run with if they resonate with you. If they don't, they'll surely trigger fresh ideas that *do* have meaning for your experience. Regardless, let this section guide you and affirm your growing instincts, too.

1. Energy Booster

2. Healing Broken Heart

3. Anti-Septic Stones

4. Healing for Any Type of Cancer

5. Immunity Booster

6. Healing for Prostate

7. Memory Booster (Long-Term, Short-Term, or Both

8. Psychic Awakening

9. Diabetic Stand-By

10. Grounding After Trauma

Overall, don't limit yourself, and don't feel dejected if you can't find the information you're looking for right away! Continue striving and trust your instincts. Your future with crystal healing will surely be bright as long as you complete those steps.

Crystal Healing for the Zodiac

Without going too deep into the tenants of Western astrology, it suffices to say that each person being born at a particular time and place, under a particular zodiac sign, has a stone or set of stones that correlates to their astrological intricacies. This section will reveal its details as it goes.

Basics of Western Astrology

Within the study of Western astrology, there is more than just one sign per person. When you think of your zodiac sign, you likely think of one sign, so this may sound especially confusing for you. Essentially, what you think of as your one and only zodiac sign is actually just what's called your "sun sign." It describes the zodiac sign the sun was in the month you were born. However, you're more than just that, for the other bodies in our solar system were in other zodiac signs on the instant of your birth, and those associations affect your personality, interests, and life experiences, too.

All of these constellations, or zodiac signs, relate to planets and bodies in our solar system, too, so you can go back to the section on "Solar System Associations" to ascertain which planetary energy infuses your Sun Sign, Moon Sign, and Ascendant with the following guide:

Aries = Mars
Taurus = Venus
Gemini = Mercury
Cancer = Moon
Leo = Sun

Virgo = Mercury
Libra = Venus
Scorpio = Pluto
Sagittarius = Jupiter
Capricorn = Saturn
Aquarius = Uranus
Pisces = Neptune

In the study of Western astrology, people often talk about the "big three." The big three talks about the three so-called "biggest" astrological and astronomical influences on your personality at the moment of your birth: the monthly position of the sun (**your Sun Sign comprises your personality as others perceive it**), the daily position of the moon (**your Moon Sign relates to your emotional states, your dreams, and your impulses**), and the exact position (to the minute) of the sun, based on what zodiac constellation it was moving through the *moment* of your birth (**your Ascendant or Rising Sign relates to who you are as a deeper personality that others may not immediately perceive**).

You call this arrangement of your "big three" and beyond your "natal chart" or "birth chart." You can have your birth chart calculated online using such websites as Astro.com, Café Astrology, Astro-Charts.com, and more. Once you know at least your big three, you can come to incorporate crystal healing for every aspect of yourself. You can work on just your sun sign and its struggles, but with the aid of these websites (or simply the knowledge of your other placements), you can heal your emotional state via your moon sign and your deeper personality via your ascendant, too. The possibilities with crystal healing are limitless!

Stones for Sun Signs

Basically, **if your sun sign is Aries**, look for stones related to fiery Mars energy. As a reminder, some crystals of this nature are bloodstone, garnet, hematite, sardonyx, and red tourmaline. Some other crystals for Aries Sun include carnelian, citrine, iron pyrite, jasper, and topaz.

If your sun sign is Taurus, look for stones related to earthy Venus energy. As a reminder, some crystals of this nature are moss agate, calcite, emerald, green jasper, malachite, watermelon tourmaline, and turquoise. Some other crystals for Taurus Sun include boji stone, kyanite, lapis lazuli, peridot, and tiger's eye.

If your sun sign is Gemini, look for stones related to airy Mercury energy. As a reminder, some crystals of this nature are most agates, aventurine, jasper, mica, and pumice. Some other crystals for Gemini Sun include calcite, dendritic agate (in specific), howlite, and tiger's eye.

If your sun sign is Cancer, look for stones related to watery Moon/lunar energy. As a reminder, some crystals of this nature are aquamarine, beryl, mother of pearl, pearl, quartz, sapphire, and selenite. Some other crystals for Cancer Sun include calcite, jasper, moonstone, opal, pink tourmaline, and rhodonite.

If your sun sign is Leo, look for stones related to fiery Sun/solar energy. As a reminder, some crystals of this nature are diamond, sulfur, sunstone, topaz, and zircon. Some other crystals for Leo Sun include amber, citrine, garnet, kunzite, onyx, quartz, and tiger's eye.

If your sun sign is Virgo, look for stones related to earthy Mercury energy. As a reminder, some crystals of this nature are green aventurine and green jasper. Some other crystals for Virgo Sun include dioptase, garnet, moss agate, sodalite, and smithsonite.

If your sun sign is Libra, look for stones related to airy Venus energy. As a reminder, some crystals of this nature are yellow jasper and citrine. Some other crystals for Libra Sun include aventurine, bloodstone, jade, lepidolite, sapphire, and topaz.

If your sun sign is Scorpio, look for stones related to watery Pluto energy. As a reminder, some crystals of this nature are kunzite, malachite, and obsidian. Some other crystals for Scorpio Sun include apache tear, beryl, garnet, hawk's eye (a variation of tiger's eye), and rhodochrosite.

If your sun sign is Sagittarius, look for stones related to fiery Jupiter energy. As a reminder, some crystals of this nature are fire opal, hematite, purple flash labradorite, lava, lepidolite, lodestone, and purple flash obsidian. Some other crystals for Sagittarius Sun include amethyst, citrine, (any colored flash) labradorite, lapis lazuli, and sodalite.

If your sun sign is Capricorn, look for stones related to earthy Saturn energy. As a reminder, some crystals of this nature are coal/anthracite, jet, salt, and black tourmaline. Some other crystals for Capricorn Sun include amber, fluorite, malachite, ruby, and some tourmalines.

If your sun sign is Aquarius, look for stones related to airy Uranus energy. As a reminder, some crystals of this nature are aventurine, diamond, and mica. Some other crystals for Aquarius Sun include fluorite, labradorite, moonstone, and quartz.

If your sun sign is Pisces, look for stones related to watery Neptune energy. As a reminder, some crystals of this nature are amethyst, celestite, lepidolite, and mother of pearl. Some other crystals for Pisces Sun include agate, bloodstone, calcite, selenite, and turquoise.

Stones for Moon Signs

With Moon signs, things get a little different; the section on Solar System Associations is less of a helpful guide for these lunar placements.

For those with Aries Moon, try aventurine, bloodstone, jasper, magnesite, or sunstone. The crystal most aligned with your intuition will be Ametrine.

For those with Taurus Moon, try apache tear, green agate, calcite, lepidolite, or rhodonite. The crystal most aligned with your intuition will be Selenite.

For those with Gemini Moon, try blue selenite, snowflake obsidian, topaz, or tourmaline. The crystal most aligned with your intuition will be Aqua Aura Quartz.

For those with Cancer Moon, try carnelian, jasper, or sodalite. The crystal most aligned with your intuition will be Moonstone.

For those with Leo Moon, try ametrine, citrine, larimar, or tiger's eye. The crystal most aligned with your intuition will be Yellow Calcite.

For those with Virgo Moon, try amethyst, carnelian, citrine, or peridot. The crystal most aligned with your intuition will be Blue Kyanite.

For those with Libra Moon, try calcite, jade, larimar, or rhodochrosite. The crystal most aligned with your intuition will be Opal.

For those with Scorpio Moon, try agate, apache tear, labradorite, malachite, or obsidian. The crystal most aligned with your intuition will be Herkimer Diamond.

For those with Sagittarius Moon, try garnet, lapis lazuli, lepidolite, moss agate, or sodalite. The crystal most aligned with your intuition will be Lapis Lazuli.

For those with Capricorn Moon, try ametrine, calcite, magnesite, moonstone, or rose quartz. The crystal most aligned with your intuition will be Phantom Quartz.

For those with Aquarius Moon, try beryl, boji stones, rhodonite, or selenite. The crystal most aligned with your intuition will be Aquamarine.

For those with Pisces Moon, try aventurine, fluorite, jasper, sunstone, or tiger's eye. The crystal most aligned with your intuition will be Celestite.

Stones for Ascendant / Rising Signs

The section on Solar System Associations is once again helpful when considering your rising sign or Ascendant. **If you have Aries Rising**, look to stones with fiery Mars energy like bloodstone, garnet, hematite, sardonyx, and red tourmaline as well as the stone Jasper.

If you have Taurus Rising, look to stones with earthy Venus energy like moss agate, calcite, emerald, green jasper, malachite, peridot, watermelon tourmaline, and turquoise as well as Boji Stones.

If you have Gemini Rising, look to stones with airy Mercury energy like agate, aventurine, jasper, mica, and pumice as well as the crystal Kyanite.

If you have Cancer Rising, look to stones with watery Moon/lunar energy like aquamarine, beryl, mother of pearl, pearl, quartz, sapphire, and selenite as well as the crystal Moonstone.

If you have Leo Rising, look to stones with fiery Sun/solar energy like amber, diamond, sulfur, sunstone, tiger's eye, topaz, and zircon as well as the crystal Citrine.

If you have Virgo Rising, look to stones with earthy Mercury energy like moss agate, green aventurine, and green jasper as well as the crystal Blue Tourmaline.

If you have Libra Rising, look to stones with airy Venus energy like yellow jasper and citrine as well as the Rose Quartz crystal.

If you have Scorpio Rising, look to stones with watery Pluto energy like kunzite, malachite, and obsidian as well as the Smoky Quartz crystal.

If you have Sagittarius Rising, look to stones with fiery Jupiter energy like fire opal, hematite, purple flash labradorite, lava, lepidolite, lodestone, and purple flash obsidian as well as the crystal Topaz.

If you have Capricorn Rising, look to stones with earthy Saturn energy like coal/anthracite, jet, salt, and black tourmaline as well as the crystal Garnet.

If you have Aquarius Rising, look to stones with airy Uranus energy like aventurine, diamond, and mica as well as the crystal Amethyst.

If you have Pisces Rising, look to stones with watery Neptune energy like amethyst, celestite, lepidolite, mother of pearl, and turquoise as well as the stone Aquamarine.

CONCLUSION

As you make it to the final page of *Crystal Healing for Beginners*, you deserve another thanks. You were thanked for the download when you were welcomed to the text in the introduction, but now, it's a different story. Thank you for engaging with this text and for making it through to the end! Hopefully, it was as informative and as helpful as I intended it to be.

At this point, you should feel confident that there are ways to incorporate crystal healing into your life or daily routine, and you should have several tools at your disposal for this new and exciting phase of your life, thanks to this book. In order to achieve all the goals you likely now have for crystal healing, the next step is to take things into your own hands.

See if there are any crystals or semi-precious stones that you've unconsciously collected or drawn to you over your lifetime. See if there are any metaphysical or mineral stores in your town and go check it out! See what stones appeal to you intuitively or go with a plan in mind. Whatever tactic you use, just make sure you get out there and get started without hesitation.

Thanks again for both making it to this point and for the download! If you found this text useful in any way, please feel free to leave a review on Amazon. I can't improve without your help, and I'm also eager to know what works for you and what doesn't. Send those thoughts my way, and congratulations again!

Your future has been altered for the better through the act of reading this book, and you now have every tool (knowledge-wise) that you need to succeed. It's all up to *you* on the next phase of this journey, and I can't wait to see where you end up.

DESCRIPTION

Have you been seeing pictures of gorgeous crystals on social media and then found yourself wondering what each one was and, even more, what it did? Have you ever simply wondered what the whole "crystal healing" thing was all about? Did you know that crystals and minerals are used today for storing information, for the building of electronics, for watch-making, and more?

When it comes to crystal healing, things are a bit wild in the best possible way. It might sound crazy to think that these (sometimes very tiny) stones can heal us, but it's much more natural than you could ever imagine. In the following pages, you'll be introduced to crystal healing, its history, and its multiple modalities so that you can find the right style and technique for you.

You'll learn about...
- The statistics and abilities of over 100 unique crystals & stones.
- How to feel the energy of your crystals to begin working with them.
- How to create healing grids with your crystals.
- What chakras and crystal healing have to do with one another.
- Diagnosing & curing illness or disease.
- Reiki healing, ancestral healing, and trauma healing.
- How astrology and crystal healing correlate.
- What crystals, minerals, and stones work well with each other.
- How to create your own healing pouches of crystals.
- And much, much more!

By downloading this book, you will enable yourself to learn, grow, and heal in ways you may never have thought possible and you allow yourself to begin a beautiful adventure with crystals for the sake of incredible benefits. Every day, I thank my lucky stars for my experiences with crystal healing, and I wouldn't trade them for anything and that's why I choose to share them with you now. Good luck, and happy healing!

www.ingramcontent.com/pod-product-compliance
Lightning Source LLC
Chambersburg PA
CBHW071425070526
44578CB00001B/5